POSTSOCIALIST MODERNITY

Postsocialist Modernity

Chinese Cinema, Literature, and Criticism in the Market Age

JASON MCGRATH

STANFORD UNIVERSITY PRESS

Stanford, California

2008

Stanford University Press
Stanford, California
© 2008 by the Board of Trustees of the
Leland Stanford Junior University

Library of Congress Cataloging-in-Publication Data

McGrath, Jason.
  Postsocialist modernity : Chinese cinema, literature, and
criticism in the market age / Jason McGrath.
      p. cm.
  Includes bibliographical references and index.
  ISBN 978-0-8047-5874-1 (cloth : alk. paper)
  ISBN 978-0-8047-7363-8 (pbk.   )
  1. Popular culture—China. 2. Motion pictures—China.
3. Culture in motion pictures. I. Title. II. Title: Chinese cinema,
literature, and criticism in the market age.

HM621.M372 2008
306.4'810951—dc22

                                         2007031057

Printed in the United States of America

Typeset at Stanford University Press in 10/15 Minion

Contents

Table and Figures

Table

Figures

Acknowledgments

This book began as a Ph.D. project at the University of Chicago and continued during my first years of teaching at the University of Minnesota, and I am indebted to many people and units within both institutions as well as elsewhere.

I had several sources of generous financial support. A Century Fellowship from the Division of the Humanities of the University of Chicago sustained me through five years of graduate school, including the early stages of dissertation planning and writing. The Center for East Asian Studies awarded me a predissertation travel grant that allowed me to lay the groundwork for my year of research abroad. My 2002–2003 academic year at Fudan University in Shanghai was funded by a Fulbright-Hayes Doctoral Dissertation Research Abroad Fellowship from the U.S. Department of Education. My final year of dissertation writing was supported by a fellowship from the Whiting Foundation, awarded through the Division of the Humanities. Later, at the University of Minnesota, the project continued with the support of a Faculty Summer Research Fellowship and a McKnight Summer Fellowship in 2005. Final revisions were completed during my semester as a resident fellow at the Institute for Advanced Study in the spring of 2007. I am grateful to all of these programs and the people who staff them for their confidence and generosity.

Much of Chapter Five appeared in somewhat shorter form in the volume *The Urban Generation: Chinese Cinema and Society at the Turn of the Twenty-first Century*, edited by Zhang Zhen and published by Duke University Press. Chapter Six appeared in article form in the fall 2005 issue of the journal *Modern Chinese Literature and Culture*. I am thankful for the permission to reprint that material here. I also thank Chris Berry, Prasenjit Duara, Tom Gunning, Kevin Latham, and Robin Visser for generously sharing their works in progress.

Several chapters were presented in one form or another at workshops and conferences. I am grateful to the coordinators and participants of the China's Long 20th Century, Mass Culture, and Arts and Politics in East Asia workshops at the University of Chicago, all of which served as crucial forums for the working out of ideas. I also thank my fellow panelists at the 2001 Annual Meeting of the American Association of Chinese Studies in Chicago, the 2003 Annual Meeting of the Association for Asian Studies in New York, and the 2003 International Junior Scholars' Conference on Sinology in Taiwan, and in particular the panel discussants Cui Shuqin, Robert Chi, and Liao Binghui for their helpful critical comments. Other scholars who provided greatly appreciated advice, encouragement, and criticism for one or more chapters include Chris Berry, Maghiel van Crevel, Song Mingwei, Robin Visser, David Der-wei Wang, and Zhang Zhen.

During my year of research at Fudan University, I benefited from the assistance, friendship, and intellectual guidance of many people. I am especially appreciative of Professor Chen Sihe, who agreed to serve as my faculty advisor despite his many other commitments. The (then) Ph.D. students in that department, most notably Nie Wei and Zheng Jian, helped me with countless matters. I am grateful for their companionship, and the same goes for Professors Gao Yuanbao of Fudan University and Zhang Sheng of Shanghai Jiaotong University, with whom I shared many excellent meals and conversations. In addition, Professor Wang Xiaoming, of Shanghai University and East China Normal University, was very generous with his time and advice.

My thanks go to all the students and faculty of the Department of East Asian Languages and Civilizations at the University of Chicago for providing a uniquely challenging and stimulating learning environment in addition to indispensable camaraderie and encouragement throughout my time there. Among students of Chinese culture, I was inspired and spurred on over the years by Bao Weihong, Max Bohnenkamp, John Crespi, Anup Grewal, Krista Van Fleit Hang, Paize Keulemans, Lam Ling Hon, Kevin Lawrence, Eugenia Lean (an honorary member), Hyun-jeong Lee, William Schaefer, Song Xiang, Ting Chun Chun, and Zhang Hongbing. A major part of my training at the

University of Chicago also came from the program in Cinema and Media Studies, where I learned a great deal from all the faculty whose classes I took or informally audited, including Tom Gunning, Miriam Hansen, and James Lastra, as well as many CMS graduate students. Among the latter, I especially thank Daniel Morgan, who provided key feedback on early versions of my cinema chapters.

As members of my dissertation committee, Tom Gunning and Judith Zeitlin were enormously helpful for both this project and my professional development in general. The former's encouragement, productive criticisms, and reading recommendations helped me to become (I hope) somewhat more of a film scholar and less of a literature student who dabbles in cinema, while the latter offered indispensable guidance, both practical and intellectual, throughout my graduate training. In their own exemplary scholarship, both also provided valuable proof that deep thought and impenetrable prose are not the same thing.

At the University of Minnesota, my senior colleagues Michael Molasky, Paul Rouzer, and Ann Waltner read all or part of the manuscript and provided encouragement at a key postdissertation stage of the project. Of great help during later revisions were conversations with many others, including Chris Isett, Hiromi Mizuno, Bali Sahota, and Tom Wolfe, all of whom provided feedback, inspired thoughts, or recommended sources. Special thanks to Chris Swader, who read and made suggestions on the introduction and conclusion at a very late stage, and Sumanth Gopinath, who did the same and made key recommendations as well as being a critical sounding board and source of new ideas throughout the final revisions. Thanks also to all the members of the Film Collaborative of the Institute for Advanced Study, to every member of the Gated Community, and to my colleagues Joe Allen, Mark Anderson, Leo Changjen Chen, Maki Isaka, Christine Marran, and Simona Sawhney for their friendship and stimulation.

At Stanford University Press, I would like to thank Muriel Bell and her assistants Kirsten Oster and Joa Suorez for guiding me through the acceptance process, John Feneron for doing the same during the production process, and Mary Ray Worley for her truly expert copy editing. Two anonymous readers provided extremely useful advice, and I am deeply grateful for their time and serious engagement with my project. I fear that I have failed to fully live up to some of the most challenging suggestions, but I at least have no doubt that the text has benefited from the attempt. Any remaining errors are mine alone.

I must also give credit to my usually first—and in some ways most critical—reader as well as my partner and best friend, Stacey Burns, who provided all sorts of help and solace. Also on a personal note, I thank my mother, Jean Harris, for giving me an early love of literature and art, and my father, Michael McGrath, for imparting the spirit of critical thought and intellectual curiosity.

Finally, I would like to acknowledge three teachers and mentors who were absolutely vital at different points in my education, and to whom I dedicate this book. First, everyone who learns a language as different as Chinese is from English can point to an outstanding language instructor who made all the difference. For me that teacher was Wen-hua Teng, and for that I am always grateful. Second, my undergraduate advisor at the University of Texas, Sung-sheng Yvonne Chang, not only first exposed me to the fields of modern Chinese literature and film but also set a fine example with the integrity and seriousness of her own scholarship. Finally, Xiaobing Tang, the chair of my dissertation committee, was the single most crucial influence on my development as a scholar, and I am especially proud to have been among the lucky handful of people under his continuous advisement during shared years at the University of Chicago. Beyond his wide knowledge and incisive intellect, what I most hope to have learned from him is a deep empathy with historical subjects who, at however different a place or time from our own, nevertheless reflect and respond to the unique historical necessities of their moment in a way that cannot help but reveal something about our own human existence.

POSTSOCIALIST MODERNITY

1

Worlds in Fragments: Culture and
the Market Under Postsocialist Modernity

China has seldom loomed so large in the Western imagination. During the early stages of the post–Cultural Revolution era of "reform and opening" (*gaige-kaifang*) the mainstream view of China in the West wavered between patronizing approval for Deng Xiaoping's introduction of limited market reforms and equally condescending disapprobation for the continuation of authoritarian political rule. And yet, by the turn of the century a scant two decades or so later, China suddenly appeared as an economic juggernaut destined to overtake the United States as the world's largest economy. Whether viewed with alarm or with excitement at the possibility of cashing in on China's success, what is now unquestioned is that China has transformed from a secondary player in the second (or third) world to a central force—perhaps eventually *the* central force—in the global capitalist system.

This book is about Chinese culture during the latter stage of the reform era, when cultural production itself went from being largely socialized to mostly marketized. My study makes no claim whatsoever to being comprehensive—no single book could possibly do that—nor even to being representative. Instead, through close readings of a relatively small number of critical essays, films, and works of fiction, I hope to examine how various cultural texts have reflected, and reflected *on*, the "going to market" of Chinese culture and society in general during the postsocialist period. In this introductory chapter, I argue that not only have the forces of marketization resulted in a new cultural logic in China, but this development is part of a global condition of postsocialist modernity and must be understood in the context of the history of the global capitalist system, which not only transforms China but also is thereby transformed. To comprehend the processes shaping Chinese culture in the market age, we do not necessarily have to make recourse to relatively recent academic and media discourses such as postmodernity and globalization so much as we need to reexamine the fundamental nature of capitalist modernity, the meaning of a market society, and the ways these articulate themselves to a previously social-ist mode of production. In the realm of culture, we find that the postsocialist condition is fraught with experiences of fragmentation and anxiety in addition to the awakening of new desires and identities. In terms of material economic practices, as I will argue in my concluding chapter, global postsocialist mo-dernity may represent a new era of globalized barbarism, or it may eventually prove not to be as "post" as it at first seemed.

The Culture Industry and Market Reforms

China's reform era—from late 1978 to the end of the century and beyond—has from the start been characterized by the ever-expanding reach of the mar-ket in society. The initial market reforms of Deng Xiaoping were limited to pro-duction in rural households and villages, where formerly collectivized farmers were allowed to sell their surplus produce privately on the local market and villages were encouraged to set up small industries and keep any profits for themselves. Throughout the Deng era and the Jiang Zemin era that followed, these market reforms expanded inexorably (if not steadily) to the point that the Chinese economy was formally integrated into the global capitalist system by its admission to the World Trade Organization (WTO) at the turn of the century.

Notwithstanding the apparent continuity signaled by the "reform era" ap-pellation, however, it was not until the early 1990s that the fundamental *cul-tural* logic of the People's Republic of China underwent a basic market-driven rupture. The profound political and economic changes of post-Mao China had resulted in significant new cultural developments as early as the late 1970s; yet, despite major innovations in cultural expression during the 1980s, from the aesthetic accomplishments of the "Fifth Generation" in cinema to new directions such as the "root-seeking" (*xungen*) and avant-garde (*xianfeng*) movements in literature, the circumstances of cultural production through the 1980s remained shielded from the effects of the market. For example, even major Fifth Generation films such as *Huang tudi* (Yellow earth; dir. Chen Kaige, 1984) and *Hong gaoliang* (Red sorghum; dir. Zhang Yimou, 1987), regardless of their innovations in cinematic style and narrative approach, were nevertheless produced within the existing socialist studio system, the filmmakers being salaried employees of the state whose constraints did not include an overriding concern with box-office profitability. Similarly, writers of literature remained largely in the state sector of cultural production, occupying positions and drawing salaries according to the literary institutional system that had been established in 1950 based on the Soviet model. This socialist Chinese literary system met its demise not at the beginning of the reform era in the late 1970s, nor during the period of intense cultural innovation in the 1980s, but rather in the 1990s, when it became largely irrelevant.[1]

There are many reasons for viewing the transition from the 1980s to the 1990s—specifically, the period of 1989–92—as a turning point in the history of Chinese culture. Some observers take 1989 as a pivotal moment due to the student protests and the June 4 violence in Tiananmen Square. The resulting disillusionment and cynicism among intellectuals and artists, according to this line of thinking, led to an abandonment of high cultural ideals and an embrace of commercialism and the profit motive in the following decade. However, in terms of the underlying forces shaping cultural production, 1992 serves as an even more important turning point. In January of that year, Deng Xiaoping made his historic "southern tour" of the coastal special economic zones that had been on the cutting edge of free market economic reforms. With this tour Deng symbolically reaffirmed the course of the reforms and removed any lingering hesitation in the state bureaucracy after the turmoil of 1989. In the Fourteenth Party Congress later in 1992, the "socialist market economy" became the official label for the new organization of social resources, and various policies were instituted to extend market reforms to new areas of the economy. Most significantly, the culture industry was for the first time placed on the front lines of economic restructuring, and thus in the course of the next few years cultural production in general was subjected to the imperatives of market competition.

The various texts of criticism, fiction, and cinema examined in the present study come almost exclusively from the period after Deng's southern tour in 1992, with the exception of a few earlier works that serve as context and contrast. A similar political endpoint in cultural history that frames most of the content of this book would be the enshrining of Jiang Zemin's "Three Represents" in the amended constitution of the PRC in 2004.[2] The "theory" of the Three Represents states that the Party must represent the development of China's "advanced productive forces" (code for capital) and China's "advanced culture" in addition to the interests of the masses. In his address on the Three Represents to the Sixteenth Party Congress, on the matter of culture Jiang emphasized the importance of "encouraging diversity" and "letting a hundred flowers blossom and a hundred schools of thought contend," thus endorsing the already well-established trend of cultural pluralization (more on that later). The dependence of this diversity on "the growing socialist market economy" was clear from Jiang's demand that the Party "deepen cultural restructuring," "improve the system of markets for cultural products," "deepen the internal reform of cultural enterprises and institutions and gradually establish a management system and operational mechanism favorable to arousing the initiative of cultural workers, encouraging innovation and bringing forth more top-notch works and more outstanding personnel."[3] The promulgation of the Three Represents did not signal any dramatic new direction but simply consolidated existing trends and stamped them with Jiang's own ideological authority. However, for the purposes of the present study, the incorporation of the Three Represents (and thus the legitimacy of capital and of the emerging private culture industry) into the PRC constitution in 2004 serves well as a bookend for the transitional period begun in 1992 and an indication that the new, marketized cultural conditions of the intervening years had grown entrenched enough to become the law of the land.

Many of the details of the institutional restructuring that began in the early 1990s are discussed in later chapters, but an important point to be made at the outset is that market reforms in China have not been dominated by the privatization of entire industries in the sense that happened, say, in Russia during the same period. Instead, many changes occurred as publicly owned enterprises were forced to earn profits and adapt to market demand, while others resulted from the emergence of new private cultural enterprises that often found ingenious ways to exist symbiotically with, and to find shelter in the legitimacy of, the state sector itself.

In the arena of literary production, for example, the existing publicly owned literature journals that published new authors and helped to extend the careers of established ones faced ever-fiercer competition with each other and with the explosion of new, lower-brow magazines and other forms of popular entertainment.[4] As for books, all publishing houses remained in the state sector, but the market demands for entertainment and variety were met partially through the manipulations of private book dealers (*shushang*), who worked with publishing houses to get around the ongoing restrictions imposed by state ownership in order to take advantage of profitable opportunities. For example, the practice of book number trading (*maimai shuhao*), by which publishing houses and private dealers bypassed restrictions imposed by the state system of distributing Chinese Standard Book Numbers (CSBN, the Chinese version of the International Standard Book Number [ISBN]), though technically illegal, spread through the publishing industry. In this way a book could be conceived, printed, and distributed entirely with private funds but have the nominal stamp of a licensed state-owned publisher, which would profit only from the sale of its name and its officially allotted book number. Through such transactions, as well as the related phenomenon of "cooperative publishing" (*banzuo chuban*), the literature industry as a whole reacted to the profit imperative imposed by market competition.[5]

The film industry offers a parallel case of complex new public-private arrangements rather than wholesale privatization. All the major studios in China remained under state ownership, and domestic film productions could be distributed only under one of the official studio labels. At the same time, the studios were now expected to be profitable, even as their environment became vastly more competitive after the introduction of imported Hollywood and Hong Kong blockbusters beginning in 1994. The studios were thus given the incentive to produce as entertaining a product as possible, and one way they met the demand was to work with private film production companies. As we will see in Chapter Six, by the end of the 1990s some of the most popular films in China were actually private productions that simply shared the label of an official studio in order to receive domestic distribution. As in the case of book number trading, the state-owned enterprise earns its profits not by creating a product but essentially by selling its own official legitimacy and then sharing in the product's success.

Postmodernity or Modernity?

In the face of all the changes sweeping the Chinese economy and cultural scene by the early 1990s, some Chinese critics began to distinguish the "new era" (*xin shiqi*) of 1978–89 from the "post–new era" (*hou xin shiqi*) that was dawning.[6] The "post" of this post–new era was also linked to the suggestion that China was entering a *postmodern* phase in its cultural life, as the essentially modern intellectual ideologies of the 1980s, and the modernist works of art that accompanied them, were felt to have been surpassed and discredited. Much English scholarship on Chinese culture since 1989 takes a similar view, with postmodernism as the guiding theoretical approach.[7] Indeed, the concept of postmodernism is often useful in the analysis of contemporary Chinese culture. As I will argue in the next chapter, there is a fundamental sense in which postsocialist China is intrinsically postmodern, insofar as it closes the door on the particular vision of modernity offered by the Maoist revolution. It is also true that an aesthetic of postmodernism has been evident in various art movements in China since the 1980s, and that postmodernism as an academic theoretical discourse became common in some quarters by the early 1990s.[8] Finally, it is obvious that by the turn of the century the sort of globalized society of superficial media spectacle that we often associate with postmodernity was very much in evidence in China, particularly in its largest and richest cities.

However, despite all the evidence for the existence of postmodernism in China, to say that postmodernity is postsocialist society's fundamental condition would be misleading. In fact, when the discourse of postmodernism became prevalent in the late 1980s and early 1990s, the term often seemed to be used interchangeably with *modernism* to simply point to some vaguely avant-garde quality. As Gao Minglu notes, in China "postmodernity has been just an alternative version of modernity. Postmodernity was perceived as a newer version of modernity proper, instead of as an essential critique of or a break with it."[9] While postmodernism as an aesthetic or critical pose may have been adopted by various Chinese artists and writers, its meaning in relation to modernism and modernity is very different than in the Western discourse on postmodernity. As a result, bearing in mind Fredric Jameson's insistence upon "the radical distinction between a view for which the postmodern is one (optional) style among many others available and one which seeks to grasp it as the cultural dominant of the logic of late capitalism," I maintain that the central cultural logic of China at the turn of the twenty-first century is not essentially postmodern, but rather is largely consistent with the fundamental dynamics of capitalist modernity itself.[10]

Postsocialist Modernity

For the above reasons, my exploration of the cultural logic of China from the early 1990s into the new century will occasionally engage Western theoretical models of modernity and modernism. But even more important, I consider it essential to start with some basic concepts that contemporary Chinese cultural critics have applied in their own observations of culture since the early 1990s. For me, the most central of these are *shichanghua* (marketization), *duoyuanhua* (pluralization), *gerenhua* (individualization), and *fenhua* (division, differentiation, disaggregation). As these terms indicate, there has been a basic sense that culture was not only transforming, but actually breaking apart, diversifying, and becoming ever more difficult to describe simply or to pin down. These abstract processes characterize the dynamics of transition from state socialism to a postsocialist market society, and it is through them that we can revisit some basic observations regarding the very nature of capitalist modernity.

Differentiation and associated concepts such as rationalization and secularization have of course long been key to sociologists of modernity from Durkheim to Weber to Habermas. In *The Differentiation of Society*, Habermas's sometime foe Niklas Luhmann outlined a theory of social modernity that takes as its defining dynamic a process of differentiation which "is not simply decomposition into smaller chunks but rather a process of growth by internal disjunction."[11] That is, an inherently expansionist capitalist modernity is marked by the separation of different spheres of life into relatively autonomous subsystems such as politics, education, religion, art, and so on, in contrast to the preceding historical state of a relatively unified premodern feudal system in which, for example, political, economic, religious, and cultural authority tended to coincide. Central to this process is the rise of economic markets, which drive the differentiation of society as a whole, and which make "impersonal" relations possible through the abstraction of exchange value. In this way the market "removes the mutually binding moral controls that evaluate persons and thus moral *engagement* as well."[12] People and commodities (and people as commodities) meet on the market as moral-neutral abstractions always reducible to exchange value.

In his epic wartime analysis of the history of modern liberal capitalism, Karl Polanyi also saw the false utopia of the "self-regulating market" as the driving force in the transformation of society under industrial modernity. According to Polanyi, what is entirely unique to modern capitalism is not the presence of markets, which of course had long existed, but rather the fact that they run society rather than the reverse; in all previous known forms of social organization, the economic system was a function of social organization as a whole, but under modern capitalism we have "the running of society as an adjunct to the market. Instead of economy being embedded in social relations, social relations are embedded in the economic system."[13] Among other things, the ideal of the self-regulating market requires "the institutional separation of society into an economic and political sphere," whereas in other forms of social organization the economic is ultimately subordinated by the political.[14] Here again we see how the market drives the differentiation or disaggregation of society, through which different spheres of social activity are separated *by* the logic of the market, which therefore becomes determinate for the society as a whole. In terms of people's social and cultural lives, capitalist modernity brings massive dislocation and the collapse of many previous social ties and cultural codes, as relations and values are increasingly reduced to abstract market functions. The paradigmatic description of this underlying dynamic of capitalist modernity rings as true as ever a century and a half later: "All fixed, fast-frozen relations, with their train of ancient and venerable prejudices and opinions, are swept away, all new-formed ones become antiquated before they can ossify. All that is solid melts into air, all that is holy is profaned."[15]

The distinctive and irony-laden twist that a postsocialist society puts on this formulation is that what was holy and is now profaned by capitalism is not just the premodern value system but also Marxism itself, insofar as a particular version of it was enshrined as a totalizing ideological system (Stalinism, Maoism) and then largely discarded. Nevertheless, despite the peculiarities of the postsocialist condition, the basic processes characterizing Chinese culture and society since the early 1990s—marketization, differentiation, individualization, pluralization—are consistent with a transformation from a unified social system, in which the political, the economic, and the cultural are all intimately intertwined, to a market society in which the economic differentiates itself and in turn drives the differentiation and pluralization of many other aspects of society and culture. A different way of putting all this would be in terms of the distinction Gilles Deleuze and Félix Guattari make between the *code* and the *axiomatic* (to be discussed in the next chapter), which in many ways simply reiterates Polanyi's insight into the distinguishing characteristics of modern capitalism. According to Deleuze and Guattari, the ethical and ideological "codes" that governed precapitalist societies give way to the primacy of the abstract "axiomatic" operations of the economy in capitalist modernity: "unlike previous social machines, the capitalist machine is incapable of providing a code that will apply to the whole of the social field. By substituting money for the very notion of a code, it has created an axiomatic of abstract quantities that keeps moving further and further in the direction of the deterritorialization of the socius."[16] In this light, *fenhua,* or differentiation, might also be glossed as a *deterritorialization* driven fundamentally by the logic of capitalist marketization.

Heteronomy and Autonomy

In view of the processes just outlined, in the following chapters the transformation of China's planned economy and ideologically unified culture into a market economy and pluralized culture will be described in part as a transition from (state) heteronomy to (relative) autonomy. By heteronomy—literally, subjection to the rule of another power—I mean that under the Maoist social organization all the various spheres of politics, society, economics, and culture were theoretically, and in most cases actually, subsumed under the total project of revolution; hence, for example, the oft-critiqued instrumentalization of art, through which films and novels became vehicles for political propaganda. By autonomy, on the other hand, I mean the various types of autonomy generated by the market-driven differentiation of society and culture, which will be discussed in more detail below and throughout later chapters. But by this brief discussion it should be clear that, somewhat paradoxically, the heteronomy of various spheres of society and culture implies an overall condition of homogeny, or totalization, in that some central ideological power unites the social field, while the autonomy of these spheres implies heterogeneity or pluralization. Yet, as I argue above, the apparently diverse and disconnected phenomena that appear in the new, pluralized cultural field are in fact all related in that they are manifestations of the logic of marketization; capitalism, as has often been noted, thrives on its own occultation by virtue of becoming naturalized and invisible as a total system. At the height of Mao's rule, nobody doubted that all spheres of society and culture were being united under the banner of the Communist revolution, but the driving power of the current revolution is dispersed in the flows of money, capital, and commodities.

In the realm of the arts, one thing we see as new in contemporary Chinese culture is the sort of relative autonomy of the aesthetic that was part of the process of modernization in the West. Thus the various modernist, postmodernist, or otherwise avant-garde movements in Chinese culture in the reform era follow much the same logic of increasing artistic autonomy as that of the various Western modernisms—an autonomy which takes its place under the more global logic of the differentiation of society in general, through which the arts stake out their autonomous spheres just as do politics, religion, and so on. In Chapter Three, we will examine such an avant-garde movement in literature, in which the "Rupture" writers, in manifesto-like fashion, declared their independence from all external forces and influences. The early films of director Jia Zhangke, examined in detail in Chapter Five, also represent an attempt to make art that is independent of both political power and market forces, in that it neither seeks the support of the state studio system nor tries to entertain a mass audience.

Equally important—in fact even more so in China at the turn of the century—aside from the aesthetic autonomy sought by relatively elite art, there is the much more visible phenomenon whereby the market engenders new autonomies of *popular* culture, allowing new genres of entertainment cinema and literature to appear, for example, to occupy an increasingly large space in the public imaginary distinct from officially sanctioned discourse. Thus in Chapter Three we will see that not only did the growing market for popular fiction alter the aesthetic and career choices of a major writer such as Chi Li, but even the "Rupture" writers themselves, in flamboyantly proclaiming their artistic autonomy, were in part engaged in a publicity stunt to gain attention in the ever more market-driven mass media. Even "independent" filmmaker Jia Zhangke, though he did not make films in a popular genre, nonetheless soon became dependent upon the transnational market for art films, insofar as his producers expected his films to gain success through screenings at film festivals and subsequently in art-house theaters around the world. As for the increasingly competitive domestic market for filmmaking, in Chapter Six the early "new year's celebration films" of Feng Xiaogang will serve as examples of a new popular genre that appeared in the late 1990s to contend with Hollywood and Hong Kong imports for the Chinese mass audience.

As already noted, the new autonomies of Chinese culture must be viewed as contingent, relative, and apparent autonomies, and I by no means intend the term to be taken at face value or regarded as intrinsically positive. The growing relative autonomy of culture in the reform era is generated by, and ultimately must adjust itself to, various market conditions, from the demands of domestic consumers to those of a global cultural market. Culture since the early 1990s must therefore be explored in terms of two countervailing movements—a deterritorializing trend from heteronomy to autonomy in the relationship between cultural production and state institutions and ideology, and a simultaneous reterritorialization as culture is commodified and subjected to the market mechanism and the profit imperative. In fact, following Theodor Adorno, we should understand the new autonomies of culture under marketized conditions as not just being the negation of the previous heteronomous condition, but as in fact containing ultimately their own heteronomous negation. The autonomous modernist artwork—whether in the form of Zhu Wen's individualized, existentialist novels or Jia Zhangke's aestheticized art films—in fact is yet heteronomous to the society that necessitates its very autonomous form;

even the most apparently "autonomous" work of modernist art is a product of social labor that cannot help but reveal its own historicity. More concretely, it too becomes a commodity on a market (however elite that market may be), leading to a different sort of heteronomy in Adorno's sense—that works of art are ultimately determined by the culture industry itself under capitalist conditions.[17] Thus the autonomy of culture as either high art or entertainment in postsocialist China, insofar as it is only a relative autonomy, can be simultaneously read as but an aspect of or appearance within an underlying transition from a *state* heteronomy to a *market* heteronomy,[18] the latter of which presents itself as autonomy and pluralization in part by reference to the previous totalized condition of state Communism.

Moreover, what may be provisionally called the autonomy of culture in postsocialist China is not simply a condition but rather a trend or tendency, generated by the market yet always in tension not just with the deeper market heteronomy as just described, but also with the political power that first unleashed it but nonetheless periodically attempts to contain it and reassert state heteronomy in various ways—banning certain novels or filmmakers, patrolling the Internet, and so on. In other words, culture and the arts in contemporary China must both respond to the dominant trend of marketization *and* cope with the remnants of state heteronomy. Without question, however, the pressures of the former are generally now felt much more broadly and deeply than those of the latter (no matter the lengths to which the Western media continue to hype any instances of the latter they can find), and the censorship of the market now functions at least as effectively as that of the state.

Although political control of culture has now been vastly reduced in most cases, works resulting from the relative autonomies of culture in the market age often still reflect their prehistory in the earlier revolutionary age. Indeed, it is only in contrast to the previous collectivized society and totalizing ideology of Maoism that so many observers feel compelled to remark on the "pluralized" state of contemporary Chinese culture at all. (In contrast, nobody bothers to point out that American cultural production is "pluralized," since that is a given.) Even as economic transformation accelerates, both popular and elite postsocialist culture continue to be marked by the memory of socialism, which can often serve as a source of nostalgia under contemporary conditions. More significantly, the preceding state of socialism means that the trends generated by the arrival in China of capitalism (though the preferred euphemism for the new formation is "socialism with Chinese characteristics") run up against a capacity for critique that is, among some intellectuals at least, somewhat different than in the West, insofar as a generation of Chinese have experienced a market-dominated society as a new—and often disturbing—phenomenon, rather than as a given condition of socioeconomic life.

Postsocialism as a Global Condition

This brings us to the phrase "postsocialist modernity" itself. It is with some reservation that I use the term *postsocialist*. "Socialism" can take a wide variety of forms, some of which in the course of the twentieth century's upheavals became obscured by a particular strand of Marxist-Leninist communism, others of which have quietly existed and continue to be practiced elsewhere (as in the social democracies of Northern Europe), and still others of which may well remain to be realized in the future. Obviously in the Chinese context it is the specific form of state socialism pursued by the Chinese Communist Party (CCP) in the last century that has been largely abandoned in the post-Mao period. In many ways, this postsocialist condition is shared with the societies formerly subsumed under the Soviet Union and its allies and satellite states, in that, despite their differences, all these states were under the rule of Communist parties with origins in the 1919 Comintern and the Bolshevik model of the "dictatorship of the proletariat." In fact, some scholarship on Eastern and Central Europe, Russia, and other former Soviet republics prefers the term *postcommunism* to *postsocialism*, which would indeed seem to be more specific.[19] Yet to use the term *postcommunism* in the case of China would be confusing, since single-party Communist political rule has remained constant throughout all the social and economic transformations of the post-Mao era. Another difference between contemporary China and other postsocialist states is that the state-owned portion of the economy, though shrinking, is nonetheless still substantial. As a result, as Kevin Latham has argued, "The 'post' of 'postsocialism' in the Chinese context does not signify a straightforward 'after' in either logical or chronological terms."[20]

Despite the important distinctions between Chinese postsocialism and that of societies which have gone further in terms of economic privatization and rule by new political parties, many crucial commonalities remain. In China as elsewhere, the ideology of global communist revolution has been replaced by that of capitalist economic growth (i.e., endless accumulation) and individual consumerism, and the complexity and contradictions of this transition are reflected in the media and the arts. As Slovenian aesthetics scholar Aleš Erjavec has pointed out, "Today, these [postsocialist] countries share very similar problems, such as rising unemployment, a crisis of values, a loss of identity, commercialization, nationalistic ideas, and a resurgence of sympathy for the former political system, but they also share something else. At the historical turning point that marks the beginning of their transition to capitalism, these countries also possessed a similar cultural and ideological legacy. From this legacy there emerged similar kinds of artistic endeavors."[21] Thus postsocialism is a cross-cultural phenomenon that reveals striking parallels—the films of Jia Zhangke and Hungarian director Bela Tarr, for example (Chapter Five), or those of Feng Xiaogang and Russian filmmaker Aleksei Balabanov (Chapter Six).

In a broader sense, I would go further to say that postsocialism is not just a condition that characterizes nearly all of the formerly communist "second world" but is rather a global, universally shared condition. The international communist movement represented the only really serious threat and alternative to the spread of capitalism—as synonymous with modernity—around the world. The failure of the global communist movement and the apparently overwhelming triumph of capitalism are therefore conditions affecting the entire planet. In fact, from the perspective of postsocialist states, the term *globalization* often appears to be simply a label for the rapid, technologically enabled spread of capitalism into areas it had not previously penetrated—or had previously been kicked out of.

Postsocialist modernity is thus a global condition, and a condition that, with the collapse of the "alternative modernity" of communism, inexorably returns us to the "singular modernity" that is, in the final analysis, synonymous with capitalism.[22] Chinese postsocialist modernity is an integral part of global postsocialist (capitalist) modernity, and it is a fantasy to celebrate it as primarily an example of diversity or difference, as an "alternative modernity" or one of "multiple modernities" that is fundamentally separable from global capitalist modernity (which is not to say that a genuine "alternative modernity" of this sort could never arise in China, or elsewhere, in the future).

At the same time, we must be careful not to jump from this to the mistake of hypostatizing capitalist modernity itself, as if it has some abstract, constant form that simply reappears to reiterate itself in various societies, postsocialist ones being merely the latest manifestation. Global capitalism is always in flux, and postsocialist modernity represents a fundamentally new stage of capitalist development, not just for China but for the world. Indeed, as a volume on contemporary Eastern Europe has argued, the postsocialist condition provides us with an opportunity to rethink classical sociologies of capitalism, especially since "the most unlikely agents [former communists], starting from the most inconceivable point of departure [communism], are the ones who are building capitalism."[23] If there are universals of capitalist modernity (as I have argued above in the case of market-driven differentiation and the generation of relative autonomies of culture, for example), postsocialist societies would seem to offer a telling test case for finding them. Yet even any universal characteristics of capitalism always appear in new social and cultural environments with which they must cope. Even more important, the global conditions of capitalist accumulation have periodically undergone radical shifts since the beginning of capitalism a half millennium in the past, and these shifts mark fundamental changes in the structure of global capitalist modernity itself.

While it is no doubt hazardous to identify the precise nature and ultimate direction of these shifts while they are under way, it is still possible to discern some basic trends guiding the transformation of global capitalism under postsocialist modernity. First, the fall of communism as an international alternative to capitalism has, somewhat ironically, coincided with the gradual decline of American hegemony in the world. Although the destructive power of the American military is still many times greater than that of any actual or potential rival, American control of the global capitalist economy has slipped in many respects (the decline of American manufacturing, the rise of alternative currencies to the dollar, the vulnerability created by massive public and private debt, and so on) even if it remains strong in others (control of key institutions such as the World Bank and the International Monetary Fund, for example). Moreover, when one considers hegemony in Antonio Gramsci's sense of not simply *domination*, but also *leadership* that gains the consent of others by claiming a universality in which other states share in a system that benefits all, the decline of American hegemony in fact appears to be tied to the end of the Cold War. As David Harvey has argued, the Cold War provided a rationale for all capitalist states to rely upon American leadership for protection against the threat posed by communism.[24] Now that the threat has been removed, one of the most important bases for consent to American hegemony has been lost as well. Of course, to the extent that the United States' position of world leadership relied upon a moral claim to represent justice, democracy, and so on, the dominance of neoconservatism in American foreign policy during the Bush presidency—with the subsequent horrors of "preemptive" war, torture, demagoguery, extreme unilateralism, and so on—accelerated the decline of American hegemony, but the process already had been well under way.

Concomitant with the gradual decline of American hegemony has been the rise of other regional concentrations of capitalist economic power: the formation of the European Union, the remarkable ascent of the Japanese economy during the 1960s through the 1980s, the economic growth of the "Four Tigers" (also known as "Little Dragons": Singapore, Hong Kong, Taiwan, and South Korea) in East and Southeast Asia, and finally the explosive expansion of the Chinese economy since around 1990. Particularly if we accept Giovanni Arrighi's narrative of the history of capitalism as a succession of "long centuries," each dominated by a particular center of capitalist power driving the world economy, it is tempting to speculate whether China will prove to be the economic hegemon of the twenty-first century and beyond, replacing the United States as the center of the global capitalist economy.[25] Indeed, it is a testament to the suddenness of the Chinese rise within the global capitalist economy that—after barely mentioning China when writing *The Long Twentieth Century* in the early 1990s, focusing instead on Japan as the main Eastern threat to American hegemony—Arrighi himself more recently suggested that we may well be in the early stages of a "re-centring of the global political economy on East Asia and, within East Asia, on China."[26] In this view, China will present what David Harvey dubs a new "spatio-temporal fix" for global capitalism. Here *fix* is intended to have a double meaning, in that the international economic system becomes "fixed" in a new place as a means of "fixing" a cyclical problem of overaccumulation, in which its previous configuration had played itself out and led to unused surpluses of capital, labor, and commodities that had no outlet in a saturated market.[27] As the previous center of capitalist accumulation then goes into decline, with rising debt and unemployment and a decaying infrastructure, global capital seeks new spaces ripe for profitable development. Countless mainstream media reports have trumpeted popular versions of essentially the same argument—that we are beginning an "Asian Century" dominated by China—on the basis of China's economic growth as well as its rapidly expanding importance as a trading partner—not just to other states in the region, nor to other key northern economies such as those of the United States and Germany, but even to a growing number of southern economies in Latin America and Africa.

The sort of overarching narrative of the history of capitalism offered by Arrighi and Harvey allows us to conceptualize postsocialist China as neither presenting an "alternative modernity" to global capitalism, nor simply being assimilated into some unchanging, essentialized abstraction called *modernity* (or *capitalism*), but rather as becoming an integral part—and perhaps eventually the center—of a global capitalist system in the midst of epochal transformation. In other words, postsocialist China does not simply partake of global postsocialist modernity but may well prove to define it more than any other state, and the capitalist modernity to come may be as different (and as similar) as those under America's long twentieth century and the United Kingdom's long nineteenth century were in comparison to each other.

At the same time, however, several problems with this account must be acknowledged. As critics of Arrighi and Harvey have pointed out, it is by no means certain that American hegemony will decline smoothly or quickly, or even that it will necessarily decline definitively at all, and in any case unforeseen economic crises or wars could change the global outlook—and that of China—quite suddenly.[28] Even more important, this narrative of the "rise of China" reifies "China" itself and relies too heavily upon the idea that global political economy is a drama in which the main actors are internally homogenized nation-states. The real situation is much more complex, and this complexity is reflected in much of the cultural production examined in the following chapters. Rather than describing China as gradually becoming the new center of a postsocialist global political economy, it may be more accurate to say that a new potential "center" is dispersed among East Asian hubs of capital including Beijing, Shanghai, Shenzhen, Hong Kong, Taipei, Singapore, Seoul, and Tokyo, while within mainland China there remains a vast underdeveloped periphery that provides the raw resources of materials and labor to be exploited by the emerging East Asian concentration of capital.[29] The dominant images of the "new China," whether promulgated in China or abroad, come largely from its urban hubs, while the comparatively impoverished rest of the country is often ignored. Indeed, the largely neglected areas of China, outside the major urban hubs of commerce and culture, amount to a constitutive absence in most representations of contemporary China. As soon as one considers them, what had appeared to be a commendable economic success story often turns out instead to be an instance of the worst abuses of "primitive accumulation" in capitalist development (see Chapter Seven). Thus, while "China" may indeed rise to a position of unparalleled prominence in the coming century, the real question will be whether economic growth and capital accumulation will benefit a large enough portion of the population in the medium to long term to maintain the legitimacy of the new concentration of capital and the political system that upholds it. While observers on the right no doubt overestimate the extent to which market reforms have helped the poor in China, critiques from the left must not underestimate the appeal of the new imaginary of consumer capitalism even to those in China who so far have benefited from it only modestly or not at all.

The Role of Culture

If, with the above caveats in mind, we nonetheless accept the stunning rise of the Chinese economy as one of the central, defining phenomena of global postsocialist modernity, the question that arises in the present context is what role culture plays in all this. In fact, a notable trait of contemporary Chinese culture evident in many examples in the following pages is its still often hesitant and anxious nature in contrast to the relentlessly forward march of the Chinese economy. In intellectual and cultural life we find much second-guessing, auto-critique, and even a persistent inferiority complex in relation to the more "advanced" capitalist cultures of the West. Deserved or not, the perceived inferiority of Chinese intellectual and cultural life betrays ambivalence over the "going to market" of culture itself. At the same time, it shows that economic hegemony, however incipient, by no means corresponds directly to cultural hegemony. Pascale Casanova, following Fernand Braudel, points out that in the history of capitalist modernity, the center of world artistic space at any given time often has not necessarily coincided with the contemporaneous center of political or economic power.[30] To cite just one example, while Great Britain was at the height of its global power in the nineteenth century, the center of "world literary space" was nonetheless Paris, not London.

Even in economic terms, for the moment China remains mainly a regional hegemon with the possibility of global dominance still perhaps decades away. However, even within the East Asian region, Japan, South Korea, Taiwan, and Hong Kong appear to be much more culturally dominant than mainland China, at least in terms of their measurable impact in commercial culture. Korean gangster films and melodramas, Japanese anime, Taiwanese popular music, and Hong Kong entertainment cinema all have been embraced much more widely in China than similar mainland Chinese cultural phenomena have elsewhere in East Asia. Thus Chinese officials are reportedly "fretting" over China's "cultural deficit"; in the realm of literature, for example, "Officials are looking for a success story that would firmly reestablish China on the literary map of the world and make foreign publishers engage in bidding wars for the translation rights."[31] Even domestically, as markets open up to foreign competition, the issue is not simply whether domestic culture can compete economically, but whether it can continue to even seem relevant in people's minds. Susan Larsen has made this point about the "crisis" in postsocialist Russian cinema—which has parallels with the situation in China since the mid-1990s—noting that what concerns filmmakers and critics is not simply the economic difficulties of the domestic film industry, but also "a catastrophic drop in the audience's perception of the social relevance and cultural significance of contemporary [Russian] cinema," which led to a drop in the domestically produced share of the box office market to only 10 percent in 1996.[32] As postsocialist societies not only marketize their cultural industries but also expose those markets to the global cultural economy, they face competition from culture producers that often have much greater resources, more experience at appealing to mass consumers, or long-standing high status in what Casanova calls the "world structure" or "world space" of culture. In China, this phenomenon combines with the vulgarizing effects of the market in general (see Chapter Two)—and the sheer upheaval that goes with the shift from cultural heteronomy to cultural autonomies—to provoke a deep ambivalence among many artists and intellectuals about the role of domestic culture even as the economic marvel continues.

Fragmented Worlds, Worlds Within Fragments

The processes of deterritorialization and differentiation associated with the spread of capitalist modernity are frequently experienced as profoundly disorienting and destructive, and postsocialist China is no exception. Thus—aside from the buzzwords mentioned earlier such as *shichanghua* (marketization), *duoyuanhua* (pluralization), *gerenhua* (individualization), and *fenhua* (differentiation)—other terms that often appeared in cultural criticism in the 1990s conveyed a sense that the differentiation of culture and society was in many cases experienced as a disturbing disintegration. For instance, terms containing the character *beng* (collapse, split) were used to describe the breakdown (*bengkui*) of values in contemporary society[33] or the collapse (*bengta*) of a sense of social totality[34] or of a frame of reference for authors of literature.[35] Other terms employ the character *sui* (break, fragment) to convey a similar perception, as in the shattering (*posui*) of spiritual convictions[36] or of all past beliefs.[37] In these instances, the objective differentiation of society is experienced subjectively as the crumbling of value systems or ideological reference points that previously served to orient thought and behavior.

Many of these examples are drawn from the "humanist spirit" debate among intellectuals to be discussed in the next chapter, and one thing they reveal is an ideological void that inevitably appears when the heteronomous organization of communist culture ceases. This seems to be a generic feature of postsocialist societies, as Erjavec argues: "An essential part of the 'postsocialist condition' was the ideological, political, and social vacuity of the ruling utopian political doctrine, a doctrine that exceeded plain political ideology, for it held in its grasp the whole of the social field and hence spontaneously affected all social realms."[38] When such a totalizing doctrine is voided, it leaves an immense ideological vacuum, which is of course partially filled by commodity culture. Indeed, Erjavec argues, the role of the commodity in capitalist cultures is in some ways equivalent to the role of political ideology in communist cultures, in that "each permeates all pores of the respective society. In the former, the billboards promote consumer products, while in the latter, they display ideological slogans and promote political ideology."[39] Both even have similar "languages of banality" that fill the social space.[40]

Here we also run into a peculiarity of the postsocialist condition that only reinforces the loss of "ancient and venerable prejudices and opinions" that occurs generally under capitalist modernity. In China, the Maoist revolution itself, as an alternative utopian vision of modernity, advocated the systematic and sometimes violent replacement of the old with the new, of "feudal" culture with revolutionary culture. Thus, when postsocialist capitalist culture arrived, with its own need to continually revolutionize both production and consumption, it confronted a population that already had been cut off from much traditional culture while being immersed in the totalizing culture of revolution. Consequently, the loss of both traditional *and* revolutionary ideological reference points contributes to a persistent feeling of disintegration that accompanies the breakneck building of a new economy.

In fact, in today's China the most iconic character of all is arguably *chai* (demolish), which seems omnipresent in contemporary Chinese cities, painted on buildings slated for destruction to make way for the runaway construction boom, causing entire neighborhoods to disappear seemingly overnight. Considering the sociopsychological implications of the crumbling of ideological anchoring points in addition to physical infrastructures, it is tempting to psychoanalyze the cultural trends of contemporary China in one way or another. For example, given Jacques Lacan's definition of psychosis as the loss of such ideological *points de capiton*, one might follow Deleuze and Guattari and diagnose contemporary (postsocialist) capitalist culture as schizophrenic. Alternatively, beginning from the view of totalitarianism as pathologically collectivizing precisely that which should remain private—individual desire itself—one might characterize the postsocialist period as, at least in this sense, a *return* to sanity after the madness of the Cultural Revolution.[41]

But here I will only recall the classic C. T. Hsia essay "Obsession with China:

The Moral Burden of Modern Chinese Literature," which ends with a critique of Chinese communist literature, the writer of which "equates a bright socialist future with whatever little dreams of personal happiness still lurk in his heart," thereby losing even "a minimal personal life" or the possibility of simple "domestic and individual happiness."[42] A quarter century into the reform era, we might often note that the loss of a "bright socialist future" was no small sacrifice, given the anomie, hedonism, and nihilism apparent in much postsocialist Chinese culture, just as in Western capitalist culture. Yet it is also clear that the domestic and individual pleasures of personal life have at long last returned to mainland Chinese cultural representation with a vengeance. The autonomies of various industries, markets, artworks, and artists are accompanied by a new psychology of autonomy in which visions of desire and fulfillment have become highly individualized.[43] After the merging of the public and private spheres under the totalizing ideology of communism, in which even the individual psyche is explicitly expected to be heteronomously determined by revolutionary politics, the transformation to postsocialist modernity requires the excavation of a new psychological interiority that had been previously repressed.[44] I have argued elsewhere that one result of this is the rise of romantic love to, in a sense, replace the political in popular cultural representations.[45] In Chapter Four we will see how, in the "cinema of infidelity," adultery and divorce became tropes for representing not just the new interior desires and anxieties awakened in the market age, but implicitly the very social and economic processes generating these desires and anxieties.

In the final analysis, of course, no matter how highly individualized people's aspirations become, they are nonetheless rooted in a wider social imaginary and tied ultimately to the material processes transforming China in the reform era. One challenge in any attempt to describe postsocialist Chinese culture is how to give an overall account of something so pluralized, fragmented, and riddled with contradictions. The title to this introduction, "Worlds in Fragments," is intended to convey something of the sense of disintegration implied by the Chinese characters *beng, sui,* and *chai* mentioned above. However, this title also echoes more specifically two sources to which the present study is indebted, one Western and the other Chinese.

First, it recalls a favorite phrase of Cornelius Castoriadis, "world in fragments," which was used as a title for a collection of his writings in English translation.[46] Although I was not familiar with Castoriadis' work until the present book was well under way, it provides a precedent to my emphasis on modernity as a transformation from social and cultural heteronomy to autonomy. The notion of heteronomy as developed by Castoriadis, in particular, is related (though not identical) to mine. For him, heteronomy meant a certain "'closure' of meaning and interpretation" characteristic of both premodern and "totalitarian" modern societies, in which meanings and values are posited as given absolutely by a seemingly outside force in which the subject is cathected—a role which the Communist Party or Chairman Mao himself played during much of the earlier history of the People's Republic.[47] *Autonomy*, on the other hand, is for Castoriadis an "emancipatory project" that began in ancient Greece, is taken up again with modernity, and is meant to represent a society's full consciousness of its own self-constituting nature, and therefore its ultimate freedom. As a socialist, Castoriadis felt that modernity as autonomy was merely "contaminated" by its association with capitalism.[48] In contrast, the *relative* autonomies of culture that I explore are intimately connected to the trend of capitalist marketization, and I am more apt to follow Adorno's conception of autonomy and intend to imply no relation to a wider "emancipatory project."

The second, and for me earlier, inspiration for this chapter title comes from Chen Sihe's *Zhongguo dangdai wenxue shi* (History of contemporary Chinese literature), in which he describes the state of literature after 1990 as *yige suipianzhong de shijie*, or literally "a world in fragments," in which some authors uphold literary elitism, others embrace the commodification and vulgarization of literature, and still others capture entirely singular private lives.[49] The image of a world in fragments captures well the differentiated, pluralized state of Chinese culture since the early 1990s, and thus the impossibility of representing or narrating it in any way that can approach a tidy whole. However, the phrase *suipianzhong de shijie* can also be used to mean "a world *within* a fragment." In other words, each of the fragments of contemporary culture in the following pages presents us with a semiautonomous world, and the hope is that by critically reconstructing this world, we gain insight not just into the fragment but also into the unrepresentable totality, if only in some fractal form.

If a common thread links these fragments together in the present study, it is the logic of the market, and my suggestion is thus that while China in the advanced reform era no longer has any master ideological signifier or overarching cultural "fever," it does have the central cultural *logic* of the market, which, for the first time in the history of the People's Republic, leaves its traces virtually everywhere. Thus, through the exploration of some key moments in postsocialist cinema, literature, and criticism—various "worlds within fragments"—the marketization of culture emerges not just as a condition of production but as a historical horizon that is imagined and negotiated in diverse ways through individual works of art, from new genres of entertainment cinema and popular literature to renewed strategies of modernist negation and cultural critique.

2

Ideologies of Popular Culture:
The "Humanist Spirit" Debate

When one is searching for a path, there are two possible
situations. In the first instance, one knows clearly what one
wants and can even see it in the distance already, so that
one can systematically describe it and even invite others to
pursue it together; in the second instance, one has only the
faint feeling that one needs something without knowing
where it ultimately lies, and the only certain thing is that
one must go ahead and search, since one is already lost.[1]
—Wang Xiaoming

As the 1990s began, the intellectual world in China was in disarray, the nearly
unanimous consensus regarding the orientation of intellectuals during the
1980s shattered by events disturbingly beyond the control of the intellectuals themselves. Previously, despite the fluctuations of official Chinese cultural
policy in the 1980s, from periods of relative laxity to the mild crackdowns of
"antispiritual pollution" campaigns, there had been a steady overall alliance between the world of scholars, critics, and artists on the one hand and the reform-
minded CCP (Chinese Communist Party) leadership headed by Deng Xiaoping on the other. Although intellectuals might sometimes have been frustrated
by the pace of change, the policy of "reform and opening" was understood to
be the common project of enlightened intellectuals and progressive officials,
and this policy was assumed to consist of the inextricably linked components
of free market economic reforms, a more liberal policy toward the arts and
scholarship, and gradual democratic political reforms. The self-perceived role
of intellectuals was to enlighten the masses and modernize their thought while
also spurring officials further down the road of reform and modernization on
a Western liberal model.

This feeling of sharing a common goal with the reform-minded CCP leadership ended with the bloody crackdown on the Tiananmen Square demonstrators on June 4, 1989. Intellectuals in general had backed the student protesters in the belief that their demands were consistent with the reform project as a whole, and the government violence against idealistic youths from within their own ranks taught intellectuals the stark lesson that their alliance with the Party leadership only went so far. In short, June Fourth severed the perceived link between the enlightenment (*qimeng*) movement among intellectuals during the "culture fever" (*wenhua re*) of the 1980s and the democratic and ideological reforms that were assumed to be its political counterpart. After a decade of effort in carrying out the former, the latter suddenly seemed to have been an illusion, which in turn called into question the worth of the intellectuals' enlightenment movement itself.

As political reform shifted into reverse in the post-Tiananmen crackdown, and as the intellectual liberal consensus foundered as a result, the third component, economic transformation, strangely continued unabated, even accelerating as the Chinese economy grew at close to double-digit annual rates throughout the early 1990s. Any question of whether free market economic reforms would be stalled by the more conservative post-Tiananmen mood among the top CCP leadership was unequivocally laid to rest by Deng Xiaoping's celebrated 1992 "southern tour" of the special economic zones, during which he praised the economic changes under way and called for the quickening and expansion of reforms nationwide. However, the fact that such capitalist policies (though never thus called) could be pressed further even as cultural liberalization was pushed in the opposite direction only helped to split up the previous consensus that political, economic, and cultural reforms were inseparable markers along one path of modernization.

Further alienating many intellectuals from the apparent direction of economic reforms was the increasing visibility of the effects of commercialism in the culture industry, which was itself in the midst of a growing trend of marketization. By the late 1980s and early 1990s, the cultural manifestations of the intellectual enlightenment movement—such as the early Fifth Generation films and the "root-seeking" (*xungen*) and avant-garde (*xianfeng*) schools of literature—had given way in social prominence to new cultural phenomena perceived by many intellectuals as vulgar and lacking in any enlightenment value. Most notable were the "Wang Shuo phenomenon" in literature and cinema (see also Chapter Six) and the rise of popular television series as touchstones in mass culture. The critical and scholarly elite were forced into the realization that the free market reforms they had endorsed as part of the overall project of enlightenment and modernization had the unfortunate effect of bringing the most visible cultural expressions down to the level of the common consumer, who seemed to value entertainment and sensory stimulation over enlightenment. Furthermore, amid the economic boom, many academics were themselves engaging in side businesses or stock market speculation in addition to their usual teaching and research duties, or even quitting the field of scholarship altogether. Finally, within critical discourse itself, the sense of any central set of concerns had been lost with the dissipation of the 1980s "culture fever."

Against this rather bleak background of post-Tiananmen Chinese intellectual discourse, the lack of a core issue in cultural criticism was finally filled, at least partially, with a lengthy and wide-ranging debate over the state of the "humanist spirit" (*renwen jingshen*) in contemporary China. The phenomenon started with a series of oral discussions in 1992 and 1993 during which several Shanghai-based scholars cast a critical eye on the current cultural scene. However, the topic attracted wide attention only after the publication of a panel discussion among some of these scholars in the journal *Shanghai wenxue* (Shanghai literature) in June of 1993.[2] In this and subsequent articles—most importantly in a series of issues of the influential Beijing-based literary journal *Dushu* (Reading) in 1994—many scholars from various disciplines lamented what they perceived as a "loss" (*shiluo*) or "obscuring" (*zhebi*) of the humanist spirit in contemporary China. Soon their concerns were countered by an opposing group of diverse scholars and writers, based largely in Beijing, who denied any such loss had occurred and called into question the motives of the critics raising the alarm. The debate roiled and swelled over the following two years, involving a wide array of writers and periodicals and spawning well over a hundred different published essays and discussions.[3]

The debate was broad and complex, but the central issue was succinctly expressed by a participant in one of the early *Dushu* panel discussions: "After the fading of ideology, how do humanist intellectuals face the upsurge of popular culture?"[4] A related but largely unstated question was how humanist intellectuals should redefine their relationship to the official reform policy in the wake of June Fourth and the explosive growth of capitalism in Chinese society. The humanist spirit debate is therefore worthy of detailed discussion not simply because it constituted a significant period of contemporary Chinese intellectual history, but more importantly because it marked the beginning of a shift in the very configuration of cultural power in China under postsocialist modernity. In turning a critical eye on the spread of the market to cultural production, the "humanist spirit" intellectuals offered a preview, however hazy, of many of the critical positions that would be taken up later, whether by intellectuals such as those of the "New Left" (*xin zuopai*) or by artists in the realms of literature, independent cinema, and even mainstream commercial cinema, as we will see in the following chapters. In recognizing the new centrality of the market to China's cultural life, the "humanist spirit" critics were in fact coming to grips with the new condition of postsocialist modernity and the fundamental dynamics of capitalist society that were now shaping the People's Republic.

The Humanist Scholars' Case for a Cultural "Crisis"

The humanist spirit controversy was launched by an alarmist cry over an emerging "crisis" in the state of literature, the humanities, and Chinese culture in general, a predicament that was summed up as a crisis of the "humanist spirit" itself. The opening salvo of the debate was fired by Wang Xiaoming, who began the *Shanghai wenxue* panel discussion with the following dire overview:

The crisis of literature today is already quite apparent. Several literary periodicals are losing their direction, the quality of new works is in general decline, and appreciative readers are growing fewer by the day, while those among writers and critics who realize they've chosen the wrong profession and "leap into the sea" [of business] are ever more numerous. . . . [W]ith this all-embracing tide of "commodification" with Chinese characteristics about to practically pull the literary world out by its roots, the discovery is suddenly made that the great majority of people in this society have already long lost any interest in literature.[5]

Proceeding to a passionate justification of the arts as "each and every person's basic path to a state of spiritual freedom," Wang Xiaoming concludes that "the crisis of literature in fact exposes a crisis in the humanist spirit among contemporary Chinese, and the indifference of society as a whole toward literature proves in some respect that we already have lost interest in the development of our spiritual life."[6]

Thus, a perceived crisis in the state of Chinese literature is extended to the arts in general and then on to the very spiritual life of the Chinese people. Such a connection between literature and the state of the nation was of course hardly a new or unusual thesis in modern Chinese intellectual life. In the same passage, Wang Xiaoming noted that, "particularly in twentieth-century China, the vast majority of people's interests in philosophy, history, and even music and art all were clearly weaker than the interest in literature, so that literature became a crucial method in the development of our spiritual life."[7] Such a notion of literature as an embodiment of the modern national spirit began with the twentieth century itself, in particular with Liang Qichao's 1902 call for fiction to take on the burden of molding a modern Chinese citizenry.[8] Later, the New Culture Movement of the May Fourth Era was launched by Hu Shi's 1917 proposals for literary reform, understood to be a means of spurring cultural modernization in general.[9] Consequently, the perceived "crisis in literature" in the 1990s conveyed a sense that an entire century's tradition of literature's importance in the life of the nation was coming to an end, while the metonymic relation of literature to nation meant that a crisis for one implied a crisis for both.

The original *Shanghai wenxue* panel discussion—which included Zhang Hong, Xu Lin, Zhang Ning, and Cui Yiming in addition to Wang Xiaoming—went on to identify two negative trends perceived in contemporary Chinese cultural products: "pandering to the vulgar" (*meisu*)[10] and "self-indulgence" or "self-amusement" (*ziyu*). The panel strongly criticized two artists in particular for exemplifying these trends: the novelist and culture industry entrepreneur Wang Shuo and the Fifth Generation filmmaker Zhang Yimou. They attacked Wang Shuo for simply "mocking everything" (*tiaokan yiqie*), which the panel distinguished from legitimate satire (*fengci*), the latter being backed by serious critical judgment and ultimately "reaching an affirmation of universal life values." Wang Shuo's novels, in contrast, were said to lack any transcendent viewpoint whatsoever and merely to "identify with the ruins" of the depravity they depicted.[11] Zhang Yimou's films were similarly attacked for a perceived lack of a transcendental viewpoint, the director being accused of offering visions of a backward China for consumption by Western audiences without including any true humanist vision of progress or enlightenment. Instead, the films were said to be concerned only with sensory stimulation and "toying with technique."[12] Panel participant Xu Lin concluded that artists such as Wang Shuo and Zhang Yimou lacked the "artistic imagination" necessary to "reconstruct values in this age in which preexisting values are undergoing comprehensive disintegration."[13]

In the following months, as the discussion spread to other publications, a number of advocates of the "humanist spirit" further developed their critique of the current situation in popular culture, the arts, and the academy. In explaining their vision of the "humanist spirit" and its decline, several critics frequently referred to another key term, "ultimate concerns" (*zhongji guanhuai*)[14]—or, sometimes, "ultimate values" (*zhongji jiazhi*)—which were said to be expressions of the humanist spirit. Consequently, according to philosophy professor Zhang Rulun, the "gradual flagging and even disappearance" of the humanist spirit in turn "causes ultimate concerns to lag far behind the concern for money in stirring the human heart," particularly with the ascendancy of instrumental reason (*gongju lixing*) and consumerism (*xiaofeizhuyi*).[15]

There was also the implication that certain academics had been complicit in the decline of the humanist spirit and the loss of ultimate values. Most strongly critiqued were scholars who used imported new theoretical approaches such as poststructuralism and postcolonialism—often ridiculed en bloc as "postism" or "postology" (*houxue*)—theories that were not necessarily attacked as such but rather only in their "immature" Chinese forms.[16] As one critic put it, mainland intellectuals failed to "use their own language to raise their own questions," instead following the lead of overseas scholars who were not necessarily in touch with Chinese realities. "This has led to the following situation: the questions are in mainland China, but those who raise them are overseas; the phenomena are in mainland China, but their explanations are overseas."[17] Chinese scholars who used fashionable theoretical jargon were accused of applying it "completely without analytical critical facility"[18] and of trying to remove "the shame of retreat and instead give oneself a sense of pride as a 'vanguard.'"

Retreat certainly is not a good thing, but it is nothing to lose face over. When one encounters too great an adversary, sometimes one cannot help but retreat. However, when one is clearly in retreat, yet one tries to deceive oneself and whitewash it by sticking a big layer of foreign signboards over it, that's just a little bit pathetic. In my view, this kind of retreat followed by self-deception is as remarkable as anything else in the current crisis of the humanist spirit.[19]

Here Wang Xiaoming's description of the "postists'" stance as a "retreat" reveals the underlying dynamics of the cultural politics at stake. The postmodernist scholars—most notably Zhang Yiwu and Chen Xiaoming (to whose counterarguments I will soon turn)—generally took a deconstructionist position toward the idealistic philosophies of intellectuals in the 1980s while celebrating the rise of a market-driven consumer culture as a welcome dose of pluralism and practicality. For the humanist scholars, however, such a stance was not simply irritating for all its use of foreign theoretical buzzwords, but in fact constituted a capitulation both to the violent suppression of the intellectuals' aspirations and to the great wave of commodification and "money worship" that was sweeping Chinese society and drowning out the voices of the cultural elite. In short, the deconstruction of the liberal humanist ideals of the 1980s was seen as profoundly cynical, a disguised retreat from idealism that, like works by artists such as Wang Shuo that "mocked everything," constituted merely an "Ah Q-style spiritual victory."[20]

Consequently, the humanist scholars' ridicule of theoretical trendiness was not simply a form of xenophobia or intellectual nativism, as is evident from the frequent references to Western philosophers and theorists in their own arguments.[21] In fact, the very idea of the "humanist spirit" had obvious connections with the Western liberal humanism that had inspired the enlightenment movement among Chinese intellectuals in the 1980s. At the same time, the humanist scholars were careful not to collapse the humanist spirit (*renwen jingshen*) in their discourse with the Western philosophy of humanism (*renwenzhuyi* or *rendaozhuyi*), and they took pains to theorize the relationship between the universalism of the humanist spirit in principle and the individualism of it in practice, including the particularity of its historical and cultural expressions.[22] Moreover, the Chinese intellectual heritage was invoked by the humanist scholars as much as Western philosophical sources, with Confucius and Mencius sometimes serving as exemplars of the humanist spirit in Chinese tradition.[23] In the end, the issue of the cultural sources of the humanist spirit was resolved by casting it as a universal essence that is nonetheless manifested only in particular and diverse historical and cultural forms, from (early) Confucianism to Western enlightenment philosophy. The task was thus to reinvent it for the contemporary condition: "In terms of tradition, [the humanist spirit] is related to the spiritual heritage of both Chinese and foreign intellectuals, but it is also a topic of study under a new historical environment."[24]

A related question in the humanist spirit discussion, and one on which the humanist critics expressed many and often contradictory viewpoints, was the issue of when precisely the humanist spirit had been lost or eclipsed. In some discussions and essays, the answer seemed to be with modernity in general—that is, with the radical break from Chinese tradition that occurred in the course of the decline and fall of the Qing Dynasty, the iconoclastic May Fourth Movement, and the wars, revolutions, and upheavals of the twentieth century. For instance, Meng Fanhua described the situation this way: "The problem we face is: with traditional ethical values having lost their effectiveness as a measure, a deficiency of values on the level of culture will appear in society."[25] In such a formulation, which was stated or implied in one form or another by many of the humanist critics, the loss of humanist spirit becomes merely a new way of talking about the familiar problem of changing values in a modernizing society. This view would of course coincide with an emphasis on the sources of the humanist spirit within the Chinese philosophical tradition, in which case the dilemma confronting intellectuals is the loss of the traditional role of the Confucian scholar/official who both guides the cultural life of the nation and provides enlightened advice for the state.

However, the "crisis" that suddenly so alarmed the humanist critics was clearly not merely a matter of nostalgia for premodern conditions, and the perceived "loss," for many at least, had occurred specifically with *postsocialist* modernity rather than simply with modernity in general, as should be obvious from Wang Xiaoming's original framing of the problem (quoted above). Most of the humanist spirit advocates took its decline to be a new characteristic of the 1990s, the main loss being not the traditional Chinese value system but rather the "enlightenment" consensus of the 1980s, and the main culprit being the "vulgarization" (*cubihua*) or "secularization" (*shisuhua*) brought on by the commodification of culture in the market economy. Zhang Zhizhong's statement of the problem is representative: "What [the humanist spirit thesis] implicates is the Chinese reality of the 1990s, the phenomena that surface with the rise of the great tide of the market economy and business: money worship, the sacrifice of principle for profit, the loss of ideals, the disintegration of ethics, . . . it is precisely that the concern for money is far, far greater than the concern for spirit."[26] In fields such as literature, the result is that "spiritual products are turned into commodities."[27] The operative contrast in such a formulation is not with pre–twentieth century China, but rather with the "culture fever" of the 1980s, when high-brow literature was flourishing, intellectual discourse enjoyed high social visibility, and neither seemed sullied by crass market considerations.

Nevertheless, as I will argue later, the question of exactly when the humanist spirit was lost becomes an issue in the humanist spirit discussion precisely because the 1990s marked a *return* to questions of capitalist modernity that had been bracketed for decades by the very different utopian vision of modernity offered by Maoism. That is, on the one hand, the view that "ultimate values" were lost and the humanist spirit obscured with the original arrival of modernity in China oddly ignores the intervening decades of Maoist ideology (which indubitably posited ultimate values) in addition to the idealism of the 1980s. On the other hand, such a view also implicitly recognizes that the conditions of the 1990s, including the rise of an urban commodity culture and the jarring integration of China into the global capitalist system, were in some senses a return to the earlier arrival of Western modernity in China through imperialism during the late Qing and Republican eras. With the general sense of the arrival of new circumstances, what was sought was a renewal, or "sublation" (*yangqi*), of the "humanist spirit" of the 1980s intellectual scene, which had itself been considered a "renaissance" (*fuxing*) of the enlightenment aspirations of the May Fourth Movement.[28]

Rebuttals of the Humanist Critique

A sustained counterattack on the humanist scholars was inevitable given that many of the targets of their criticism were contemporary artists and critics who either were explicitly named or whose identities were implicitly obvious. The riposte came from two broadly defined sources: first from the artists whose work was under attack and their supporters within the liberal intellectual establishment; and second from the literary scholars whose theoretical slant had been accused of complicity in the decline of the humanist spirit.[29] The most notable representatives of the former camp were Wang Shuo himself and his defender Wang Meng, the respected elder liberal writer and cultural critic, while the latter camp included the leading "postist" scholars Chen Xiaoming and Zhang Yiwu.

From Wang Shuo and his supporters came a passionate defense of the increased cultural freedom and diversity they saw as the fruits of free market reforms and consumerism, along with an often acerbic attack on the humanist critics as promoting a dangerous "subconscious cultural despotism," as Wang Meng put it.[30] In an interview published in *Shanghai wenxue* in the spring of 1994, Wang Shuo and two of his partners in a new television and film production company were given a chance to respond to the charges against them within the same journal that had originally published the attacks. Their rebuttal can be summarized by two broad themes: a defense of the quality of, and motivations behind, the commercially successful artistic works under attack, and a justification of the popular artists' aesthetic and career decisions as a matter of "free choice" upon which the self-styled humanist critics were unjustifiably trying to encroach. In the first case, they insisted that "making money is no object" for their company compared to "putting out some good things," "helping other people spend money ... and get a reasonable return," and "offering our hard work as a contribution to the prosperity of the country."[31] Meanwhile, Wang Shuo's partners defended his novels as having plenty of "humanist spirit," and Wang Shuo himself defended the quality and humanism of Zhang Yimou's films, the other main target of the humanist critics' original attack.[32] In the second case, the "free choice" of Wang Shuo and his colleagues was set against the background of the social trend of "pluralization" (*duoyuanhua*), in which each person had a new "autonomy" (*zizhuquan*), conditions that were said to actually spur higher quality in cultural products.[33] The humanist critics, in contrast, were accused of hoping for a return to a "singularized" (*yiyuanhua*) condition, using the humanist spirit as a weapon to meddle in other people's choices and reassert their own authority at the center of the cultural life of the nation. Thus, according to Wang Shuo, the real "loss" lamented by his opponents was not that of the humanist spirit at all but rather "the loss of the line of sight that pays attention to them, the loss of the gaze that worships them."[34]

Almost simultaneously, Wang Meng published his own rebuttal of the humanist scholars in the journal *Dongfang* (Orient), in which he elaborated upon many of the same points Wang Shuo and his associates had made, adding an even stronger caustic edge. Wang Meng not only also labeled the idea of the "humanist spirit" a "weapon," but called it the same weapon used by leftist ideologues and artists during the "Stalinist age." He warned that "to sanctify the humanist spirit and make it absolute, just like making any abstract concept or dogma absolute, is merely to wrap oneself in a cocoon."[35] Here, as with Wang Shuo's own intervention, the idealism of the humanist scholars was depicted as a potential path (back) to the tyranny of a centrally engineered society, which "in essence uses an imaginary 'capitalized Human' utopia to ignore and obliterate human wants and needs."[36] In contrast to the actual inhumanity of a utopian planned economy, the free market economy was praised for acknowledging the "pluralism, multiplicity, and multifaceted nature of the human spirit" itself.[37] If market economies have such a deleterious effect on culture, then why, Wang Meng mockingly wondered, have market economies in other states produced a succession of great writers, artists, thinkers, and cultural figures for hundreds of years?[38] If the humanist spirit was lost, then in fact it was lost with the end of free markets and the beginning of collectivization in the 1950s, so that "while it was lost, nobody said it was lost, but now that it has returned a little bit, there's an outcry about its loss."[39]

Such powerful faith in the superiority of the free market echoed the contemporary global discourse of post–Cold War capitalist triumphalism and constituted a Chinese form of what one American leftist critic has labeled the "market populism" of the 1990s. Market populism is based on the premise that markets are not merely mediums of exchange but, like democratic elections, also mediums of consent that promote a basic equality among citizens.[40] In this view, any criticism of the market's functioning is "elitist," while the market itself is celebrated as a mechanism that efficiently bypasses the meddling of people who may just be resentful that their fortunes before the blind justice of the market are not as good as those of others who have struck it rich.[41] Thus, like Wang Shuo and company, Wang Meng frequently questioned the motives of the humanist critics and suggested they were simply whining because they could not keep up with the times. A similarly minded critic, Qu Weiguo, also accused the humanist critics of "elitism" (using the English word), and speculated further that, "in this sense, the crisis of literary criticism is probably the progress of society, and furthermore a sign of democratization in our country."[42] Even the critique of Zhang Yimou as pandering to foreign art film audiences with exotic visions of a backward China was turned on its head by depicting the critics as judgmental elitists and the art cinema world as the democratic market mechanism in action; as Wang Shuo put it, "If foreigners are willing to watch something and Zhang Yimou is willing to direct something, what's wrong with that?"[43]

The other counterattack on the humanist critics, besides that from Wang Shuo and his supporters, was launched from within the academy itself, as the postmodernist standard-bearers offered a more theoretical and systematic critique of the humanists' terms and their underlying metaphysical and ontological assumptions. Chen Xiaoming argued that the humanists were simply making a move to seize or preserve discursive power by asserting a province of knowledge ("ultimate concerns") and narrating their own subject position as the "humanist spirit" uniquely capable of undertaking such knowledge. In this way they narrated themselves as the subject of history within a metaphysical and teleological context of modernity in the Western Enlightenment tradition.[44] The phenomenon of the humanist scholars and their ultimate concerns was identified as "constituting a highly significant cultural symbol of this era," as, "against the background of commercialism in the 1990s, . . . the position of humanism has taken on a narrative function for the political unconscious." However, Chen Xiaoming's critique also personalizes the position of the humanist critics to the extent that the "narrative function" in question is mainly to preserve their professional status, further revealing the "elitist tendencies of intellectuals."[45] In a brief essay the following year, Zhang Yiwu echoed Chen Xiaoming's deconstructive analysis, describing the "humanist spirit" as a "mythology" that pretends to stand in an absolute position outside of discourse, obscuring the fact that it is itself generated by the discourse of modernity. Zhang Yiwu also added a postcolonialist critique, accusing the humanist scholars of a self-Orientalizing argument that accepts a discursive position as "Other" by repeating a Western master narrative of enlightened modernity in which China will always occupy a subordinate, backward position.[46] These counterarguments by Chen Xiaoming and Zhang Yiwu, while often using a similarly exaggerated rhetoric, in the end constituted a more challenging critique of the humanist position than the defenses of Wang Shuo and his supporters. Thus, while I have sketched them only briefly here, I will periodically return to them in the remainder of this chapter.

The Terms of Debate

As the humanist spirit discussion proceeded throughout 1994 and much of 1995, battle lines were drawn and redrawn as offended figures on both sides either exaggerated the arguments against them or retreated from certain positions for which they had been most severely critiqued. We have seen, for example, how many of the arguments made by Wang Shuo and his supporters were based on the premise that the humanist critics advocated a full-scale return to a collectivized planned economy (which none of them had in fact done), as if criticism of popular cultural commodities were conceivable only to Stalinists. In fact, these repeated accusations led some of the humanist scholars to deny in later articles that there had been any relationship whatsoever between the loss of the humanist spirit and the rise of the market economy, a position clearly contradicted by their original framing of the problem.[47] Wang Shuo and his business partners were particularly incensed at the "unethical" personal nature of some of the humanist critics' attacks, in which they had implicated the individual morality of figures such as Jia Pingwa, who had recently published the sensationalized and mildly lascivious novel *Fei du* (Ruined capital).[48] However, Wang Shuo and the other opponents of the humanist scholars were also guilty of personalizing the debate, insofar as they repeatedly insisted that the real motives of the humanists were entirely selfish ones only disguised as high-minded concern for the spiritual life of the Chinese people.

Leaving aside the personal and professional politics of the "humanist spirit" debate, the most convincing arguments against the humanist critics were those that focused on their theoretical grounding. Simply put, the crucial terms in which the original problematic had been framed—"humanist spirit" and "ultimate concerns" or "ultimate values"—had never been adequately defined, but rather tended toward both a zero-degree metaphysical claim and a generality that made them hard to apply in any concrete way. An example of an early attempt at a definition went as follows:

What I understand by "humanist spirit" is the contemplation of the "existence" of "humans"; it is the concern with the value of the "human" and the meaning of "human" existence; it is the contemplation and investigation of the fate, suffering, and emancipation of humanity. The humanist spirit is largely above the phenomenal world, belonging rather to the ultimate concerns of humanity and manifesting the ultimate values of humanity. It is the foundation and starting point of moral and ethical values, not those moral and ethical values themselves.[49]

Given such a broad and vague description, it is not surprising that one critic noted shortly thereafter that "the humanist spirit is a concept that is impossible to define, and everyone who uses it will not necessarily have the same thing in mind."[50] In fact, some of the attempts at a definition directly contradicted each other, as when Zhang Rulun repeatedly put the split between human civilization and nature at the very essence of the humanist spirit, whereas Wang Yichuan lists "the identity of human and nature" as one of the essential elements of his "working definition" of the humanist spirit.[51] The inability to pin down the meaning of the term was sometimes claimed as the very strength of the concept: "It is precisely the indeterminacy and vagueness of its denotation that makes it possess such a limitless power of extension."[52]

However, the critics of the concept of humanist spirit were unlikely to be swayed by the argument that approaching meaninglessness was a virtue, and the humanist spirit advocates' attempts to either define it or justify its ineffability sometimes amounted to mere mystifications. Zhang Rulun, in particular, was fond of resorting to Daoist mysticism in justifying the metaphysical a priori status of the humanist spirit:

The humanist spirit is certainly not some clear-cut rule or norm, but rather "a formless form, a shapeless shape." Without it, the world could not become.[53]

It is precisely because the humanist spirit is a "how" [rather than a "what"] that it appears as if there's nothing there, just as Chapter 21 of the *Dao de jing* states: "As a thing, the Dao is vague and obscure. Though vague and obscure, in it there is form." We certainly cannot say that it isn't there, but saying precisely what it is is also impossible, and unnecessary.[54]

It thus sometimes appeared that the concept of the humanist spirit would be-come rarified to a point approaching vacuity. Considering the centrality of the term combined with its lack of fixed content, there was much justification in Zhang Yiwu's observation by May 1995 that "the 'humanist spirit' has already become a great mythology, an omnipresent central term," that "is both a kind of mysterious, inexplicable theory and, in critical practice, used as a synonym for such terms as 'sublime,' 'idealistic,' 'sincere,' and so on."[55]

Similar problems arose with the question of "ultimate concerns" or "ulti-mate values," and with the relationship between these terms and the "humanist spirit." Wang Xiaoming grappled with the problem in this way: "If we under-stand concern with the ultimate as our own inner need for ultimate values, and if from this standpoint we make ceaseless efforts to grasp these ultimate values, then the humanist spirit we refer to is precisely the manifestation of this concern, which is thus inseparable from practice, or one could even say it is pre-cisely the self-consciousness *of* this kind of practice."[56] Thus, to the extent the "ultimate concern" of the humanist spirit advocates was defined, the definition bordered on the tautological: the ultimate concern of the humanist spirit turns out only to be manifested by the very humanist spirit that pursues it; or, slightly more intelligibly, the humanist spirit is the self-consciousness of the search for ultimate values. The tortured nature of such formulations leaves the humanist critics open to legitimate critical analysis and deconstruction of the key terms in their discourse, yet it also indicates what was truly at stake for these intellec-tuals in the early 1990s, which was precisely the sense of *loss* (*shiluo*)—perhaps the real key term, and one to which I will return. Early in the discussion, Chen Sihe, one of the leading humanist critics, openly stated the feeling of being un-certain as to what the concerns ultimately were: "As for ultimate concerns, what can we take up as a concern? In the West they have religion, so that whether true or not, at least they have something to believe in, but what about us?" He goes on to state that "what the May Fourth tradition has given us is a sense of mission and a sense of justice," but not a substantive tradition, and, "if we're not clear on these things, our sense of mission and sense of justice are powerless. Our courage does not amount to knowledge, nor to power."[57]

The above comments by both Wang Xiaoming and Chen Sihe emphasize the sense of the "humanist spirit" as something that searches for rather than something that arrives at an ultimate value. In a sense, the humanist spirit was impossible to define because it had not yet arrived, and the nature of what it would arrive at was not yet known; thus the term necessarily carried more messianic promise than concrete applicability. The reasons the ultimate concerns were unknown, and hence the search by the humanist spirit necessary, were of course grounded in the very social and cultural circumstances critiqued by the humanist scholars. The "loss" of ultimate concerns was manifold: the loss of Chinese tradition, the loss of the May Fourth tradition, the loss of Maoist utopianism, and finally the loss of the renaissance of the May Fourth tradition in the 1980s. In the 1990s, the intellectual heirs to the heritage of modernit(ies) in China simply did not know the term for which they were searching—hence the lack of definition—yet they insisted on the idealism of believing there was such a term, or such an ultimate concern. The problem, however, was that the conditions that led to the "loss" of ultimate concerns also precluded, for the moment at least, the very possibility of arriving at any kind of ultimate concern that possessed cohesive social force. In fact, the humanist critics' own formulation of ultimate concerns or values conceded in advance the atomization of society in the reform era, insofar as it reduced these concerns to a strictly individual level. Thus Wang Xiaoming gingerly approached the issue of ultimate concerns as follows:

This is perhaps the most profoundly felt problem facing Chinese intellectuals today. In China at least, from ancient times up until now, the vast majority of interpretations of ultimate values had in common the fact that the interpreters took themselves to be social representatives and spiritual guides, and they firmly regarded their own set of beliefs as the ultimate truth that everybody should acknowledge, even to the point of doing many terrible things on that basis. Thus, as for the ultimate concerns we are discussing today, I wish to emphasize their individual nature, or to put it specifically: (1) the pursuit of an ultimate value can only begin from one's real personal experience; (2) the fruits of this pursuit will only be one's own interpretation of such a value, which should by no means be equated with the ultimate value itself; (3) one only goes on such a pursuit in one's capacity as an individual, and nobody can monopolize the right to such pursuit and interpretation.[58]

With these strict provisos, Wang Xiaoming effectively inoculated the humanist critics against the anticipated attacks of those who would accuse them of intolerance and absolutism (which came anyway), yet the same restrictions call into question the very idea of "ultimate values": if access to them is so strictly individual and contingent, in what sense can they be said to be "ultimate"? The same panel discussion went on to address this question, with the resolution that although "interpretations" might be entirely individual, the ultimate "meaning" of even individual practice would eventually be decided by the social consensus of a community and hence by history itself.[59] Of course, this eventuality being postponed for the moment—as a pluralized market society was rapidly scrambling any consensus value system beyond the monetary—any final definition of "ultimate concerns" would have to be deferred.

Postsocialism, Ideology, and the Market

To summarize my discussion of the "humanist spirit" debate thus far, the loss of critical grounding and utopian vision which the humanist scholars lamented in the cultural products of the 1990s in fact becomes equally evident in the aporias of their own conceptual apparatus. This does not lessen the significance of their critique; rather, it powerfully demonstrates the historical necessity underlying the cultural phenomena that aroused these critics' concern in the early 1990s. That is, the very inability to define the "ultimate concerns" of the humanist spirit must itself be read symptomatically. As we have seen, the quest of the humanist spirit for ultimate concerns consisted not of a clear collective mission but more of a commitment by each individual to pursue some transcendental truth in his or her own way. This vision of the ultimate concerns, then, is no vision at all but rather the hope that such a vision will still be possible by a scholar or an artist imbued with the humanist spirit. It is not so much a substantive utopian imaginary as a tentative effort to hold open a space where such an imaginary can still arise, even if those who sought "ultimate concerns" could not clearly foresee them in the current environment.

Such a negative utopian vision has itself been viewed as a characteristic of postmodernism, and it is in this specific sense that the humanist spirit debate was symptomatic of a postsocialist condition that is in this respect postmodern. As Fredric Jameson has put it, if modernism had its utopias, postmodernism has "utopianism after the end of utopia."[60] In this postmodern utopianism, "the conception of a Utopian anticipation is foregrounded in a theoretical, non-figurative way," so that what is produced is not some positive form of utopian space but rather "the concept of such a space," "a new kind of mental entity" that cannot be assimilated by "any kind of positive representation."[61] The reason a postmodern utopian conception cannot achieve a positive representation but only a theoretical, nonfigurative space for utopian anticipation lies in the perceived foreclosure of modernist utopias. It is in this specific sense that I here apply the condition of postmodernity to China: by the 1990s, there was a general perception that the previous, powerful idealistic anticipation of the approaching arrival of a transcendent modernity in all its plenitude had been shattered or revealed as illusory. Such utopian illusions included not only the communist paradise envisioned by revolutionary Maoism but also the ideals of enlightened progress held by intellectuals in the 1980s in a reprise of the "science and democracy" faith of the May Fourth Movement. In discussing early 1990s works by novelist Wang Anyi, Xiaobing Tang has theorized the resulting mood as a postmodern historical melancholy, in which the object lost is precisely the passion previously evoked by such utopian expectations of modernity.[62] Far from extolling China's entry into a leveling, global postmodernity, this postmodern melancholy of shattered idealism serves rather to critique a transnational postmodernism that represses the preceding historical loss. Such a critique is possible insofar as, in postmodern melancholy, the lost idealism of the modern continues to haunt the postmodern present and reproach it as lacking.[63] The idea of the humanist spirit and its ultimate concerns may in fact be understood as an attempt to name this postsocialist loss and thus to offer a provisional ground of critique.

In this context, the intervention in the humanist spirit discussion by a group of critics from Jiangsu is particularly interesting. These critics—Wu Xuan, Wang Gan, Fei Zhenzhong, and Wang Binbin—strongly emphasized the *negativity* (*foudingxing*) of the humanist spirit, which was said to have power only in its critical capacity. The "loss" in question thus becomes a loss of theoretical grounding from which to oppose and transform the present reality—a grounding that is the true function of utopian vision. The Jiangsu discussion, moreover, was one of the few instances in which the loss of the humanist spirit was narrated as a global problem of the late twentieth century. Citing Frances Fukuyama, the participants describe the crisis of the humanist spirit as one that involves all of humanity, since "human history today has already reached a mature condition." This end-of-history perception, however, far from calling for complacent acceptance, requires rather a principle of the humanist spirit which "can be understood as a principle of negation, a principle of rejection."[64] Moreover, in the contemporary globalized situation these critics argued for ending a century-long practice of "using Western concepts to 'negate' Chinese traditional culture" and instead finding a critical stance of negation that "belongs to our own existence," even if the negation only prepares the way for "a reality that is not as yet realized."[65] The concept of the humanist spirit, then, functions as a provisional, local stance of negation as well as an anticipation of the future reappearance of utopian vision. Such an approach to the humanist spirit entailed *both* the recognition of a new global condition of postsocialist modernity *and* the necessity of attending to the specificity of the Chinese historical context and developing a local critical and theoretical response.

Consequently, despite the specificity of its Chinese intellectual and historical context, the humanist spirit discussion nonetheless reflects the reality of China's integration into the neoliberal capitalist world-system of postsocialist modernity, in that the problem of a lost ground of negation or critique was a general post–Cold War phenomenon. In the Chinese case, if the Maoist revolution was the negation of semicolonial capitalism in China, then the postsocialist situation was the negation of the negation, and the new world order apparently required an entirely new critical approach (as the failure of the return to liberal enlightenment values in the 1980s may have proved). More broadly, the collapse of "actually existing socialism" in the communist world in general seemed to undercut Marxism as the favored ground from which to critique a now truly global capitalism. This sense of a new worldwide condition calling for a new critical approach in part explains the sensation in Western critical theory of the 2000 work *Empire*, in which Michael Hardt and Antonio Negri argue that the contemporary situation calls for "finding once again an ontological basis of antagonism."[66] Their very formulation of Empire as a total system with "no outside," however, makes this task seem almost impossible: "It seems that there is no place left to stand, no weight to any possible resistance, but only an implacable machine of power."[67] It is in this sense of completed or arrested history that the humanist scholars' struggle to find a new critical stance toward global capitalism is indicative of China's condition as an element of a more global postsocialist modernity. Where Marxism appears outdated or delegitimized due to its association with the abandoned ideologies of the Soviet Union and Mao-era China, there suddenly seems to be no practical or conceptual bulwark from which to launch a critique of capital.[68] Thus, in a landmark essay launching the "New Left" intellectual movement in contemporary China, Wang Hui lamented that "the proponents of various alternative theories . . . have begun to recognize in the course of their heated debates that the very idea of 'critique' is gradually losing its vitality." He nevertheless called on Chinese intellectuals to seize the current "historic opportunity for theoretical and institutional innovation."[69]

Although I have argued that the humanist spirit debate arose in response to conditions of postsocialist China that can be called postmodern in the specific sense outlined above, as I argued in the previous chapter, in my view the social and cultural transformations in China since the early 1990s are not best understood within a framework of postmodernity. While much about the "crisis" addressed by the humanist scholars must be grasped in the context of postsocialist Chinese society, including the particular sense in which it is "postmodern," many of the basic issues involved are in fact characteristic of modernity itself—modernity here being understood to mean capitalist modernity, including a market economy and the concomitant commodification of culture. In short, the postsocialist condition of late twentieth-century China does not supersede but rather resurrects the fundamental questions of capitalist modernity in China.

The cultural issues raised by a growing commodity economy have a history in China that far predates the reform era and the PRC itself. As early as the late Ming Dynasty, a commercial revolution and the growing influence of the merchant class were raising concerns among literati-officials who saw a general vulgarization of culture as it was increasingly assimilated into commerce. This trend was brought about by many factors, including the rapid growth of a literate proto-bourgeoisie on the demand side and improvements in mass production printing technologies on the supply side. Together, these led to the rise of a commercial publishing industry that changed the nature of literary culture, previously almost exclusively the province of the elite literati-officials.[70] While these so-called sprouts of capitalism in the late Ming cannot be equated with capitalism itself, they do have much to do with a bustling market economy, and the relationship between commerce and perceived cultural vulgarization is already apparent. Thus, in considering exactly when the "humanist spirit" was lost, the humanist critics occasionally traced the origins of the crisis back to the late Ming period.[71] Although the Qing Dynasty asserted a stricter cultural orthodoxy for a long period, by the late Qing, commercial literature was booming once again, with phenomena such as serialization and the proliferation of sequels showing the power of the market in driving literary production.[72]

In the more recent and more indisputably "modern" past, many of the same issues were clearly visible in the Republican era, from the May Fourth Movement to the rise of a bourgeois material culture exemplified by Shanghai in the 1930s. The May Fourth Movement took literature to be a serious endeavor of enlightenment and social transformation; yet during the same period there was a thriving urban market for low-brow popular literature, the "Mandarin Duck and Butterfly school" (*yuanyang-hudie pai*) of commercial fiction that the leading intellectual figures of the day dismissed as reactionary in both form and content but the new urban-dwelling literate masses found highly entertaining. Even at the level of "serious" literature, the tension between cultural elitism and commercialism was evident. In fact, Robin Visser has noted strong parallels between the "humanist spirit" controversy of the 1990s and the debates between the *Jingpai* and *Haipai* (Beijing and Shanghai schools) of the 1930s. For instance, the accusations of Zhou Zuoren and Shen Congwen that Shanghai writers were merely "playing with life" or "fooling around" presaged the humanist critics' condemnation of Wang Shuo for simply "mocking everything" or "playing with literature"; and the earlier Shanghai writers were similarly accused of putting commercial interests ahead of literary concerns.[73] The progressive cultural elites' distrust for market-driven literary production was not so different in the 1990s, when, to cite just one instance, humanist critic Cai Xiang would argue that "the 'commercial passion' has in fact invaded literature. Literature's combination with commercialization thus makes the trend of pandering to the vulgar."[74]

In the same panel discussion, however, Xu Jilin pursues a different connection between the May Fourth Era and the reform era that places much blame for the current "crisis" on the elite intellectuals themselves. Both the May Fourth intellectuals and those of the 1980s, however iconoclastic and interested in a Western-style "enlightenment" they may have been, were actually following the old Chinese literati tendency toward a "singularized moral tradition" (*yiyuan-hua de daotong*) in which intellectuals have the "social mission" to guide the nation as a whole. Thus, while the content of the Dao, or "moral truth," may have changed drastically, the tendency among intellectuals to consider themselves its spokespersons had remained consistent from Confucianism through neo-Confucianism, the May Fourth Movement, the Maoist era, and on up through the 1980s. In each case, intellectuals would "reconstruct an integrated (*yitihua*) ideological structure" and identify themselves in some way with political power.[75] Cai Xiang adds that the tendency was particularly severe in the Maoist era, in which integration into a singularized state system was so great that "intellectuals became state cadres." In the end, he argues, intellectuals became dependent on the system, and although "the ideology maintaining the system has already lost its idealistic fervor and utopian allure, many of contemporary intellectuals' latent ideals still have a close inner relationship with this." Consequently, regardless of their stated theories, this latent "fundamental life attitude" had left intellectuals with a strong feeling of being "deflated" or "evacuated" (*bei choukong*).[76]

This kind of narrative describing the intellectuals' marginalization from a previously central role in society was in fact repeated often, both by the humanist scholars' critics, who accused them of mere selfish whining, and by the humanists themselves, as we have just seen. Both sides also tended to agree on why this had happened: the explosive growth of the private economy and consumer culture. The irony, of course, was that in the 1980s intellectuals had been among the most ardent supporters of the free market reforms that in the 1990s would leave them feeling so "deflated." Cai Xiang again offered the following narrative of this process:

Intellectuals of that time [the 1980s] did not imagine the future in terms of social practice but rather more importantly in terms of their own spiritual tradition and system of knowledge, and in such an imagination there was a strong utopian mood. However, once the economy gets started, it naturally takes on its own characteristics. The market economy that followed not only failed to fulfill the utopian imaginings of the intellectu-als but toppled the intellectuals' discursive power with its profuse commercialist and consumerist tendencies. Several of the slogans that intellectuals had bestowed with such idealistic fervor—such as freedom, equality, impartiality, and so on—had now taken on the secularized interpretations of the urbanites, producing or resurrecting the most primitive money worship, so that the trend toward individual self-interest received a practical boost, spirit and flesh began to separate, the cruel laws of competition reen-tered social and human relations, a kind of mediocre taste in life and value orienta-tion were quietly being established, and the spirit was wantonly taunted and mocked. A vulgarized age had already arrived. . . . The romantic imagination intellectuals had about society and the individual was altered beyond recognition in the realm of reality. Under the sway of spontaneous economic interests, the masses were pursuing sensory satisfaction and rejecting the "tireless instruction" of the intellectuals; the bell had rung and class was dismissed, and the status of the intellectual as "mentor" had already disap-peared of itself.[77]

What is notable about such a description is that an obvious disdain for the cultural mediocrity engendered by the market (here as elsewhere the humanist critics' positions echo Horkheimer and Adorno) is combined with a kind of sardonic self-disdain as well, in which intellectuals deride themselves for hav-ing been duped. Unlike the sense of betrayal by the Communist Party leaders in the wake of 1989, however, in this case it is more difficult to determine precisely what is to blame, other than the simple, blind logic of the market. In a lengthy contribution to the humanist spirit discussion, Wang Yichuan first theorized this logic as "disaggregation" or "differentiation" (fenhua): "Put simply, this is an evolution from the pure to the mixed or from the one to the many, with differentiation as its focal point."[78] Here Wang describes "differentiation" as an overall cultural logic of the 1990s that embraces, rather than springs from, the "pluralization" of the economy, and he argues that the humanist spirit itself must "differentiate," presumably in order to match the spirit of the age.[79]

However, as I argued in the previous chapter, this comprehensive logic of "differentiation" can be glossed instead as deterritorialization in order to em-phasize that the logic of the market determined the overall cultural logic that took hold in the 1990s, rather than the other way around. Deterritorialization, as used by Gilles Deleuze and Félix Guattari, refers to the tendency of free market capitalism to dissolve social structures into abstract flows—flows of free labor, capital, information, money, and so on. What is important in the present context is that those structures deterritorialized by capitalism include ideological systems constituted by some kind of *code* or ethical symbolic order. Capitalism, in contrast, operates according to what Deleuze and Guattari call an *axiomatic* logic, in which purely abstract formulas are determinate and the law of universal equivalency through money reigns supreme. In this view, although capitalism may opportunistically gain ideological justification through some preexisting code—such as the "Protestant work ethic" or "neo-Confucianism"—in its essence these codes are equally interchangeable insofar as they are ultimately subservient to the axiomatic. In fact, one might say that the real ideology of capitalism is precisely that all ideologies and values are subservient to the axiomatic—which is the reason capitalism can so opportunistically adapt and reproduce itself across so many times, spaces, and cultures.[80] As I argued in the previous chapter, this deterritorializing property of free market capitalism is manifested in turn-of-the-century China by the generalized shift from *heteronomy* to *autonomy*—or from integration (*yitihua*) to differentiation (*fenhua*) and singularization (*yiyuanhua*) to pluralization (*duoyuanhua*).

The axiomatic nature of the market mechanism, with its tendency to deterritorialize preexisting values and social systems, was of course noted long ago by Marx. In *Grundrisse*, for example, the power of community bonds is held to be inversely proportional to the "social power" of money itself.[81] With the dominance of exchange value and the fetishization of the medium of exchange, social life is alienated from individuals, who become "indifferent to one another" and express their actual social bond through exchange value, so that "the individual carries his social power, as well as his bond with society, in his pocket."[82] As the last chapter noted, other critics of capitalist modernity have linked the market to the breaking apart of social bonds as well; Karl Polanyi, for example, argued that it is only with modernity's market society that "social relations are embedded in the economic system" rather than the reverse.[83]

As ever more sectors of society were subsumed by market forces in China in the 1990s, the accompanying loss of social bonds and values was noted in various ways by those who viewed the new cultural conditions under the globalized market economy as a "crisis." The terms *humanist spirit, ultimate concerns,* and *ultimate values* often stood in for the *absence* produced by the deterritorialization of a heteronomous ideological field by the rise of the market. For example, Yuan Jin remarked that after "the market economy took its dominant position, ... by the principle of commercial society that equalizes all people before money, money itself became the value measurement by which everything was weighed." Thus, with the rise of consumerism, "the quality of life is turned into the quantity of life, the pursuit of quantity becomes the meaning of life, the satisfaction of desires substitutes for the pursuit of meaning, and ultimate concerns naturally decline."[84] The concern for "quality," which implies an ideology capable of making such judgments, is replaced by, or rather *is always reducible to*, mere "quantity," or the universal equivalency by which everything can be substituted or satisfied by a monetary value (commodified), including human desires. This reducibility of everything to the same abstract measure is the essence of the axiomatic of capitalism as well as the means by which it tends to generate autonomy or atomization. Notions of "quality of life" or "ultimate concerns," on the other hand, imply an extraeconomic code or value system that collects disparate elements into a heteronomous ideological field.

A Chinese theoretical language for this shift from heteronomy to autonomy was provided later in the decade by Chen Sihe, who analyzed modern Chinese cultural history in terms of the distinction between a "common name" or "shared denominator" (*gongming*) and a condition of "namelessness" (*wuming*).[85] "Common name" refers to a key ideological concept in relation to which the entire cultural field is oriented. This would correspond to a *point de capiton* in the Lacanian theory of ideology, an "anchoring point" or signifier that appears to the subject as a fixed reference point and thus serves to stabilize the entire symbolic realm. In the ideology of the May Fourth Movement, this function was served by "science and democracy"; in the Cultural Revolution, by "class struggle"; in the 1980s, by "reform and opening." In the 1990s, however, Chen Sihe describes the absence of such a common name and the shift to a cultural condition of "namelessness," in which there is no *unifying* key ideological signifier (although there may be several competing, semiautonomous ones that organize divergent discursive fields). This shift in culture from centering around a common name to being dispersed in a nameless condition corresponds to the end of centralized state-sponsored cultural production and the arrival of the privatized culture industry in the PRC.

My detour through these theoretical languages is intended to highlight the nature of the "loss" felt by the humanist critics and to relate it to the level of ideology, or the loss thereof in the face of the deterritorializations of the market. In the words of Chen Sihe, "After the great tide of the commodity economy has shattered traditional values, a giant void has appeared in the human spiritual side."[86] This "void," the space vacated by the ideological support of an idealistic, unifying value system, was felt particularly strongly by a social class that had viewed itself as the privileged caretakers and purveyors of such a transcendent code. One critic described this new condition as a kind of homelessness: "Economic factors have become too strong within the workings of society, and the status of money has increased expansively, which has left other, noneconomic social factors, including the humanist spirit, at a loss. In consequence, we can say that intellectuals have lost their status as 'lawmakers,' and have not even preserved their status as 'explainers,' but rather have suddenly become 'vagabonds.'"[87]

This raises the question of whether the "humanist spirit" itself was being advocated as the master signifier of a new ideology in an effort to resist the deterritorializing trend of contemporary culture and organize the cultural field according to a new "common name." That was certainly the view of its critics, which is especially evident in the postmodernist scholars' discursive analyses of the "humanist spirit" phenomenon. For example, Zhang Yiwu began his own critique with an exaggerated description of the influence of the previous two years' discourse on "humanist spirit": "In the present cultural context of the 'post-new era,' the 'humanist spirit' has already become a giant mythology, an omnipresent central term, the newest cultural fashion, and also a kind of premise and condition for ethical critique. The set of discourses established around this phrase have taken on a kind of irrefutable authority."[88] The essence of the deconstructive critique of the "humanist spirit" discussion was precisely to reveal it *as a discourse*, and thus historically contingent and strategically motivated. Advocacy of the "humanist spirit" and "ultimate concerns" was seen as an attempt to impose universal principles or permanent moral truths and thus assert control over cultural discourse in general. Although this criticism ignored much of the humanist critics' provisos regarding the individual nature of "ultimate values," it effectively raised the important question of how, or whether, the humanist spirit and its ultimate values could be distinguished—in their abstract discursive functions—from the ideological master signifiers of the recent past, whether they be "enlightenment" or "class struggle."

In one example, Chen Xiaoming concluded his critique published in *Shanghai wenxue* by accusing the humanist critics of attempting, "in a pluralized age," to put "everything under the command of the creed of the 'humanist spirit,' rejecting and belittling other forms of knowledge and discourse."[89] The term I have translated here as "creed"—*gangling,* or "guiding principle"—is roughly equivalent to what I am calling *code* after Deleuze and Guattari. Moreover, *gang*—literally, the headrope of a fishing net—offers a figurative image similar to that of *point de capiton*—literally, a stitched nodal point that holds various fabrics together. The same term was used in the Maoist maxim "take class struggle as the headrope [or 'basic principle']" (*yi jieji douzheng wei gang*), a slogan Wang Meng would refer to in an effort to connect the "humanist spirit" more closely to leftist extremism than to its ostensible enlightenment inspirations. Thus warning of the dangers of creating a new ideological verity along the lines of "class struggle," Wang Meng argued that "there is no omnipotent key or panacea," and "the humanist spirit is also not omnipotent."[90]

Some of the major humanist critics acknowledged the question of the ideological claims of the "humanist spirit" directly, though not in the same terms. Chen Sihe, for instance, asked, "Today should we still seek to construct a set of universal value norms, a new spiritual center," or should intellectuals "simply set a basis for getting on with their own work within their own work stations?"[91] Chen himself was somewhat ambivalent in his answer. On the one hand, in response to accusations that the notion of the humanist spirit was an attempt to establish an oppressive new orthodoxy, he emphatically denied that the humanist critics were trying to resist the "pluralization trend" or control anyone's "lifestyle choices." On the other hand, he insisted that "no matter how great the liberty society grants humans in the choice of their own lifestyles, humanity will always have some fundamental life principles that cannot be destroyed or shaken."[92]

As we have already seen, however, these fundamental principles were open to the criticism of being overly mysterious and inadequately defined by their advocates. As Zhang Yiwu put it, "without undergoing any sort of argument, the 'ultimate value' is arrived at through some sort of inner need; it is a product of faith, a transcendental realm which intellectuals arrive at through an inner mystical cultivation." He then quotes the following passage from a *Dushu* panel discussion: "what is important is that one has faith."[93] This element of nonempirical belief, making the humanist spirit a leap of faith, is certainly not inconsistent with a possible role as a new ideological *gang*, or *point de capiton*, insofar as any powerful ideology is likely to contain a kernel of passionate, irrational commitment (the cult of Mao being a prime example). However, Zhang Yiwu neglects to quote the full sentence regarding faith: "As for where the individual humanist spirit is applied, whatever kind of faith is chosen is of no great importance; what is important is that one has faith."[94] That is, what finally keeps the humanist spirit and its ultimate concerns from becoming the "despotic" new totalizing ideology feared by its critics is precisely what I have called its postmodern utopianism. The "humanist spirit" labels not an *object* of faith so much as the *act* of faith itself, and the real object—the "ultimate concern"—remains undiscovered, or certainly undefined in any collective or coercive way ("whatever kind of faith is chosen is of no great importance"). Thus, in a sense the humanist spirit concept turns its weakness into a virtue; the gaps in its conceptual structure ensure that it maintains a latent utopian potential without becoming a full-fledged ideology. This is why its advocates repeatedly returned to the notion that the humanist spirit appears only within individual practice and cannot be imposed collectively. In a *Shanghai wenxue* panel discussion toward the end of the debate, Wang Hongsheng insisted that "at least we can distinguish between an individual utopia and a collective utopia" and concluded that "in this pluralized world, . . . each humanist intellectual is choosing his or her own mode of existence, and likewise searching for his or her own mode of discourse."[95] Meng Fanhua labeled this noncollective utopianism the "new idealism," which he asserted was completely different from "traditional" idealism: "Traditional idealism is an idealism combined with political theology, a part of the ideology within the system, and moreover ideology gives this idealism a quality of coercion, using various methods to transform the beliefs and quests it narrates into a collective imagination." The "new idealism," in contrast, although it "has a utopian nature," simply provides a "space" for "pursuing a spiritual outlet."[96]

The idealist element to such a "space," then, makes it first and foremost an attempt to insert some discursive content into the "void" left by the crumbling of old value systems. This void (the space vacated by the anchoring points of previous ideologies) and the cultural products that seemed to thrive within it were perceived as raising the threat of nihilism, a specter that returns frequently in the "humanist spirit" discussion. In the initial *Shanghai wenxue* panel, Wang Xiaoming recounts the problem of the loss of ideological grounding:

[The cultural phenomena that "mock everything"] are logical consequences of the course of our spiritual development. It is as if you come to a sober realization after having been shaken to your core by a series of events, realizing that you've been led up the wrong path by your ignorant beliefs, and thus you leap up and flee toward another, opposite set of beliefs. But then very quickly you discover that these new beliefs are still of no use, and you're still continually on the losing end and cannot find a way out. At such a time, wouldn't your first instinctive reaction most likely be simply to give up all conviction, to give up the search for a way out? On the contrary, you will even mock such a search in order to free yourself of the preceding deep sense of loss. In such a bitter environment, self-ridicule can become an effective means of self-consolation. Compared with idealism, nihilism always appears to be more forceful, since it does not have to trouble itself with any verification.[97]

This account essentially relates the intellectual history of the PRC without naming names.[98] The events that left intellectuals shaken to their core would be those of the Cultural Revolution, causing the collapse of the preceding faith in Maoist ideology, while the "opposite set of beliefs" refers to the enlightenment pro-reform coalition with the new Party leaders during the 1980s. This latter ideology turned out to be "still of no use," so that in a sense we have another account of a "negation of the negation" that leaves intellectuals at a loss. Cultural phenomena such as Wang Shuo and critical stances such as postmodernism were seen as simply embracing the void or "identifying with the ruins" and thus equated with nihilism.[99] In a further discussion of nihilism, Wang Hongsheng argued that it had its positive side in that, although intellectuals who still had "faith" but faced a "rupture between this faith and its object" faced a "nihility," that "nihility is really the foundation of freedom," if only in an absolute sense. For advocates such as Wang, the concept of the humanist spirit was an attempt to exercise that freedom in order to transcend the nihility itself by establishing some primary act of faith or belief, which "is the only choice possible for a person facing nihility."[100]

To conclude this discussion of the ideological status of the "humanist spirit," it is best seen not as a new "common name," or anchoring point, but rather as a name for the idealistic search for an adequate one, and thus an emblem of its lack. If anything, the so-called ultimate concern of the humanist spirit may be considered such an ideological linchpin, but the ultimate concern is not so much defined by the humanist scholars as posited as existing. What they were more immediately troubled by was the problem of the void, or nihility, left in the wake of departed ideologies. The "humanist spirit," then, functions most importantly not through any positive content, but as a substitute that both signifies and attempts to fill this lack. This fetishistic nature of the humanist spirit is brought to the fore in one of the 1994 *Dushu* panel discussions by Wang Binbin, who first posits a primordial state of wholeness, when "Chinese intellectuals were originally in possession of their own humanist spirit," referring to early Confucianism as a "manifestation of Chinese-style humanist spirit." However, Confucian philosophy was corrupted by its association with political power, which sought both to make Confucianism serve its own ends and to "emasculate" (*qushi*) it: "This is like the requirements of the imperial court regarding eunuchs: a man was needed, but a castrated man." The "thing" lost to castration, identified also as the true Dao, or moral truth, "was perhaps precisely the humanist spirit."[101] This account of the "loss" of humanist spirit as a "castration" evokes the figurative meaning of *yange,* or castration, as "depriving a theory of its essence." The "humanist spirit," then, stands in for the lost anchoring points, or "essences," of past value systems and thus simultaneously signifies and fills in the void left by their absence. The discussions about the specific sources (or lack thereof) of the concept of "humanist spirit" in Chinese intellectual history were beside the point, insofar as the humanist spirit arises at the same time as its "loss," produced by a narrative of loss and thus existing not as a presence but as a named absence. Thus, the answer to Wang Meng's sarcastic question about the "loss" of humanist spirit—"How can you lose something you never had?"—is simply "through narration."[102] As we have seen, the postmodernist critics seized on the status of the humanist spirit as narrated in order to deconstruct it. Zhang Yiwu, for example, charges that the humanist spirit "places all its hopes in a mythological 'past,' the word 'loss' demarcating a kind of fantasized heavenly kingdom."[103] However, such a nostalgic—even melancholic—narration not only repositions the past but also productively resituates the present via the past, and the discursive function of the "humanist spirit" was equally to hold open a space for the reappearance of idealism in the future.

Conclusion

The acrimonious nature of the debate over the meaning of the "humanist spirit" and the goals it was intended to serve is itself perhaps the best illustration of the concept's incapacity to become the focal point of a new ideological consensus. In May 1995, as the discussion was winding down, Gao Yuanbao, himself a participant in some of the previous year's *Dushu* panels, published an essay that looked upon the entire discussion with some critical distance. He noted that the phenomenon as a whole revealed a surprising and growing division within the academic world, in which vast differences in background, scholarly approach, and interests were appearing, "making it very difficult for the discussion to form a distinct center of thought." Moreover, due to the lack of a "productive 'public space'" in academia, "nothing having real cohesive force has yet come in sight." Gao Yuanbao thus shifted the emphasis from the humanist spirit itself as a new theoretical construct to the problem of the environment in which the debate took place, concluding that "how to nurture this kind of 'public space' is a major humanist question confronting Chinese intellectuals."[104]

This reframing of the issue raises again the paradoxical nature of the "humanist spirit" debate, in that the humanist critics' position itself manifested the transition from heteronomy to autonomy generated by free market economic reforms. The perceived loss of the centrality of high cultural discourse in Chinese society under the market economy was accompanied by the desire to establish an independent public sphere of academia, the lamented *loss* of heteronomy thus being simultaneous with the desire for the *gain* of autonomy. This was evident in one of the major *Dushu* discussions, in which Xu Jilin noted that, unlike the West, China lacked any "independent academic tradition of academics for academics' sake, pursuit of knowledge for its own sake."[105] Chen Sihe, who pointed out the irony of the intellectuals' marginalization by the very force (the market economy) that they had fervently supported as part of the overall reform program of the 1980s, nevertheless proposed that, "whether or not the previous planned system has collapsed, intellectuals should have a space of existence that is their own."[106] In fact, as Wang Xiaoming would later note, the humanist spirit debate may well mark the first instance in the history of the PRC in which a major academic topic of discussion was conceived and pursued on such a scale with no official political backing.[107] This is perhaps the clearest evidence that a welcome new autonomy was the counterpart to the perceived marginalization of academic discourse under market reforms.

To recapitulate, in the course of the two-year discussion of the "humanist spirit," the debate itself manifested the very characteristics of the 1990s that imbued the objects of its critique. On the one hand scholars lamented their marginalization, yet on the other they asked, at long last, to be left alone to pursue ideals that would not be enlisted in the service of political power. They critiqued popular cultural products for a profound loss of idealism and pursuit of self-interest, yet they were unable to systematically conceptualize their own ideals without including individual pursuit of individual truths as a central feature. And, in a final twist, the cries of being forgotten by society as a whole were belied by the wide interest generated by the debate itself. Thus Gao Yuan-bao pointed out that "being able to attract such broad attention and response within such a short time demonstrates that people still maintain a valuable interest in serious academic inquiry."[108] At the same time, it threatened to vulgarize academic criticism itself, as the catchphrases of the "humanist spirit" discussion themselves began to appear even in commercial advertisements.[109] Geremie Barmé goes so far as to call the debate itself "a media mini-sensation," in which the print media realized that, like sensational or titillating novels, hot "cultural debates and literary causes célèbres could also be exploited to sell newspapers and books."[110] This danger had in fact been noted by Chen Sihe as the debate picked up steam. He warned that "it has become standard practice in the intellectual world to take serious theoretical thoughts and vulgarize them into fashionable slogans, simplifying them into seemingly obvious subjects conventionalized by popular usage. If the humanist spirit also becomes a kind of fashionable subject, then it will become meaningless."[111]

While not rendering the discussion meaningless, the widespread media attention did blur the line between elite critical discourse and the vulgarized popular culture it was attempting to critique. The unforeseen popularity of the topic, moreover, indicates that the perceived loss of idealism and ideological grounding addressed by the humanist spirit discussion was felt far beyond the confines of academic conferences and scholarly journals. As Gao Yuanbao put it, the "intense social impact" of this academic debate "was not so much the motive of the discussion itself, but rather the discussion unintentionally activated a kind of structure of expectation within the social consciousness of the 1990s." At its worst, what was activated may have been a militant need to "establish an absolute value," but in the spirit of the original discussions, the need was more simply to find a new ground for cultural critique within a confusing, rapidly changing, and often disillusioning society.[112]

The "humanist spirit" sensation burned itself out soon after the peak of its cultural prominence, ceasing to be a central topic of discussion in the latter half of the decade. Or rather, the same issues continued to be addressed, but not necessarily in the same terms, and in fact various ripples of the discussion could be seen in virtually all the other major cultural debates of the 1990s.[113] For example, the critique of the Chinese "postist" school begun by the humanist critics was renewed and continued by various humanist scholars, both inside and outside mainland China, in 1995 and beyond.[114] Meanwhile, the humanist critics' calls for the development of a more specifically Chinese critical discourse in the humanities and an autonomous sphere of scholarly activity were continued by the "Chinese national studies" (*guoxue*) movement, one of the major intellectual trends of the decade. Finally, the concerns over the social transformations wrought by the market economy continued to be the focus of the "New Left" (*xinzuopai*) critics of the late 1990s and beyond, making them in some sense inheritors of the "humanist spirit" tradition, while their "liberal" (*ziyoupai*) opponents continued the pro-market stance taken by Wang Meng against such criticism.[115]

The ongoing relevance of these positions in the postsocialist era is a testament to the significance of the humanist spirit discussion itself, for raising important new issues if not for resolving them. As the first large-scale debate in the PRC that took the marketization of culture (rather than some aspect of the relationship between culture and politics) as its central concern, the humanist spirit debate marks the entry of what I am calling postsocialist modernity itself—that is, the new condition of global capitalism in the post-Soviet, post-Mao age—into critical consciousness in Chinese intellectual discourse. To explore some ways in which marketization played out in actual cultural texts of this time, we will turn first to some trends in literature that began in the early 1990s and remained relevant well into the new century.

3

Adaptations and Ruptures:
Literature in the New Culture Industry

> As for "nihilism," we shall acknowledge that our epoch
> bears witness to it precisely in the way that by nihilism we
> understand the *rupture of the traditional figure of the bond*,
> un-binding as a form of being of all that pretends to be of
> the bond. Our time indubitably sustains itself with a kind of
> generalized atomism because no symbolic sanction of the
> bond is capable of resisting the abstract potency of Capital.[1]
> —Alain Badiou

> Thus isolation is a project.[2]
> —Jean-Paul Sartre

As the previous chapter has shown, there was a general sense during the first half of the 1990s that the Chinese literary scene was in the midst of a large-scale transition. The literary trends of the previous decade seemed to have spent their energy, while the spread of market reforms to the culture industry presented a new set of challenges and opportunities for writers and publishers. As we have seen, while virtually all prominent literary scholars and critics agreed that the conditions of literary production were undergoing a massive transformation, they were sharply divided in their evaluation of the new situation, including the desirability and predicted effects of market reforms as well as the degree to which contemporary Chinese literature was meeting the new challenges it faced.

While the Shanghai-based scholars who launched the "humanist spirit" debate sounded the alarm over an emerging "crisis" in the state of literature, the humanities, and Chinese culture in general, others were arguing that much new literature was in fact making precisely the adjustment to new conditions that the humanist scholars had found lacking. This position was exemplified by Zhang Yiwu, Wang Gan, and Zhang Weimin, who proclaimed the arrival of "New-State-of-Affairs literature" (*xin zhuangtai wenxue*), which was held to be a dynamic and appropriate "transition mechanism" through which literature articulated the transformation of society and culture.[3] "New-State-of-Affairs literature" was said to go beyond the "New Realist" (*xin xieshi*) and "experimental" (*shiyan*) schools that had dominated the elite literary scene at the turn of the decade, and it was in fact one of several new labels that proliferated in the 1990s as critics attempted to come to grips with emerging literary trends; others included "Post-New-Era literature" (*houxinshiqi wenxue*), "New Urbanite fiction" (*xin shimin xiaoshuo*), and "New Experiential fiction" (*xin tiyan xiaoshuo*). Among the most noted traits of the new fiction were an urban and contemporary setting, an aversion to allegory and symbolism, and a narrative perspective that focused on—and arose from—personal experience rather than either formal artistic concerns or explicit ideological programs.

Despite the optimism of critics such as Zhang Yiwu, literature was undoubtedly going through a severe institutional readjustment—if not an outright "crisis" as the humanist critics claimed—by the early 1990s. As early as the mid-1980s, the literature industry had followed other sectors of the economy in undergoing market-based economic reforms. In 1984 the government signaled that literary journals should move toward becoming more financially self-sustaining, and around the same time there was an explosion of popular entertainment literature, which responded directly to the mass market and helped spur a decline in readership among journals of elite literature. However, it was not until 1992 that literary institutions were placed firmly on the agenda of economic reform, with authors, literary periodicals, and publishing houses expected to sever their reliance upon state subsidies and squarely face market forces.[4] A new era in publishing was signaled when Wang Shuo was compensated through royalties rather than a one-time fee for publication of his collected works. Legions of less popular writers were expected to wean themselves from public stipends, and thus many authors of "pure" or "serious" literature began to "leap into the sea" (*xiahai*) of private business, writing more lucrative but less prestigious forms of literature such as popular fiction, film and television scripts, advertising copy, and reportage. Given the profusion of new entertainment options—such as television, through which increasingly diverse programming was available to more households than ever—competition for the public's attention was fierce, and economic pressures pushed both authors and literary periodicals to change their standards and adapt to the emerging consumerist leisure culture. To cite one example of the new set of economic incentives faced by authors, the fees paid for literature published in the new, profit-oriented popular periodicals began at a rate over three times that of the elite, state-funded journals of "pure" literature.[5] Meanwhile, those elite journals themselves tried to overcome dwindling state funding, making efforts to attract more readers and financial support through such means as improved layout design and paper quality, much-hyped writers' contests, corporate sponsorship, advertising, and the introduction of new, more popular genres of writing. Critics such as Zhang Yiwu himself became celebrities who could reliably generate controversy, and thus sell periodicals, so that the careers of top literary critics and scholars were in many cases also beholden to the logic of the market. The very proliferation of new "schools" of literature—each championed by one or another literary journal—was as much a reflection of the journals' efforts to attract attention and appear on the cutting edge as it was a result of real, significant changes or distinctions within literature itself.[6] In other words, such labels were appearing no longer as positions taken on an ideological or aesthetic battleground, but rather as name brands to help journals and critics compete on the cultural market. For the writers themselves, as was the case with visual artists during the 1990s, there was an absence of self-conscious "movements" (*yundong*) through which artists participated in common projects.[7] Instead, artistic production shared in the general cultural and social trends toward autonomy, atomization, and pluralism in the new market economy, and the various "schools" of literature hailed as new and cutting-edge were largely an invention of critics and editors rather than the result of collective self-positioning by authors.

In fact, many of the newly labeled "schools" of literature were characterized even by critics in terms which themselves brought into question the presumed unity of the set of works or writers thus grouped. In particular, the writers of "New-State-of-Affairs literature," "New Urbanite fiction," and "New Experiential fiction" (categories which largely overlapped) were praised as proceeding from direct, observable, individual experience rather than from an overarching ideology or ideal. As a result of the individualized styles and concerns of writers, the "schools" thus defined not only encompassed a wide variety of expressions but paradoxically even took individualized expression as one of their defining common characteristics.

In this chapter, I will use the works and career paths of two very different contemporary authors, Chi Li and Zhu Wen, as a means of exploring some of the new schools or genres of literature that were significant from the late 1980s to the turn of the century. These included "New Realist fiction" (*xin xieshi xiaoshuo*) and "popular" or "common literature" (*tongsu wenxue*) in the case of Chi Li, and the "late-born generation" (*wanshengdai*) or "newly born generation" (*xinshengdai*) and the "Rupture" (*duanlie*) group in the case of Zhu Wen. By moving between readings of these writers' fiction and examination of the larger phenomena they were said to exemplify, I hope to highlight some of the broader dynamics of the literary world under postsocialist modernity in China. Both writers will be viewed as constituting specific adaptations to the new environment of the culture market. In particular, the career trajectory of Chi Li will be used to illustrate how some authors met the challenges of the breakdown of the elite literary institutions by pursuing success in the popular cultural market. Zhu Wen, in contrast, will be viewed as an instance of resistance to the trend of popular, commodified culture and part of a modernist effort to assert the autonomy of the aesthetic and the possibility of a radical break from the past and even from the present "state of affairs." Despite their obvious differences, both writers developed strategies to adapt to the drastic change in the status of literature within contemporary Chinese culture in general, and in the end both found it expedient to branch out from literary production into other media to pursue new creative and financial opportunities.

The "New Realism" of Chi Li's Emasculated Heroes

In terms of literary style, thematic concerns, and even the way in which a new "school" was christened, the "New Realist fiction" that began in the late 1980s was a forerunner to many of the new schools of literature that would be hailed in the following decade. New Realist fiction was described as partly a reaction against the avant-garde fiction (*xianfeng xiaoshuo*) of the mid to late 1980s. Whereas the avant-garde writers were said to have left many baffled readers behind in their pursuit of pure experimentation with language, New

Realism was commended for returning to the concrete daily life of contemporary China and thus attaining a legibility and appeal to readers in general that other elite fiction of the time had lost. When the editors of the literary journal *Zhongshan* published a special issue on New Realist fiction, which was defined in an editorial preface, the journal was not simply aligning itself with the new "school" it was trumpeting, but helping to constitute, partly through the sheer act of naming, the very object of its study, which in turn would serve as a marketing tool for the journal.[8] As Hong Zicheng points out, "it is evident that the posing of 'New Realist fiction' was not just an outline of a new writing trend, but also a literary phenomenon formed by the 'manipulation' [*caozuo*] of critics and literary journals."[9] Many of the characteristics claimed for New Realist fiction were in fact reiterated and elaborated within the various new schools of literature in the 1990s, as those were in turn generated by subsequent editorial and critical "manipulations," making much fiction of the 1990s an outgrowth of sorts to New Realist fiction.

Despite his skepticism toward the initial hailing of New Realism, Hong Zicheng himself acknowledges a trend in Chinese literature that began in the late 1980s and continued, under various names, throughout the 1990s—a new literature that "expressed the material reality of modern urban life."[10] There were important differences between the new literature and the preexisting tradition of "realism" in modern Chinese literature. According to Hong, one of the most notable characteristics of the new trend was the fragmentation of the "realist" world depicted into an entirely individual perspective: "individual experience became the key reference upon which writers based their descriptions of reality." This fragmentation of perspective, in which the "reality" of the realist work is incapable of transcending individual perspective and achieving a sense of social totality, is ascribed to the breakup of all-encompassing ideologies by the end of the 1980s as well as the growing prominence of "commercial society."[11]

One manifestation of this newly individualized perspective among the New Realist authors was an important subgroup of the school, namely two new women authors from Wuhan, Chi Li and Fang Fang. As two of the most oft-cited examples of the new literary trend, Chi Li and Fang Fang were notable both for their attention to the individual life struggles of ordinary urban dwellers and for the regional setting and language of their fiction. In their attention to seemingly trivial life events as well as the peculiarities of local customs and slang, they constituted an irruption of "feminine detail" and provincial color into the narrative of contemporary Chinese literary history.[12] The attention to detail by these Wuhan writers exemplified the turn of New Realism as a whole away from the master narratives of either Maoist revolution or the subsequent "Enlightenment" movement of the 1980s—which, even as it opposed the ideological excesses of the Cultural Revolution, still produced writers who "emphasize[d] only social problems from a reformist approach," which had its own teleological ideology.[13] New Realist novelists such as Chi Li abandoned all obvious ideological objectives in favor of close but carefully limited attention to the trivialities of daily life in a very particular provincial setting. These details not only assert contingent individual subjectivity against a totalized view of society but also foreground local culture in a way that is not then integrated into a broader national identity. A look at some of Chi's characteristic New Realist works will illustrate these and other aspects of the new trend in literature.

Chi's short story "Leng ye hao, re ye hao, huozhe jiu hao" (Hot or cold, it's good to be alive), first published in 1991, perhaps best exemplifies the regional flavor and attention to detail of the author's early works.[14] The story spans less than a day, relates no dramatic events, and is peppered with sometimes salacious local slang and discussions of local customs and cuisine. Much of the action, such as there is, revolves around the long-standing Wuhan habit of sleeping outside on the edges of the streets to seek relief from the oppressive summer heat (a custom soon on the decline, as air conditioners became more common). The main characters are a cheerful young drugstore clerk named Maozi, his somewhat haughty bus-driver girlfriend, Yanhua, and their friends and family members. Maozi is notably feminized by his worshipful, domesticated devotion to Yanhua, expressed by his willingness to cook and clean for her and uncomplainingly absorb her scoldings. However, more than anything the story celebrates the sweaty passion of the couple's young love as well as the community spirit of people who survive extreme heat by mingling together on the street.

Chi Li's most famous early story, and the one with the most paradigmatic status in the New Realist movement, was *Fannao rensheng* (Troublesome life), first published in the elite literary journal *Shanghai wenxue* in 1987. Like "Hot or Cold, It's Good to Be Alive," the novella carefully limits its scope, this time to a single day in the life of an ordinary man, Yin Jiahou, a factory technician who struggles to make ends meet and raise his young son while coping with his judgmental and perpetually unsatisfied wife (whose name is never given). As Yin goes through the various tribulations of his day at work, his wife's domestic nagging and lack of physical attractiveness are contrasted with the seductions of three other women: Yin's assistant, who professes her sexual availability to him; a beautiful young worker Yin flirts with at the factory kindergarten where he leaves his son for the day; and a mysterious former lover whom the kindergarten worker resembles, dredging up painful memories of love lost. At the end of the day, however, lying in bed beside his spouse, Yin realizes that he is inseparable from her and concludes that "the wife of an ordinary man should be just this coarse, this cranky, without a bit of pretension."[15]

The theme of a man coming to terms, through the daily struggles of marriage, with life as ineluctably "ordinary" is also common to two other novellas that, with *Troublesome Life*, are sometimes grouped together by critics as Chi Li's "life trilogy" (*rensheng sanbuqu*). In *Bu tan aiqing* (Don't mention love), first published in 1988, a doctor named Zhuang Jianfei, who has gotten married only in order to have a sexual outlet, in the course of a long falling out with his wife and in-laws comes to face the need to compromise and sacrifice for the sake of a marriage. Similarly, in *Taiyang chushi* (The sun comes out), published in the literary journal *Zhongshan* in 1990, young Zhao Shengtian is gradually transformed from a fun-loving hooligan into a responsible husband and father by the normal experiences of adjusting to marriage, childbirth and child rearing, and the financial burdens of maintaining a household. In each case, as with *Troublesome Life*, the "reality" of ordinary daily life not only is sketched to the exclusion of high drama or heroic action, but also is implicitly *chosen*—or at least consciously acquiesced to—by the male protagonists in an act of sacrifice of some previous preference or ideal—the lost romance of Yin Jiahou's past (still attainable in the substitute form of adulterous affairs), the no-strings-attached sex which was Zhuang Jianfei's past as well as his unrealistic expectation of marriage, and the friendships and wild evenings out that Zhao Shengtian had enjoyed before marrying and settling down.

During this early stage of her writing career, Chi Li articulates a new concern with representing the everyday life of mostly ordinary working-class townsfolk. However, these stories notably do not focus on the everyday lives of women, for example, by capturing the trivial details of the domestic life of housewives or mothers. Rather, they feature male characters who are explicitly *feminized* in the sense that they turn away from stereotypically masculine sexuality and male friendships to adapt instead to the rhythms of the domestic household and the material and emotional needs of their wives. Thus there are frequent incidents in which a male protagonist is emasculated by a humiliating incident or a cutting comment, and the narratives trace a gradual repression of those characters' extramarital sexual desires and dreams. In other words, these "realist" stories enact a demasculinization of their protagonists, who are forced precisely to become "realists" who must give up an imaginary phallic power in order to cope with an everyday domestic and vocational sphere that demands constant compromise and humility. In *Troublesome Life*, for example, Yin Jiahou's day begins in early morning, when his son falls out of bed, leading to a series of mishaps that soon have his wife roundly scolding him for the poor quality of housing he provides the family, ending her tirade with "What kind of a man are you!" Moments later, after using a screwdriver to turn off a broken light fixture, Yin Jiahou has murderous fantasies of violent masculine reempowerment: "The instant the light went out, Yin Jiahou's eye caught the gleam of the screwdriver in his hand, which was followed by a fleeting thought. He dared not take another look at his wife, he was so badly frightened by his own idea."[16] The day that follows, ending with the mental reconciliation of Yin Jiahou to his family life mentioned above, amounts to an exercise in the repression of the forbidden desires, both violent and sexual, that apparently fill his fantasy life.

This subsumption of stereotypical masculinity by a feminized domestic sphere coincides with the broader role of New Realism in modern and contemporary Chinese literary history, and specifically in the historical dialectics of "the heroic and the quotidian," as described by Xiaobing Tang.[17] Chi Li's attention to domesticity and the personal politics of love and marriage necessarily means that, as in Zhang Ailing's narratives of "feminine detail" analyzed by Rey Chow, "'big' historical issues tend to recede into the background," an approach that "stands at the opposite extreme of the 'revolutionariness' that we often associate with modernity in the Chinese literary context."[18] New Realist fiction distinguishes itself from the classic May Fourth form of modern Chinese literature by rejecting the possibility of attaining a transcendent, enlightened critical view of society. At the same time, it is the antithesis of the later Maoist version of socialist realism, with its imperative to demarcate positive characters from negative characters and its focus on heroism in the service of revolution. In renouncing the fantasy of empowerment through enlightenment or revolutionary consciousness in favor of engagement with an intractable daily reality, New Realism conforms to what Fredric Jameson refers to as "the idea of realism as a decoding" or "demystification of some preceding ideal or illusion."[19] In short, the "ordinary life" of New Realist fiction constitutes an irruption of the nonpolitical, unheroic, and essentially nonnational everyday life that had been previously repressed by conceptions of literature as a tool for narrating Chinese national modernity from the May Fourth Era to the Cultural Revolution to the various politically tinged literary movements of the 1980s.

This view is supported by the sole book-length Chinese critical study of Chi Li's fiction, by Liu Chuan'e, whose main purpose, however, is to contrast this New Realist phase of Chi Li's career with her work a decade or so later, in the late 1990s, to which we will turn shortly. According to Liu,

in [Chi Li's] *Troublesome Life* stage at the end of the 1980s, her stories describing the life vicissitudes of ordinary people contrast with the "grand narratives" and "false grand narratives" of the preceding scar literature, introspection literature, literature of reformers, root-seeking literature, and realist literature, building a new focal point for writing out of the most valueless daily life processes of urbanites. . . . Chi Li's household chitchat narratives perfectly match the mentality of practical, day-to-day getting-by when the old idealisms have been smashed and new idealisms have yet to be born.[20]

For Liu, the disillusion expressed by New Realism consists partly in the realization that the "Four Modernizations" and the era of "opening and reform" were offering promises that they would fail to keep, as "the dreams of modernization in people's hearts began to be dispersed by the much more concrete details of individual life." Consequently, "the hardships of reality shook the foundations of the 'grand narratives.'"[21] Indeed, literary critic Zhang Yiwu proclaimed "the end of idealism" in early 1989 *before* the violence in Tiananmen Square broke out that same year, indicating that literature was already manifesting a gen-

eral weariness with teleological or utopian concerns; the idealistic reformist
ideology which earlier in the decade had held the promise of an imminent,
enlightened transformation of society and culture was being eroded by the
monotony of everyday life.[22] The emasculated daily lives of Chi Li's early New
Realist protagonists bespeak a larger loss of faith in the master signifiers of the
reform era.

Success and "Vulgarization"

Liu distinguishes this New Realist phase of Chi Li's writing from her later
career as a celebrity writer of best-selling novels and television scripts, exemplified by the 1998 novel *Lailai wangwang* (Coming and going). These later works
of Chi Li are said to be representative of a newer prevalent mentality in Chinese culture, so that tracing Chi Li's career becomes a method of mapping the
cultural changes wrought by postsocialist modernity itself: "Her urban legend
stories of recent years have catered to the aspirations for wealth and curiosity
about the world of decadence among that majority of readers who hope to get
rich but have not done so."[23] While critical of the quality even of Chi Li's earlier
fiction, Liu especially dismisses the "fast-food aesthetic" of her later works, the
popularity of which is only seen as further evidence of the trend of "pandering
to the vulgar" (*meisu*) in society as a whole.[24] Between the earlier, New Realist
works and the novels of the late 1990s, Liu sees several important changes. First,
there was a clear shift in class emphasis from relatively low-status "ordinary"
people and their life troubles to the "successful personages" (*chenggong renshi*) of the new urban market economy. In plot and language, there was a shift
toward "common literature" (*tongsu wenxue*) as opposed to "pure literature"
(*chun wenxue*). Finally, in terms of literary style, Liu sees a shift from the slight
and unadorned prose of the New Realist period to an extravagant and exaggerated style in the later "legends of wealth."[25] These changes in the stories themselves are accompanied by a shift in Chi's status as a novelist, which was transformed from that of a young writer taken seriously by the elite literary scene
in the late 1980s to an emblem, for critics such as Liu, of the vulgarization of
culture during the 1990s. At the same time, in terms of popular reception, Chi
Li became the name of a "phenomenon" whereby the writer herself becomes "a

trademark, is a selling point," and, indeed, is publicly imagined as the very type of "successful personage" of the 1990s that she was now writing about.[26]

Nothing represents the change in the status of Chi Li as a writer, and the changing role of literature within the culture industry, better than the phenomenon of *Coming and Going*.[27] Within two years of its publication in August 1998,[28] this novella had sold two hundred thousand copies and had been turned into an eighteen-episode dramatic series that was the nationwide television sensation of the summer of 1999.[29] In contrast to the modest narratives of Chi's earlier New Realist stories, with their depictions of daily life over the course of as little as a single day, *Coming and Going* is no less than a national allegory spanning several decades and describing the rise of a humble clerk in a frozen meat warehouse in the mid-1970s to become a successful, wealthy businessman in the booming new urban economy of the 1990s. The focus on a male protagonist and his struggles with his wife and his own desires had not changed from the earlier works of the New Realist period; however, the life circumstances of the male hero and, most remarkably, the ways he negotiates the gap between his fantasy life and his real life all were in remarkable contrast to the previous works.

As we have seen, in Chi Li's important New Realist narratives such as *Troublesome Life*, the protagonist learns to suppress his extramarital longings in order to squarely face the ordinary life—and ordinary wife—that is his lot as an average person. *Coming and Going*, on the other hand, presents a portrait of a common man who becomes a very successful businessman and in the process is able to reverse the power relationship between himself and his wife. When Kang Weiye first meets his future spouse, Duan Li'na, she is a well-connected Party member and daughter of an army officer. After the two have sex, she blackmails him into marrying her and continues to dominate him in their early married life. Later, however, after he has begun his ascent as a businessmen to the highest reaches of the new economy, Weiye begins to ignore Li'na and instead falls in love with a beautiful business associate named Lin Zhu. Lin Zhu serves as an ultimate fantasy object who introduces Weiye to a whole new refined, cosmopolitan lifestyle during their torrid romantic affair. The relationship only falls apart when the two try to set up an alternative domestic space together in an apartment he buys for her. Disillusioned by the complications of quotidian routine as well as Weiye's reluctance to divorce his wife, Zhu eventually leaves him. Weiye is still unable to repair his marriage, as he is permanently estranged from his wife, whose conservative values, including an ongoing attachment to revolutionary ideals and a tendency to quote Mao Zedong, appear hopelessly outdated to a successful businessman in the reform era. Finally, Weiye takes yet another lover, but this time it is an attractive young woman, Shi Yupeng, who provides neither powerful connections nor romance but simply physical intimacy, and who in turn receives a cash allowance from Weiye in what amounts to a straightforward commercial arrangement. In quickly consenting to the cash gifts, the fun-loving but none-too-deep Yupeng herself breezily muses, "So I'm a commodity; who isn't a commodity?"[30] Meanwhile, Weiye himself does not worry about the fact that Yupeng obviously fakes orgasms during sex—her hollow responses "probably all gathered from watching TV"—but instead decides "just pursuing his own pleasure is fine."[31]

In the course of Coming and Going, then, rather than repressing his masculine desires in favor of a quotidian domestic reality, Kang Weiye enters a series of sexual relationships—first with a conservative wife who continues to act as a kind of revolutionary superego (the threat of which is embodied in a dagger she owns, which Weiye at one point fears she will use to kill his girlfriend); then with a glamorous lover who shows him a new world of luxury living and passionate desire fulfillment; and finally with a kind of compromise mistress who becomes a mere commodified plaything. In contrast to the repression of forbidden appetites and acceptance of an "ordinary" life by the protagonists of Chi Li's earlier works, Weiye freely acts upon his desires, so that the story of his life becomes not a confrontation with daily reality but rather its opposite—an exercise in fantasy fulfillment. At the same time, his final arrangement with Shi Yupeng makes clear that this fulfillment will be incomplete, consisting more in boundless commodity consumption than in the permanent consummation of idealized romantic passion, as embodied by Zhu.

Far from her earlier works' sense of history's arrested development—of the need to cope with the immediate, repetitive problems of an intransigent reality—in Coming and Going Chi Li attempts not so much a more ambitious form of writing (indeed, it is less so) but rather a blatant effort to create a fable-like narrative of modernization all the way from the Mao era to the century's end.

Readers are reassured that the repressive and judgmental revolutionary super-ego can be ignored, or at least kept at bay, while new material wealth offers the possibility of endless pursuit of physical pleasures and psychological de-sires. However, the novella fails to completely exorcise the specter of historical judgment, insofar as the disapproving wife, Duan Li'na, remains as a kind of atavistic yet unavoidable drag on the protagonist's libidinal trajectory, forcing him to face the impossibility of the permanent possession of any true object of passionate desire and instead satisfy his wants only in substitute commodity form.

In fact, in spite of all the romance, wealth, and sex enjoyed by Kang Weiye in the course of the narrative, *Coming and Going* has an oddly muted and prosaic ending. It is as if, even after the breathtaking sweep of historical change he has witnessed and embodied, ultimately Weiye is still unable to overcome the stasis of everyday life. In the last chapter he remains both in his loveless marriage, although the pair have long since separated, and in his extramarital relation-ship with Shi Yupeng, although by this point their sex life has cooled and he has realized she is far too childish for him. In an effort to further normalize the situation, he arranges a dinner in which his wife and mistress must meet and be civil to each other, but the clueless Yupeng gets drunk and offends Li'na's political consciousness by making one of Mao Zedong's famous poems into an off-color joke in which Mao's ode to a "fairy cave" is said to really be a sexual reference to the anatomy of his wife, Jiang Qing, of Gang-of-Four notoriety.[32] Weiye thus fails in his attempt to reconcile the women in his life and the his-torical epochs they embody when Li'na, the conscience of his revolutionary youth, cannot bear to have the Great Helmsman's words reduced to the level of ahistorical hedonism represented by Yupeng and her generation of 1990s youth. In the end, Weiye flees the dinner, goes on a drinking binge, and passes out by himself on a riverbank. Waking up, he reflects on the women he has known in his life, frets over the state of his business, and then, in the novel's final line, "Kang Weiye stood up, took a big stretch, and returned to his busy daily life."[33] With this oddly unsatisfying ending, a best seller packed with melodrama fails to provide much of a sense of resolution, but in the end points only to the mo-notony of quotidian routine that apparently afflicts even so successful a person-age as Kang Weiye. It seems that even the new heroes of the late reform era must be left in the rather unheroic state of neither achieving their ultimate desires nor paying for their moral failings but instead simply plodding on beyond the horizon of the narrative.

Interestingly, the television adaptation of *Coming and Going* attempts to give much more dramatic closure and moral clarity, although it almost pleads for the viewer's assistance in providing these. Among the several new subplots that embellish the TV series is a late one in which Weiye pledges his company's resources to help fight the massive flooding that struck Hubei province in 1998. (He explains to his colleagues that "it's also to publicize our company, publicize our brand," in what amounts to a facile reassurance to the audience that there is no essential contradiction between the welfare of the masses and the self-inter-est of the new capitalists who control more and more resources.) While Weiye is personally overseeing his company's contributions in Hubei, accompanied by his mistress, his father falls ill and dies in his absence. Consequently, after returning home, Weiye melodramatically displays his repentance by kneeling under his father's funeral portrait, weeping repeatedly, muttering "I'm not wor-thy," and so on. This penultimate episode of the show ends with a voiceover narrator appealing directly to the viewer: "Friends in the audience, can you help him to choose a new path in life?" In the final episode, as if to sample ev-ery possible ending, Weiye and Li'na finally divorce, Weiye asks Yupeng if she wants to live with him and is turned down, and Weiye and Li'na subsequently rediscover their love for each other and reunite under the very pavilion where they had first met decades earlier. Thus, the final resolution appears to offer the safe, conservative message of eventual repentance and fidelity that one would expect from a series on state television. Nevertheless, this message is partially undercut by an awkward metatextual modernist quirk inserted into the final show: the actor playing Kang Weiye repeatedly appears in inserted scenes shot in black-and-white, in which, dressed in a Chicago Bulls t-shirt, he speculates directly to the camera about both how the narrative will end and what the audi-ence will think of the ending. After the reunion of the married couple, for ex-ample, he wonders if they will find happiness together and concludes only that "many viewers will have a question mark on this." Then, in the final diegetic scene, Kang Weiye goes alone to a movie theater to try to buy a ticket to *Titanic* (which had shattered every box-office record in China) and is turned away, as if to emphasize the ultimate inaccessibility of a romantic ideal even to the most successful winners in the new economy. Consequently, although the television version of the story ends with the conventional resolution of a reunited married couple, it complicates any sense of closure or reassurance with its wild swings in the final episode (in which Weiye had also gotten divorced and essentially proposed to his mistress), its metatextual distanciation and suggestions of doubts among the audience, and its odd final scene in which the hero, though reunited with his wife, goes by himself to try to see a Hollywood blockbuster.

The sensation of *Coming and Going* as both a best-selling novel and a television series shows the extent to which the public imagination of the late 1990s was aroused by a new kind of imaginary identification, if not hero worship, in the form of the wealthy and powerful entrepreneur—the much ballyhooed "successful personage" of the new economy—to whom a multitude of attractive women are available, if only for consumption. At the same time, it also suggests a fundamental suspicion toward the new ideal lifestyle, a discomfort or anxiety that finds expression in ambiguities and irresolutions in the text as well as in the hostile responses of critics such as Liu Chuan'e within the wider cultural context. Finally, insofar as it allows us to trace the career trajectory of one writer from a young exemplar of the New Realist school of fiction in the late 1980s to a popular culture brand name herself a decade later, *Coming and Going*, along with its television spin-off, shows us one possible strategy through which literature could adapt to the profoundly changed environment during the age of cultural marketization. By appealing directly to popular fantasies and hitching themselves to the more prominent audiovisual entertainment media, writers with luck and perseverance could maintain both a high income and a large readership, but perhaps only at the expense of drawing the repugnance of devotees of "pure" literature.

The New Modernist "Rupture"

In contrast to Chi Li and the phenomenon of commercialized "common" or even "vulgarized" literature that she represents, a quite different adaptation to the new cultural environment was attempted by a group of writers who launched what they called the Rupture (*duanlie*) movement. This affiliation was led by their senior member, Nanjing-based poet and novelist Han Dong, and his friend Zhu Wen, also a poet and novelist. In contrast to the "schools" of literature of the preceding years—which, as noted above, were the creations of critics and literary journals rather than the self-identifications of authors— the Rupture phenomenon was at least partly a self-conscious effort by authors themselves. The impression of a group movement was created in 1998, when the journal *Beijing wenxue* (Beijing literature) published the results of a question- naire distributed by Zhu Wen to a variety of young writers across China who, in their responses, starkly and virtually unanimously denied any debt whatsoever to a series of normally presumed influences and powers: founding figures of modern Chinese literature such as Lu Xun, later Chinese writers of the 1950s– 80s, contemporary Chinese criticism and literary scholarship, recent idols of the radical literary scene such as Haizi and Wang Xiaobo, Western literary and critical theory, religious influences of any kind, the Chinese Writers Associa- tion, elite literary journals including *Dushu* (Reading) and *Shouhuo* (Harvest), and the Mao Dun and Lu Xun Prizes for Literature.[34] Geremie Barmé called the Rupture salvo "nothing less than a condemnation of both official and non- official culture that rivals the ferocious, mass denunciations of the Cultural Revolution."[35] Hailing largely from Nanjing and Shanghai, the Rupture writers also represented a regional resistance to the hegemony of Beijing as the center of Chinese literary institutional authority and cultural discourse. As a Chinese critic sympathetic to the movement stated, the questionnaire amounted to no less than a "declaration of independence," by which writers asserted the "nega- tion" of all previous influences and powers in the literary scene in favor of a pure "literature for literature's sake," free from all ideologies and institutions that might seek to manipulate it.[36]

The Rupture movement was thus in part a revival of the occasionally re- pressed modernist or avant-garde impulse in modern and contemporary Chi- nese literature, the predecessors of which can be traced back to the Creation Society of the early 1920s—the original standard-bearers of "art for art's sake" aestheticism in China—as well as the Shanghai "New Sensationists" a decade later. As China faced ever greater historical crises, these modernist impulses in the Republican era were soon subsumed by the view of art as a tool for revolu- tion and resistance to Japanese occupation. After 1949, the modernist Chinese literary tradition continued in Taiwan but disappeared from the mainland until the 1980s, when it was revived by the "residual modernism" of "experimental" or "avant-garde" writers such as Yu Hua and Su Tong, who conveyed an intensified interiority that resisted the inhuman objectification of both revolutionary political and postrevolutionary consumerist culture.[37]

Despite its occurrence during a period in which the trend of consumerism was much more advanced, the Rupture movement focused its ire on the perceived manipulation of literature by political ideology and the various institutions and organs that were viewed as its servants. For example, one colorful rant by Zhu Wen went as follows: "For several decades the fat ass of ideology has sat squarely upon Chinese literature as if for a single day, and several crops of writers have been thus suffocated, because there was no air, just farts. . . . Now it is as if this ass has been raised just a little, allowing some air in, but Chinese literature inevitably still bears the imprint of that ass."[38] Asserting that in China, even "outside" writers always had to be co-opted by the "inside" if they were to survive at all, Zhu Wen concludes that the traits of individuality and creativity have always been weak in Chinese letters. This is particularly lamentable since "the spirit of modern literature, of modern art, is precisely individuality and creativity!"[39] After further decrying that "this is an age generally lacking in heroism, perhaps even an age that no longer needs heroism," Zhu Wen concludes with the assertion that he and his contemporaries in the Rupture group are nonetheless "the most mature, most sound generation of authors of the last half century, possessing a spiritual position of true independence."[40]

In the final analysis, Zhu Wen contends, even the distinction between authors "inside" and "outside" the literary institution is meaningless, insofar as the only distinction that matters is that between good and bad writers.[41] His argument in general is a proclamation of the autonomy of the aesthetic that goes hand in hand with the insistence on a radical "rupture" with all past literary influences and present extraliterary concerns. The positing of such an absolute break with the past, the manifesto-like form in which it is made, and the claim of being the first to "possess a spiritual position of true independence" are all of course prototypical modernist rhetorical tropes. It is here, in the emphasis on the autonomy of "good" literature, that the position of the Rupture movement follows the overall logic of differentiation (*fenhua*) that, as the previous two chapters have argued, is a central characteristic of postsocialist modernity in China. Fredric Jameson, drawing upon Niklas Luhmann, has described how capitalist modernization can be conceptualized as a process of endless differentiation, or "the gradual separation of areas of social life from each other, their disentanglement from some seemingly global and mythic (but more often religious) overall dynamic, and their reconstitution as distinct fields with distinct laws and dynamics."[42] This logic of differentiation appears as a radical temporal "rupture" from the perspective of an aesthetic field declaring its "independence," and it manifests itself as an "autonomization" by which the field marks itself off as a "small-scale whole" or "totality" distinct, say, from the realms of politics, economics, or religion.[43] Unlike modernisms in the West or in Republican-era China, the modernist schools of the reform era mark out their autonomy not against a premodern totalized society but against the alternative modernity of Maoism, in which all spheres of social and cultural activity are subjected to the global dynamic of revolution and collectivization. In either case, the process of differentiation, though receiving its driving force from marketization under capitalist modernity, nevertheless embraces the modernist assertion of the (relative) autonomy of the aesthetic. This autonomy is then experienced by artists as both a clean break with a past period of artistic heteronomy *and* an insistence on the distinction of "pure" art from the mere commodities that fill the mainstream of any modern capitalist culture.

However, a tension arises here between the goal of autonomy and the ostensibly collective nature of the Rupture movement itself. Although the autonomy of the Rupture writers is evident in the highly individual nature of their various styles, genres, and concerns, this very individualism calls into question the plausibility of any meaningful identity as a singular Rupture group. This tension between the goal of radical autonomy and the necessarily collective nature of any self-defined school of modernism may indicate in part a contradiction inherent to modernist movements in general; to the extent that any artistic *school* by definition implies some degree of heteronomy of individual artistic vision in relation to the group, the rallying around common manifestos, labels, or symbols may even represent an atavistic longing for the very linchpins of meaning that modernity has destroyed. Moreover, in the case of reform-era China, any self-declared revolutionary movement faces further problems having to do with the particular political context of the postsocialist situation. In fact, the leaders of the Rupture group avoided the term *movement* (*yundong*) altogether, with its connotations of collective revolutionary action that seemed outdated in the 1990s, referring instead to a group "performance" or "action" (*xingwei*). In this sense, stunts such as the manifesto-like Rupture questionnaire take on the aspect of a kind of one-time "performance art" (*xingwei yishu*) rather than a coherent, ongoing artistic movement. The collectivist nature of the Rupture group was in fact necessarily diluted by the pronounced dissimilarities among its members. Indeed, aside from their insistence on independence from past influences and present institutions, there is little literary basis for linking, say, Han Dong with Mian Mian, the young author of naively written, sensationalist autobiographical accounts of sex and drug abuse among contemporary urban youth; nevertheless, both were grouped under the same Rupture banner.

Not surprisingly, some observers accused the Rupture group of simply attempting to attract attention and create a media sensation. As one novelist and scholar acquainted with the Rupture writers put it, the entire affair could be seen less as a declaration of the purity and autonomy of literature than a return of the very "hero complex" that long drove Chinese literature to overestimate its centrality to society as a whole.[44] Here, as in the case of the "humanist spirit" advocates of the early 1990s, a longing for autonomy (of literature or of humanist scholarship) from the rest of society is perhaps accompanied by a barely concealed fear of marginalization, which in turn leads to alarmist outcries about a "crisis of the humanist spirit" (in the case of scholarship) or an exaggerated gesture of "Rupture" through a mass-mediated performance.

Other critics nonetheless took the Rupture event as a landmark moment in Chinese cultural history that represented a fundamental change in the position of literary authors within society. Chen Xiaoming, who (as discussed in Chapter Two) had hailed the very cultural transformations of the early 1990s that others had viewed as evidence of a spiritual crisis, now considered the Rupture action as heralding an entirely new state of literature in China. As Chen gleefully proclaimed, with the Rupture group, "The Chinese literary scene unexpectedly had a community of people dare to suddenly make public an attitude which clearly defined themselves as an 'alternative' [*yilei*] outside of dominant culture, the first time in over a half-century such a bizarre absurdity had appeared."[45] With the Rupture authors, "those serving as the subject of literature, those literary writers most able to hit the mark on contemporary life, are no longer part of the general literary institution," and yet "they have suddenly emerged on the surface of history to occupy the primary position in contemporary literature."[46] This was clear evidence that "the tradition of literature from its socialized organizational structure to its spiritual essence" had "undergone a fundamental transformation."[47] It also indicated "a legitimacy crisis occurring in the general institution of contemporary Chinese literature"—that is, a welcome one in which the enfeeblement of the official literary system corresponded to a new, unprecedented degree of self-determination by authors.[48]

Chen Xiaoming's enthusiasm for the Rupture action notwithstanding, even he acknowledged that the group's novelty was exaggerated, viewing it more as clear evidence that a change had *already* occurred than as the agent of that change itself. He noted that the stance of radical independence had crucial precedents in the reform era. A decade earlier, Wang Shuo had already "changed the attitude of the author toward literature and toward society. From Wang Shuo onward, in its essence literature was no longer an affair of the nation-state, a symbol of the spirit of the age, but rather a career choice or an amateur hobby of the individual." The transformation was pushed further by the example of the iconoclastic Wang Xiaobo, who symbolically "shattered the mystery enshrouding the literary institution and demonstrated the multifaceted feasibility of writing outside the system."[49] Aside from the *institutional* autonomy presaged by the two maverick Wangs, the *aesthetic* autonomy of a modernist style in some of the Rupture writers owed much to the innovations of various avant-garde poets and fiction writers of a decade earlier.[50] In short, "In actuality, the rupture had long since occurred, but people had not taken much notice of it. Rupture is an objective historical fact, whereas to declare rupture is to make a break indicating subjective initiative."[51] The Rupture group's achievement, therefore, was less to instigate the rupture in question than to assert its self-consciousness.

In the praise of critics such as Chen Xiaoming and Li Xianting (cited above), one cannot help but detect a measure of personal investment in the brief sensation that was the Rupture phenomenon. Clearly the expression of a dramatic break from the past and autonomy from the hoary literary institution by the

Rupture authors intersected symbiotically with Chen Xiaoming's own self-positioning as a postmodernist gadfly at odds with the critical establishment. As noted above, in the end even he felt compelled to moderate his hype of the group with an acknowledgment of the paradoxical dependence of their "rupture" on vital antecedents such as the avant-gardists Su Tong, Yu Hua, Ge Fei, Sun Ganlu, and Bei Cun, after whom "the likes of Zhu Wen and Han Dong could not possibly produce many more innovations on the level of form." In fact, Chen argued, stylistically even the best Rupture writers were more conventional than the innovators of the late 1980s, which was not due to a lack of individual creativity, but rather to the fact that "the resources that could be unearthed in the fictional form were already drawing near exhaustion."[52] Instead, he argued, what was genuinely new about Zhu Wen and Han Dong was the unique narrative perspective of their stories, which "take the most meaningless segments of life as the core of the narrative."[53] In this sense, these Rupture writers can be said to have as much in common with the earlier New Realist fiction as with the avant-garde fiction of the 1980s, except that the details of daily life now become magnified to the point of achieving an estranging perspective that gives the stories a modernist sensibility despite their relative lack of formal experimentation.

Zhu Wen's Narratives of Boredom

It is beyond the scope of this discussion to analyze a range of Rupture literature in order to sketch the full scope of the Rupture school (if such a thing exists at all in a literary sense); however, a closer look at the fiction of the "Rupture" questionnaire instigator himself, Zhu Wen, should suffice to bring out some of the implications of the new autonomy manifested and represented in his literature, including the perspective of an emergent form of free-floating subjectivity associated with urban youth in postsocialist China. Zhu Wen, in fact, had already been assigned by critics to other schools of literature before participating in the Rupture movement. Besides sometimes being lumped under broader categories such as New-State-of-Affairs literature, he was also grouped with writers of his particular generation—those who were born in the 1960s and began writing in the 1990s—as the "late-born generation" (*wanshengdai*) or "newly born generation" (*xinshengdai*). These authors were distinguished from both older writers, whose careers dated to the 1980s or earlier, and an even younger generation of writers who were born after 1970 and began attracting attention by the late 1990s. Many of Zhu Wen's early stories were written in the first person and in some cases appeared partially autobiographical.[54] However, in an overlapping series of short stories and one novel published in the mid to late 1990s, Zhu Wen depicted a protagonist, or rather a series of protagonists, named Xiao Ding, a young man whose life is marked by a melancholy lack of motivation and direction. In these stories, the anomie-ridden Xiao Ding goes through a series of seemingly random encounters and experiences that add up to a plot in which events occur with little sense of cause and effect or goal-seeking.

Xiao Ding is an intellectual—in some of the stories he is still attending university; in others, he is a freelance writer—but he is in fact a new class of intellectual that appeared in China in large numbers only after the employment system established during the Mao era was more or less dismantled in the 1990s. With students no longer assigned to work units upon the completion of their education and full employment no longer maintained even as an appearance, what might be called a new educated youth underclass appeared in Chinese cities. Either high school graduates who failed to test into universities, or college and technical school graduates who failed to find jobs, these educated but unemployed youth often continued living with their parents while participating in an emerging youth subculture marked by hedonism and individualism and dependent partly upon the images of Taiwan, Hong Kong, Japan, South Korea, and the West promulgated by a new youth culture industry in China.

Discussions of Zhu Wen's stories by critics in China generally feature the terms *wuliao* (boredom), *yihua* (alienation), *xuwu* (nihility) or *xuwuzhuyi* (nihilism), and *gerenhua* (individualization)—which together capture the spirit of Xiao Ding's existence and the perspective (if not the sense of humor) of the narrative. *Wuliao*—which can mean either "bored" or "boring," with the latter further connoting a judgment of silliness or stupidity—is not just a mood but a pose struck by disengaged youth in turn-of-the-century China.[55] An *wuliao* attitude implies not only a lack of interest in an object (or lack of an object of interest) but also a pose of superior dismissal toward any such object, so that an overall *wuliao* attitude embodies the paradoxically world-weary boredom of youth who refuse to legitimate the values or goals endorsed by mainstream society. Wang Xiaoming, in particular, considers *wuliao* the essence of Zhu Wen's characterization of Xiao Ding, whose "boredom" is actually a symptom that "we live at the tail-end of a momentous age" in which life "is truly a pool of stagnant water that breeds boredom."[56] In other words, youthful boredom is yet another manifestation of the postsocialist crisis in meaning that Wang Xiaoming saw afflicting his own generation, who had at different times been filled with utopian hopes for revolution and then for cultural enlightenment, only to have them shattered each time.[57] By the 1990s, the age of great hopes had been exhausted, so that Xiao Ding's boredom and lack of purpose in fact represent "an extremely great spiritual problem" and thus a worthy subject of literature (the unique mission of which should be to explore spiritual problems).[58] Wang Xiaoming sees in Zhu's Xiao Ding a self-conscious exploration of the "problem" of boredom and therefore the spiritual crisis it represents, pointing out that only a narrative that is highly self-aware of the meaninglessness of the life depicted could express it so vividly.[59]

And yet, in a character like Xiao Ding, Zhu Wen presents at the same time both a dark vision of boredom and nihilism *and* a potentially enticing model of a new subjective freedom, the protagonist's lack of material motivation or ideological direction being accompanied by a genuine autonomy of both mental and physical movement. Xiao Ding's freedom often appears nomadic in the utopian sense of the "schizophrenic" lifestyle glorified by Deleuze and Guattari—a capacity to wander aimlessly along various lines of flight and make rhizomic random connections with others rather than simply circulating within stable social hierarchies of family, school, and workplace. However, rather than identifying this form of being with the claims made for the decentered postmodern subject, we might instead recognize in Xiao Ding the long-familiar figure of Benjamin's *flaneur*, with the same lifestyle of boredom and ambivalent relations to the commodified urban milieu in which this wandering subject finds himself.[60] Here the very precondition of the individual's new freedom is the disappearance of stable social institutions as anchors for the individual subjectivity, which becomes evident in Xiao Ding's sense of melancholy (an implicit narrative of loss) and nihilism (an implicit structure of lack).

To cite just one example from Zhu Wen's novella *Xiao Ding gushi* (Stories of Xiao Ding; actually a series of short sketches with unrelated plots), as the eponymous protagonist eats by himself in a noodle shop, a mentally unbalanced woman at a nearby table begins talking to him as if he is her son who has run away from home.[61] Though he has never seen the woman before and tries to escape her, the scene plays out in public in a way that leads anonymous bystanders to believe the woman is correct and Xiao Ding is simply trying to avoid going home with his mother. As the incident builds to an increasingly riotous climax, Xiao Ding finally agrees to accompany the woman "home" just to temporarily defuse the situation. Oddly, however, he suddenly begins to feel comforted in being with her, even thinks she looks familiar and agreeably pretends to have memories of her and the absent "father" to whom she refers. Inevitably, just when Xiao Ding has become truly attached to her during their walk "home," the woman disappears while Xiao Ding is using a public toilet. Having made this random connection with a stranger who has suddenly left him "orphaned," Xiao Ding looks around helplessly and calls to her in the hope of continuing the journey home. Although humorous, the incident carries unmistakably disconsolate undertones, as a "lost" young man apparently unconsciously yearns for a family with whom he feels at home.

Aside from illustrating the melancholy nature of Xiao Ding's nomadic freedom, this incident also indicates a typical combination of setting and characterization in Zhu Wen's stories. Xiao Ding's sardonic adventures consist largely of trivial situations shared with anonymous others in pedestrian public spaces like the noodle shop where he was accosted by the presumptuous "mother." In the novel *Shenme shi laji shenme shi ai* (What's trash, what's love), experiences as generic as eating at a KFC restaurant are related in exhaustive, fascinating, and amusing detail. This particular scene ends with Xiao Ding engaging in another temporary, purely fantasized family relationship. A woman and her two bratty young children have shared Xiao Ding's table in the crowded restaurant. After first being irritated by the children's antics, Xiao Ding is struck by the thought that the four of them at the table make up a perfect nuclear family: "Xiao Ding suddenly felt that a family of four is sometimes formed just this way; as difficult as it sounds, it could also be this incredibly easy."[62] Nevertheless, the reality of the relationship consists only of brief, awkward small talk between strangers brought together arbitrarily and fleetingly.

These random anonymous connections Xiao Ding experiences as his personal relationships, and the settings in which they occur, foreground a particular form of sociality that emerges in the conditions of modernity. This form of sociality—which is virtually a given in urban, capitalist societies but notable in mainland China precisely for its contrast with the dominant rural, collectivist social imaginary that preceded it—is captured well by Jean-Paul Sartre's concept of a "serial mode of co-existence" of the kind that happens, for example, among a random crowd waiting at a bus stop. In contrast to a group united by some kind of active practice or collective enterprise, this kind of assemblage of people is a mere "plurality of isolations," all of whom are made in some sense interchangeable in relation to the urban environment that in effect orchestrates their movements and interactions.[63] In this sense, the material environment both structures the alienated, isolated subjectivity of each individual *and* joins them together in "serial unities" determined only by the material infrastructure around which they orient their activities. In the case of the bus stop crowd, "the unity of the collection of commuters lies in the bus they are waiting for; in fact it *is* the bus, as a simple possibility of transport (not for transporting *all* of us, for we do not act together, but for transporting each of us)." The people gathered are all waiting for the same bus, but "their acts of waiting are not a communal fact, but are lived separately as identical instances of the same act."[64]

In Zhu Wen's stories, Xiao Ding's alienation is in a sense inseparable from the serial collectivities to which he temporarily belongs—such as the arbitrary group of people eating chicken sandwiches and French fries at a KFC restaurant. The narrative's detailed descriptions of the food, plastic trays, napkins, tables, fast-food workers, restaurant loudspeakers, and other customers all suggest that Xiao Ding is intimately engaged with the artificial environment even as he experiences his fundamental isolation from all the other customers with whom he is temporarily joined. Ironic glimmers of genuine collective belonging only reinforce the fundamental "seriality" of the gathering, as when Xiao Ding imagines himself in a family with the strangers at his table, or when, at the urging of the KFC loudspeakers, everybody joins in the singing of "Happy Birthday" to some random, unseen child in the crowded restaurant.

In Sartre's theory, the serial collective is contrasted with a "group-in-fusion," a group actively united in a common practice or project that has the revolutionary potential to overcome the alienated structure of society. Such a "group-in-fusion" in fact brings to mind the collective "actions" and the "declaration of independence" of the Rupture group itself. In other words, Xiao Ding's nomadic subjectivity and the serial, inert nature of his relations with anonymous others can be contrasted with the assertive, collective activities of Zhu Wen himself on the literary scene. This is by no means necessarily a contradiction, or rather it is perhaps merely one that can be seen in nearly all modernist aesthetic movements in the sense described earlier as the tension between autonomy and collectivity. The newly proclaimed radical autonomy of the aesthetic as well as the autonomous subjective consciousness often expressed in modernist literature are both generated by the overall dynamics of differentiation and autonomization of capitalist modernity itself—while the heroic collective *pose* is the means by which a particular avant-garde movement seeks to overcome, by presenting itself as a revolutionary group-in-fusion, the very inertia and serial alienation that it may well simultaneously document in its art. The artist might try to spur a collective movement, yet the art itself has no choice but to take as a starting place the fragmented world it inhabits and the loss of the global coherency of the world that preceded it, whether that be the totality of a premodern worldview or that of Maoism.

The quality of taking the fragment rather than a now-foreclosed whole as the starting point was in fact one of the characteristics of Chinese literature most praised by critics after the 1980s. As we have seen, New Realists such as Chi Li were hailed for sticking to the details of individual, ordinary lives rather than trying to sketch grand narratives through allegory, history, "root-seeking" mythology, or politically charged tales in which individual lives or families stand synecdochically for the upheavals of national history. Whereas, as I have argued, Chi Li later went on to offer grand narratives of modernization in her very different works of the 1990s, other successors to the New Realists such as the New-State-of-Affairs writers were praised again for beginning with fragmentary experience rather than any vision of totality: "The possibility of writing the totality exists only within the writer's life situation; history and reality are condensed within the ephemeral tide immediately rushing past him or her, and only by grasping the fragments washing by on this tide can the writer grasp this age, grasp himself or herself, and thereby grasp the totality."[65] Here the New-State-of-Affairs writers were said to go further than the New Realists by writing from a more engaged position of personal experience rather than taking a distanced narrative viewpoint. Indeed, in Chi Li's early stories and novellas the world inhabited by the characters is that of fragmented ordinary life, but the third-person omniscient narrator stands above that world, taking a remote, objective perspective that approaches naturalism.[66] The narration in Zhu Wen's stories of Xiao Ding, in contrast, while generally in the third person, is not omniscient but limited, drifting along with the protagonist, never claiming any sort of epistemological transcendence. Consequently, even more than in the case of New Realism, the writers of Zhu Wen's generation were seen as practicing a rigorous form of "individualized writing" (gerenhua xiezuo). In an essay on this aspect of the "newly born generation," Zhang Jun asserts that such an individualized perspective is in fact the normative condition of literary and cultural production, and even had been evident in earlier modern Chinese writers such as Lu Xun and the New Sensationists of the 1930s, but that artists in China had lacked it in recent decades due to their condition of being subsumed within a "singularized" culture under the master signifiers of collectivist ideology.[67] In current conditions, however, since "the 1990s are an age of individualization, it is only natural that individualized writing will appear in this age."[68]

Yet the "individualization" of writing such as Zhu Wen's is a trait that is obviously intimately related to the isolated, "serial" mode of subjectivity evoked in his fiction. In an essay on What's Trash, What's Love, Huang Fayou traces the "feeling of boredom" and "nihilistic attitude" conveyed in Zhu Wen's fiction ultimately to the alienation (yihua) of the character Xiao Ding, whose freedom is inseparable from an essential uselessness he feels in relation to society. Huang cites the episode in which Xiao Ding volunteers for a charitable organization in an effort to overcome his anomie. As Xiao Ding tells the secretary at the agency: "I want to connect with people, to really connect, because I feel like I no longer have any relation to this society, to other people. No trace of a real 'relation' at all. I want to feel like I have some use."[69] Xiao Ding's subsequent experiment with assisting a handicapped boy soon ends when the wealthy family he is trying to help treats him with contempt. Huang attributes Xiao Ding's inescapable feelings of uselessness to the supremacy of exchange value in a market economy: "The tide of turning people into commodities is the real cultural root cause miring Xiao Ding in the bog of alienated freedom. In this age when the principle of exchange becomes the highest norm and the snares of mutual exploitation are all around, if a single frail individual does not want to turn himself into a thing, then it seems the only choice is to find freedom in the fragmentary."[70] Recalling the description of postsocialist China as a "world in fragments" discussed in Chapter One, this finding "freedom in the fragmentary" (*canquezhong ziyou*) that characterizes Xiao Ding's lifestyle does not simply represent an obliquely oppositional stance of an alienated youth. It is in fact an exaggerated representation of the utopian shards available to any subject under the conditions of modernity; in the midst of a serialized, alienated existence, individual "freedom," as it is concretely lived in daily life, amounts to the freedom to attach oneself to the fragments of one's choosing, whether those of private fantasy or public amusement, as compensation for the estranging effects of commodification.

Huang Fayou's discussion leads us to the most powerful sense in which Zhu Wen's fiction takes on an unmistakably modernist feel: the axis of the narrative lies only in Xiao Ding's free-floating subjectivity, and Xiao Ding is a classically modernist (anti)hero. In Fredric Jameson's words, we can "grasp the modernist impulse as the symbolic anticipation of a unity of individual experience (completely comprehensible in its own terms) whose condition of possibility is the dissolution of the older traditional communities or groups and the emergence of individualism and anomie."[71] Pausing to reassemble our various terms of analysis, then, it is clear that the individualization, alienation, and boredom narrated by Zhu Wen in the figure of Xiao Ding all contribute to an overall modernist orientation that is rooted ultimately in the process of capitalist modernization itself, as the latter unfolds on the unique ideological terrain of postsocialist modernity in China. Whether autonomy is seen positively (freedom) or negatively (alienation), it results from the same process of differentiation/fragmentation of a society in an age of market-driven pluralization and the delegitimization of communal ideologies. For a character such as Xiao Ding, "uselessness" coincides with autonomy of movement and thought and becomes an emblem of resistance to reification, but the modernist antihero must still grapple with—indeed, must face even more directly than Chi Li's Kang Weiye—the loss of grounded meaning in favor of the ceaseless flux of equivalencies in capitalist modernity. In short, the underlying problem facing such a character is that of meaninglessness, or nihilism.

The previous chapter noted that the specter of nihilism in both popular and elite culture was one of the chief concerns of the prominent intellectuals who decried a new "crisis" of the spirit and society in China of the 1990s. At the same time, many of the same intellectuals acknowledged a certain unavoidable, historically determined nihilism in themselves. Wang Hongsheng, for example, remarked that "the historical facts of the twentieth century have shattered everything ever believed in by humanity" without, however, shattering the *need* to believe, thus making the resulting nihility that much more unbearable: "It is almost impossible for me to grasp the ultimate implications of the rupture [*duanlie*] between this kind of belief and the object of belief. Is it some plight of linguistics or an existential catastrophe? And how is it that problems of language and problems of existence are so strangely tangled up together?"[72] Wang thus recognizes nihilism as not simply a spiritual plight but also in some sense a crisis of naming and of representation. While the modern critic or philosopher confronts nihilism as the void left in the wake of shattered belief systems, the modernist artist confronts a crisis of faith in normative systems of representation and narrativity.

In the first significant study of Zhu Wen to be published in a major Chinese literary journal, Song Mingwei noted many aspects of Zhu Wen's fiction already touched upon above: the highly fragmented and subjective nature of the narration, the plots that are almost entirely episodic, the lack of any clear motivation or causality for the various events, making it very difficult to attain any grasp of the narratives as a totality.[73] Song also observes that the lack of any objective, totalized view is due not just to the discontinuity of the narratives but also to their subjectivized perspective, which "unavoidably has a tendency toward extreme individualization," a view echoed in many other critics' readings, as we have seen.[74] Song further notes that the various "Xiao Dings" in Zhu Wen's stories "are all prototypical 'slackers' [*youshou-haoxianzhe*], or one might say that what is most notable about their spiritual condition is its nihility."[75] The perspective is not merely narrowed from a wider cultural or social totality to an individual point of view, but that individual perspective—precisely because it is *so* individual, that is, alienated—by definition lacks any exterior goals or beliefs that can generate meaning.

Without denying the existential void Xiao Ding incarnates, Song Mingwei argues that even such a nihilism contains within itself a latent idealism: "The existence of this void is a fact, but in terms of some hopeful aspect, to maintain a nihilist spirit implies that an uncompromised personal space still exists within the human heart; identifying with a void is always more valuable than identifying with the whole and giving it the semblance of reason, and in any case nihilism is a kind of power that connotes a spirit of the unknown, with the possibility of spurring a new lease on life."[76] That is, the "uncompromised personal space" offered by a genuinely autonomous existence, however meaningless it may appear, is preferable to identifying with a "whole" in which one must be reified in order to be useful. This view partially echoes Wang Hongsheng's argument, mentioned in the previous chapter, that in an absolute sense "nihility is really the foundation of freedom."[77]

It is perhaps here at the paradoxical intersection of nihilism and idealism that we can distinguish the epistemological vision of Zhu Wen's fiction from that of the later works of Chi Li written during the same period of the mid to late 1990s. Whereas a work such as *Coming and Going* uses characters and events to represent what is *already known* about contemporary Chinese history and the widely disseminated meanings of the current socioeconomic structure, Xiao Ding and his random encounters continually push toward an *unknown*, or something inassimilable to the current condition.[78] Xiao Ding thus becomes the embodiment of a void within the symbolic economy of contemporary China. This is expressed most graphically by the character's experience, through several chapters of *What's Trash, What's Love*, with a venereal disease, genital warts. For example, this passage describes Xiao Ding just after bicycling through the main gate of a hospital:

He immediately felt that something was not right. The rather plain old outpatient services building he remembered from his previous impressions had been demolished, a tall new building was under construction, and the previously peaceful hospital now appeared to be buzzing with extraordinary activity. There were lots of guys in hardhats going in and out of the place, and big yellow trucks frequently drove over and raised plumes of dirt and dust. Xiao Ding stood under an official notice board, his hands gripping his handlebars, and took a moment to adjust his mood. He said to himself, yes, everything was changing, but it was not directed at him. The world had always been this way, it was just that previously he had understood too little. Xiao Ding couldn't comprehend why he would be so deeply upset by these quite normal changes before his eyes, which were hardly even worth mentioning. It suddenly occurred to him that his mother had once predicted he would catch a venereal disease. She knew nothing about venereal disease, and even less about Xiao Ding's personal life, so her line of thought was simply bizarre, pathological, without the slightest bit of reason, and yet she had hit the nail on the head. For someone to stand in front of your face, open her mouth and completely randomly blurt something out, but then to in fact perfectly target one's most vital point—this really could drive one to distraction, make one go crazy. Could it really be that my life has already become even more bizarre than my mother's ossified mind? Xiao Ding's nervousness and alarm rose. Standing in front of that message board, he was completely unable to gain control of his chaotic thoughts. He finally said to himself, why do I feel I'm like a wart on this society? Alive, but not a part of this body, breathing but with no temperature, unable to feel this body's metabolism, I'm a growth, a wart. Has my life really come to this? Xiao Ding unconsciously shed a tear. This made him even more dissatisfied with himself; why would he shed tears for no apparent reason in this place? What the hell was this all about?

This passage brings out a number of salient features of Zhu Wen's writing. First, it demonstrates that Zhu's innovation lies not in a radically new use of language itself—Chen Xiaoming is correct in his previously mentioned observation that the Chinese avant-gardists of a decade earlier had been more innovative in form than were the Rupture writers—but rather in the way language is used to capture a certain mode of postsocialist subjective experience, that of the superfluous *wuliao* generation of youth in a society undergoing relentless transformation. As already mentioned, the point of view is generally third person, limited rather than omniscient, but the flow of the text switches freely between objective narration, free indirect discourse, and even first-person inserts without quotation marks. In this way the reader, even without the benefit of a directly confessional voice, nonetheless becomes thoroughly familiar with Xiao Ding's way of thinking. The casual use of colloquialisms (e.g., "guys," *jiahuo*) and profanity (e.g., "what the hell," *zhe tama*) in the third-person narration shows a frequent slippage into free indirect discourse, which can sometimes then slip into the first person ("Could it really be that my life has already become even more bizarre than my mother's ossified mind?"). By these means, the narrative captures the often chaotic flow of Xiao Ding's consciousness, as when his anxious thoughts about the construction site at the hospital change suddenly into the memory that his mother had predicted he would catch a venereal disease. The fiction thus reveals how even the seemingly innocuous and pedestrian events of contemporary urban life—eating at a KFC restaurant, walking near a construction site—may in fact be subjectively experienced as profoundly estranging and anxiety-provoking.

The subjective effect of the construction site is particularly noteworthy precisely because passing by a construction site or seeing that a once-familiar building has been torn down would in fact be *so* common and unnoteworthy an event for any resident of contemporary urban China. As noted in Chapter One, the character *chai* (demolish, used in the passage translated above) is arguably *the* iconic character of postsocialist China since the early 1990s, being painted everywhere on buildings slated for destruction, as whole neighborhoods are torn down and rebuilt almost more quickly than one can even register the multitude of transformations simultaneously occurring in one's physical environment. Xiao Ding scolds himself for being thrown into something like a panic attack for being "so deeply upset by these quite normal changes before his eyes, which were hardly even worth mentioning," but it was perhaps precisely the fact that "everything changing" had become the "normal" condition of life that made it so traumatizing.

The shift in Xiao Ding's attention from the anxiety-provoking demolition and construction at the hospital to the memory of his mother's prediction of his venereal disease leads him to articulate a self-image that graphically represents his alienation from his elders, his society, and the "normal changes" occurring everywhere around him. His estrangement from his mother is clear from his aghast frustration that she could possibly have guessed anything crucial about his life, much less its most private fact of all. But all this leads Xiao Ding finally to draw a metaphorical meaning from his own disease: his real problem is not simply that he has warts on his body, but that he himself is like a wart on the body of society, alive on its surface but unable to feel its "metabolism." Indeed, in the course of the novel, the disease gradually becomes a structure for Xiao Ding's subjectivity, as if it has reproduced as a symptom on his own body the relation he has to the body politic—an inexplicable and vaguely obscene excrescence, an element foreign to the system. Xiao Ding, in all his "uselessness," serves as a pathological excess, a Lacanian *sinthome* that cannot be accounted for within the normal order of society, just as his genital warts defy the normal functioning of the organism.[79] It is in this sense that I understand Song Mingwei's detection of a latent idealism to Zhu Wen's nihilism: in the condition of postsocialist modernity, to reverse the fragmentation/demolition of the previously unified cultural and social sphere is impossible, so rather than maintaining a "semblance of reason"—a representation of totality, an implicit endorsement of the new ideology along the lines of *Coming and Going*—it is better to write precisely *as sinthome* (the specific concept of which Lacan worked out through the fiction of the archetypical modernist author himself, James Joyce). Though this may appear as nihilistic, it may in fact be the most idealistic position possible for one who confronts a thoroughgoing disintegration of previous identifications and meanings, yet still seeks some sort of meaning or truth through art.

Conclusion: From Literature to Media

The autonomy of art sought through the modernist vision of Zhu Wen and other Rupture writers should not obscure the fact that commercial authors such as Chi Li were also attaining a different form of autonomy in the new conditions of the reform era. With the boom in entertainment literature that began in the 1980s and accelerated after the culture industry reforms of the early 1990s, popular authors like Chi Li achieved their own "rupture" with the previous literary establishment. Indeed, if Chen Xiaoming's appreciation of the Rupture group was partly based on the associated change in the status of writing from an instrument of a totalized society to simply a career choice, then a popular writer such as Chi Li should be even more worthy of his praise. By reaching her readers through the mechanism of the popular culture market rather than just through the top-down, state-linked literary associations, prizes, and journals, Chi Li represents the relative autonomy generated by the logic of the market—or, as described in Chapter One, a release from *state* heteronomy that nonetheless amounts to a new *market* heteronomy. In writing best sellers and popular television scripts, Chi Li has no need for the approval of the elite literary critics—which, indeed, she lost after her New Realist phase. As the "Wang Shuo phenomenon" proved, what critics might condemn as "vulgarization" can be both liberating and lucrative for a writer willing to sully him- or herself with the crass interests of commerce.

The autonomies of Rupture writers such as Zhu Wen and popular fiction writers such as Chi Li are in fact each belied in some fundamental respects by their mode of appearance within the public sphere. Even as the Rupture writers declared the independence of their aesthetic pursuits from all social and historical influences, they nonetheless made their case in the attention-grabbing form of a media event. The radically detached subjectivity of the fictional Xiao Ding, who drifts aimlessly through serial encounters with anonymous others, is set off by the group-oriented Rupture movement itself, which attempts to gain notoriety by creating the impression of a collective antiestablishment movement. Even Xiao Ding's sometime profession as a freelance writer indicates a new position championed by the Rupture crowd but only made possible by the new postsocialist cultural economy—what Geremie Barmé identifies as "the category of 'freelance writer' (*ziyou zhuangaoren*) or, rather, 'independent' or 'free writer' (*ziyou zuojia*), accrued the status of the fringe, with all the attendant possibility, resistance, and éclat . . . , not to mention commercial viability."[80] Under market conditions, the "free" artist as *sinthome*—embodying an inassimilable, useless, perhaps even subversive excess in the manner of Xiao Ding—can all too quickly become the latest, brief sensation if market conditions are ripe. The market, unlike the communist state, does not police the boundaries of ideological correctness so much as constantly expand them in whatever direction sales are to be made.

Turning again to Chi Li, in the context of the cultural scene of the 1990s, the greatest measure of her own success perhaps lies not in her novellas and stories themselves, but rather in the succession of television and film adaptations made from them. During the decade, *The Sun Comes Out*, *Don't Mention Love*, *Coming and Going*, and *Xiaojie nizao* (Good morning, miss) all were adapted into television scripts by others, while *Ni yiwei wo shi shei* (Who do you think I am) was turned into the film *Jia shi* (Family affair). After the great popularity of *Coming and Going* as both a novella and a television series, Chi Li co-wrote the follow-up *Kou hong* (Lipstick) as a twenty-episode television script. At the demand of her publisher, she also adapted it into a novel, which was rushed out just fourteen days after she had submitted the manuscript in order for it to be on bookshelves when the television show aired.[81] So anticipated was the novel that the publisher increased the original print run from thirty thousand to one hundred thousand, and the book became an early landmark for the fledgling online bookseller industry in China.[82]

If the example of Chi Li shows the extent to which, during the 1990s, popular literature was integrated into the newly profit-oriented culture industry as a whole, the career of Zhu Wen turns out to point no less to the growing importance of visual media in Chinese culture and the corresponding drop in the profile of "pure" literature. Even while writing some of his most notable works of the 1990s, Zhu Wen turned to film screenwriting as another source of income and outlet for his creativity. His first script was for the minimalist thriller *Wushan yunyu* (Rain clouds over Wushan; dir. Zhang Ming, 1996), an independent production that, in retrospect, was on the cutting edge of two broader movements in Chinese cinema—a wave of mostly independent *noir*-inflected films about mysterious identities or unsolved crimes as well as a partially overlapping "new formalism" that would characterize many of the notable mainland Chinese films released at the turn of the century and beyond.[83] Zhu Wen later worked on the screenplay for the major studio release *Guonian huijia* (Seventeen years, 1999), by the previously pioneering underground director Zhang Yuan.[84] Finally, in 2001, Zhu Wen himself directed his own script with *Haixian* (Seafood), an independent production that was well received at international film festivals, jointly winning the top prize in the Cinema of the Present section at the Venice Film Festival in 2001. By now virtually a full-time film director, Zhu Wen followed *Seafood* with *Yun de nanfang* (South of the clouds, 2004), a film that managed to reap more success at international film festivals—winning two prizes, including the FIPRESCI Prize, at the 2004 Hong Kong International Film Festival—while also attaining domestic release under an official studio label.

Thus, if Chi Li's career traced a trajectory from the New Realist movement hailed by elite literary critics of the late 1980s to the popular mass culture of best sellers and television series by the late 1990s, Zhu Wen's shorter career followed a parallel path from "pure" literature with an essentially modernist aesthetic to the Chinese film scene, with ties to both the transnational art-cinema market and the domestic studio system. Both authors illustrate, in very different ways, how literature simultaneously pursued and coped with new modes of autonomy imposed by the elemental restructuring of the Chinese economy and the separation of the culture industry from state socialism. At the same time, the careers of both authors demonstrate—again, in quite different ways—how the new economy was fundamentally undermining the leading role "serious" literature had played in Chinese culture for a century and directing the energies of many writers—great talents and hacks alike—into other endeavors that were both more profitable and more vital in a transformed cultural scene.

4

The Cinema of Infidelity:
Gender, Geography, Economics, and Fantasy

The previous chapter described how the theme of marital infidelity, or the threat thereof, was used by novelist Chi Li as a means of exploring how people in postsocialist China confronted an obdurate everyday life on the one hand and the desires awakened by a new imaginary of global capitalism on the other. Particularly with the novel and TV series *Coming and Going*, Chi Li used the figure of a successful, sympathetically portrayed, yet adulterous businessman to dramatize both the allure and the moral quandaries of consumer capitalism for those benefiting from the new economy of the reform era. Such a character—the successful, urbane, contemporary man with one or more extramarital mistresses—had in fact become a stock figure in Chinese popular culture by the turn of the century. Moreover, narratives featuring this kind of character were only a subset within a broader body of films, TV shows, and works of literature centered upon the themes of adultery and divorce.

This chapter will examine the trope of marital infidelity in a number of films of the reform era, with two distinctive narrative patterns emerging according to the variables of chronology, class, gender, and geography. Although several films will be discussed, I will concentrate in particular on a close reading of the 1994 film *Ermo* (dir. Zhou Xiaowen), which both exemplifies a more general narrative structure and stands as one of the most accomplished Chinese popular films of the 1990s. In all its varieties, the postsocialist cinema of infidelity articulates both the new desires awakened in the midst of urbanization and economic restructuring and the new anxieties associated with them, including the individual anxieties aroused by private desire as well as collective anxieties over the very privatization and commodification *of* desire and fantasy—along with economic production—during the reform era.

The Mistress as Accessory to Urban Success

The culmination of the popular cultural preoccupation with infidelity may well be the blockbuster film *Shouji* (Cell phone; dir. Feng Xiaogang, 2004), in which a famous TV personality named Yan Shouyi, the host of a talk show, tries without success to maintain the delicate network of lies and concealments that allow him to have two different mistresses in addition to his estranged wife. As had been the case for the character Kang Weiye in *Coming and Going*, Yan Shouyi is a highly successful and prominent figure in the new reform-era society, and his beautiful mistresses serve as both emblems of his achievement and rewards for his competitive triumph in the market economy.

Given the history of concubinage and courtesan cultures in traditional China, it is worth noting the implications of the return of the successful man's mistress—not to mention the prostitute (see Chapters Five and Seven)—to the popular cultural imagination as well as social practice. In the course of the reform era, the gender equality that had been part of the utopian vision of both the May Fourth Movement and Mao-era revolutionary culture was abandoned in favor of a return of sorts to the traditional notion that rich and powerful men may avail themselves of mistresses in addition to their wives, and even poorer men may hire readily available prostitutes for their sexual satisfaction. Whatever might be said of the supposed oppression of women through the suppression of "femininity" during the Mao era, the fact that countless women may now choose or be forced by circumstances into the social role of the mistress or prostitute does not augur well for the prospects of women's liberation under the conditions of postsocialist modernity.

In fact, the Maoist leanings of the wife in *Coming and Going*, as discussed in the last chapter, add another layer to her function as vengeful superego precisely because of the taboo on concubinage in revolutionary culture; Kang Weiye's mistresses, as much as his capitalist business ventures, show his distance from collective revolutionary values, and those values haunt the guilty conscience of protagonist and reader alike. As had been the case in the TV version of *Coming and Going*, *Cell Phone* also ends with an act of contrition and renunciation of the duplicity and selfishness associated with infidelity. Having made his life a mess through deceptions largely carried out through cell phone calls and text messaging with his wife and mistresses, in the midst of getting caught in yet another lie Shouyi gets a message saying that his dear grandma has died back in the rural village where he had grown up before going to Beijing to become a TV star. After returning to the village for her funeral, stricken with grief and dressed in a traditional white funeral robe and headband, Shouyi kowtows and pays his last respects to the matriarch, then dramatically throws his cell phone into her cremation fire, vowing never to use one again. Despite the novelty of incinerating a cell phone, such an ending plays to cultural touchstones that are obvious to the point of being clichés: Shouyi's repentance (which arguably should be directed at his wife) takes on the extra symbolic baggage of filial piety through the show of remorse to an older generation, while its setting in his old home village mobilizes a familiar urban/rural dialectic in which the Chinese countryside is seen as embodying a traditional, ethical national essence that is endangered by the immorality of the modernized city.

Of course, in a film like *Cell Phone*, no less than in a TV series or novel such as *Coming and Going*, tacking on a climax that delivers a moral sermon on family values cannot fully eclipse the attractions of the libertine lifestyle portrayed up to that point. *Cell Phone* condemns its eponymous devices as instruments of deception and ends with a fanciful vow to forswear the use of them, yet the film is also one long advertisement for cell phones (literally so, in fact, since Motorola was one of its sponsors) and the lifestyle associated with them.[1] Similarly, the playful young mistresses that populate these tales of infidelity are an integral part of the tableau of professional success and material wealth that audiences enjoy as they follow protagonists who are no less sympathetic for their unfaithfulness. These narratives are thus undoubtedly vulnerable to the criticism that they propagate an attractive image of the "successful personage" that has become the "new ideology" of contemporary China, an image which in fact hides a reality of growing class differences and income disparities.[2] *Cell Phone*'s ultimately critical stance toward the self-centered and deceptive habits of a "successful personage" such as Yan Shouyi cannot fully negate the audience's previous identification with him. Indeed, the ambiguities of *Cell Phone* helped to make it a major phenomenon in popular culture, provoking wide media attention with sensational reports of couples fighting, demanding to see each other's cell phone logs, and even breaking up after seeing the film, which soon became the biggest box-office hit yet for China's most popular director.[3]

The basic narrative structure of *Cell Phone* already had become so common by the end of the 1990s as to constitute a cinematic genre in itself, a genre that offers fable-like narratives of the moral dilemmas confronted by protagonists facing dramatic changes in personal economics as well as libidinal possibilities in the reform era. In such films, a man takes on one or more extramarital lovers after achieving some sort of economic success and social elevation. In many cases, the man's success and ability to defy his wife are implicitly contrasted with a previous position of parity or even subservience within the marriage. An early and typical example is *Lihun le jiu bie zai lai zhao wo* (After divorce; dir. Wang Rui, 1997), a relatively commercial family drama that remained a common offering in Chinese video stores well into the new century. Made by the "Sixth Generation" director Wang Rui, the film tells the story of a middle-aged aspiring writer in Beijing named Li Haoming. At the beginning of the film, Haoming and his wife, Shihui, are getting a divorce because he has failed to support the family through his writing despite spending their meager savings on a computer. Shihui allows Haoming to stay in their apartment, which actually belongs to her family, until he has found his own place to live. However, living with him drives her so crazy that she soon trades living abodes with her younger sister, Shihong, who has recently come to Beijing to perform in a solo dance recital. Shihui thus moves out of the apartment along with their son and leaves Haoming to contend with Shihong, who at first treats him with contempt and takes over the apartment in a way that accentuates the powerlessness of the destitute Haoming. Shihui taunts him for his failure as a writer, husband, and father, and Haoming's sense of futility is (overly, one feels) dramatized when late one night he goes to a completely deserted city intersection and pretends to be directing nonexistent traffic, as if he is losing his mind.

After a string of humiliating professional rejections, Haoming's fortunes begin to turn one day when his work is finally published in a newspaper. After learning of this, Shihong begins to be kinder to him, even helping him to find more writing jobs without telling her sister. Haoming shares his views on the arts with Shihong, who impresses him with her own artistic integrity when she refuses to use advertising from corporate sponsors in her dance show. She helps him to break out of his "cocoon," for example, by taking him to a disco and getting him to dance to a raucous Cui Jian song, and a romance soon blossoms between them. With Shihong as his muse, Haoming writes a best-selling novel (entitled *A Woman Who Burst into My Life*) and becomes famous. Everything falls apart, however, after Shihui learns of Haoming's romance with her younger and more attractive sister. Shihui shows up at their apartment to say she is taking the property back, and Shihong quickly gathers her things and leaves. Haoming pursues her, while Shihui proceeds to smash everything in the apartment, including Haoming's computer. The film's final sequence crosscuts between Shihui's violent destruction of the domestic space and Haoming's failed search for Shihong amid the busy traffic of the city.

Many later films would repeat the plot pattern of *After Divorce*, in which a male protagonist enjoys a beautiful younger mistress as a measure of his success in some realm of intellectual or artistic endeavor, but complications eventually ensue to fatally threaten his enjoyment. In *Zhao Xiansheng* (Mr. Zhao; dir. Lü Yue, 1998), a professor of Chinese medicine married to a now-unemployed factory worker has an affair with an attractive former student, but discovery by his wife, the unexpected pregnancy of his lover, and finally a terrible car accident intervene to destroy his deceitful lifestyle. In addition, besides *Cell Phone*, another one of director Feng Xiaogang's extremely successful "New Year's celebration films" (*hesuipian*) features male adultery as its main theme.[4] *Yi sheng tanxi* (Sigh; 2000) depicts the convoluted relationships of a famous writer named Liang Yazhou with his wife and his mistress. As was the case with the protagonists of *Mr. Zhao* and *Coming and Going*, Yazhou continually makes promises to both his wife and his lover, but he cannot bring himself to either remain faithful to the former or get a divorce and marry the latter. The result is that all parties, and the man's confused young daughter as well, face repeated crises and recriminations, even though Yazhou's material success allows them all to live the lifestyle of Beijing's new rich.

Finally, this group of urban films of infidelity might include *Shuohao bu fenshou* (Agreed not to separate; dir. Chuan Jingsheng, 2000), which, like the later

Cell Phone, features a TV personality as a hero, in this case TV sports journalist Teng Yuanfeng. In *Agreed Not to Separate*, however, it is the wife who has had an affair years before and, consumed by guilt over the identity of her son's real father, finally files for divorce. As with the other films, in *Agreed Not to Separate*, marital infidelity is depicted as an integral part of a lifestyle that is clearly marked as urban, modern, sophisticated, successful, and sometimes featuring an alluring sense of Westernized bohemianism. All take place in either Beijing or Shanghai, and the globalized and consumerist nature of those cities at the turn of the century is emphasized through settings such as Starbucks, KFC, discos, luxurious hotel rooms, and spacious apartments in housing complexes with names like "Euro Classic." In *After Divorce*, when Shihong throws a party for all her artist friends, a long-haired young man strums a guitar and sings Bob Dylan's "Knocking on Heaven's Door," while in *Agreed Not to Separate* the wife's illicit lover is again a shaggy-haired guitarist who not only sings a pop song with the English chorus "My love to you . . ." but also ends the song by dramatically smashing the guitar, like a rock star, to demonstrate the depth of his romantic frustrations (if not the imagination of the filmmakers). In this context, the women who become mistresses to the heroes are the ultimate accessories to the new successful lifestyle in the booming urban economy of the reform era. They are invariably younger and more beautiful than the protagonists' wives, and the screaming accusations of the latter during marital arguments contrast with the adolescent, flirtatious pouting and simpering of the young mistresses when they are competing for the attentions of the hapless heroes.

Again, however, these films inevitably display some ambivalence toward the lifestyle of excess they simultaneously celebrate, and without exception they end on a note of moral comeuppance, in which the protagonist must face the price of his infidelity and make a vow to be a good, faithful husband and father in the future. We have seen how, in *After Divorce*, the wife returns at the end as an avenging maternal superego who sends the mistress out to get lost in the streets and then physically demolishes the man's workplace and love nest. In *Mr. Zhao*, the protagonist is left in a vegetative state in a wheelchair, while his wife and former mistress join forces to rifle through his things and discover his secrets. *Agreed Not to Separate* ends with the male protagonist rushing to the airport to prevent his wife from leaving town for good with their son, but she boards her plane while he is still stuck in traffic. At the end of *Sigh*, the hero has finally come to his senses, gone back to his wife and daughter, and broken up with his mistress. Everything seems ideal in the final scene, when he is on vacation at the beach with his family, but in the final shot of the film he answers his ringing cell phone, then turns to stare at the camera, mouth agape and a look of fear on his face, at which point the film ends. (Perhaps his lover is simply intervening in his life again, or possibly she has even committed suicide, something with which she had threatened him earlier.) Finally, as previously mentioned, *Cell Phone* ends with the protagonist's ritual destruction of his own cell phone as an embodiment of his sins.

Fables of Forbidden Lovers and Rural Transformation

The films discussed so far—in which a successful urban male commits adultery and faces at least the threat of divorce—actually constitute only a subset of a larger group of films featuring the theme of marital infidelity in the reform era. Equally numerous, and for the most part chronologically preceding the films already discussed, were films about rural women in adulterous relationships. In both cases, the trope of infidelity offers a means to narrativize a highly ambivalent attitude toward the reform era itself, which offers enticing new freedoms and the promise of satisfaction of intense new desires while simultaneously arousing fears of social disintegration and loss of cultural identity in the face of global consumer capitalism.

Even well before the reform era, the connection between modernization and changes in marriage norms and practices had long made marital difficulty a favorite trope for artists who sought to depict the contradictions of a changing society. In the decades preceding the establishment of the PRC, the genres of both elite May Fourth literature and popular "Mandarin Duck and Butterfly" fiction frequently used issues of love, marriage, and related generational conflict to stage confrontations between traditional practices and new social and economic forces. A typical plot device, with precedents in both premodern Chinese literature and well-known Western sources such as *Romeo and Juliet*, was a distinction between the arranged marriage partner and the true object of romantic passion, through which was staged a dramatic confrontation between social norms and family expectations on the one hand and individual desire on the other.[5] Rey Chow has noted in particular that the main concerns of Mandarin Duck and Butterfly literature "are frequently refracted, sentimentally and didactically, through a focus on 'woman' as the locus of social change."[6] Thus much popular fiction of the Republican period featured the social issue of arranged marriage as a problem to be overcome by modernity, and specifically the woman as a site of interiority and potential resistance to neo-Confucian social normativity in the name of a new, modern form of subjectivity spawned by the conditions of semicolonial capitalism.

From the early years of the reform era until well into the 1990s, many important films employed the figure of a woman protagonist and the trope of marital infidelity for rhetorical effects reminiscent of those narratives of arranged marriages in the Republican era. In these cases, however, the suffocating social constraints confronting women were not simply the conservative values of premodern feudalism, but also the communal pressures of residual communism enforced by local party cadres in a way that often reinforced the traditional patriarchy. All of these rural films of infidelity involve a rural woman engaged in some kind of manual labor who becomes sexually involved with someone other than her (first) husband. In each case, the economic activities of the woman and her lover play a key role in the plot, and the liberation of sexual desire through an affair is in some fundamental way tied to an effort to liberate the woman's entrepreneurial ambitions as well. Consequently, these films anticipate their urban counterparts discussed above insofar as the trope of infidelity and divorce is used to narrativize much broader issues of the reform era, particularly the new market economy and its promises of upward mobility combined with its threats to existing social norms and ethics.

The rural cinema of infidelity can be traced to the film *Ye shan* (In the wild mountains; dir. Yan Xueshu, 1985), a groundbreaking "Fourth Generation" work that has been perhaps unfairly overshadowed by the contemporaneous debut films of the Fifth Generation.[7] *Wild Mountains* features a potentially scandalous plot that sympathetically portrays spouse-swapping among peasant couples as they adjust to the rural economic reforms of the early Deng Xiaoping era. Huihui is a relatively conservative peasant who works the land, while his younger brother Hehe is seized by the entrepreneurial spirit and continually hatches new moneymaking ventures. Unfortunately, Huihui's wife, Guilan, is comparatively progressive, while Hehe's more traditional wife, Qiurong, is fed up with his often ill-fated business schemes. In a resolution as rational as it is implausible, the two couples divorce and remarry in the configuration that most suits their individual dispositions: Qiurong with Huihui, and Guilan with Hehe. The first couple then goes on with the more traditional peasant life, while the latter eventually overcomes community prejudice by bringing in a labor-saving mechanical grain mill that represents economic progress for the whole village. With its happy ending, *Wild Mountains* is a testament to the optimism stirred by the economic successes of the early reform era. As Xiaobing Tang observes, the film "illustrates the liberating impact of the market and urban culture on the mentality of peasants living in remote rural areas."[8]

This early example introduces many elements that would be central to later rural films of infidelity of the early 1990s. The focus on a distinction between the socially approved marriage partner and the actual, secret love object effectively reintroduces private desire into cinematic discourse after the end of Maoism. Moreover, this private desire is strongly associated with private *enterprise* in the realm of home economics, as the couple that first develops an extramarital intimate bond is precisely the pair drawn to household entrepreneurial activities. Finally, private desire is also connected with the allure of the urban, as when Guilan accompanies Hehe to the county seat and is stimulated by the spectacle of life in the city. Consequently, in the context of the early Deng Xiaoping era, *Wild Mountains* can be seen as a film less about partner-swapping and remarriage than about the modernization of rural China through the unleashing of the entrepreneurial spirit and the desire for a more fulfilling life among the peasantry. This theme is not secondary to so much as dramatically narrativized *by* the more salacious plot involving spouse-trading, and the eventual acceptance of the latter by the fictional rural community thus conveys the impression that the Chinese countryside is ready for change and progress.

While the overall message of *Wild Mountains* is reassuringly positive, very similar plot elements would be deployed in much more ambivalent ways by the major rural films of infidelity I will examine from the early 1990s, *Xianghun nü* (Women from the lake of scented souls, *aka* Woman sesame-oil maker; dir. Xie Fei, 1992) and *Ermo* (dir. Zhou Xiaowen, 1994). In both of the later films, the heroine is a rural woman engaged in some kind of household entrepreneurial activity. The woman in each film is married to a fundamentally flawed husband—physically crippled and either sexually abusive or impotent—and in each case the protagonist has a secret lover. Remarkably, both lovers drive trucks that make the trek from the local village to the city, so that the attraction of the lover in each case is linked to the promises and freedoms of the urban world in general.[9] Also in both films, the economic production of the woman's household industry in the course of the film becomes articulated to a larger business enterprise with an international bent, thus fundamentally changing the nature of the woman's labor and its relation to capital.

The heroine from *Women from the Lake of Scented Souls* (hereafter *Scented Souls*), Xiang Ersao, is a middle-aged woman with a household industry manufacturing sesame oil from the plants growing naturally on the local lake. Her husband is both lame and lazy. He walks with a crutch, is often drunk and abusive, and occasionally awakens Ersao to sexually molest her after drinking and watching illegal pornographic videos with his buddies. In contrast to his efficient and industrious wife, he rarely works but is generally seen lying about, playing chess, drinking with friends, and the like. Far from having chosen this partner herself, Ersao had been sold into her husband's family as a child bride, so that her marriage is a personal tragedy reminiscent of countless precedents in both premodern and modern Chinese popular culture. Her real passion goes to her secret lover, the truck driver Ren Zhongshi, who usually stays in the city but arranges trysts with Ersao when he comes to her village. Ersao has two children, a schoolgirl daughter named Zhi'er, the father of whom is in fact Zhongshi, and an older son named Dunzi, who suffers from epilepsy and mental retardation.

It is the truck-driving lover, Zhongshi, who brings change to Ersao's situation early in the film when he puts her in contact with a Japanese businesswoman whose company decides to invest in Ersao's sesame oil enterprise and export the product for sale in Japan. During a trip to the provincial capital, Xi'an, Ersao finalizes the deal and tours the company's oil factory, with its gleaming modern industrial machines. Soon the nature of her own household production is changed when the Japanese firm provides her with labor-saving machines as well. The city is thus depicted as the rural woman's source of increased wealth as well as sexual satisfaction, both of which are facilitated by the handsome trucker, who both literally and figuratively traverses the distance separating the rapidly modernizing city and the relatively backward and conservative countryside. The promise of a better life represented by Zhongshi proves to be unreliable, however. During one of their liaisons, Ersao angrily accuses him of treating her merely as his mistress, saying that, had he been willing, she would have divorced her husband to create a life together rather than simply serving as his "concubine." Eventually Zhongshi breaks off their relationship altogether, most likely because he has taken another lover. When he promises to take care of their daughter financially and attempts to pacify Ersao by giving her a thousand yuan, she angrily refuses the money.

Ersao's miserable predicament is narrated in melodramatic style, with many scenes of weeping and emotional confrontation, and it is placed in a mythical context by reference to a local legend about women during the Qing Dynasty drowning themselves in the lake to escape arranged marriages—hence the name "scented souls" (*xianghun*), a flowery traditional term for a female spirit. Ersao, it is suggested through such techniques as dissolves from a close-up of her face to long shots of the lake scenery, is a contemporary incarnation of these female ghosts of the lake, caught in a bitter cycle of gender oppression, having in fact tried to drown herself as well after being sold as a child bride. Moreover, she apparently keeps the cycle going when she manipulates an attractive young local girl from a poor family into marrying her own mentally handicapped son as a means of paying off the poor girl's family debt—incurred through failed investments that had made the girl's family losers in the newly competitive rural economy. In the end, however, after seeing how her daughter-in-law, Huanhuan, is physically abused by a debilitated husband she does not love, thus suffering just as Ersao herself has suffered, Ersao finally decides to break the cycle of misery and offers to release the young woman by allowing a divorce. The story nevertheless ends in yet more tears, as Huanhuan laments that she is now spoiled goods and could never find another husband.

In the context of this chapter, what is notable about *Scented Souls* is how it represents the process of rural economic reforms through the figure of a sympathetically depicted female entrepreneur who also has an extramarital affair. Ersao's household industry is precisely the kind of market-driven production that was most encouraged in the early stages of Deng Xiaoping's rural economic reforms. Indeed, it is this kind of rural industry that was the "flagship of the rural reforms and engine of rural growth" in the early reform era.[10] However, when Ersao's household industry is connected to an international market through the Japanese investors, in effect it represents China's transition from the early, localized market experiments to a more comprehensive entry into the age of globalized capital. And yet, through the failures of Ersao's affair and her personal life in general, the film suggests that the new promises of the reform era may fail to lift even such a clever and industrious rural woman out of her misery.

Ermo: Desire, Production, and Black Comedy

The plot of *Ermo* is in many ways remarkably parallel to that of *Women from the Lake of Scented Souls*, and like that film, it echoes many story elements of the earlier *Wild Mountains. Ermo's* director, in fact, had gained experience as the assistant director of *Wild Mountains* a decade earlier. Although Zhou Xiaowen is generally labeled a Fifth Generation filmmaker—in contrast to the Fourth Generation directors of the other two films—he is actually one of the few major directors whose career in filmmaking began during the Cultural Revolution, placing him between the Fourth and Fifth Generations.[11]

Ermo itself is an interesting hybrid in terms of its mode of production. The film was not assigned to Zhou Xiaowen by his studio, but rather was inspired by the director's own reading of the little-known novel of the same title by Xu Baoqi. Having worked in both genres for the Xi'an Film Studio in the 1980s, Zhou has said that by the end of the decade he had "thought a lot about the categories of 'art film' and 'entertainment film' and came to the conclusion that it's a false dichotomy." As a result, "I looked for a middle way between the two."[12] This philosophy resulted in *Hei shan lu* (Black mountain, 1990), the release of which was long delayed by negotiations with censors. Zhou was cut loose from the Xi'an Film Studio after a later studio project, *Cehuangqi* (Lie detector, 1993) proved to be an incoherent disaster. The director decided to make *Ermo* as his next film, but he found no takers when he shopped it around to all sixteen major film studios in China. As a result, he produced the film himself, with key

postproduction help coming from a pair of Beijing entrepreneurs with operations in California and Hong Kong. In this sense, Zhou Xiaowen was part of the
first wave of independent filmmakers in China in the early 1990s (see Chapter
Five), despite vast differences in almost every other sense—including generation (Fifth versus Sixth), subject matter (rural versus urban), and filmmaking
style (closer to the lyrical naturalism of *Wild Mountains* than to the *cinéma
vérité* realism of most other independent films of the early 1990s). *Ermo*, which
eventually did obtain a studio label and distribution in China, represents a Fifth
Generation studio director's attempt to endure after changes in the studio system made it impossible to continue working as he had in the 1980s.

The eponymous heroine of *Ermo* lives in a rural village with her impotent
husband, who had been a village chief in the past but is now an invalid incapable of contributing substantially to household production. Ermo, on the
other hand, works tirelessly at the household industry of making *mahua* (fried
and twisted) noodles from scratch to sell on the street market to fellow villagers. Her next-door neighbors are comparatively well off, owning a TV set as
well as a truck, and Ermo's son often goes to the neighbors' house to watch TV,
despite the fact that Ermo frequently feuds with the neighbor's wife and resents
the attraction their home holds for her son. This leads Ermo to desire a TV set
of her own, an ambition that gradually consumes her and leaves her physically
and emotionally exhausted. *Ermo* thus generally is viewed as an allegorical fable
of capitalist rural modernization centered on Ermo's single-minded quest for a
TV set, in the end amounting to an entertaining yet devastating critique of the
way commodification and the global imaginary of consumer capitalism distort and dehumanize both productive labor and desire. Several observers have
noted the Marxist underpinnings of *Ermo*'s rhetorical message, and indeed in
both its broad plot and several telling details the film can serve almost as an
illustration of Marx's key chapter on "The Commodity" in the first volume of
Capital. However, as I will argue later, the film's interest lies also in the compel-
ling ambiguities that serve to mitigate its own critique, particularly through its
comedic elements and its implicit historical consciousness.

Ermo's plot and rhetoric both begin with Ermo's position as a laborer who
single-handedly supports her family through hard work and entrepreneurial
initiative. Besides making her noodles to hawk in small bundles on the street,

she weaves baskets to sell on the side. Her work is represented in all its physicality in an early sequence in which she arises from bed before dawn to begin the laborious process of making noodles. A close-up of her bare foot stepping right next to her prone husband's head symbolizes in an almost sensual way her dominance within the household and arguably eroticizes the image of Ermo's feet—a point of significance for the next part of the sequence, in which the noodle-making process is filmed in a manner that presents Ermo's laboring body to the viewer as an eroticized spectacle. The scene begins with another close-up of Ermo's bare feet, now kneading dough in a large bowl beneath her. In the next series of shots, punctuated by jump cuts that emphasize the duration of her physical labor, Ermo's upper body is framed as she continues kneading the dough with her feet. In these shots, the sweaty, heaving body of the attractive Mongolian actress playing Ermo, Ailiya, exudes a sensuality reminiscent, for example, of the way the early films of Zhang Yimou displayed the body of the Chinese sex symbol Gong Li. Indeed, if not for the previous shots and the soundtrack continuing the sound (now out of scale) of her feet's work, these shots could be interpreted as depicting actual sexual stimulation.

This exhibition of Ermo's laboring body in an almost masturbatory fashion leaves Zhou Xiaowen open to the criticisms leveled at Zhang Yimou and other Fifth Generation icons, namely that the director films his rural heroine in a way calculated to appeal to the voyeuristic and fetishizing gaze of the audience as well as the orientalizing gaze of the West.[13] I argue, however, that on the contrary this sexualized scene of physical labor is most importantly the symbolic nexus from which the remainder of the film extends the parallel plot strands of Ermo's labor and her sexual desire. For, in retrospect after later plot developments, this scene posits Ermo in an autonomous state in which, despite her solitude and the hardship of her toil, she at least is in possession of her own sexuality as well as her own labor power, which even seem to be momentarily fused into a singular exertion. At this moment in the film, Ermo's work is immediately invested with the full force of her sensual existence—in short, it is presented as an instance of unalienated labor. The function of such a scene is to set the stage for, and serve as an implicit contrast to, the later directions taken by her libido and her social production, both of which become commodified and thus in some basic sense alienated from herself.[14]

FIG. 4.1. Ermo as she kneads dough with her feet.

The truck-driving neighbor, Xiazi, begins the transformation of Ermo's labor when he drives her to the nearest city to sell her noodles and baskets for a higher profit. Ermo, her aspirations raised by the increased income combined with her new consumer desire to buy the largest TV set in the county, later accepts Xiazi's suggestion that she go to work making noodles for a restaurant in the city, an establishment that signals the encroachment of a global imaginary by its name, the "International Grand Restaurant." Significantly, it is not until shortly after Ermo begins selling her labor at the restaurant that she consummates an affair with Xiazi himself, who, it later turns out, is also subsidizing her wages at the restaurant. Thus the expansion of Ermo's productive ambitions in the service of her desire for a TV set goes side by side with the unleashing of her libidinal desires in her brief but passionate affair with Xiazi. However, the commodification of both her labor and her sexuality leave her in a state of fundamental self-alienation—a state dramatically illustrated (in somewhat clichéd fashion) by a shot of her reflected face split in half by a large crack in a hotel-room mirror during one of her urban liaisons with Xiazi.

To understand precisely what happens to Ermo's labor, in parallel with her sexuality, it is worth considering in more detail her original mode of production, particularly given the Marxist flavor of the film's overall rhetoric. Strictly speaking, although at the film's beginning Ermo's *mahua* noodles are already commodities insofar as they are sold on the market, it is only when she begins working in the urban restaurant that her labor becomes capitalist labor. At the opening of the film, the noodles sold by Ermo are simply what Marx would call precapitalist "excess produce," resulting from the "independent individual production" of goods, some of which are consumed and the rest sold to other producers as commodities.[15] In other words, it is a somewhat less capital-intensive form of the type of rural industry we have seen in Ersao's modest sesame oil production enterprise at the beginning of the earlier film *Scented Souls*. In that film, household production was fundamentally changed when Japanese investment partners added labor-saving machinery and packaged the product for export. Similarly, when Xiazi gets Ermo the job making noodles at the International Grand Restaurant in the city, the essential nature of her production changes. Whereas Ersao continued to make her sesame oil at home, but with machines provided by an outside firm, Ermo goes to where the machines are and contributes only her labor and expertise. In fact, she now enters the marketplace as a free laborer rather than an independent producer since, strictly speaking, the commodity she sells is no longer her own noodles but rather her commodified labor power to make noodles to be sold by the restaurant.

Ermo's labor and her sexuality, which had seemed to merge in the early noodle-making sequence, continue to be tied together through parallel plot developments that show her unwitting alienation from each through a process of commodification. Soon after taking the restaurant job, Ermo begins her sexual affair, which she later realizes is a form of prostitution insofar as Xiazi covertly subsidizes her wages while she serves as his mistress. Ermo's shock at the realization of her alienation from her own sexuality through its commodification is particularly poignant due to the importance she had clearly placed on her own sexual agency in a previous scene: When Xiazi had tried to seduce her for the first time in his truck, she had forcefully rejected his aggressive physical advances with a blow to his genitals; only after he had been thus subdued did she methodically remove her own clothes to reveal that the desire was mutual—but would be consummated only at her own pace. When she later realizes that her twin desires for economic gain and sexual fulfillment have led her to be unwittingly compromised, her sexuality and labor both commodified, she defiantly reasserts her independence in a restaurant meal scene that mirrors in reverse an earlier scene. In the same restaurant, Xiazi had bought Ermo a sumptuous lunch just before the initiation of their affair; now, she treats him to an equally lavish meal as she ends the affair and returns all his money, pointedly showing that she refuses to be put in his debt or to sell her sexuality. As a contemporary critic in China approvingly noted, "*Ermo* is the story of a female with an independent character and an autonomous individual dignity."[16]

If Ermo's labor and sexual desire have now come full circle after a lucrative but temporary stint in the capitalist labor market and a passionate but unsustainable love affair, her recently discovered consumerism nevertheless proceeds along its inexorable course, as she continues to horde and obsessively count her savings with the aim of buying the large TV set from the city. It is this plot arc that generally receives focus as the essence of *Ermo*'s critique of global capitalism, and the manner in which it is resolved indeed suggests that the danger of commodity fetishism constitutes the moral of the film's Marxist fable. The TV set seems almost to be a character in the story, with a magnetic aura that attracts the other characters and makes them gawk at it in wonder. Thus, during Ermo's periodic visits to the department store in the city to view the set she is saving up to purchase, there are repeated shots of Ermo and other gaping shoppers as if from the point of view of the TV set itself, which consequently seems to be returning their gaze.[17] Its wondrous range of attractive images (most notably the soft-core eroticism of the American soap opera scene that engrosses Ermo the first time she lays eyes on the TV), its ability to speak in different languages and reveal wonders like "every strand of the foreigners' blond hair"—all make the TV set appear almost magical. To recall Marx's classic description of the commodified wooden table, the TV set seems to evolve grotesque and wonderful ideas out of its mysterious electronic brain, otherworldly images of eroticism and exoticism that leap impossible distances to suddenly appear before the rural villagers as conceivable, alluring lifestyles.[18] Ermo, in her first encounter with the TV and its love scene from the American soap opera *Dallas*, darts her eyes quickly to each side, as if to make sure none of the other shoppers has taken notice of her particular voyeuristic enjoyment, then widens her eyes as she looks directly back at the scene on the TV, letting herself be immersed in its erotic fantasy world. Ermo's fetishization of the TV set also extends beyond the images it presents to embrace its brute presence as an object, an imposing piece of furniture the very size of which represents symbolic social value; her insistence on buying the department store's largest set, with a twenty-nine-inch screen, results not from an aesthetic appreciation for large-screen images but from the prestige of having the largest TV set in the county. As an imposing, high-tech object, the TV embodies wealth and status even when turned off—as is vividly shown by the real-world example of a group of remote Sri Lankan fishermen who have purchased unusable TV sets to show their wealth even though they have no electricity.[19]

Ermo's obsession with the TV is only the most central of an array of plot elements that make the film easily read as, in Judith Farquhar's words, "a sophisticated Marxist critique of distortions of use value and the fetishism of commodities in capitalism."[20] Several moments in the film highlight the ways in which the commonsense primacy of use value is corrupted by the attractions of commodities and the greed for the purest realization of the commodity form, money itself. For example, in response to Ermo's desire for a TV set, her husband repeatedly argues that they should instead be saving to upgrade their house, pointing out that a TV set is only an "egg," a final product to be consumed, while a house is a "chicken" with long-term productivity. In a tragicomic scene during one of the commutes of Xiazi and Ermo between village and city, Xiazi's truck strikes and fatally injures a donkey owned by an old farmer. When Xiazi repeatedly offers to compensate the farmer monetarily, the farmer protests, "What good is money? He can't work now," thus refusing to substitute the exchange value of money for the use value of the animal. Ermo herself, in her obsessive drive to save enough for the TV set, all too eagerly transforms her physical being into money. After she learns she can sell her blood for money at the hospital in the city, she does it so frequently as to endanger her health. Though her ultimate fetish is the TV set, in the interim Ermo fixates on the physicality of the cash earned by the sacrifice of her sweat and blood. In no fewer than nine scenes, Ermo is shown counting her money, her enjoyment of it a sensory experience that includes licking a torn bill and appreciatively inhaling the scent of fresh currency. As Anthony Giddens has put it, "money is a mode of deferral," and Ermo's deferred satisfaction of owning the TV set is itself turned into a pleasure through the surrogate enjoyment of the cash that represents both past labor and the future commodity.[21]

The fetishization of money epitomizes the replacement of use value by exchange value that is critically depicted throughout *Ermo*—most importantly, as I have argued, in the commodification of Ermo's own labor as well as her sexuality. An allegorical reading of the film's plot suggests that, by extension, the labor power and social relationships of the Chinese peasantry in general are in danger of being sold out to the promises of capitalist modernization. The ultimately illusory nature of these promises is dramatized in the film's devastating final sequence, in which Ermo finally buys the TV and brings it home during the Spring Festival celebration. Long desired for its very size, the set turns out to be so big that it cannot be brought through the door of Ermo's house but must be handed through a large window instead. Once inside, since there is no other convenient place to put it, the TV eventually is placed on the *kang,* or bed, on which the whole family sleeps. Through these details, the TV set that had projected such magnetism with its images in the urban department store becomes an awkward, oversized physical presence that colonizes the little rural home of Ermo and her family. Formerly the ultimate object of desire, once obtained, it has perversely metamorphosed into almost the reverse—"a gigantic metaphor for Ermo's *blocked* desire."[22] The subsumption of household use values by this invading commodity is demonstrated when the large ladle Ermo uses in making noodles is employed to make an antenna, causing Ermo to ask, "How will I make noodles?" Once the TV is hooked up, the entire village crowds into Ermo's house to witness the spectacle of a televised game of American football. However, the game results in less enjoyment than confusion, as the villagers debate what exactly they are seeing (a gang fight among foreigners? a basketball game?)—the illegible foreign entertainment contrasting with the traditional Chinese New Year festivities with which the city streets had bustled during the trip to buy the TV set earlier in the day.

After an ellipsis during which all the neighbors have left the house, Ermo and her family remain slumped on the floor, dozing while the still-blaring TV occupies their bed. The TV is again broadcasting an erotic scene from an

American soap opera, much like the scene that had fascinated Ermo in the department store when she first laid eyes on the TV set. Now, however, instead of having a rapt crowd of gawking shoppers, the scene of a couple showering together plays out without attracting a single diegetic gaze, a point emphasized by repeated cuts from a frontal view of the TV screen to a reverse shot of the family sprawled, eyes closed, on the other side of the room. After the soap opera ends, the TV goes to a typical end-of-broadcasting sequence showing the weather forecast for major cities around the globe. As an offscreen voice reads the temperatures, a map of the world highlights the various locations, with iconic architectural images from each global site accompanying the forecast. The sequence would seem to reinforce the notion of the TV as having the almost magical power to connect a small village in the Chinese countryside with the great cultural centers of the world, from Beijing to New York City—except that Ermo and her family continue to snore throughout the broadcast. Only when the station goes off the air and the TV switches to an image of snowy static accompanied by the blare of white noise does Ermo suddenly open her eyes and return the blank gaze of the TV. In the film's final three shots, the image of the TV going to static cuts to a close-up of Ermo awakening, then back to a shot of the static, into which the camera zooms until the entire frame is filled with snow. Against this background, just before the film ends, we hear the distant echo of Ermo's voice hawking her noodles in the distinctive melody that has been heard repeatedly throughout the film and thus has come to represent Ermo's industry and her livelihood. With this final combination of image and sound, then, *Ermo* links the labor of its peasant heroine not with some fantasy world of desire such as the sex scenes she had watched in the city, nor even with the TV itself as object, but rather with a close-up of "a vacuity," "the emptying out of meaning."[23]

Anne Ciecko and Sheldon H. Lu view this vacuity as "an index of a problematic, pervasive, existential, and ideological emptiness as a result of the kind of economism and pragmatism of the Deng era"—in other words, the crisis of cultural meaning and sense of nihilism that I have explored in various ways in the previous chapters.[24] More specifically, with this final image, Ermo—who had remained oddly passive and vacant as her neighbors, and even her now-enthusiastic husband, had celebrated the arrival of the TV—confronts the collapse of the phantasmic structure that she had built up around the fetishized television, which, when seen in the department store, had held what Benjamin would call the displayed commodity's implicit promise of utopian plenitude.[25] In contrast, after it has taken its awkward position in her real living space, in the film's final image of empty static Ermo for the first time sees through the fetishistic nature of the TV.[26] In a strictly psychoanalytic reading we might say that she now "traverses the fantasy" and sees the real void at the heart of any impossible object of desire; in the particular sociohistorical context of *Ermo*, by extension she also suddenly recognizes the globalized consumer paradise the TV represents as a fleeting illusion that ultimately fails to fulfill the desires it arouses in the Chinese countryside. As Zhang Yiwu summarizes, "In the end, [Ermo] discovers that this myth [of modernity] contains nothing but those twinkling, befuddling specks of white light. The TV contains everything, yet it contains nothing."[27]

Given the obvious Marxist bent of *Ermo*'s rhetoric and its fable-like narrative of the dangers of commodity fetishism, it is not surprising that most overseas commentators have read it as fundamentally critical of the reform era and the effects of the economic transformation of the countryside.[28] Like *Women from the Lake of Scented Souls*, *Ermo* apparently suggests that neither the entrepreneurial initiative nor the sexual agency of a clever rural woman will be sufficient to free her long-pent-up desires and give her some degree of autonomy from the oppressive social forces around her. Like Ersao in *Scented Souls*, Ermo has a passionate affair with a man for whom she has genuine affection and also betters herself economically by articulating her labor with the resources of outside capital, yet in each case the affair is stifled and a higher income fails to change the basic nature of each woman's dependence upon a fundamentally inadequate husband and a backward community. It is as if the new freedoms of the reform era allowed a brief utopian moment, a glimpse of a new life of romantic satisfaction and economic progress, but the utopian potential of the vision was lost with the realization that this new life would take debased commodity forms including the prostitution of sexual agency, the commodification of labor power, and the fetishization of consumer goods.

Nonetheless, for all its apparent Marxist critique, the message of *Ermo* is far from straightforward. If the narrative is viewed as a starting point (rural household production and marital fidelity), followed by complications (urban wage labor and marital infidelity), followed by an ending point (a return to rural household production and marital fidelity, with a new TV)—the disturbing final shots of the film cannot be taken simply as an indication that Ermo should have been happy where she started. The viewer's sympathies are closely aligned with Ermo, and her affair with Xiazi appears as a welcome release for Ermo's repressed passion. Similarly, Ermo's ambition and business competence are depicted favorably, and her work in the city does not strike one as debased, at least not until the revelation that it is subsidized partly by her lover. In fact, the abstraction of Ermo's labor through its commodification in the city is directly tied to the increased freedom of her sexual agency, and if we will eventually be disappointed by the ending of her affair, her employment, and her quest for the TV set, we nevertheless are unlikely to yearn on Ermo's behalf for the purity of her original state of being. Instead, the audience may feel that her dreams of a more autonomous and fulfilling life were stifled and that the unleashing of her economic ambition and her libidinal desire were lamentable only in their failure.

In this context, it is interesting that while English studies of *Ermo* tend to emphasize its Marxist critique of capitalism, the film's critical reaction in China tended to see it more as a tragicomedy about the *incompleteness* of modernization in the countryside. Luo Yijun compared the character Ermo to a caterpillar cocooned in the "natural economy" of traditional society that ultimately is unable to metamorphose into a modern butterfly, since "her distant grasp of the pulse of the modernized market economy is still too remote!"[29] Similarly, Tao Dongfeng interprets the final scene of the film, with its spatially dramatized gap between the static-filled TV set and the snoring family, as symbolizing the mutually uncomprehending chasm between "modern industrial civilization" and "agricultural civilization."[30] Even a more nuanced critical reading by Zhang Yiwu interprets the shot of Ermo's split reflection in a cracked hotel mirror as showing that Ermo has failed to achieve the "comprehensive rupture" necessary to establish a new subjectivity suited to the "the myth of 'modernity'" promised by the TV set—an interpretation that still implicitly critiques modernization's incompleteness in rural China rather than capitalist modernity itself.[31]

The reasons for Ermo's fundamental dissatisfaction and the necessity of change become evident through the political subtext of the film. In a fairly straightforward psychoanalytic reading, Ermo's commodity fetishism as well as her secret affair arguably are driven by the fundamental lack she suffers in the figure of her impotent and sickly husband. The dynamics of sexual power in their household are characterized by the husband's lack of phallic power, both in the literal sense of being impotent and in the symbolic sense of being politically and socially disempowered. Ermo herself at one point directly taunts him for not being able to "do what a man does," and she sometimes orders her bumbling husband about, telling him to cook a meal after her first day of making profitable sales in the city, for example. As a former village chief, the husband repeatedly goes through the rather craven ritual of reminding his neighbors that he is no longer in office each time they habitually address him as "Chief" (*cunzhang*).[32] Now useless as a household provider and out of touch with the times, the chief embodies a more general marginalization of Communist political power, formerly the center of meaning generation and moral authority in the countryside. During one scene in which Ermo fights with Xiazi's wife as dozens of neighbors watch the violence, the film cuts to a shot of the chief observing from the distance of his own window and muttering that "they should all be legally punished." The comedy of the moment comes in part from the understanding that he is an irrelevant old man who no longer has power even over his own household, much less the power of legal sanction. In the vacuum left by the chief's emasculation, it is no surprise that Ermo seeks sexual satisfaction as well as symbolic meaning and social status elsewhere. The tall and strong Xiazi, whose dapper Western-style clothes contrast with the chief's generic blue cotton Maoist uniform,[33] offers temporary fulfillment but ultimately proves to be unreliable as a long-term source of satisfaction and stability, just as the TV set proves equally disappointing in the end. Thus it is easy to see the husband's phallic power as a state of original fulfillment which, once lost, sets in motion the logic of substitution of the fetish for Ermo: "The biggest TV set is intended to replace the dysfunctional phallus of her husband, the former village chief, in the symbolic order."[34] Or, as a reviewer in China put it, "In *Ermo*, the TV set becomes a symbol for man, a symbol of power."[35] *Ermo* might even be read as a feminist critique of phallic power in general, or of patriarchy in rural China in particular. However, upon consideration of the sexual politics of

Ermo, it seems that if *Scented Souls* presents the dilemma of a woman seeking to break out of an endless cycle of gender oppression by the forces of patriarchal tradition, *Ermo* suggests a more subtle reading, in which gender is not so much a baseline category of oppression as a figurative trope to represent the relationship between the rural people and the larger economic and political forces they face in the reform era. Ermo's awakened sexuality and economic productivity both figure as markers of a newfound autonomy and interiority that contrast with the previously heteronomous and quite public organization of resources, meaning, and subjectivity—a Maoist past that is suggested only obliquely in the decrepit figure of the former political leader. Although the disappointing conclusions of Ermo's dalliances with both her neighbor and her TV set hardly give one great hope for the future of rural China caught in the thrall of a new global consumerist imaginary, the figure of a washed-up and feeble former village chief/husband suggests neither the possibility nor the desirability of a return to the previous order of things.

For this reason I do not completely agree with Dai Jinhua's interesting argument that what Ermo seeks is not actually a new life at all, but rather a return to the old order, in which her family's status was higher than that of her neighbor's due to the political power of her husband, which she now seeks to replace by her higher consumptive power.[36] While this rings true insofar as it brings out the logic of substitution inherent to any fetish, it does not entirely account for Ermo's enjoyment of her new sexual and economic autonomy during the middle section of the film. Indeed, to take the logic of the fetish too far—seeing Xiazi and the TV set as merely interchangeable substitutions for an imaginary, desire-organizing phallic signifier that had earlier been associated with the chief—would be to fall into the trap of structuralist stasis that is the danger of any ahistorical psychoanalytic approach. Rather, the system of substitutions the film presents as the trajectory of Ermo's desire is only readable against the broader backdrop of the social conditions and historical transformations that in fact help to determine Ermo's individual libidinal economy. Her enjoyment of the new autonomy of her libido as well as her labor is both an intense personal experience and a marker of a new public imaginary in reform-era China. And, however seriously we must take the Marxist critique of consumerism raised by *Ermo*'s conclusion, to reduce Ermo's enjoyment and the wider public imaginary associated with it to the status of mere false ideology would be to underestimate not only its intensity but also its power to shape the very historical circumstances that generated it in the first place. It is this type of reduction that is often the blind spot of the New Left in the field of Chinese cultural studies, both in China itself and in Western academia. Our critique of postsocialist modernity must also come to terms with the extent to which its autonomization offers real personal satisfactions which work indirectly to legitimize the official ideology of market-driven modernization among much of the public.

There is a final and most important way in which a reading of *Ermo* as a moral or political condemnation of capitalist reforms must be problematized, which is a consideration of the role of humor in the way its message is configured. Unlike *Scented Souls*—essentially a variation on the maternal melodrama in which Ersao endures her miserable fate but releases her daughter-in-law from the same—*Ermo* is a comedy, and a funny one at that.[37] In fact, as Xiaobing Tang has shown, *Ermo*'s generic precedents include one of the classic Chinese comedies of the early 1960s, *Li Shuangshuang*, which also featured a strong-willed young married woman coping with social change in the countryside.[38] Close attention to *Ermo*'s humor reveals that the film is aimed at a sophisticated audience that would take as a given condition the changes in values that Ermo herself was only beginning to embody. Thus, for example, the punch line in the scene with the injured donkey comes when, after repeatedly protesting the reduction of his animal's use value to exchange value, the old man suddenly bargains for a little *more* money in compensation from Xiazi. With that detail, the moral authority of the elderly peasant is undermined by the realization that he is merely pursuing his own self-interest like everyone else and values cold cash as much as anyone. When rural people are depicted as genuinely innocent and ignorant in the film, their naïveté itself becomes the grounds for a joke. For instance, the villagers' ignorance of what they are watching on TV is sometimes humorous to the point of stretching credulity, as when they mistake American football for basketball. (While the former may appear alien to most Chinese, the latter certainly would not.) Similarly, when Ermo brings some nicely packaged dress shirts home from the city market to give to her son and husband, the latter is humorously befuddled by the thin strip of cardboard he finds inexplicably tucked under the shirt collar. How are we to understand such humor at the expense of rural naïveté? Fredric Jameson has argued that the modern urban West condescendingly imagined the countryside as the site of rural idiocy, sexual repression, provincial boredom, and so on, but by the end of the Cold War, the now-postmodern West had transferred this role to the "imagined drabness" of "the Second World city and the social realities of a nonmarket or planned economy."[39] In the case of *Ermo*, from the perspective of an urban Chinese audience, it seems that the two imaginaries operate together, with stasis and naïveté represented by the vestiges of communism *in* the rural village.

Through its comedic form, then, *Ermo* clearly anticipates a viewer who is a fully formed subject of the reform era rather than someone who stands on its brink in the way Ermo, her family, and their neighbors do. This acknowledgment does not necessarily lessen the significance of the film's critique of commodity fetishism, but it does change its valence, in that it takes the globalized commercial society under critique as an already given condition. In fact, the film's apparent harsh critique of consumerism did not stop the American *Journal of Global Marketing* from reading it as a useful guide for global corporations hoping to increase sales in China. Instead of taking the final shot of Ermo's view of empty static on the TV as the devastating implosion of her fantasy of consumerist fulfillment, the authors optimistically speculate that "perhaps a new desire for another consumer good will drive her to seek work, once again," and go on to suggest lessons Western marketers might draw from the film to help them peddle their products in China.[40] The same study speculates that, "were the character of Ermo to magically see this movie herself, she probably would not get much of it and would fail to see most of its humor."[41]

The Rural Cinema of Infidelity

In fact, the cynicism that lends *Ermo* its comedy—as well as its dubious utility as a guide for marketing strategists—is itself an indication of changed historical circumstances when compared with the earlier films of rural economic reform and extramarital dalliances. *Wild Mountains*, made early in the Deng Xiaoping era, represents the hopes raised by the introduction of rural economic reforms during the late 1970s and early 1980s. The newly unleashed entrepreneurial spirit of the peasantry is celebrated, and the marital difficulties of the two couples work themselves out in a way that suggests new personal freedoms will not lead to major social problems in a modernizing countryside. *Scented Souls*, though made in the early 1990s, continues to reflect many of the concerns of the latter half of the 1980s, when various works of film, literature, and even television directly or indirectly raised the question of whether the modernization of the reform era would be able to overcome the tenacity of essentially premodern conservative values in traditional communities.[42] Thus the heroine's happiness is stymied not by her own greed or the false promises of capitalist modernity, but rather by the patriarchal family system through which she was sold as a child bride and thus condemned to a lifetime of misery with a man she did not love. *Ermo*'s heroine, on the other hand, is made miserable precisely by the failure of the new imaginary of the capitalist reform era to live up to its initial promise of personal fulfillment. The disappointing endings to both her affair and her quest for the TV set thus indicate a growing cultural ambivalence toward the more advanced state of economic transformation during the Jiang Zemin era of the mid-1990s.

As we progress, then, from *Wild Mountains* through *Scented Souls* to *Ermo*, we go from optimism to pessimism in message and from realist drama to maternal melodrama to black comedy in genre. There are some other potential additions to this list of rural films of infidelity in the reform era.[43] For example, Xie Jin's 1986 melodrama *Furong Zhen* (Hibiscus town) depicts a strong-willed, hardworking female entrepreneur who runs a successful tofu restaurant in the years before the Cultural Revolution, loses everything when attacked as a rightist by an extremist local Communist Party secretary, and later, after her husband dies, has an illicit sexual relationship with another rightist outcast who is subsequently imprisoned for their transgression. This film's story ends at the dawn of the reform era in 1979, when the heroine's lover is released from jail to become her legitimate husband and the restaurant is returned to her as well. *Hibiscus Town* thus does not feature adultery per se but rather a widow's illicit extramarital sex, and the reform era is represented directly only in its closing scenes. Nevertheless, being released in the time in between *Wild Mountains* and *Scented Souls*, *Hibiscus Town* is no less a product of the reform era that clearly shares several generic features with those films of rural infidelity, most notably a "rich peasant" heroine whose private sexual desire confronts public sanction and whose entrepreneurial spirit is unleashed by the new market economy.

Another potential addition to the rural cinema of infidelity is *Tianguo nizi* (The day the sun turned cold; dir. Yim Hou [Yan Hao], 1994). Although made at the same time as *Ermo*, *The Day the Sun Turned Cold* is a noir crime mystery that depicts scandalous events in the frozen, remote countryside in 1980, near the beginning of the reform era, as well as their repercussions a decade later.[44] A woman named Pu Fengying (played by Siqin Gaowa, who had also played Xiang Ersao in *Scented Souls*) is suspected by her son of having poisoned his father, who suddenly fell violently ill while eating a meal at home just after discovering his wife's infidelity. Ten years later, in the film's present, the now-grown son finally reports the crime to the police, who launch an investigation that eventually leads to the arrest and execution of the mother as well as her lover, whom she had married after her husband died. Despite its generic distinction as a mystery revolving around a violent crime, *The Day the Sun Turned Cold* shares all the key plot elements of the rural cinema of infidelity. Again the family is engaged in small-scale rural industry and entrepreneurship, in this case manufacturing tofu in a primitive home workshop, and again the mother in the family engages in an adulterous affair with a man who helps to transport her, this time by sleigh, from her small village to the market in the county seat, where she sells her tofu to provide the family income. As with *Scented Souls* and *Ermo*, the woman feels no sexual attraction to her husband but lusts passionately after her lover. Moreover, as in the case of *Scented Souls*, the cuckold husband is an abusive man who takes full advantage of the patriarchal power granted him within the traditional rural family system. The slaying of the husband thus amounts to the violent overthrow of symbolic phallic power to allow free rein to the passions it has forbidden, while the son's betrayal of the mother a decade later represents a more fundamental filial devotion to the father and thus a return of the law of the father to punish the transgressive couple (a plot device that echoes the role of the son in Zhang Yimou's *Ju Dou*). Consequently, though it seemed Fengying had managed to escape her unhappy marriage in a way the heroines of *Scented Souls* and *Ermo* had not, in the end her fate is the most bitter of all, as she pays for her betrayal by going before the firing squad. Again, the apparently innocuous freedom to produce a surplus good and sell it on the open market in the city has led by turns to the dangerous unleashing of repressed desire at an eventually high cost to a woman pursuing happiness through dubious means. Due to its official nation of production, however, *The Day the Sun Turned Cold* can only be provisionally added to the Chinese rural cinema of infidelity; although it was set and filmed in mainland China, with Mandarin dialogue and mainland Chinese actors, the director and production funding both came from Hong Kong.

Conclusion

We can summarize the preceding discussion of the cinema of infidelity by dividing it into two structural forms, which, as Table 4.1 illustrates, break down remarkably consistently according to the variables of chronology, geography, gender, and class to constitute distinct narrative patterns.

TABLE 4.1

The Cinema of Infidelity

Film	Year	Setting: Rural/Urban	Adulterer:* Female/Male	Class: Laborer/ Intellectual
Wild Mountains	1984	R	F	L
Hibiscus Town	1986	R	F	L
Scented Souls	1992	R	F	L
Day the Sun Turned Cold (Hong Kong)	1994	R	F	L
Ermo	1994	R	F	L
After Divorce	1997	U	M	I
Mr. Zhao	1998	U	M	I
Agreed Not to Separate	1999	U	F	I
Sigh	2000	U	M	I
Cell Phone	2004	U	M	I

*This category is used loosely to mean spouses who have extramarital sexual relations either before or *after* divorce or the death of a spouse. Since the plot of *Wild Mountains* involves the switching of two pairs of spouses, both genders eventually stray sexually from their original marriage partners. However, it is the female Guilan who is accused of adultery and beaten by her husband because she is perceived as having too intimate a friendship with another man. Similarly, in *Hibiscus Town*, the heroine is widely suspected of committing adultery while married, but she only actually has extramarital sex after her husband's death. In *After Divorce*, a man takes his ex-wife's younger sister as a lover soon after his divorce.

As we have seen, the first narrative pattern involves a rural woman engaged in some kind of manual labor who becomes sexually involved with someone other than her (first) husband, while the second pattern, which became prominent later in the reform era, features an urban male intellectual whose liaisons with a mistress are depicted as part of a lifestyle of economic success and social prominence in the new economy.

This subcategorization of the cinema of infidelity in reform-era China suggests several conclusions based on both its synchronic, structural characteristics and its diachronic permutations. In the first sense, we see an obvious geographical distinction. Xiaobing Tang has noted that, beginning in the 1980s, "the gap between country and city entered rural films as an inescapable pathos," and the rural films examined here are exemplary instances of this.[45] In *Scented Souls*, *Ermo*, and *The Day the Sun Turned Cold*, the dramatic traversal of the distance between the rural village and the city as a space of economic opportunity and romantic fulfillment is only temporary, the ultimate impossibility of the city's promise being underlined by somber or tragic narrative conclusions that suggest the unavoidable fate of life in a countryside that steadfastly resists modernization. In contrast, the urban films of infidelity often depict a modernization process that has already gone too far, causing the intellectual protagonists to lose their ethical moorings and potentially destroy their families. Thus, if the rural setting invokes the anxieties of incomplete modernization, the urban milieu presents both the attractions and the dangers of a modernization that may be out of control. Consequently, when the diachronic dimension is added to this geographical distinction, the films of infidelity examined here trace a historical arc in the imagination of progress in the reform era, from the concern that the Chinese nation is not adequate to the task of modernization, to the consciousness that a new capitalist modernity not only has arrived but also has become a problem to be dealt with in its own right. Finally, the way the category of gender in this structural analysis corresponds so closely with the variables of chronology, geography, and class cannot but be ideologically significant. Clearly, the agonies and inadequacies resulting from incomplete modernization are most easily marked as feminine, while the triumphs and enlightened contrition of overheated modernization are given masculine form—both of which point to an overarching patriarchal master narrative.

In any case, the ambiguities and conflicting signals within the cinema of infidelity, in both its urban and rural varieties, reflect a more general ambivalence toward the new vision of Chinese modernity that rapidly unfolded in the reform era. On the one hand, the initial improvement in material well-being in the countryside due to early rural economic reforms, as dramatized in *Wild Mountains*, is indisputable, and it is equally difficult to ignore the astounding and often impressive transformations in the urban environment throughout the 1990s and beyond. In spite of the forceful critiques by New Left intellectuals and the growing discontent among poor farmers, laid-off factory workers, and the "floating population" of new urban migrants (see Chapter Seven), it is nevertheless safe to say that the reform era's rapid economic growth and the multiplying sources of entertainment and stimulation that have accompanied it have generally legitimized the reform agenda in the eyes of much of the public in the post-Mao era (although indications of simmering class discontent make this a very tenuous observation). On the other hand, it is equally true that the mainstream public is well aware of the dislocations that have resulted from massive social and economic transformation, and in particular the sense that value systems are crumbling and a firm moral order is no longer available to guide behavior. Films from *Ermo* to *Cell Phone* thus simultaneously dramatize the excitement of transformation and the enticement of material progress as well as the anxiety that too much is possibly being abandoned or betrayed in the process. The trope of adultery, a behavior that embodies both the allure of exhilarating new desires and the ethical dangers inherent in their pursuit, is an ideal vehicle for conveying the ambiguities of the reform era itself.

The theme of adultery also epitomizes a wider phenomenon in the cultural imaginary of the reform era that is no less significant for its obviousness—namely, the privatization of desire itself. The *privacy* with which a character such as Ermo pursues extramarital sexual gratification out of sight of a disapproving public gaze is but an extreme example of a more comprehensive postsocialist reimagining of individual desire and personal fulfillment precisely *as* individual and personal. Intense desires and their satisfaction were certainly represented in a wide range of art, literature, and cinema of the Mao era, but they virtually always had a pronounced public dimension and indeed often related directly to a social or political agenda—the attractiveness of a potential lover, for example, being directly tied to his or her level of commitment to the project of revolution. Moreover, the options for private sexual fulfillment were limited in very concrete ways in a highly collectivized society that offered very little room for private space or discreet freedom of movement.[46] Thus it is not surprising that with the gradual privatization of the material economy in the 1980s and 1990s, there was an accompanying privatization of the libidinal economy, which is evident in the cinema of infidelity we have explored here. Of course, cinema itself being arguably uniquely distinguished by its very public-ness,[47] what we have in the case of the cinema of infidelity is a public negotia-tion and representation of the privatization of desire and the anxieties it pro-vokes. The trope of infidelity, with its inherent aspect of ethical transgression, manifests a broader anxiety over the ethical consequences of the privatization of desire, and in particular over the accompanying divestment of commitment to the good of a larger collective, whether it be the nation, the commune, or the family.

Interestingly, the cinema of infidelity engaged these issues with some consis-tency over not only a long period of time but also a wide range of modes of cin-ematic production. The films I have explored in this chapter, while sustaining several consistent plot elements and cultural concerns, are in fact significantly varied in terms of their film-industry backgrounds. *Wild Mountains* is a prod-uct of the state studio system during the time of its post–Cultural Revolution renaissance in the 1980s. It made several technical and artistic breakthroughs in keeping with the contemporary concern with "modernizing cinematic lan-guage" in the People's Republic during the early reform era.[48] It was thus artisti-cally ambitious and, in its message promoting the modernization of both eco-nomics and values, sanguine to the point of being instructional. In this sense it typifies the "culture fever" of the 1980s, during which artists, intellectuals, and the state-owned culture industry saw their role as advancing artistic standards while educating the public in order to modernize the nation. A few years later *Scented Souls* continued to reflect many of the same concerns. Produced by a state studio, its director, Xie Fei, was a major "Fourth Generation" auteur and senior member of the film industry establishment—teaching, for example, at the Beijing Film Academy. At the same time, compared to *Wild Mountains*, *Scented Souls* betrayed an awareness of a global audience brought about by the international success of several Fifth Generation films in the intervening years. *Scented Souls* itself went on to win the Golden Bear at the 1993 Berlin Film Festival, its melodramatic excesses apparently being sufficiently balanced by its spectacular cinematography and the Western audience's ongoing fascination with the suffering of rural Chinese women under feudal social oppression. Some of the films of urban infidelity, while attracting no attention abroad, are also middle-brow products of the state-run film industry; *After Divorce*, for example, was produced by the Youth Film Studio of the Beijing Film Academy.

Other films discussed in this chapter, however, collectively indicate the striking pluralization that occurred in the film industry beginning in the 1990s. *Ermo*—though made by a Fifth Generation director and sharing many aesthetic and thematic concerns with such landmark studio films as *Wild Mountains* and *Yellow Earth*—was in fact privately funded and only received a studio label later for distribution purposes, as mentioned earlier. *Mr. Zhao* was a very subtle and accomplished independent film directed by the eminent cinematographer Lü Yue, yet it never received a studio label and was never distributed in China. *Sigh* and *Cell Phone*, in contrast, were popular entertainment films that were distributed throughout China. As with Feng Xiaogang's other "new year's celebration films," they were coproductions resulting from a mutually profitable cooperation between the state studio system and well-connected private production companies who obtained sympathetic—perhaps even preferential—treatment by officials in charge of censorship and distribution (see Chapter Six). *Cell Phone* was a marketing strategy as much as a film from its inception. The director collaborated with the respected and successful novelist Liu Zhenyun to write the film script, and he persuaded the writer to adapt it into a novel as well to be published simultaneously with the film's release.[49] Sales of the book quickly reached hundreds of thousands of copies, and synergy with both the novel and the Motorola product tie-ins helped to market the film and thus make profits for both its private investors and its state-owned coproducer, the Beijing Film Studio.

Feng Xiaogang's combination of private, profit-seeking enterprise with state-studio legitimacy shows how fluid are the boundaries in the newly pluralized mainland Chinese film industry. In addition, the same fluidity applies to aesthetic preferences in the cinema of infidelity. The present chapter, being

mainly a structural analysis of the narrative themes and plot elements in a selection of films, has largely ignored the issue of film style. However, it is worth
noting the degree to which styles of photography and mise-en-scène traversed
the boundaries of the various modes of industrial production. Despite being an
independently produced film, *Ermo* was filmed in the style of detached, ethnographic realism characteristic of the more celebrated state studio art-films of
the previous decade, including *Wild Mountains* and *Yellow Earth*. *Mr. Zhao*, on
the other hand, another independent production, very effectively used hand-
held camera work to maximize a feeling of claustrophobia in its mostly interior
spaces. Its shaky handheld close-ups and lack of depth do not so much increase
our sympathy for the characters as give us a sensory analogy to the lack of perspective or critical distance of a man who is allowing secret desires to wreck his
life. Although Feng Xiaogang's commercial films *Sigh* and *Cell Phone* had much
higher budgets and greater mass appeal than *Mr. Zhao*, they actually applied
many of the same cinematic techniques to similar situations involving domestic deception and conflict. Whether this is due to direct influence or just similar
solutions to common problems of representation, it points to the increased fluidity and pace of change in film aesthetics in the new pluralized situation, and
the difficulty of drawing clear correspondences between modes of production
(state, private, or "underground") and artistic styles. In the next chapter, I will
explore the complexity of the issue of style in the case of a single "independent"
filmmaker who emerged in the late 1990s and achieved acclaim abroad while
initially remaining an "underground" artist at home.

5

"Independent" Cinema: From Postsocialist Realism to a Transnational Aesthetic

> I'm not willing to use that sort of commercial method, or a
> stylized method to tell a story; I will tell it sincerely, and in
> this realist method do it best.[1]
>
> —Jia Zhangke

> But realism in art can only be achieved in one way—
> through artifice.[2]
>
> —André Bazin

One of the films considered in the previous chapter, *Women from the Lake of Scented Souls*, was produced within the state studio system and achieved recognition at international film festivals. In this sense and others (its spectacular rural setting, its fable-like narrative), that film followed the model set by the sensation of Fifth Generation films in the 1980s. In fact, the emergence of an internationally recognized Chinese art cinema during that decade constituted one of the most notable Chinese cultural phenomena of the post-Mao era. Since that time, art films (and more recently artsy martial arts films by China's most famous directors) have been China's most visible cultural export to the rest of the world, and consequently the concept of a Chinese national cinema has taken shape on a global level to an unprecedented degree. Although this new Chinese national art cinema was first exemplified by the works of the Fifth Generation—in particular those from the decade 1984–93, or from approximately Chen Kaige's *Huang tudi* (Yellow earth, 1984) to his *Bawang bie ji* (Farewell my concubine, 1993)[3]—beginning in the early 1990s the role of mainland Chinese art cinema auteur was played increasingly less by the Fifth Generation directors and more by a diverse new group of filmmakers, including He Jianjun, Jia Zhangke, Jiang Wen, Ning Ying, Wang Xiaoshuai, Zhang Yang, and Zhang Yuan. Several among them shared to varying degrees labels such as "Sixth Generation," "independent," "urban generation," and "underground." In contrast to the Fifth Generation, many of these filmmakers worked entirely outside the state studio system, and thus ironically they presented the face of "Chinese cinema" to the world despite the fact that many of their films remained undistributed in mainland China itself.

In this chapter I will examine the phenomenon of independent filmmaking that emerged with the 1990s and competed with Fifth Generation productions to become a major part of the mainland Chinese presence in the international art-house scene. After describing the rise of independent production and a postsocialist realist aesthetic in contemporary Chinese cinema, I will focus on the films of one "Sixth Generation" director, Jia Zhangke, who until 2004 remained completely independent of officially recognized studios in China but garnered increasing attention overseas.[4] I will explore the rich thematics of Jia's films and place them in the context of both the domestic "underground," or independent, film movement and the global art-cinema market. As one of the most prominent young directors to emerge from China around the turn of the century and attract global attention, Jia obtained funding from production companies and government ministries from Japan to Europe, and major Western critics pronounced him to be among the finest of new directors and his films landmarks of Chinese cinema.[5] Within China, however, the same films could be seen only on pirated video disks, with viewings in their original formats limited to a handful of locally organized screenings in major cities. Nevertheless, these films remain deeply engaged with Chinese society in the postsocialist era, making implicit claims regarding the nature of Chinese urban reality today and the ethics and aesthetics of its documentation and memory.

It is generally agreed that Jia's films embody a bold new style of realism in contemporary Chinese cinema, both in terms of their stripped-down aesthetic and in terms of exposing and documenting a raw, sometimes unpleasant contemporary reality. In fact, I will argue that the realism of Jia's works must be understood as drawing upon two very distinct sources. The first is a broader indigenous movement of postsocialist realism that arose among both documentary and fiction filmmakers in China in the early 1990s. Significantly, the same artists who pioneered this postsocialist cinematic realism were also the first independent filmmakers in the history of the PRC. In many ways, Jia's films continue, and even epitomize, the concerns and accomplishments of this movement. However, the realism of these films must also be understood in the context of a second source, namely the tradition of international art cinema, and particularly a type of aestheticized long-take realism that became prominent in the global film festival and art-house circuit by the late 1990s. Of these two foundations of Jia's realism, the former is most evident in his early projects and short films, while the latter is exemplified by his epic *Zhantai* (Platform, 2000)—which was thus not surprisingly the work that garnered the rave reviews from Western critics referenced above. Consequently, while the director's career resists a narrative of a clear-cut successive progression from one form of realism to another, his films can nonetheless be understood as constituting, each to varying degrees, both an intervention into a specifically Chinese cultural discourse and a cultural commodity that appeals to contemporary global art-film aesthetics. In the end, the striking new autonomy staked out by independent artists such as Jia Zhangke beginning in the 1990s nevertheless had to articulate itself to a global cultural market in order to sustain itself and reach an international audience. Moreover, by the time of his film *Shijie* (The world, 2004), Jia had also joined a Chinese state studio in order to reach a domestic audience as well. Thus while the rise of "independent" cinema is a crucial feature of postsocialist Chinese film culture, the label itself is a slippery one, illustrating the point that the autonomies of culture under postsocialist modernity are always relative and contingent ones that ultimately must adjust to market conditions of one sort or another.

Independent Cinema and Postsocialist Realism

Independent film production did not exist in the PRC before the 1990s. During the Mao era all studios were state-owned and all production therefore subject to the political priorities of the national leadership. With the 1980s, the ideological control loosened, allowing pioneering studios to produce the more individual expressions of the new Fourth and Fifth Generation auteurs such as Xie Fei, Tian Zhuangzhuang, Huang Jianxin, Chen Kaige, and Zhang Yimou. Nevertheless, even those films that constituted a new Chinese national art cinema in the eyes of the international film community were made with studio funds by directors who were state employees. It was not until Zhang Yuan's *Mama* (1990) that a filmmaker, trained in the Beijing Film Academy yet lacking in postgraduation directing opportunities within the state studios, actually self-produced a low-budget, privately funded feature film. While *Mama* did subsequently get distribution under the label of the Xi'an Film Studio, some of Zhang Yuan's later independent works did not, and yet, from *Mama* on, the director took the unprecedented and brash step of entering his films in international film festivals without official sanction in China. Through these efforts, Zhang Yuan was able to make a series of independent films that received partial funding and considerable attention from abroad despite being largely unseen in China and occasionally drawing the ire of the authorities.[6] Other young directors who followed this path in the 1990s included Wang Xiaoshuai, He Jianjun, and, shortly later, Jia himself.[7] However, the careers of all these directors demonstrate how "independent" filmmaking, almost as a requirement for reaching any audience, will necessarily be drawn into cooperation with the state studio system or with the international production companies that supply the global art-cinema market.[8]

Jia's early career follows the model of Zhang Yuan not just in its independent mode of production but also in its filmmaking style, which can be described as postsocialist critical realism.[9] This aesthetic is postsocialist both in the sense of being a successor and contrast to the previously dominant aesthetic of socialist realism and in the sense that it is a realism of the postsocialist condition. In the first respect, this style of realism directly contradicts the tenets of socialist realism, the remnants of which could still be seen in state media representations and officially sponsored patriotic "main melody" (*zhuxuanlü*) films even well into the reform era. Socialist realism, as borrowed from the Soviet Union and later elaborated into a combination of "revolutionary realism and revolutionary romanticism" during the Mao era, claims to depict not merely the raw, visible surface of reality but more importantly an underlying ideological truth composed of class struggle and the inexorable historical movement toward a communist utopia. In contrast, the postsocialist realism of independent cinema of the 1990s essentially flips the relationship between the two levels: rather than professing to show an ideological truth that underlies apparent reality, it seeks to reveal a raw, underlying reality by stripping away the ideological representations that distort it.[10]

In this sense, the aesthetic of postsocialist realist cinema is reminiscent of the literary school of New Realism (see Chapter Three) that arose as the 1980s drew to a close. The term *New Realism* was proposed by the editors of the literary journal *Zhongshan* (Zhong mountain) in early 1989 and was used to label a group of young novelists who were said to share a style that, "while still taking realism as its distinctive feature, nevertheless particularly emphasizes a return to the original condition of real life in its primary form, genuinely and squarely facing reality and human life." The New Realist aesthetic was contrasted with both the avant-garde literature of the 1980s and the "bygone fake realism," with its "straight road" and "politicized appeal"—that is, the state-sanctioned revolutionary realism that was the legacy of the Mao era.[11] This idea that there was an "origin" to "return" to (*huanyuan*), a "primary" or "natural" form (*yuansheng xingtai*) of real life that the artist could squarely face, bypassing the distortions of political ideology, was evident also in the realist movement in cinema that began around the same time. Later the critic and film scholar Yin Hong would describe the new independent films of the 1990s, including Jia Zhangke's *Xiao Wu* (1997; occasionally titled *Pickpocket* in Western markets), as a "return to original life conditions" (*shengming zhuangtai de huanyuan*), which he contrasts with the "prolonged political passions of the last century"; and another critic, Lü Xiaoming, would describe Sixth Generation films in general as conveying "primary life conditions" (*yuanshengtai*).[12]

Of course, the claim to oppose received ideological representations with the revelation of real life in its primary condition is itself ideological, and we need not belabor the point that the "real" ostensibly unearthed by a postsocialist realist filmmaker must be understood as a historically situated construct rather than as some nondiscursive thing-in-itself that actually appears before the audience. However, to admit as much is not to deny the particular strengths of the realist aesthetic; a realist film does not convey the real itself any more than an oneiric film delivers an actual dream, but each style is potentially powerful and illuminating. In this sense, to point out the constructed nature of even the most raw documentary footage only debunks the theory of realism in its most naive form. Even André Bazin, in his classic essay championing the ontological realism of the photographic image, attributes the power of photographic realism to a "need for illusion" that is "purely psychological," the origins of which "must be sought in the proclivity of the mind towards magic"—a far cry from a simple claim of some essential scientific objectivity of cinema.[13] Bazin compares a filmmaker not to a scientist but to a novelist and describes cinematic realism as a means of manipulating and modifying reality, not simply revealing it, so that even the Italian neorealists "demonstrated that every realism in art was first profoundly aesthetic."[14] Indeed, despite the claimed revelations of "primary life conditions" among the critics already mentioned, Jia himself was equally aware of the impossibility of true objectivity for even the most realist style, calling it simply an "attitude" and an unattainable "ideal" of the filmmaker.[15] Thus the question raised by Jia's realism is not whether it divulges an elemental reality so much as *how* it constructs the powerful impression of a confrontation with reality through the rhetoric of a film's narrative and its cinematic style.

A realist impulse in contemporary Chinese cinema had in fact manifested itself from the very beginning of the reform era. During the 1980s, in the struggle to carve out some space for artistic autonomy after the overwhelming politicization of the Mao era, many filmmakers and critics championed the supposed indexical realism of cinema—that is, the ability of the camera to directly record the likeness of objects through a physical, scientific process. The immediacy of representation that this made possible was implicitly opposed to the ideological truth claims of socialist realism. In 1979 the journal *Dianying yishu* (Film art) published the groundbreaking article "On the Modernization of Cinematic Language," by Zhang Nuanxin and Li Tuo, which introduced the breakthroughs of Italian Neorealism and the French New Wave and sympathetically described Bazin's theory of cinematic realism and his advocacy of a long-take style as best exploiting the inherent photographic realism of cinema.[16] For many in a film community long cut off from developments in the noncommunist world, the article attained a manifesto-like status, and its use of the buzzword of the emerging reform era, "modernization" (*xiandaihua*), in the very title tied the project of transforming Chinese cinema to the broader officially sanctioned reform movement. For the following decade many films by both Fourth and Fifth Generation directors incorporated elements of Bazinian-style realism, including on-location shooting, natural lighting and sound, long shots and long takes, and enough narrative ambiguity to require active audience engagement and interpretation. Meanwhile, other photographic theories of realism, including those of Roland Barthes and Siegfried Kracauer, were translated into Chinese and taught in the Beijing Film Academy, often by visiting Western scholars.[17]

With the turn of the decade, however, just as the New Realist school was emerging in Chinese literature, a more radical wave of cinematic realism appeared, taking at least three forms: a documentary video movement rising out of Beijing's marginal artist colonies, the related phenomenon of low-budget independent cinema exemplified by Zhang Yuan's early directorial career, and finally even a turn toward a new sort of realism among established Fifth Generation directors by the early 1990s. The new documentary movement was launched in 1990 by Wu Wenguang's *Liulang Beijing* (Bumming in Beijing), which depicted the struggles of marginal artists and other young intellectuals at a time of uncertainty and political turmoil.[18] Zhang Yuan, the pioneering independent fiction film director, traveled in the same artistic circles in Beijing and pursued a similar raw realism in his early films. The groundbreaking *Mama*, for example, appearing in the same year as *Bumming in Beijing*, intercuts a fictional narrative with documentary interview footage. Finally, by the late 1980s and early 1990s, despite their usual association with rural and historical subject matter, several major directors of the Fourth and Fifth Generations began to tackle contemporary urban subjects with a realist style. Most important, with *Qiu Ju da guansi* (The story of Qiu Ju, 1992; dir. Zhang Yimou), a leading Fifth Generation director shot a major film in an unprecedented quasi-documentary style, using a large number of nonprofessional actors, radio microphones, and hidden cameras to elicit naturalistic performances in actual contemporary settings. While younger directors in the 1990s hoped to distance themselves from their Fifth Generation predecessors in general, *The Story of Qiu Ju* nevertheless helped to set a new standard for realist technique in Chinese fiction filmmaking.

Aside from its technical devices, *The Story of Qiu Ju* is also significant as a work of *critical* realism, insofar as it depicts the life struggles of the marginal and powerless. Similarly, the independent cinema movement of the 1990s was concerned with laying bare the contradictions of postsocialist modernity in China. In this sense the cinematic realism of the 1990s carried on the modern Chinese legacy of social (as distinct from social*ist*) and critical realism, an aesthetic that was especially dominant in film and other arts of the 1930s. Marston

Anderson has described the critical realist style of that time as seeking not necessarily "to promulgate a new ideological vision of the world" but rather "to
explore . . . the gap between a discredited worldview and the actual functioning
of society."[19] Similarly, postsocialist realist cinema does not directly promulgate
an oppositional ideology but rather indirectly critiques mainstream ideology
by foregrounding ordinary people's experiences that normally go unrepresented by either the officially sanctioned media or the entertainment industry. This tactic of exposing rather than opposing rests on the belief that social
contradictions are apparent in everyday life but elided in mainstream representation. The postsocialist realist films of the 1990s are thus imbued with the faith
that just going out into public with a camera and capturing the unvarnished
street life one finds there serves to unmask ideology while documenting the
realities of contemporary China.

Shooting in the Streets

Exemplifying this documentary impulse was Jia's first work, a fifteen-min-
ute Betacam video entitled *You yitian, zai Beijing* (One day, in Beijing, 1994).
Produced as a student project by a small group of friends calling themselves the
Beijing Film Academy's Youth Experimental Film Group (*Qingnian dianying
shiyan xiaozu*), the video documented passing crowds in Tiananmen Square on
a random day in early summer.[20] The main concern of the project was simply
to record the movement of ordinary people in perhaps China's most quintes-
sential public space. The layers of symbolism accumulated by official representations of Tiananmen are thus belied by the quotidian activities of the people
passing through, and the work as a whole serves as a gesture of the capacity of
the videographer to directly capture "real" life even in the most ideologically
encumbered of settings.

Jia Zhangke also directed the group's next project, *Xiao Shan huijia* (Xiao
Shan going home, 1995), the beginning of which recalls the previous work with
a still shot of a woodcut depicting a person holding a camera in profile against
the background of Tiananmen—an image that served as the emblem of the
Youth Experimental Film Group.[21] This vision of the filmmaker's empowerment is further reinforced during the opening credits montage, one shot of

F I G . 5.1. Opening image of *Xiao Shan Going Home*; logo of the Beijing Film Academy Youth Experimental Film Group.

which shows a military policeman walking directly toward the camera and gesturing to stop the filming. Instead, the camera stubbornly documents his approach right up to the moment his hand is about to block out the lens. Such images establish a basic rhetoric of opposition between the officially sanctioned point of view and the view revealed by the independent filmmaker's camera, or quite simply between ideological narratives and the reality they ostensibly mask.

Xiao Shan Going Home is a fifty-eight minute narrative video, also shot on Betacam for less than US$2,500, about a restaurant worker in Beijing who wants to return to his home in the provincial city of Anyang for the Spring Festival. In a series of encounters, Xiao Shan drinks with friends, has a brief fling with a young woman, and repeatedly tries but fails to find a ticket to go home for the holiday during the busiest travel season of the year. The fact that Xiao Shan never in fact goes home, despite the title of the video, indicates that the main interest is not in tracing a narrative arc but in documenting the lives of a few of Beijing's "outsiders" (*waidi ren*), or migrant workers (*mingong*), and in the process recording some of the sights and sounds of Beijing as the Spring Festival approaches. To this end, the video frequently follows its small nonprofessional cast out into the streets, subways, and train stations, trailing them with a jerky handheld camera amid hundreds of unwitting extras. As was the case with the documentary project in Tiananmen Square, much of the work's energy and interest come directly from the exhilaration of taking a camera into an uncontrolled public space and documenting its random events and objects—an old man playing harmonica, a subway station newsstand, an angry, unexplained confrontation between people on a crowded sidewalk.

This documentary tone is set early in the video when Xiao Shan and a hometown acquaintance, now a prostitute in Beijing, walk together through the streets. The segment begins with a shot facing a crowded stream of foot traffic out of which the two characters appear. The shot thus recalls the celebrated opening shot of *The Story of Qiu Ju*, in which a stationary camera records the flow of a similar street crowd for nearly two minutes, only at the end of which does movie star Gong Li herself emerge from this unstaged, real-world crowd to enter the film as its heroine. However, as the street sequence in *Xiao Shan Going Home* progresses, a major difference becomes apparent. In *The Story of Qiu Ju*, though documenting real people, the camera itself is camouflaged so that it does not draw the attention of those it records passing by. As a result, the random "extras" remain unaware of and thus unengaged with the camera, while part of the spectacle is the very fact that the famous and glamorous Gong Li is so well disguised as a pregnant peasant that she can walk through the crowd unnoticed, preserving the film's fictional realism. In *Xiao Shan Going Home*, in contrast, the protagonists are played by unknown, nonprofessional actors, and rather than being hidden the camera is clearly right out in the streets with the crowd it documents—as is obvious by the repeated looks random people in the crowd direct at the lens, thus breaking the "fourth wall" between the diegetic events and the camera that records them and the audience that views them.

Such looks to the camera in fact occur a total of more than eighty times during the public scenes in *Xiao Shan Going Home*. The effect of the "real" people looking at the camera while the actors do not indicates the priorities of this type of filmmaking, which implicitly values a *cinéma vérité*[22] or "on-the-spot" documentary realism,[23] with its emphasis on immediacy, over a seamless fictional realism. That is, with each scene in which bystanders look to the camera while the protagonists ignore it, the world depicted suffers from a noticeable rupture between the diegetic characters and the "extras," who in fact now are revealed as extradiegetic. As was indicated by the camera shown prominently in the woodcut of the film's opening shot, the presence of the camera in the fictional video is not concealed but rather flaunted. In one shot, the camera operator's hand even becomes visible as it parts some hanging plastic flaps while exiting a clothing store. In short, the sacrifice of *fictional* realism due to the obvious presence of the camera is trumped by the effect of *documentary* realism gained by the clear evidence that the camera was taken into an uncontrolled public space, where it documented in part real people's spontaneous reactions to the camera itself. In this project, then, the priorities of the postsocialist realist documentary impulse at least temporarily override the priorities of fictional narrative realism. Again, the effect in terms of cinematic rhetoric is to lay radical claim to a basic underlying reality that precedes the distortions of ideological representation and even of fictional narrative itself.

Xiao Shan Going Home remained just an obscure student work until a reporter from Hong Kong suggested the filmmakers enter it in the Hong Kong Independent Short Film and Video Awards competition. This eventually earned a prize for the video as well as entry into the 1997 Hong Kong International Film Festival. The exposure put Jia in contact with the Hong Kong collaborators for his following three feature films, producer Li Kit Ming (Li Jieming) and cinematographer Yu Lik Wai (Yu Liwei), himself a graduate of the Belgium Film Academy who had worked on films in Europe as well as China.[24] Consequently, even at this early stage of his career, Jia's work was drawing on both financial and artistic resources outside of mainland China and beginning the shift from exposure only to his own small circle in Beijing to participation in the international art cinema scene.

Nevertheless, the work that followed, *Xiao Wu*, showed several similarities to *Xiao Shan Going Home*. Despite a higher budget, better production values, more careful framing, and a switch from Betacam video to 16mm film, *Xiao*

Wu retains much of the on-the-scene immediacy and documentary directness of its predecessor. The episodic plot about a drifting pickpocket, Xiao Wu, in the minor county-seat city of Fenyang in Shanxi province (Jia's hometown) is played entirely by nonprofessional actors,[25] and as with *Xiao Shan Going Home*, exterior scenes are filmed amid the actual street crowds in Fenyang, without the control afforded by shooting permits, a large crew, and a compliant group of extras. The raw realist style is thus partially attributable to issues of funding and official sanction, but it is also a matter of the priorities of the filmmakers. As Jia has said, they wished to maintain a certain "crude" (*cu*) appearance "because we wanted to shoot something with a very strong on-location [*xianchang*] feeling."[26] The effort to document immediate reality and eschew obvious aesthetic or ideological manipulation contrasts with accounts promulgated by the official media, themselves represented within *Xiao Wu* by television news reports and announcements over ubiquitous public loudspeakers.

Despite the continuity in style between *Xiao Shan Going Home* and *Xiao Wu*, some stylistic differences that exceed those attributable to changes in funding and technology are also apparent. In particular, while both films tend toward shots of long duration by Hollywood standards, in *Xiao Wu* the long take becomes an especially pronounced technique in certain key scenes, with shots up to six minutes long, whereas the previous work had only once exceeded a two-minute take (and then only slightly). Chris Berry discusses the organization of time in *Xiao Wu* as a "narrative distension" that presents a radical vision of postsocialist realist time countering any master narrative of teleological progress, whether that of the march toward a communist utopia or that of official reform-era modernization. This distended postsocialist time is the time of the reform era's "losers" rather than its more oft-represented "winners."[27] My view of the rhetorical effect of *Xiao Wu*'s realism is very much in keeping with Berry's theoretical reading of the time of the film. *Xiao Wu* presents an intractable Chinese "reality" which is explicitly juxtaposed against both official media representations and the promises of global capitalist ideology. A closer look at three of the film's exceptionally long takes will illustrate how stylistic choices structure the sense of the bleak urban "reality" uncovered.

In the first instance, Xiao Wu has gone to visit his estranged friend Xiaoyong on the day before the latter's wedding. Once Xiao Wu's sworn brother and fellow delinquent, Xiaoyong is now a successful businessman who enjoys the high social standing of the nouveau riche in reform-era China, and his wedding is a major community event reported by the local news media. To protect his reputation, Xiaoyong has distanced himself from his former friend, still a petty thief, to the extent of not even inviting Xiao Wu to the wedding celebration. Nevertheless, a determined Xiao Wu goes on a crime spree in order to accumulate a cash wedding gift, which he then takes to Xiaoyong's house to confront his old friend. The meeting between the two consists mainly of a single shot lasting three and three-quarters minutes. The two sit half facing each other at a desk in a long-shot composition, both nervously chain-smoking. Xiao Wu berates Xiaoyong for failing to invite him to the wedding, repeatedly muttering, "You've fucking changed." Xiaoyong tries to refuse Xiao Wu's wedding gift. They have little to say to each other, and the tension is accentuated by the continuous take, filled with awkward silences and anxious cigarette puffing. The shot ends after Xiao Wu rises to leave, throwing his gift packet onto the desk in front of Xiaoyong and challenging the latter to look at the tattoo on his forearm that once symbolized their friendship.

This single long take dramatizes one of the central relationships of the film, that of Xiao Wu and Xiaoyong, and by extension interrogates the relationship between the new classes they represent. Having been virtually identical in social standing not so long ago, the two friends now belong to quite distinct social spheres. Indeed, their relationship, as represented in the film, forces us to contemplate the generally suppressed issue of class in reform-era China. When he makes forays from his nearby village to the county seat, Xiao Wu becomes in effect a minor provincial version of the "floating population" (*liudong renkou*) in the Chinese urban environment, peasants who lack official residency status and legitimate social standing, and who instead are widely viewed as the principal sources of problems such as rising crime rates and prostitution. Xiao Wu is thus at the bottom of the new class structure of urban China in the reform era, while Xiaoyong, an admired businessman and community leader, is at the top.

Xiao Wu, however, problematizes the class distinction between Xiao Wu and Xiaoyong by making countervailing ethical distinctions. During the confrontation, Xiao Wu appears not as a petty thief but rather as a loyal friend who fulfills his promises, and Xiaoyong seems less an admirable businessman than an evasive deceiver who has forgotten the bonds of sworn brotherhood. *Xiao Wu* thus presents two contrasting perspectives on the character Xiaoyong, one given by the media reports bracketed within the diegesis, the other the apparently objective view of the story as a whole, filmed in a realist style and aligned with Xiao Wu's point of view. These contrasting takes on Xiaoyong recall Wang Xiaoming's distinction between *xin furen*, the nouveau riche, and *chenggong renshi*, literally "successful personage." *Xin furen* names an emergent social class that has seized an inordinate share of China's new material wealth largely through questionable business practices and collaboration with corrupt officials. The term *chenggong renshi*, on the other hand, identifies a mainstream cultural symbol, a new model for admiration and emulation widely promulgated through images in commercial advertising as well as the official news media. According to Wang Xiaoming, *chenggong renshi* should thus be viewed as a representation, or "portrait," of *xin furen*, but a deceptive one that is only a "half-faced portrait" (*ban zhanglian de xiaoxiang*), presenting an image of a life of comfort and leisure without revealing the actual material practices behind such a lifestyle.[28] Instead, the function of the image of the "successful personage" is to legitimize the rhetorics of transition that Kevin Latham has argued are at the core of the hegemonic ideology of postsocialist China (see also Chapter Seven). Latham points out that both journalists and nouveau-riche entrepreneurs are complicit in perpetuating this ideology in the public sphere.[29] In *Xiao Wu*, Xiaoyong is a provincial version of the nouveau riche, celebrated by local media as their own local "successful personage" worthy of praise and emulation; his new social standing and the local media's lionization of him replicate the national discourse on how success and the good life should be envisioned in the reform era.

In the film, however, the contrast between the formulaic and superficial media reports on the wedding of Xiaoyong and the realist aesthetic of the film that frames them effectively points to the unseen half of the *chenggong renshi* portrait, the underlying material reality of class inequality that puts the nouveau riche and the floating population at opposite extremes of the social spectrum.[30]

While exposing the ideological falsehood of the "successful personage" portrait, the film undercuts any presumed ethical justification for the class divide
between the two former friends. In fact, the two characters are equalized within
the long-shot composition of their confrontation, creating an impression of
equivalence echoed in explicit comments made later in the film to challenge
any moral distinction between the two friends' professional pursuits. When
Xiaoyong later has one of his underlings return Xiao Wu's wedding gift on the
grounds that the money's origins are dubious, Xiao Wu angrily retorts that
Xiaoyong's own money is equally unclean, having been made from trafficking
in black market cigarettes and exploiting bargirls. Xiaoyong soon replies that
his so-called cigarette smuggling (*zousi*) is really simply trade (*maoyi*) and that
he does not exploit his bargirls but merely engages in the "entertainment business" (*yuleye*). Hence, by correcting the blunt language of Xiao Wu's accusations with an insistence on legitimate-sounding labels of the reform-era economy, Xiaoyong attempts to reassert the distinction between his calling and that
of Xiao Wu and thereby justify his social position as *chenggong renshi*. However,
his efforts are controverted by the film as a whole, which effectively calls into
question the boundary between legitimate business and outright stealing in the
age of free market reforms.

Our second key long take in *Xiao Wu* occurs nearly one hour into the film,
when Xiao Wu goes to visit his romantic interest, Meimei, in the dormitory
of the karaoke bar where she works. Like Xiao Wu, Meimei is a marginal figure in the urban landscape, an outsider who has come to the city looking
for opportunity but finding only exploitation. While working as a karaoke
bargirl—paid to accompany male customers in private karaoke rooms in a
role that often leads to outright prostitution—Meimei calls home and lies to
her parents that she is actually in Beijing pursuing her dream of becoming a
movie star. She meets Xiao Wu when he patronizes the karaoke bar, but their
relationship becomes romantic only when he goes to see her one day after she
has stayed home sick. In a remarkable shot lasting just over six minutes, the
two are seen visiting in Meimei's room in a distancing long-shot composition.
Although they appear awkward and listless, as the shot proceeds their yearning becomes more palpable, and a hint of hope, if not sentimentality, makes

a rare appearance in the film. As the ambient exterior noises of traffic fill the silences in their conversation, Xiao Wu and Meimei struggle to penetrate each other's loneliness. When Xiao Wu asks Meimei to sing a song, her choice—Faye Wong's "Tiankong" (Sky)—vocalizes the feelings of solitude and desire they cannot otherwise express.[31] The shot length and the persistence of the noise pollution coming seemingly from just outside the room serve to accentuate both the couple's determination to carve out a space of togetherness amid their despair and the ultimate futility of the effort, as the outside world relentlessly enters to disperse the dreams of their marginal lives.

The temporary hint of hopefulness is nevertheless carried over into the next scene, in which Xiao Wu has gone by himself to an empty bathhouse. His desires awakened and his usual deadpan guardedness discarded, he strips naked and sings loudly to himself as he wades in the bath pools. As he sings, the camera tilts up to a window high on the wall of the bathhouse that lets in a wash of light illuminating the interior mist—a surprisingly utopian image in keeping with Xiao Wu's current mood as well as the song ("Sky") sung in the previous scene by Meimei. In a later meeting, Xiao Wu and Meimei cement a new romantic relationship, and Xiao Wu buys a pager so that Meimei can get in touch with him anytime. Before long, however, in her desperation Meimei runs off with a wealthy out-of-town client, and for much of the remainder of the film Xiao Wu waits in vain for her call to appear on his pager. Instead of realizing the hopes raised by their early courtship, he eventually has lost her as well as fallen out with his former best friend and his family back in his home village.

Xiao Wu's downward spiral is inevitably concluded by his arrest for picking pockets during a government crackdown on theft. This crackdown had become apparent from the opening minutes of *Xiao Wu*, and references to it are scattered throughout the film in the form of public loudspeaker announcements, television reports, and news media interviews taking place in the streets of Fenyang. As was the case with media accounts of the wedding of the "model entrepreneur" Xiaoyong, the reports on crime—the last of which is on the arrest of Xiao Wu himself—serve as an internal counterpoint to the film as a whole, with its sympathetic portrayal of the "real" life of one of the public enemies targeted by the police crackdown. In other words, the truth claim, or effect of realism of the film as a whole, is again rhetorically bolstered by its depiction of the very layer of official ideology it ostensibly cuts through to expose the obscured underlying reality. Just as the media's "half-faced portrait" of Xiaoyong as a model of success is stripped away, the depersonalized criminals vilified in the media are fleshed out into the "real" Xiao Wu, a marginalized dreamer with a stronger moral compass than the successful businessman lionized by the same media.[32]

The television street-reporting depicted in *Xiao Wu* also puts an interesting twist on the problem of bystanders' looks to the camera of the kind that was so prevalent in *Xiao Shan Going Home*. Dozens of such looks occur in *Xiao Wu* as well, but the majority of them happen during depictions of media street interviews. As a result, since interviewers and cameras are now included within the diegesis during such scenes, the gawking spectators can be interpreted as attracted by the street interviews and accompanying cameras *within* the story rather than calling attention to the filmmaker's camera and thus the constructedness of the fiction as a whole. That is, fictional realism is here less threatened by the extras' gazes at the lens than was the case with the previous video project. The spontaneity of people's reactions to the camera seeming now to have narrative motivation, the *cinéma vérité* immediacy of on-location shooting within street crowds is maintained and yet integrated into the diegetic world.

The most notable case of bystanders staring directly at the camera, however, occurs in the film's final shot, in which the tendency of random passersby to stop and gape at a movie camera is manipulated in a different and particularly inventive way. In a shot lasting over two and a half minutes, while being led after his arrest to another location by a police station chief, Xiao Wu is temporarily handcuffed to a cable next to the street and left there alone. The handheld camera stays with Xiao Wu squatting helplessly tethered to the cable in the foreground as a few people on the sidewalk behind are gradually drawn to the spectacle. Finally the camera suddenly pans to a view of the previously hidden street, which turns out to be rapidly filling with other gawkers. From a low-angle position approximating the perspective of Xiao Wu, who is now out of the frame, the camera simply returns the gaze of the gathering bystanders for a full one and one-quarter minutes until the film ends. With this camera movement, then, despite the lack of cutting, the shot seems to change from an objective shot of Xiao Wu to a virtual point-of-view shot from his perspective.[33] This

FIG. 5.2. Final shot of *Xiao Wu*, beginning as an objective shot of Xiao Wu.

impression is achieved by the combination of the pivotal pan, the very length of the shot (which in effect allows us to forget how it began), and the subsequent pans that seem to mimic Xiao Wu's head suddenly turning. This highly effective final shot thus stages a direct confrontation between the perspective of the film's isolated protagonist and the gaze of the anonymous public for whom he is objectified and estranged by the mass media. The semisubjective camera positioning literalizes the perspective of the film's rhetoric as a whole, which puts the audience in sympathy with Xiao Wu, while the gaping spectators recall the cold and sadistic crowds of Lu Xun's short stories.[34] In addition, like the scenes of street interviews by the news media, this shot very cunningly turns the problem of looks to the camera during on-site shooting into a storytelling device in itself. The crowd of onlookers in reality was of course attracted by both the actor handcuffed to the cable and the movie camera shooting him,[35] but by having the camera face the crowd from approximately the character's point of view, the stares at the lens appear to be at Xiao Wu and are thus integrated into

FIG. 5.3. Final shot of *Xiao Wu*, ending as a subjective shot of the gathering crowd from Xiao Wu's perspective.

the diegesis. In short, the fissure opened up by looks to the camera in *Xiao Shan Going Home*—the divergence between the priorities of "on-the-spot" *cinéma vérité* realism and those of fictional realism—is largely sutured in *Xiao Wu*, with somewhat more preference now given to the latter.

Aestheticized Realism and a Global Imaginary

Despite this shift to solve the problem of looks to the camera during on-location shooting in unrestricted public spaces, the style of *Xiao Wu* continues the previous work's strong presence of the camera by the use of mostly hand-held camerawork and frequent close shooting in small interior spaces, where the maneuverings of the camera become more apparent. In many ways, *Xiao Wu* epitomizes a gritty, low-budget realist style that has since been echoed in other notable Chinese films such as Wang Chao's *Anyang de gu'er* (Orphan of

Anyang, 2001) and Li Yang's *Mang jing* (Blind shaft, 2003). For the purposes of my argument, I am distinguishing this type of "on-the-spot" realism from a related yet distinct style that also begins to emerge more strongly in *Xiao Wu*, namely an aesthetic characterized by long shots, exceptionally long takes, and a relatively immobile camera. This style is exemplified in *Xiao Wu* by such scenes as the meeting with Xiaoyong and the visit to Meimei's dormitory, scenes which more closely typify a Bazinian-style realism in which the continuity of real time is preserved and the viewer is allowed to choose what details to focus on in long-shot compositions rather than being more obviously manipulated by camera movements and close-ups. However, it was only with his next film, *Platform*, that Jia's shift toward this more measured and aestheticized realist style became apparent in the work as a whole rather than just in certain scenes. In *Platform*, camera movements are limited for the most part to slow and steady pans, looks to the camera in crowd scenes are eliminated altogether, and shot duration expands dramatically, to an average of seventy-six seconds, compared with thirty-three seconds for *Xiao Wu* and just eighteen seconds for *Xiao Shan Going Home*. Indeed, sequence shots are the rule, and thus there is little continuity editing. Close-ups are virtually eliminated, while long-shot and extreme-long-shot compositions are used frequently, so that the feeling of the physical immanence of the camera is lost in favor of an evocative distance from the historical subject.

A production on the scale of *Platform* was made possible by the impact *Xiao Wu* had in the international film festival circuit, where it won a total of seven prizes at six film festivals on three continents, most notably two awards at the Berlin International Film Festival. In the wake of this success, Jia moved decisively from being simply a recent Film Academy graduate pursuing low-budget independent productions of marginal films in China to being a significant presence on the international art-cinema scene, and *Platform* was subsequently made with a professionalism and an aesthetic that fit comfortably with the prevailing industry standards. A truly globalized production, *Platform* was financed through the combined resources of production companies and government agencies in Japan, France, Switzerland, Hong Kong, and mainland China. After *Xiao Wu*, Jia had many willing new investors, and he chose Takeshi Kitano's T-Mark Inc. as his main production company, partly in order to work with a producer who had collaborated successfully with Hou Hsiao-hsien, a favorite inspiration.[36] The result (after a much more involved production process than had been the case with *Xiao Wu*) was Jia's first 35mm film, a beautifully executed, sprawling work. *Platform*'s story spans the entire decade of the 1980s, and its playing time was reduced from an originally screened cut of 193 minutes to a still lengthy 155-minute final cut. The film traces the evolution of a performing arts, or "cultural troupe" (*wengongtuan*), from Fenyang as it negotiates the rapidly changing conditions of the early post-Mao reform era and its young members face the various disappointments and excitations of lives that always seem to be on the verge of, without ever quite reaching, some sort of promised fulfillment. By these means the film simultaneously represents and interrogates the reform era itself, in which the call for "modernization" continually invokes a goal, the arrival of modernity in all its plenitude, that nonetheless always seems to be just out of the reach of much of the Chinese population.

As the performing arts troupe evolves from a state-run enterprise performing revolutionary songs for the masses in 1979 to a privatized operation selling disco dance routines and punk rock imitations to any audience it can attract by the end of the 1980s, both the promise and the elusiveness of a new vision of modernity are exemplified for its young members by popular music. As the 1980s begin, although singing political propaganda songs in their public performances, in private troupe members listen to illegal shortwave broadcasts of Taiwan pop singer Deng Lijun (Teresa Teng). Jia Zhangke has said that his first experience of hearing the singer "was exactly as it was portrayed in *Platform*," and that it left him "utterly hypnotized."[37] On the arrival of pirated tapes of her in Fenyang, he says, "you then felt a kind of new life had begun."[38] Sheldon H. Lu summarizes the effect of Deng Lijun's songs in the mainland so soon after the end of the Cultural Revolution: "The soft, sentimental, private, and humane melodies found in popular culture struck a note that contrasted with the official language of revolution and class struggle."[39] Jia himself confirms that the songs represented a shift from the collective "we" to the individual "me," and that their "very personal, individual world" immediately "infected" the people of his generation and contrasted with the collective nature of their dormitories, workplaces, and schools.[40] Thus the Deng Lijun songs, as well as other pop music that would be heard later in *Platform*, represent for the generation of youth depicted in the film not just a new form of entertainment but a new structure of subjectivity, in which private desire and individual identity take priority over community belonging and political struggle.

Even in the context of the official performance troupe, the changing times are soon acknowledged when performances of nonpolitical "light music" (*qing yinyue*) are allowed. However, troupe members become more excited by the cassette tapes of pop-rock songs one of them brings back from a trip to Guangzhou, the cutting-edge site of "opening and reform" in China in the early 1980s. The contemporary pop-rock song from which *Platform* draws its title encapsulates the feelings of both anticipation and disappointment in the film:

> Long long platform, long slow waiting
> Long long train, carrying my love everlasting
> Long long platform, lonely waiting
> Only my love departing, never my love returning

In the image of waiting on a long, desolate train station platform for a train that never arrives, the song captures both the promise of an approaching modernity offering individual fulfillment and the frustration of waiting endlessly for it in an inconsequential (yet therefore representative) small city in China's hinterland. Indeed, at the time depicted in the film no railroad even ran through Fenyang, and thus during their travels in one key scene the performance troupe members dash across a dry riverbed and up to a bridge just to get a glimpse of a passing train. The train is thus both a literal industrial emblem of modernity and a more abstract symbol of a modernity actually experienced largely as an absence and a longing. While the train has already rushed by before the performers have even made it up to the train track, their own old truck lies broken down and idle in the dry valley.

The thematic tension in *Platform* between anticipation and disappointment also finds expression in the way the film manages to depict epochal historical change largely through scenes of trivial events and even boredom. The use of ellipses is a major part of its realist style. Jia has described how he made the conscious choice to minimize obvious cause-effect narrative progressions, instead letting the viewer gradually observe the results of historical and personal change without necessarily knowing how they came about. This preference is justified as being more true-to-life: as we observe the changes in the lives around us, we are rarely aware of the details of how they happened, but we see the results nonetheless.[41] Such an approach recalls Bazin's praise of ellipses in the films of Vittorio De Sica and Roberto Rossellini: "The empty gaps, the white spaces, the parts of the event that we are not given, are themselves of a concrete nature: stones which are missing from the building. It is the same in life: we do not know everything that happens to others."[42] What we do see of the lives of the characters in *Platform* often approaches Bazin's "cinema of time" or (as he quotes Henri Bergson) "cinema of 'duration,'" in which the priority is to organize time not according to dramatic needs but rather in accordance with "life time"—the experience of time as simple duration in a life that is more full of quotidian moments, inactivity, and boredom than spectacular events even in an era of dramatic historical change.[43] Thus the importance of ellipses in *Platform* goes hand in hand with the favored use of extremely long takes that depict temporal intervals rather than just narrative events. Such stylistic decisions produce a particular vision of the historical and geographical setting, bringing out the tension between sweeping historical change as the master narrative of reform-era China and inertia as actual lived experience in a small, remote provincial city—an inertia all the more apparent because of its contrast with the official account of the "Four Modernizations."[44]

The temporal organization of *Platform*, then, continues and even intensifies the "narrative distension" that Chris Berry discusses in the case of *Xiao Wu*, in that the combination of exceptionally long takes and limited plot movement evident in key parts of the earlier film here becomes the rule throughout the film. As was the case with *Xiao Wu*, this narrative distension amounts to a radical representation of postsocialist time, but in this case it is a remembered time of the 1980s rather than an obdurate motionlessness of the present as perceived by those whose lives are going nowhere in the 1990s. *Platform* as a whole (which Jia has often stated is based largely on personal memories of the times and places depicted) is a looking back to a bygone age and a now-transformed geography. However, the era depicted is on the contrary filled with a continuous anticipation of a coming fulfillment, as discussed above. Thus, while the time within the film is subjectively experienced by the characters as melancholy over a *future* that remains forever out of reach, the film as a whole is imbued with melancholy over a lost *past*—specifically Fenyang in the 1980s, but also the lost hopefulness of youth in general. The film is then a document not of an immediate reality but of a complex network of personally experienced temporal displacements shot through with distance and duration. The distances the film explores include both the spatial distance of a marginal geographical location far from the centers of reform-era cultural change in the 1980s, as well as the temporal distances of, on one hand, the characters from their hoped-for futures and, on the other, the filmmaker (and audience) from the past that must now be recalled. These distances are not overcome but literally *endured*, as both the characters within the film and the viewer watching it experience the empty duration of the present moment largely as the absence of some future or past, lending the film as a whole a gradually increasing sense of melancholy.

Platform is thus easily read as a product of nostalgia, but such a reading must take care not to thereby dismiss it as a nostalgia that is complacent, transparent, or reassuring. To borrow the distinction made by Svetlana Boym in her study of nostalgia in postsocialist Europe and Russia, the nostalgia of *Platform* is of the "reflective" rather than the "restorative" type: instead of being generated by a national imaginary of smooth progress and recoverable essences, it arises rather from ambivalent personal and cultural memories and embraces ambiguity, distance, irony, and fragmentation as inseparable aspects of its object of meditation.[45] It neither longs for the lost society that preexisted the reform era nor embraces the ideology of the "Four Modernizations" that underlay the transformations of the decade depicted. It is a nostalgia of the past as duration rather than as a simple, quickly recognized snapshot.[46] For example, the film eschews easily identified, monolithic changes in the characters' dress and hairstyles as the narrative (and decade) progresses; rather than all characters transparently signifying the transition, say, from 1979 to the early 1980s, some characters suddenly appear with permed hair or track suits, while others retain the earlier styles of the Mao era, reflecting the multiple temporal frames of reference that actually coexist at any particular historical moment. The predominant use of long-shot compositions and long-take cinematography, of course, is an integral part of the reflective nostalgia of the film. The almost exclusive use of long shots and extreme long shots maintains a distance between the viewer and the object of nostalgia that mitigates against easy sentimentality even in the most dramatic scenes.[47] Long takes, meanwhile, convey the sense of time as endured, demanding reflection by the viewer rather than the simple consumption of nostalgic images or narrative information.[48]

The differences in style between *Platform* and *Xiao Wu* are thus largely attributable to the divergences in historical period depicted and the changed priorities that result from trying to convey a decade of fictional time through a reflective poetics of nostalgia. A significant increase in the filmmaker's budget and human resources undoubtedly also allowed for a more thoroughgoing realization of an aesthetic vision. In any case, *Platform* arguably pursues a very different sort of realist aesthetic than that of Jia's earlier works. The compositions appear to be much more carefully constructed—sometimes using Ozu's "similar-figure" (*sojikei*) technique, in which actors appear to rhyme each other's posture and orientation, for instance—giving the film as a whole a more stylized feel than *Xiao Wu*.[49] Due to the choice of shooting locations also, Fenyang has an entirely different presence than it had in *Xiao Wu*. Instead of the ramshackle modern urban architecture and dirty, chaotic streets of the earlier film, *Platform* makes frequent use of beautiful old city walls as a backdrop for its lengthy shots. In fact, these scenes were filmed in the neighboring, much more picturesque city of Pingyao, where the city wall dates to the Ming Dynasty and enough traditional architecture survives that the town became a major domestic tourist destination in the late 1990s. In addition to this change of actual shooting location, the fictional Fenyang of *Platform* appears relatively deserted, as the use of extras is vastly reduced in comparison with Jia's previous two works (with no random crowds being used, for obvious reasons of historical fidelity). In short, due to the combination of a more controlled mise-en-scène, changed shooting locations, much longer takes, more careful framing, slower camera movement, and extreme reliance on long-shot compositions, not only the city itself but the very experience of both space and time reaches a new level of aestheticization in *Platform*.

One sequence shot will suffice to illustrate this changed filmmaking style in *Platform*. The film's main protagonist, Cui Mingliang, is atop the old city wall with his love interest, Yin Ruijuan. In a shot lasting three and a half minutes, beginning in extreme long shot, the two approach the camera, which slowly pans to follow them until they pause on the wall next to it and talk. Eventually

FIG. 5.4. Example of "similar-figure" (*sojikei*) technique in *Platform*.

Mingliang asks Ruijuan whether they can be considered a couple. Mingliang gets an ambiguous answer (and in fact is later rejected, adding to the mood of anticipation and disappointment in the film), and subsequently the pair continues along the wall, now away from the camera.[50] During the bulk of the shot, while they have paused to talk, the stationary camera frames them in a bold composition in which exactly half of the screen is filled by a large brick wall in the foreground. Behind it, the two characters take turns walking back and forth, with one of them hidden behind the looming wall in the foreground while the other leans against a perpendicular wall on the still-unobscured right side of the frame. In carefully choreographed succession, the two change places four times, with each leaning, always in the same position, on the right while the other is hidden by the wall on the left. Occasionally, when changing positions, both disappear behind the wall for a few seconds, so that the entire frame resembles an almost abstract still photograph. When they both finally leave the space, the camera again slowly pans and records their retreat without following until they are again in extreme long shot.

With shots such as this one (and several others in *Platform* could serve

FIG. 5.5. Aestheticized composition during a long take in *Platform*.

equally well as examples) the combination of shot duration, composition, and careful manipulation of mise-en-scène results in a filmic style so aestheticized as to become striking in its own right, without regard to the "reality" it allegedly depicts. In this sense, to understand the formal characteristics of *Platform*, we must at least partly shift our framework away from the documentary or on-the-spot realism movement in China and instead look at the context of current trends in international art cinema. In fact, a large number of contemporary art films have displayed formal preferences quite similar to those of *Platform*. Such films become so exclusively reliant on the long take, so concerned with showing in detail the real-time intervals between narrative actions, that Bazinian long-take realism is pushed nearly to, and sometimes past, the point that it becomes its ostensible opposite: an intriguing kind of formalism. This aesthetic was a favorite of the international art cinema and film festival circuit during the 1990s and is exemplified by directors such as Hou Hsiao-hsien, Abbas Kiarostami, and Tsai Ming-liang.[51] It overlaps at least in part with the neo-Bazinian elements of the Dogma 95 movement that arose in Denmark,[52] and it is pushed to its almost minimalist limit in such works as Hou's *Haishang hua* (Flowers of Shanghai,

1998), Tsai's *The River* (Heliu, 1997), and Béla Tarr's *Werkmeister Harmonies* (Werckmeister harmóniák, 2000).[53] To the extent that this new international style had a theoretical or academic support, it was not only the Bazinian notion of cinematic realism (which had been widely critiqued in the Western academy during the very years it held sway in China in the post-Mao period), but also, by the turn of the century, the rising influence of Gilles Deleuze's two-volume philosophy of cinema.[54] In Deleuze's terminology, a film composed largely of long takes and minimal cause-and-effect narrative movement will tend to approximate the "time-image"—an image of time itself rather than of rational or plot-driven movements in time.[55] In the Deleuzian formulation, the usual contrast between national art cinemas and the classical Hollywood style is rewritten as a binary opposition between the time-image and the "movement-image," the latter of which is at least in part yet another way of conceptualizing the classical method of plot-driven narration and "invisible" editing.

Thus, an art film such as *Platform* can perhaps best be understood not as an extension of the radical *cinéma vérité* realism of Jia's earlier works, which drew more directly on the Chinese postsocialist realism of the 1990s, but rather in this broader context of art cinema as an aesthetic and theoretical antipode to entertainment cinema. In the local Chinese context, whereas the postsocialist realist aesthetic arose in opposition to the Fifth Generation's allegorical cinema as well as the residual socialist realism of "main melody" patriotic films, the foil of *Platform*'s Bazinian long-take art cinema can be thought of as both Hollywood and the emerging Chinese entertainment cinema of directors such as Feng Xiaogang.[56] The international style of aestheticized realism, with its durations and ellipses, presents an alternative to Hollywood-style storytelling, which in fact is equally operative in the popular films of Feng Xiaogang (see the next chapter) and the state-supported ideological drills of the "main melody" films. At the same time, the aestheticized realism of the transnational aesthetic exemplified by *Platform* is unavoidably itself a commodity within the specialized market that spawned it, and it competes as such with alternative trends and aesthetics on the art-film circuit. Given its excellent critical reception and strong box-office showing for a Chinese art film, particularly in Europe, *Platform* can be said to have been a success in its particular niche market.

With the 2002 feature *Ren xiaoyao* (Unknown pleasures), Jia Zhangke and cinematographer Yu Lik Wai departed somewhat from the extremes of the slow and distanced international style of *Platform*, and perhaps not surprisingly the film received somewhat less ecstatic reviews from foreign film critics. In terms of subject matter, *Unknown Pleasures* returns to a contemporary setting in the northern Shanxi mining town of Datong. The immediacy of the period depicted is accompanied by the return of a mobile, often handheld camera that feels immanent to the environments it shoots and even occasionally indulges in devices such as whip-pans (which would have been unthinkable in *Platform*). A switch to digital video (a remarkable fourth different format among the four main films discussed here) facilitates this return of a *cinéma vérité* style of realism in many scenes, as does the reappearance of random crowds from the actual city streets, along with the occasional looks to the camera by these bystanders. In other ways, however, *Unknown Pleasures* continues the trend from *Xiao Shan Going Home* to *Xiao Wu* to *Platform*, the average shot length, for example, further expanding to nearly a minute and a half, with some shots including almost painfully slow and deliberate pans along the lines of Hou Hsiao-hsien's *Flowers of Shanghai*. In still other respects—the use of a pair of stylish and sexily presented lead characters, for example—the film seems to have a younger and hipper appeal bordering on the commercial. The director himself has said that he tried to make *Unknown Pleasures* somewhat more mainstream, with a more dramatic and tightly knit plot.[57] However, in the end the picture is as oblique and uncompromising as its predecessors, depicting young lives that seem already to have reached a dead end amid a wrecked urban landscape filled with the rubble of demolished buildings and construction sites, with nuclear reactor cooling towers looming in the background. Indeed, while *Platform* shifted shooting locations from Fenyang to Pingyao in an effort to find a more nostalgic backdrop, in Datong *Unknown Pleasures* seems to have found a contemporary urban setting even more ruined and bleak than the Fenyang of *Xiao Wu*, a bombed-out looking backdrop that silently repudiates the colorful fashions of its youthful protagonists.

Indeed, as was the case in *Xiao Wu* and *Platform*, a key theme of *Unknown Pleasures* is the gap between the imaginary of popular culture and the intrac-

FIG. 5.6. Fashion amid devastation in *Unknown Pleasures*.

table reality the characters actually inhabit. The film's Chinese title, meaning "given to wander free and easy," is borrowed from a contemporary popular song that appears twice in the film. The song title itself echoes the Daoist philosopher Zhuangzi, who used *xiaoyao*, or "carefree wandering," to describe the ideal state of spiritual freedom. One of the film's protagonists, nineteen-year-old Bin Bin, is enamored of a cartoon version of the Monkey King from the classic Chinese novel *Xiyou ji* (Journey to the west)—an embodiment of a similar ideal combination of empowerment, freedom, and enjoyment, the very qualities Bin Bin most lacks in his own life. In another poignant depiction of mass-mediated identification, a group of poor mill workers is shown wildly cheering a televised announcement that faraway Beijing has won the competition to host the 2008 Summer Olympics. The accessibility of popular media also allows the young protagonists of the film to immerse themselves in global youth culture. There is an extended scene of rapturous dancing (a motif that also appears in *Xiao Shan Going Home* and *Platform*) in a techno club throbbing to the strains of a dance-mix of the mid-1990s Chinese rock song "My Love Is Stark Naked" (*Wo di ai chiluoluo*). Wry references are made to touchstones of recent global popular culture such as Quentin Tarantino's *Pulp*

Fiction (1994), which one of the lead male characters, Xiao Ji, invokes for the daring of its restaurant robbery scene. However, when Xiao Ji and his friend Bin Bin later attempt to bridge the gap between fantasy and reality by carrying out their own heroic robbery of a bank using fake explosives, the ploy is easily countered by a security guard in what must be one of the most morose and anticlimactic bank heist scenes in cinema history. As Bin Bin is taken into custody by the guard, Xiao Ji tries to flee on his motorbike down the new highway to Beijing, but, characteristically, his motorbike breaks down in the middle of the highway outside of town. Thus, while early on in the film the Chinese title may seem to refer to the carefree lifestyle of its protagonists, by the time Xiao Ji is stranded on the highway and Bin Bin pathetically delivers on command an a cappella version of the pop song "Ren xiaoyao" while in police custody, the ironic undertones of the film's Chinese title have come fully to the surface. The poses of hipness the young protagonists strike are eventually betrayed by their own powerlessness and vulnerability to disappointment; the film's attractive and trendy-looking characters again become objects of melancholy reflection rather than idealized identification.[58] To draw a parallel between the careers of Jia and one of his inspirations, Hou Hsiao-hsien, if *Platform* recalled such films as *Lianlian fengchen* (Dust in the wind, 1986) and *Tongnian wangshi* (A time to live, a time to die, 1985), then *Unknown Pleasures* takes its place beside *Nanguo zaijian, nanguo* (Goodbye south, goodbye, 1996) and *Qianxi manbo* (Millennium mambo, 2001)—films which subject the sexy rebellion of the young lead characters to such a prolonged and penetrating gaze as to reveal an underlying despair.

Negotiating National and World Cinematic Space

Jia's two feature films following *Unknown Pleasures*—*The World* and *Sanxia hao ren* (Still life, 2006)—were released on official studio labels, and thus strictly speaking he was no longer an "independent" filmmaker—though, as we have seen, independence from the domestic studios still meant dependence on the international art-film market, and indeed even his state studio releases continued to rely on producers from abroad. Nonetheless, the fact that Jia would now have access to the domestic mass audience caused a stir in the Chinese film world. While it was generally treated as good news, there also were questions of whether going mainstream would compromise the "the valuable ability to think independently and the courage to be challenging."[59] Such fears of selling out raised by the abandonment of "underground" status further demonstrate the predicament of China's "independent" directors: if, in order to have any significant audience, they successfully move toward the international art-cinema audience, they may be accused of pandering to foreigners; if, alternatively, they move toward the Chinese studio system, they risk accusations of caving in to the authorities or catering to the mainstream audience.[60] In either case the radically independent and home-grown spirit of the original postsocialist realist movement appears to be compromised.

In the end, like Jia's earlier films, *The World* attracted little notice at home but was well received abroad. The film (which will be discussed more in Chapter Seven) in fact follows the critical realist impulse of Jia's earlier films, all of which attempt to document problems of the postsocialist condition, including the hardships of the migrant labor force, the turn to theft and prostitution among some of those left behind by the new economy, and in general the loneliness and longing among young people for whom a new autonomy and access to an emerging mass-mediated youth culture are counterbalanced by the dangers of economic marginalization and social alienation. The characters in these films are neither heroic, as are the triumphant or martyred protagonists of the patriotic "main melody" films, nor fantastical, as are the happy-go-lucky dream-fulfillers of Feng Xiaogang's romantic comedies (see the next chapter). Instead, the critical realism of Jia Zhangke claims to look behind both political orthodoxy and entertaining fantasies to show an obdurate reality that belies the comforting portraits painted by ideology—whether the ideology of the Communist government or that of global capitalism (which, indeed, are becoming ever more difficult to disentangle).

If Jia's films can all be classified as critical realism in this basic sense, however, my discussion has differentiated two distinct types of realism in terms of formal style: an "on-the-spot" *cinéma vérité* realism that draws on a wider documentary impulse among Chinese artists and filmmakers of the 1990s, and a comparatively aestheticized long-shot/long-take realism that draws more upon a contemporary international art-cinema style. I have argued that Jia's works from *Xiao Shan Going Home* to *Platform* progressed roughly from the first style to the second as the filmmaker gained wider experience, higher budgets, and access to the resources and audiences of the international art-cinema world. In the process, of course, the apparently complete autonomy of the guerrilla-style videography of *Xiao Shan Going Home* was gradually replaced by the "independence" of a director whose opportunities are nevertheless intimately tied to a transnational art-cinema market. In other words, although the institutional environment for young Chinese directors in the early 1990s provided fewer opportunities for state employment but more possibilities to realize independent projects, as the decade progressed the most prominent of these new directors were integrated into either the state studio system or the global art-film production and distribution apparatus—or, in some cases, both, leading not so much to pure autonomy as to one type or another of new *market* heteronomy (see Chapter One).

Of course, incorporation into the global art-cinema institution does not necessarily indicate any premeditation or conscious adaptation to market conditions on the part of the filmmakers. For example, Jia has never yielded "artistic freedom" in any obvious way, such as giving up the final cut or yielding any control of his scripts to producers. Moreover, the transnational fashion for an aestheticized neo-Bazinian realism is by no means necessarily the motive for its adoption in *Platform*. Indeed, as a film theory concentrator in the literature program at the Beijing Film Academy, Jia would have been well versed in the theory of Bazinian realism even before he made his early films in the more raw postsocialist realist style, and the switch to the aestheticized long-take realism of *Platform* may well be fully explained by the increased resources at his disposal combined with the demands of his own vision of the historical material, as discussed above. The fact that a product is successful within a certain market does not necessarily mean it was cynically designed for the market, but by its success it remains an indicator of that market nonetheless.

In fact, in emphasizing the match between a film such as *Platform* and a certain niche aesthetic in the global art-cinema market, I mean partly to counterbalance a more frequently repeated view, namely that "political factors are generally greater than artistic factors in the reasons these [Chinese] 'underground films' win awards."[61] Such a rule apparently assumes the artistic inferiority of Chinese films, ignoring precisely the aesthetic dimension of the appeal of a filmmaker such as Jia Zhangke, who, while he may well have been marketed on occasion as "underground," is nonetheless engaged as an active agent in the development of film art. Indeed, if obvious political subversion were the only interest foreign audiences and critics had in Chinese films, *Unknown Pleasures* would have received a more ebullient critical response than *Platform*, whereas I have argued that the reverse happened due to the latter's perfection of a currently favored aesthetic. Despite my attention to Jia's presence on the global art-cinema market, then, I do not intend to reinforce the view that such a director "makes films for Westerners" or that Chinese filmmakers who gain attention in international film festivals must be peddling self-orientalizing images of China to foreigners.[62] We should perhaps be wary of the rhetoric of national betrayal as well as the simplistic form of postcolonial theory invoked by such a view. Most Westerners do not watch art films, Chinese or otherwise, and an American director who makes an independent art-house film is often equally guilty of betraying his or her own domestic mass audience in favor of appealing to a more specialized audience composed largely of foreigners.[63] Moreover, the neo-Bazinian realist aesthetic I have referred to is by no means a Western invention; two of its progenitors are certainly Yasujiro Ozu and Kenji Mizoguchi, its contemporary masters hail from East Asia and the Middle East, and it has significant audiences in Japan and South Korea, if not in mainland China. Finally, the producers, festival organizers, and audiences who have contributed to this style's hegemony—while they can undoubtedly be criticized in various ways for the discursive and financial power they wield—should not be assumed always to make a special case of Chinese cinema, uniquely choosing films based upon their political or orientalist appeal rather than their artistic merits.[64]

In fact, insofar as either Western audiences *or* Chinese critics insist on linking every Chinese film and filmmaker to the nation—and on holding an artist such as Jia accountable as a representative of China—they in fact perpetuate a position of inferiority of modern Chinese culture on the world stage. As Pascale Casanova has suggested in the case of literature, it is paradoxically within the most hegemonic "national spaces"—those with the most accumulated cultural capital—that art is most likely to appear as autonomous in the sense of establishing "a depoliticized and (at least partially) denationalized space," or rather a "sub-space" within what she dubs "world literary space."[65] Conversely, newly emergent spaces or those lacking in accumulated cultural capital will tend toward "the pole of greatest heteronomy," in which art hews to political and national criteria, or becomes crassly commercial, but cannot compete with more established spaces on the world cultural scene.[66] In the case at hand, considering the greatly increased global profile of Chinese cinemas (including those of Hong Kong and Taiwan in addition to the mainland) beginning in the late twentieth century, not to mention the vastly enhanced centrality of China to the world capitalist order (which is a related but distinct matter), one wonders when Chinese filmmakers, and indeed artists in general, will be released from the demand, whether from within China or abroad, that they act as cultural ambassadors rather than simply as artists.

Indeed, instead of critiquing Jia's cinema according to a crude East/West or China/foreign dichotomy, it is perhaps more fruitful to see his career as characteristic of postsocialist societies both East and West. Some post-Soviet Russian filmmakers have been similarly condemned by domestic critics for offering nothing but bleak portrayals of "slaves, nothings, vagrants, and drug addicts" and constituting a "betrayal of national interests."[67] There is also an interesting parallel between Jia and the Hungarian filmmaker mentioned briefly earlier, Béla Tarr. Tarr's early films, shot in the late 1970s and early 1980s, when the communist system in Eastern Europe was in its final phase of decline and ultimately collapse, show a remarkable stylistic similarity to Jia's films in his earlier, postsocialist-realist phase of documentary-style filmmaking.[68] As with Jia's early projects, one senses that the priority was to show the raw, unattractive, and sometimes even boring lives of ordinary people in a way that would appear as a realist revelation next to the ideologically saturated images promulgated by the official media. In Tarr's own words, "There were a lot of shit things in the cinema, a lot of lies. We were coming with some fresh new, true, real things."[69] Later, however, Tarr's aesthetic evolved significantly, and by the end of the century he had developed one of the most rigorously minimalist long-take styles to be found on the international film-festival circuit, making his films appropriate for film-festival viewing alongside other masters of the neo-Bazinian realism such as Abbas Kiarostami, Lars von Trier, Hou Hsiao-hsien, Tsai Ming-liang, and Jia himself.[70] As in the case of Jia, the postsocialist art filmmaker is compelled to compete for international funding and find an admittedly small audience among the global festival and art-house public. Within those limitations, the films might nonetheless rival and even exceed the artistry of the more established art-cinema traditions of Western and Northern Europe, Japan, and North America.

The situation is, however, precarious for the postsocialist artist in the global environment. Thus Jia Zhangke gets caught up in debates over whether he is pandering to foreigners and ignoring the domestic mass audience, while Béla Tarr finds it so difficult to raise funds that he must take years in between films. With the entry of China into the World Trade Organization and the explosion of the number of Hollywood and Hong Kong films on the Chinese market, even with official sanction and domestic distribution Jia's films are unlikely to make much of a public impression in China. In the next chapter we will examine a quite different—in many senses, in fact, opposite—case study in how a Chinese filmmaker responds to the challenges of competition in the postsocialist global market.

6

New Year's Films: Chinese Entertainment Cinema in a Globalized Cultural Market

Chapter Four discussed Feng Xiaogang's *Yi sheng tanxi* (Sigh, 2000) and *Shouji* (Cell phone, 2003) as examples of the urban "cinema of infidelity" in China in the late reform era. Those films were also part of a remarkable string of commercial hits by a director who almost single-handedly created a new phenomenon in Chinese cinema: the *hesuipian,* or "New Year's celebration film." The idea, previously used in Hong Kong and Taiwan and similar to Hollywood's calculated release of blockbusters on major holiday weekends, was simply to offer audiences an entertaining film with top star talent during the holiday season spanning Christmas and the Western and Chinese New Years.[1] With a nearly unbroken series of *hesuipian* from the late 1990s into the new century, Feng established himself as the most commercially successful mainland Chinese filmmaker ever. Three of his late 1990s films—*Jiafang yifang* (Party A, party B, 1997), *Bujian busan* (Be there or be square, 1998), and *Meiwan meiliao* (Sorry, baby, 1999)—rank in the top five grossing Chinese films of the twentieth century in mainland China.[2] *Be There or Be Square* was the single biggest domestically produced box-office success ever until Feng broke his own record in the new century with *Dawan* (Big shot's funeral) in 2001.[3]

Feng's unapologetic emphasis on entertaining audiences above all else distinguishes his films both from those of the Chinese art-house auteurs better known in the West, and from the state-sponsored "main melody" (*zhuxuanlü*) films screened in China with the more didactic aims of educating the audience and instilling patriotism. Feng's stated priority is simply to entertain as large an audience as possible: "I'd rather make fun movies for one billion people than serious ones for a small group of cultural critics."⁴ Of course, the Feng Xiaogang phenomenon in China at the turn of the century was not merely the result of one director's inclinations or his gifts at pleasing popular audiences. Instead, it must be understood in the context of the profit imperative imposed on Chinese cinema by its exposure to market competition during the reform era. Entertaining the mass audience, as opposed to either educating the masses or impressing cultural elites, becomes the overriding priority when film production is subjected to the profit motive and faced with formidable competition from Hollywood imports, both of which were new conditions in the PRC at the end of the twentieth century. As a response to the subjection of the film industry to the globalized market and the demand for profitability, Feng's *hesuipian* employed many interrelated strategies: joint production arrangements involving state studios, private Chinese producers, and foreign concerns; the previously mentioned holiday season marketing tactic; choices of genre (predominantly the romantic comedy) and stars that maximized entertainment value to a mass audience; and a finely honed cinematic style based on the classical Hollywood cinema. At the same time, the narratives of several of Feng's early entertainment films are remarkable for the extent to which they comment directly, even critically, on the very transition to a fully commercialized culture industry of which they are examples. While such commentary is evident in various elements of plot and characterization, what is most striking is the way these films repeatedly deploy distanciation methods including an increasingly challenging reflexivity as well as an undercurrent of irony that mitigates the overall tone of lighthearted entertainment. Thus, although Feng takes credit for having "saved the Chinese film industry"⁵ and insists his priority is simply to entertain audiences and sell tickets, his films arguably also reveal, in both the filmmaker and the Chinese audience, a highly self-aware and multifaceted engagement with the conditions of commodified cultural production in contemporary China. Insofar as some of Feng's early *hesuipian* can be read as cinema about cinema, they mark an important moment of industrial and artistic transition (from state socialism to the market) with both a mode of narration that is aggressively entertaining (sometimes even cloying) *and* a reflexive, analytical examination of the very mode of narration they deploy. These films thus provide evidence for the thesis that metacinema often appears precisely during times of crisis in the film industry—in this case, for better or for worse, simultaneously pointing to a way out of the crisis by forging a new Chinese entertainment cinema.[6]

To the extent it is exposed to the world market, Chinese cinema, like national cinemas everywhere, can maintain its vitality and ensure its continued existence only through a complex negotiation with Hollywood that involves both resistance and co-optation. The previous chapter examined a filmmaker who more or less follows the path of national art cinemas, which counter Hollywood with an alternative viewing experience, if only to a much smaller audience. In contrast, Feng's *hesuipian* attempt to co-opt Hollywood and beat it at its own game. My discussion of the New Year's film phenomenon will thus begin with a brief review of the history of Chinese cinema's relation to Hollywood, which raises some critical questions regarding the very nature of a "national cinema." Next I will trace the domestic history of Feng Xiaogang's aesthetic, beginning with its roots in the "Wang Shuo fever" of the late 1980s, before discussing in more detail three of Feng's most successful *hesuipian*—*Party A, Party B*; *Be There or Be Square*; and *Big Shot's Funeral*. Despite their success as entertainment cinema, these films present an increasingly bold metacinematic commentary on their own form as cultural commodities. Even more interestingly, they suggest that Feng Xiaogang has seized upon a feature of popular cinema and its pleasures generally neglected in film theory and criticism: the notion that a reflexive, self-deconstructing element is *intrinsic* to the enjoyment of illusionist entertainment films. I will conclude with some observations on both the domestic and global cultural politics engaged and engendered by *hesuipian* and the implications for how Chinese popular culture has changed since the acceleration of market reforms and their extension to the culture industry in the early 1990s. The *hesuipian* phenomenon constitutes an effort to create a new vision of a Chinese national cinema, one that can simultaneously provide entertainment to the public, compete successfully with Hollywood imports and thus keep the domestic film industry financially viable, and even attempt to compete with Hollywood in its own domestic market.

Hollywood and Chinese National Cinema

Since roughly the end of World War I, world cinema has generally had to contend with the hegemony of Hollywood. National cinemas have developed various strategies for coping with the aesthetic influence and competitive strength of Hollywood, and indeed the very notion of a "national cinema" (a term rarely applied to Hollywood itself) invokes the need to assert some local response to Hollywood's global dominance.[7] Even the revolutionary cinemas of the twentieth century's communist states were heavily indebted to the "classical" Hollywood style. For example, Miriam Hansen has described how the early Russian cinema became revolutionary Soviet cinema only through the mediation of Hollywood's stylistic innovations.[8] After avant-garde Soviet montage aesthetics had been suppressed by the Stalinist state, the conservative socialist-realist style that supplanted it was deeply indebted to the classical Hollywood narrative mode.[9]

Chinese cinema also has evolved in shifting relations to Hollywood, whether directly in periods of more contact or indirectly when the Chinese market was relatively protected. The golden age of Shanghai cinema, which thrived in the 1920s–40s, was an exemplary instance of the "vernacular modernism" that the example of Hollywood spread to film cultures throughout the world, as Miriam Hansen and Zhang Zhen have shown.[10] Here the influence of Hollywood cinema must be understood not just as a market force to resist or a style to imitate, but rather as a "global vernacular" through which the very experience of modernity, with all its contradictions as well as aspirations, is articulated in a variety of local sites. In the case of Shanghai, the influence and artful co-optation of Hollywood film conventions was evident in both the entertainment films of the 1920s (derided as frivolous and reactionary by the intellectual elite) and the politically progressive films of the 1930s and late 1940s that became canonized in Chinese film historiography.

After the establishment of the PRC, the legacy of Shanghai cinema was largely suppressed, although elements of the Shanghai aesthetic would occasionally resurface in periods of relative relaxation of ideological control in the arts (most notably in 1956–57 and in the early 1960s).[11] Instead, the Chinese national cinema of the Mao era was constituted by a combination of Soviet socialist realism and the Maoist emphasis on indigenous popular art forms. In any case, whether through the residual influence of the earlier Shanghai cinema or the more apparent borrowing from Soviet socialist realism (partly by means of film professionals studying in Moscow during the early years of the People's Republic), Mao-era Chinese films continued a strong if indirect debt to the Hollywood narrative mode. Despite this influence of Hollywood storytelling, however, Mao-era cinema was considered primarily an instrument of revolution and a means of educating the masses. Hollywood imports, which had dominated the market before 1949, ceased completely in favor of selected imports from the Soviet Union and, later, other Communist states, particularly North Korea and Albania. Domestic production was entirely funded and controlled by the state, with all film workers being trained and paid by the state through the national studio system. Distribution was designed to make cinema available to as many people as possible, with rural projection teams taking, for example, filmed versions of the Cultural Revolutionary "model operas" to even the most remote villages for repeated viewings. Films were viewed collectively by entire work units as part of the ideological education provided by the Party.[12] For the purposes of the present discussion, then, the most notable characteristics of mainland Chinese film culture during the first three decades of the PRC were the lack of any market mechanism determining what was produced and distributed, the corresponding lack of any competition from entertainment cinemas abroad, and the paradoxically simultaneous continuation of the indirect influence of classical Hollywood cinema in terms of fundamental narrative conventions.

The circumstances of mainland Chinese cinema were changed greatly by the economic restructuring and new cultural spaces opened up during the reform era. The modes of film production, conditions of spectatorship, range of genres and filmmaking styles, availability and aesthetic influence of films from abroad, and the very horizons of experience cinema contributes to the public imaginary have all undergone drastic changes in the decades since the late 1970s. As the brief discussion above indicates, during the Mao era, cinema, like all production, was a heteronomous instrument of the Communist Party. By the early 1980s, however, as in other areas of cultural production, a measure of autonomy had returned to filmmaking. Although state-owned studios still held a monopoly on the means of production, new studio heads and younger directors began to explore new aesthetic and thematic possibilities in so-called exploratory, or innovative, films (*tansuo pian*). These included both the early masterworks of the Fifth Generation, such as *Huang tudi* (Yellow earth; dir. Chen Kaige, 1984) and *Heipao shijian* (Black cannon incident; dir. Huang Jianxin, 1985), and more overlooked groundbreaking films of the Fourth Generation, such as *Ye shan* (In the wild mountains; dir. Yan Xueshu 1985), which was discussed in Chapter Four.

With these experimental films of the 1980s—which showed a striking new *aesthetic* autonomy from the previous revolutionary culture even as they continued to be institutionally heteronomous to the state—a new vision of a Chinese national cinema began to take shape, both in China and abroad.[13] For the first time, Chinese cinema figured prominently within international art cinema, winning awards at film festivals and gaining occasional distribution on the arthouse circuit. The experimental nature of the films was in fact partially made possible *by* their origin in the socialized economy, as the studios at that time were not expected to turn a profit and thus could take artistic chances. Only in the 1990s did a new emphasis on economic profitability lead to an upsurge in the production of entertainment films (*yulepian*), culminating in the *hesuipian* of Feng Xiaogang. During the same period, not only did a number of directors begin making their films entirely independently of the state studios (see Chapter Five), but the studios themselves were pressured to become financially self-sufficient, which led them to produce a much higher number of entertainment films, often in cooperation with private production companies, both domestic and in Hong Kong or abroad.

In the brief historical narrative I have traced above, then, several very different visions of a Chinese national cinema are evident. Stephen Crofts has offered a useful typology of national cinemas, dividing them into seven varieties.[14] Following his typology, the development of mainland China's national cinema can be summarized as going from the domestic commercial entertainment cinema of the 1920s–40s, to the "totalitarian" cinema of the 1950s–80s, to a mixture of those two types along with art cinema since the mid to late 1980s. That is, in contemporary China the state-subsidized "totalitarian" cinema remains in the form of the patriotic "main melody" films, but it exists alongside the art cinema of Fifth and Sixth Generation auteurs as well as the new commercial cinema that seeks to compete with Hollywood for the domestic mass audience. The advantage of Crofts's typology, despite some inevitable overlap between categories, is that it acknowledges a much wider range of possible "national cinemas" than allowed by the usual Eurocentric understanding of the term as signifying mainly various national varieties of art cinema, which are then contrasted with Hollywood's commercial cinema. Thus, while it was perhaps easy to identify the pioneering art films of the Fifth Generation as a "New Chinese Cinema," it is equally important to understand the more recent *hesuipian* as a new model for a Chinese national cinema, even if, like most of the varieties identified by Crofts, it has "to operate in terms of an agenda set by Hollywood."[15]

The latter comment is especially relevant to the environment in which *hesuipian* arose in China in the late 1990s. Despite the fact that "opening" (*kaifang*) had been the counterpart to the "reform" (*gaige*) slogan since Deng Xiaoping consolidated his power in 1979, only a very few Hollywood films were imported and distributed in China before 1994, and those tended to be older productions bought at low, flat rates. However, in that year a new policy was instituted to annually import up to ten foreign blockbusters (*dapian*).[16] Even when restricted to such a low number (actually fewer than ten per year, considering that imported Hong Kong films fell under the same quota at the time), Hollywood films quickly came to dominate the Chinese box office. In the first year of the new policy, seven Hollywood imports (including *The Fugitive*, *The Lion King*, *Speed*, *Forrest Gump*, and *True Lies*) combined with three Hong Kong imports to seize 70 percent of the market in China.[17] While this was highly profitable for the China Film Export and Import Corporation, a state monopoly, it dealt a further blow to the domestic film production industry, already threatened by a loss of audiences to television, which had only recently become common in ordinary Chinese homes, and home video viewing, particularly in the new video compact disk (VCD) format that swept through China in the mid-1990s. Chinese studios now would also have to compete for theater audiences with the productions of foreign studios with vastly greater resources and budgets.[18] The sudden dominance of Hollywood imports at the Chinese box office culminated with the runaway success of *Titanic*, which grossed an unprecedented US$44 million in China. In the face of competition from the blockbusters, by 2001 only one in ten Chinese productions turned a profit, with 10 percent breaking even and the remaining 80 percent losing money.[19] To make matters worse, in the same year China's entry into the World Trade Organization (WTO) doubled the annual quota of imports to twenty, forcing the domestic industry to contend with even greater competition from abroad. In this context, the high profitability of Feng Xiaogang's *hesuipian* is all the more remarkable, and his claim of having saved the domestic film industry is not mere hyperbole.

Feng Xiaogang and the Aesthetic of Postsocialist Irony

Although Feng's string of successful *hesuipian* began with the release of *Party A, Party B* during the 1997–98 holiday season, an important part of his aesthetic formula for commercial success can be traced to a decade or so earlier, when the "Wang Shuo phenomenon" erupted on the cultural landscape. In a series of extremely popular works of fiction, Wang Shuo changed the rules of the literary scene by showing that great market success could come with or without the endorsement of either the academic literary establishment or officialdom. Labeled as "hooligan" (*liumang* or *pizi*) literature, Wang Shuo's style was irreverent, humorous, and highly ironic.[20] This aesthetic of irony appeared suddenly in Chinese cinematic production in 1988, known as the "Wang Shuo year" after four of the novelist's stories were adapted into feature films.

In fact, as Aleš Erjavec has argued, irony has been the dominant trope of representation in postsocialist cultures in general, from the former Soviet Republics to Eastern Europe to China.[21] Xiaobing Tang also has discussed the rise of irony to become "the dominant mode of writing and reading" in China by the early 1990s. Tang relates the phenomenon to a "historically wrought absence of cultural normativity" that results from the debunking of both capitalism and socialism as legitimate value systems, the former by Marxist analysis and the latter by the historical experience of Maoism. Consequently, any "self-important discursive production can be immediately subjected to irony because the situation is such that any positive value has already been thoroughly dismantled or made mockery of."[22] In Chapter Two I explored at length the great cultural debate over Wang Shuo's aesthetic of "mocking everything" (*tiaokan yiqie*) and the crisis it was perceived as representing in Chinese culture, which was said to have lost any moorings in "ultimate values" by the early 1990s. In this light, the rise of irony marks the arrival of a postutopian era that would reject the premises of the modernist allegories of the Fifth Generation in the 1980s as well as the melodramatic-revolutionary narratives of the earlier socialist cinema. A new generation of cynical consumers could neither buy into the myth of socialist progress under the Communist Party nor accept the leadership of self-appointed intellectual elites who increasingly betrayed an anxiety over their own continued relevance in the face of ever-widening market reforms. For Wang and his collaborators in the film and television industries, discursive authority in all its forms became the target of mockery. At the same time, Wang's was a "profitable mockery" that, with its "conscious appeal to the entertainment and commodity value of storytelling," made the author "the first specimen of a 'marketized' literature that promotes 'best-seller consciousness' (changxiao yishi) above all else."[23] In short, he showed that irony sells in the postsocialist market age.

The exemplary early example of the new ironic aesthetic in cinema was *Wanzhu* (Troubleshooters, or literally, Masters of mischief), a 1988 adaptation of a Wang Shuo novella directed by Mi Jiashan.[24] The story of a group of male youths who launch a highly dubious service company, *Troubleshooters* aptly captures the irony-drenched humor of Wang's style. The "Three-T Company" of the film specializes in solving other people's problems, no matter how trivial or bizarre, through substitution, artifice, or deception. The business amounts to a parody of a pure capitalist service economy in which any service will be performed for the right price. In the film's most extravagant sequence, the Three-T Company organizes a sham awards banquet for a mediocre writer who feels his work has gone unappreciated. Stand-ins are recruited to play the part of famous writers in attendance, and the awards ceremony is inexplicably preceded by an elaborate fashion show in which a catwalk is crowded with people costumed as workers, peasants, preliberation landlords, female bodybuilders, police officers, Nationalist and Communist soldiers, Red Guards, fashion models, figures from traditional opera, and so on. Nothing could better express the principle of value-neutral universal equivalency in consumer capitalism than this spectacular reduction of so many eras and ideologies to sameness within a superficial postmodern parade. Importantly, however, the entrepreneurial leading characters who organize such travesties—and the narrative viewpoint that follows them and guides audience identification—maintain a distinct ironic distance from the absurd spectacle around them. Such postmodern irony, the film suggests, could become the only viable stance to take in the face of the inexorable decline in cultural normativity at a time when massive economic transformation is accompanied by the delegitimization of political and cultural authority.

Feng Xiaogang himself broke into the scene of commercial culture in early collaborations with Wang Shuo. The son of a Communist Party college professor and a nurse, Feng had painted sets for an army theatrical troupe during his military service, then found a civilian job in the art department of a television station. He eventually moved on to script writing, most notably for the groundbreaking, extremely popular television series *Bianjibu de gushi* (Stories of an editorial board; dir. Zhao Baogang and Jin Yan, 1991), China's first sitcom and an archetype for many later shows.[25] Subsequently, Feng codirected and coproduced the television series *Beijing ren zai Niuyue* (Bejinger in New York), an extraordinarily popular adaptation of a semiautobiographical 1991 novel by Cao Guilin (Glen Cao, a Beijing expatriate living in America), first broadcast on the CCTV network in October 1993. The series fascinated viewers with its on-location view of contemporary New York City and its vision of Chinese power, success, and masculinity projected onto the symbolic center of global capitalist culture.[26] After these successes, Feng attempted a series of relatively serious film projects, some of them also collaborations with Wang Shuo, but each one was struck down by the censors.[27]

Repeatedly thus frustrated, Feng was nonetheless encouraged by Han Sanping, the head of the Beijing Film Studio, who promised that if Feng made something lighter and more entertaining as a New Year's celebration film, Han would smooth its path through the bureaucracy and ensure its release. Feng responded with his first *hesuipian*, *Party A, Party B* (also sometimes referred to in English as *Dream Factory* or *Dreams Come True*), which, following in a sense the dual influences of Wang Shuo and Han Sanping, manifested the tension between cutting irony and entertaining fluff that would coexist, sometimes jarringly, in most of Feng's *hesuipian*. Feng, who later wrote that Wang Shuo's works "produced a profound and far-reaching influence on my later career as a director and became programmatic texts that guided my shooting of *hesuipian*," not surprisingly proposed to adapt the Wang Shuo novel *Ni bu shi yi ge suren* (You're not a commoner) into his first New Year's film.[28] However, Wang's reputation for "mocking everything" and the dangerous nihilism that many cultural mandarins saw in his work could easily have clashed with Han Sanping's practical concern for getting the picture past the censors. Consequently, Han approved Feng's proposal to adapt Wang's novel only with the stipulation that the film must show characters learning from their experiences, and that these lessons must not be "negative" but rather "positive" and "full of sincerity."[29] Important consequences of this juggling act included the decision (reluctantly approved by Wang Shuo) to change the title of the film, the failure to even list Wang or the original novel in the film's credits, and a drastically changed fictional ending in which a sugar-coated "sincerity" indeed wins the day over ironic detachment.[30]

In however compromised a form, *Party A, Party B* was released in late 1997 in time for the 1998 New Year's holiday season.[31] Made with a budget of less than half a million U.S. dollars, the film grossed five times that amount, paying for itself several times over in Beijing alone.[32] In retrospect, it is a landmark in Chinese cinema history, if only for putting in place for the first time all the essential elements of the *hesuipian* formula: the holiday marketing strategy, the use of popular stars, and an aesthetic of irony and parody uneasily grafted on to what is in many ways a Hollywood-style romantic comedy. Perhaps the most important precedent, however, was the film's mode of production, which amounted to a marriage of state and private interests that maximized profitability while minimizing the likelihood of obstacles in censorship and distribution. *Party A, Party B* was ostensibly a coproduction between the state-run Beijing Film Studio and the private production company Forbidden City (Zijincheng yingye gongsi), but the latter was in fact itself closely linked to the Beijing municipal government, being funded by the Beijing Television Station, the Beijing Film Distribution and Exhibition Company, and the Cultural Affairs Department— all publicly owned municipal agencies. As Yingjin Zhang notes, such government protection gave Forbidden City privileged access to financial resources and distribution channels in the capital, leading to such eyebrow-raising phenomena as the appearance of movie promotion advertisements in hundreds of street locations that had previously carried slogans such as "Building Socialism with Chinese Characteristics."[33] In short, the production company, which would go on to back Feng's later films as well, provided filmmakers with the new degree of autonomy that comes with working in a private environment rather than a state studio, but without cutting off their access to relatively high budgets or the benefits of being connected with political insiders. The role of the official Beijing Film Studio as coproducer, in turn, as Han Sanping had promised, helped ensure smooth sailing through the censors and made Feng's *hesuipian* the legal equivalent of any state-funded movie, with access to nation-wide distribution.

Simulation and Parody from the Dream Factory

The concept of *Party A, Party B* is in many ways a continuation and refinement of that of *Troubleshooters* almost a decade earlier, even starring one of the same actors, the popular Ge You.[34] Again the protagonists run a fanciful service company that goes to great lengths to fulfill the idiosyncratic requests of various customers—at the right price. But whereas the Three-T Company in the earlier film had taken on all kinds of odd jobs, such as substituting for a man too busy to take his girlfriend on a date, the "One-Day Dream Trip" (*Hao-meng yiriyou*) company in *Party A, Party B* specializes exclusively in fantasy fulfillment along the lines of the writer attending his own awards ceremony in *Troubleshooters*. The customers of the "One-Day Dream Trip" company include a man who wants to be General George S. Patton for a day; a man who wants to live out a fantasy of not revealing a secret even under torture; a man who wishes to serve as a submissive servant to feudal landlords to compensate for the fact that he bullies his wife in real life; a rich man who hopes to see what it is like to live desperately poor and eat "coarse foods"; and a movie star who wants to get rid of all the attention she is paid and live like a normal person. In each case, the company partners go to extraordinary lengths, and seemingly unlimited expense, to realize the fantasy for their customer, even if in several cases the client comes to regret the fantasy once it becomes reality.

The first "dream" sequence in *Party A, Party B* is the most elaborately staged of all. After an opening credits segment during which the protagonist, Yao Yuan, introduces himself and his new company in voice-over, the film begins with several dramatically lit, high contrast shots of the actor Ge You and a jeep in a dark garage. Both are revealed mostly in close-ups: a military boot, a gas can, a steering wheel. The man is preparing the jeep by spray-painting four stars onto it and attaching a small tattered American flag (upside down) to its antenna. Several guns and helmets are thrown in, and finally the man starts the ignition and moves out. The company's first customer is a portly bookstore owner who wants to be Patton for a day. To realize his fantasy, the "One-Day Dream Trip" team—the four people who launched the company and a group of extras they have hired for the project—have organized an implausibly comprehensive, high-budget simulation of a World War II desert battlefield tableau, including several tanks and other military vehicles, makeshift troop barracks, and a military headquarters. Dressed up as a four-star general, the customer rides around in a jeep, barks orders, chats condescendingly with lowly soldiers, leads a strategy session in a conference room (in which a map of Nanjing substitutes for a map of Germany), and even orders the executions of underlings who have angered him.

What makes this sequence most remarkable—giving it its humor and taking the dream fulfillment depicted in *Party A, Party B* from the level of fantasy imitating reality to that of a play of simulations—is that the bookstore clerk is clearly not pretending to be the historical General Patton so much as the character depicted by George C. Scott in the 1970 Hollywood biopic *Patton* (dir. Franklin J. Schaffner).[35] This film was among the limited number of old Hollywood films imported at a flat rate in the 1980s, when it was "received with unqualified admiration."[36] It was one of the Western films most regularly broadcast in dubbed version on Chinese television throughout the following years, and thus it would have been very familiar to audiences for *Party A, Party B*. Certain details of plot and mise-en-scène from the earlier film are either alluded to or directly parodied in Feng Xiaogang's comedy. For example, the customer playing Patton is told he can go visit the wounded in a military hospital so that he can kick a cowardly soldier—a riff on one of the key scenes in *Patton*. At another point, the Chinese "Patton" approaches an at-ease soldier who only notices him at the last moment and quickly rises to attention. In a direct quotation of the earlier film, the "general" then angrily uses his riding crop to strike down a pinup on the wall behind the soldier. The level of intertextual play and

FIG. 6.1. Desert shot in *Patton*.

simulation, of course, involves not just the Chinese character imitating George C. Scott playing Patton, but also Feng Xiaogang playing at being the director of a big-budget Hollywood war movie, for example, by filming scenes of army vehicles bunched together in a desert landscape in a style reminiscent of *Patton*, with the vehicles rumbling through the swirling dust toward the camera through a telephoto lens.[37] If this reveals Feng's "all-too-apparent reliance on transnational cultural imaginaries," as noted by Yingjin Zhang in a different context, it also attests to the director's ability to manipulate these images for his own purposes, not to mention the Chinese audience's capacity to process such parodic allusions for their own pleasure.[38]

In fact, *Party A, Party B* must be read in part as a reflexive commentary on the production and consumption of the very entertainment cinema of which it is an example. As we are told in Yao's voice-over narration, he is an unemployed actor, while his partners in the "One-Day Dream Trip" enterprise all had previously worked in the film industry as prop assistants, scriptwriters, and so on. This serves not just to make the proficiency of their fantasy simulations more believable but to suggest an obvious parallel between the "dreams" bought by their customers and the usual consumption of fantasies by moviegoers, with actual role-playing by the consumer taking the place of spectatorial

FIG. 6.2. Desert shot in *Party A, Party B*.

identification. It is thus fitting that an alternate English title of the film has been *Dream Factory*, recalling the classic description of Hollywood itself,[39] while the "(Good) Dream" (*haomeng*) part of the fictional company's name is in fact borrowed from a film and television production company that had been started by none other than Feng Xiaogang and Wang Shuo in 1993. All this makes for a strong metacinematic element in *Party A, Party B*, which, while by no means amounting to a high-modernist critique, nevertheless has the film call attention to its own status as both fantasy and commodity, as a transient daydream purchased by a consumer.[40] It thus fits Robert Stam's broad definition of "reflexivity as the process by which texts, both literary and filmic, foreground their own production, their authorship, their intertextual influences, their reception, or their enunciation."[41] In terms of Stam's useful typology, the cinematic reflexivity in Feng Xiaogang's early *hesuipian* is clearly of the *ludic* variety, a "playful self-referentiality," rather than an aggressive aesthetic modernism or a didactic political radicalism.[42]

Returning to the opening episode of the film with this playful metacinematic element in mind, we can distinguish three different levels of performance or apparent degrees of "staging" in *Party A, Party B*. From the opening shots of the jeep in the garage to the moment the "general" is told his time is up and he must return his costume, a tension is established between the actual playing out of the fantasy and all the associated backstage activities, as when the jeep is being spray-painted, stand-in soldiers are made up in blackface, or company employees are simply chatting among themselves. For example, after ostensibly being taken out of the headquarters conference room and shot on Patton's orders, the protagonist Yao Yuan casually smokes a cigarette behind the building and tells his attractive co-worker, Zhou Beiyan, that his father is threatening to give the family house to Yao's sister unless he gets married soon. Yao half-seriously asks Zhou to marry him in what would be a sham wedding, and the two engage in the kind of rapid-fire, barbed, humorous repartee characteristic of Beijing verbal comedy, consisting of playful, mutual mocking or *tiaokan*.[43] In keeping with the time-tested conventions of romantic comedy, as the film progresses Yao and Zhou must eventually confront the real mutual attraction that lies behind their sparring. In the end they get married and move into Yao's family house, but not before he has first lent it out to another married couple in which the woman has a terminal disease and wants only to share a nice house with her spouse for a time before she dies. This maudlin subplot serves to show the soft side beneath Yao's snide exterior and helps to bring him and Zhou together.

The three levels of performance that can be distinguished here are thus (1) the obvious role-playing in the process of helping the customers to act out their fantasies; (2) the sarcastic *tiaokan* performances of the leading couple, which serve as sublimated expressions of their actual romantic attraction, the consummation of which is deferred until the end of the film; and (3) the behavior of the characters once they have dropped their pretenses and begun "discovering their own inner sincerity."[44] As long as we remain immersed in the world of the diegesis, the authenticity of the performances ranges from the obvious falsity of the fantasy role-playing for the customers to the genuineness displayed in the "real" marriage of Yao and Zhou at the end of the film. Yet the meta-cinematic implications of, for example, the staging of the *Patton* parody lead to the recognition that as soon as we step back from diegetic immersion and consider the film as a whole, the scale of authenticity potentially reverses itself: the blatantly fabricated simulations staged for the dream-realizing customers more "authentically" foreground the film's mode of production and thus fictitiousness to the audience, while the sappy union of the romantic couple at the end is the typical feel-good illusionism of light entertainment cinema. In short, the reflexivity provided by the "dream factory" work of the company highlights the illusionism inherent in classical Hollywood "realist" storytelling, even if the latter still carries the day at the end of the film.

The Returned Ethnographic Gaze and the Pleasures of Anti-illusionism

Given the box-office success of *Party A, Party B*, not surprisingly the same investors—Forbidden City, the Beijing Film Studio, and Feng Xiaogang himself—made every effort to repeat the formula for the following holiday season. In fact, *Be There or Be Square*, released around Christmas 1998 in time for the 1999 New Year's holiday season, not only exceeded its predecessor's success but became the highest-grossing domestic production ever in mainland China.[45] For *Be There*, Feng again cast Ge You as the leading man, and this time his romantic interest was played by Xu Fan, who had played the fame-weary movie star in the earlier film. However, an equally important antecedent for *Be There* was Feng's television series of several years earlier, *Beijinger in New York*, one of the attractions of which had been that it was shot on location in New York City and featured Chinese immigrants trying to compete and survive in the West. For *Be There*, said to be the first Chinese feature film ever shot entirely in America, the producers flew in the cast and a crew of about thirty to shoot in greater Los Angeles for forty days.[46]

While *Party A, Party B* had begun with the somewhat reflexive "backstage" scene of the jeep being prepared to serve as a prop in a fantasy sequence, *Be There* begins with a more boldly metacinematic move. A crane shot moves from a high-angle view of an elevated highway stretching across a suburban Southern Californian landscape to a close framing of an empty car parked under the highway. Suddenly, one of the car's windows is shattered by a crowbar, which is followed by a close-up of a hand quickly extracting the car's stereo. The following shot of the thief running away, however, is quickly disrupted by the presence of a boom microphone, and as the camera tracks back a camera operator, director, and other film crew members also become visible as the director shouts "Cut!" It turns out that the protagonist of *Be There*, an expatriate Beijinger named Liu Yuan, is playing a bit role as a thief in a film being made by a Chinese crew in Los Angeles. While working on the film, Liu Yuan meets a more recent arrival from Beijing, Li Qing, who is house-sitting for a friend in a home used as a location for the film-within-the-film. In the episodic narrative that follows, Liu Yuan and Li Qing each drift from job to job, with one or both of them at some point being involved in insurance sales scams, janitorial labor, tour guiding, and Chinese language teaching. As Liu Yuan says early in the film, "I do whatever makes money," and his cynicism provides *Be There* with much of its humor while simultaneously presenting an obstacle to the inevitable sentimental coming-together of the romantic pair (as had been the case with the protagonist played by the same actor in *Party A, Party B*).

Through the adventures of Liu and Li in America, *Be There* openly addresses many issues of race, gender, and cultural difference that might confront a Chinese immigrant in America. Some of the tension in the couple's endlessly deferred romance is provided by the specter of miscegenation, as when Liu Yuan pretends to have found an American fiancé named Monica, or when Li Qing is ogled by a group of hairy bikers in a trailer park. In a play on racial fears, at one point Liu Yuan is aggressively confronted by a young African-American man wielding a knife in what at first seems to be the very embodiment of the threatening ethnic other. However, it turns out that the man is joking and the two in fact are friends. Liu's FUBU[47] cap and exchanges of elaborate ethnic handshakes with the black man may embarrass a Western audience with their awkwardness and obviousness (if not downright racism), but the scene nonetheless represents at least some sort of ideal of cross-cultural identification. Such episodes present Liu Yuan as a legitimate participant in an imagined community of global hipness, with intriguing, if distant, echoes of the imagined Chinese solidarity with dark-skinned subalterns that had been celebrated during the Mao era.

In fact, much of the film's appeal to Chinese audiences must have come from the revelation of countless details—real, imagined, or exaggerated—of life in America. One senses such an exoticizing "cinema of attractions"[48] at certain moments when the camera lingers, say, on the unloading of groceries in the parking lot of a Sam's Club, the pumping of gas and washing of windows at a self-service gas station, and the feeding of coins into a parking meter, all during one short sequence. The loosely plotted, episodic narrative allows frequent space for views of America as spectacle, both mundane and fantastic, an America that appeals to the fantasies of the Chinese audience, whether frightening, enticing, or pedestrian. Feng's America is a place of excess, where violence breaks out without warning and sexual perversion looms (as, for instance, when a transvestite grabs Liu Yuan's buttocks and leers, "Come to Mama, baby!" sending Liu Yuan into a macho rage from which he must be restrained). Indeed, some aspects of American life and society appear quite exaggerated—the recurrent intrusion of random crime into everyday life, for example, or the dramatic busting of an immigration racket by a federal force so large and heavily armed that it seems more appropriate for dealing with a terrorist threat.

Consequently, viewed from an American perspective, *Be There or Be Square* presents an image of the United States that is recognizable, yet often wildly distorted, inducing a funhouse-mirror feeling no doubt quite familiar to Chinese audiences who have viewed Hollywood representations of China. The film's indulgence of the Chinese audience's ethnographic interest in America serves as an obvious role reversal with Hollywood, which had long exercised its power to construct elaborate cinematic fantasies of China to satisfy a Western audience's taste for exoticism. At the same time, *Be There* also presents a counterpoint to the representations of China promulgated by the "Fifth Generation" directors who have been widely accused of peddling self-orientalizing visions of China to foreign art-film audiences. Here, the exoticizing impulse is similar, but it is the Chinese who produce and consume a view of America. Thus, read against Hollywood and Fifth Generation depictions of China, Feng Xiaogang's vision of Southern California represents the empowerment of a returned gaze, through which the mythmaking power of America's entertainment capital is turned back on itself by a Chinese film industry that is itself under the ever-increasing pressure of competition from Hollywood. Among the lessons of *Be There*, then, is that if the studios of Southern California can tell improbable stories about China and sell them for huge profits, then China can now do the same about Southern California.

On the other hand, when we stop considering merely the origin of the capital and the nationality of the filmmakers and look instead at questions of narrative mode, genre, and cinematic style, it is easy enough to argue that Hollywood asserts its supremacy even when losing Chinese ticket sales to Feng Xiaogang's *hesuipian*. Feng's films, after all, by no means constitute a "third cinema" or a national art cinema—both of which would define themselves by their opposition to Hollywood in terms of narration and style—but instead are highly dependent upon Hollywood tradition for their inspiration and legibility to audiences. A producer of *Be There*, for example, told the *Los Angeles Times*, "We see this film as a kind of *When Harry Met Sally* romantic comedy. These kinds of films do well in China these days."[49] Indeed, if *When Harry Met Sally* (dir. Rob Reiner, 1989) is clearly a contemporary update of the romantic comedy formula forged during the classical era in Hollywood, then *Be There* (as well as Feng's preceding *Party A, Party B* and following *hesuipian—Sorry, Baby*—which I will not discuss here) retains all its essential features: rapid-fire, battle-of-the-sexes dialogue; sexuality represented mainly in sublimated form through verbal innuendo and physical comedy; and the deferral of any actual romance until the end of the film. The film's points of highest tension, aside from its liberal sprinkling of American-style random violence, occur when the romantic feelings of the couple finally threaten to fully surface due to extraordinary circumstances; for the most part, these feelings are suppressed, keeping the audience pleasurably frustrated. That is, as the two leading characters are kept in a state of suspended romantic tension, the main means of manipulating audience emotions is the repeated placing and lifting of obstacles between the two would-be lovers, including circumstances that lead them to part ways for years at a time. In fact, this narrative device of having the potential lovers separate and then reunite through sheer coincidence months or years later may well be taken directly from *When Harry Met Sally*. Each separation is experienced as a temporary disappointment, while each reunion presents another opportunity for the lovers to finally arrive at the inevitable till-death-do-we-part conclusion.

And yet, however much he exploits the Hollywood romantic comedy formula, Feng Xiaogang also repeatedly inserts still more distancing reflexive gestures in the form of cycles of fabulation and deflation that both exploit and foreground precisely the formulaic expectations generated by entertainment cinema, not to mention the gullibility of the audience and the skill of the filmmaker. His narrative continually undermines itself in a way that both amuses and repeatedly unbalances the audience. Narrative threads and audience expectations are skillfully set up only to be undercut by a sudden comedic twist. One example occurs when, after a long separation, Li Qing meets with Liu Yuan and is shocked to find that he has gone blind, at which point the film immediately turns mawkish. The two face each other across a table in a café, and after an establishing medium-long shot, a series of cuts and camera movements gradually close in on the couple as Liu Yuan tells the sad story of his blindness and his longing for Li Qing. A sentimental soundtrack gradually surges as the camera moves in, until suddenly Liu Yuan blows his cover by obviously ogling a passing blonde pedestrian, then instinctively lunging when told there is a dropped wallet on the floor. The mood undergoes an immediate comic collapse, its melodrama exposed as an artifice as both the audience and Li Qing realize they've been duped.

In a similarly structured sequence already mentioned, Liu Yuan invites Li Qing to dinner and tells her of his engagement to an American woman. The occasion forces Li Qing to confront her actual romantic feelings for Liu Yuan, and she soon flees to the privacy of a bathroom to break down in tears. Since the audience is as in the dark as Li Qing herself, the revelation that Liu Yuan has made up the story of the fiancé suddenly deflates a moment of high emotion for both Li Qing and the spectator. Yet another example is a saccharine flash-forward sequence in which Liu Yuan and Li Qing are emotionally reunited in their old age at a nursing home after decades of tragic separation. The heartbreaking scenario, however, is suddenly revealed to be a mere dream Liu Yuan is having while dozing off on an airplane. In the same sequence—the film's last—an apparently imminent plane crash leads the couple to openly declare their eternal love for each other at last. The crash, of course, turns out to be a false alarm, and the scene resolves itself when the couple finally consummate their relationship with a kiss—though slapstick trumps romance in the end, as the kiss dislodges Liu Yuan's false teeth.

The kind of reflexive irony with which Feng Xiaogang laces *Be There*, with its repeated creation and then deflation of dramatic situations, cannot help but eventually call attention to its own fictitiousness as a text. It might be described as a contemporary Chinese version of the form of irony celebrated by German Romanticism. As early as 1795, Friedrich Schiller distinguished naive poetry from superior ironic poetry, "in which the poet's consciousness of what he or she is doing forms part of the poem's technique."[50] Later Friedrich Schlegel, the German philosopher of Romanticism, would outline the specific concept of romantic irony, in which the text is repeatedly revealed as a capricious fabrication, undermining the artistic illusion. Such an effect requires the combination of skill at creating the realist illusion in the first place and the anti-illusionist impulse to then display the artifice that lay behind it. Romantic irony, unlike "stable," rhetorical irony, is said to call *everything* into doubt, including the stance or reliability of the ironist, leading to an epistemological quandary that edges toward nihilism—a quandary that will become relevant in my discussion of Feng Xiaogang's later film *Big Shot's Funeral*.

The reflexive cycle of fabulation and deflation in *Be There*, with its dual impulses of illusionism and anti-illusionism, offers a study in the very nature of cinema as entertainment. Tom Gunning has suggested that cinema, like its predecessors such as the "magic theater" of Georges Méliès and John Nevil Maskelyne, relied from its beginnings on a "pleasurable vacillation between belief and doubt" in an audience that appreciated the realism of the cinematic illusion all the more for knowing that it was an illusion.[51] In his more recent studies of the Phantasmagoria,[52] a direct precursor to the cinema, Gunning has reached similar conclusions, with the same implications for the later entertainment cinema. As with the magic theater, Gunning argues that the Phantasmagoria's allure consisted not simply in the remarkable realism of the optical illusion, nor in the revelatory debunking of the illusion through the spectators' knowledge that it was in fact generated through technology rather than magic; rather, the real crux of the device's appeal came precisely from the dialectic *between* the powerful illusionist sensations and the knowledge that what was being experienced was not, in fact, real. The Phantasmagoria was thus "an art of total illusion that also contained its own critique."[53]

The implications of this model of spectatorial enjoyment are relevant to any discussion of entertainment cinema. The model of film spectatorship as ideological interpellation, promulgated by the various psychoanalytic and apparatus theories since the 1960s, has little regard for entertainment cinemas, the pleasures of which can only be ascribed to the indoctrination of the audience with hegemonic ideologies of gender, race, class, and so on. By the 1980s and 1990s, several prominent film scholars countered this view with historically substantiated examples of how actual active audiences could use local tactics of co-optation and interpretation to undermine the supposedly monological power of the cinematic apparatus and its discourse. However, Gunning's description of the spectatorship of the Phantasmagoria, the magic theater, and early cinema is even more far-reaching, in that it suggests that a certain reflexive, self-deconstructing element is *intrinsic* to the enjoyment of illusionist entertainment cinema (notwithstanding any sexist, racist, or class ideologies it may well still be advancing).

Returning, then, to the cinema of Feng Xiaogang, and specifically to *Be There or Be Square*, the repeated self-undermining of the narrative, the manipulation of the audience to emotionally invest in situations which (they must know after a while) are bound to turn out to be false, emphatically should not be seen as moments of Brechtian interruption that undercut the illusion in order to raise the art from entertainment to enlightenment. On the contrary, with the push-and-pull of repeatedly and convincingly presenting and then undermining the cinematic illusion, Feng displays his virtuosic mastery of the art of entertainment cinema and his ability to get to the essence of audience enjoyment seemingly at will, and the ironic distance that periodically alerts the audience to the artifice of the cinema they are enjoying does not lessen their amusement but in fact *accentuates* it.

Who's Filming Whom? Mise-en-Abyme in the Forbidden City

Feng Xiaogang, again backed by the semiprivate Forbidden City production company, followed *Be There* with the similar romantic comedy *Sorry, Baby* in the 1999–2000 holiday season, and with the more serious *Sigh* (see Chapter Four) less than a year later. During the 2001 New Year's season, for the first time in five years the director offered no *hesuipian* to audiences, and the half dozen or so other holiday films released by Chinese studios that year were box-office disappointments. It was not until the following season that Feng would release another *hesuipian* that would break *Be There*'s record in ticket sales. *Big Shot's Funeral* was more ambitious than any previous *hesuipian* in many ways. First, it represents a landmark in the internationalization of the Chinese film industry. Released just days after China's admission to the World Trade Organization, *Big Shot*[54] was coproduced by the private Huayi Brothers & Taihe Film Investment Company, the public China Film Group, and Columbia Pictures Film Production Asia—the Hong Kong subsidiary of Sony Pictures Entertainment that had made enormous profits from its international coproduction *Wohu canglong* (Crouching tiger, hidden dragon; dir. Ang Lee, 2000) and was eager to repeat that success. Second, Feng Xiaogang, who speaks little English, would be directing two Hollywood stars, Donald Sutherland and Paul Mazursky, in addition to the Hong Kong-American actress Rosamund Kwan and the usual protagonist played by Ge You.[55] Third, the reflexivity and irony that I have discussed in the earlier *Party A, Party B* and *Be There or Be Square* would here explode into a dizzying metacinematic farce in which no target is safe from being satirically undermined, least of all the film itself. By the end, the *mise-en-abyme* structure accumulates so many layers that the audience cannot be sure whether the story they are watching is the real film or another film-within-the-film, and even the requisite feel-good, romantic-comedy ending is introduced by metacinematic distanciation and immediately deflated by more of the same.

With such a structure, the dynamic of filming—of precisely who gets to film whom—becomes a paramount concern and carries implications for the geopolitics of representation even more obvious than those of *Be There or Be Square*. In *Big Shot* a fictional, internationally renowned American film director named Don Tyler (played by Sutherland) goes to China to shoot a remake of Bernardo Bertolucci's *The Last Emperor* (1987). In the first scene of *Big Shot*, his Chinese-American assistant Lucy (Kwan) is hiring an unemployed Chinese cameraman named Yoyo (Ge You) to shoot footage for a "making-of" documentary during the shooting of the *Last Emperor* remake. In *Big Shot*'s opening shots, Yoyo looks directly at the camera, which takes Lucy's point of view, while answering her interview questions. However, after she hands him the camera he will use for the documentary shoot, he takes a light reading and turns it on her, and for the rest of the interview *Big Shot* itself takes the perspective of his handheld documentary camera, even panning back and forth with the shaking of Yoyo's head when he is asked if he can speak English. This turning of the tables in the opening segment becomes in retrospect a microcosm or *mise-en-abyme* of the film as a whole, as the American who seems to be in control of the representation turns out to be framed instead by an irreverent and unmistakably Chinese viewpoint.[56]

From Yoyo's hiring, the film skips ahead several months to the dual shootings of the *Last Emperor* remake by Tyler and the "making-of" documentary footage by Yoyo. Despite having a massive budget, an army of extras costumed in imperial grandeur, and the same access as Bertolucci to the spectacular shooting locations of the Forbidden City, Tyler finds himself unable to shoot, paralyzed by an utter paucity of inspiration and vision. His crisis in creativity is caused by the simultaneous desire to depict an "authentic" China and the realization that he lacks the capacity to do so. His predicament represents no less than a Western auteur's sudden loss of faith in his own authority to narrate his ethnic other, an impotence that demands to be read comically against the backdrop of Bertolucci's precedent.[57] In one scene, as he, Lucy, and Yoyo stroll down a strikingly long exterior corridor that had figured in two scenes from *The Last Emperor*, Tyler issues a rambling monologue that includes both a critique of Bertolucci's aim to please Western audiences and ample evidence of Tyler's own orientalism:

I think this is the key—Chinese Imperial Palace, two colors: red and gold, red walls, gold roofs. The red stands for blood, the gold for money. Blood and money—Asian conception of power. Who could flaunt power like this? Only the emperor dared do it. You see, when Bertolucci made his film about the emperor, he empathized with the guy, treated him like he was an ordinary human being. Showed his life from the moment he was a kid and had to assume the throne as if it were a tragedy. Which in a sense is true, but mostly I think he did it because he knew that that angle would appeal to Western audiences and pretty much guarantee the film's success—you know, make money? Well, I don't think that's the right point of view. You see, the problem is, you have to break down modern prejudices, modern preconceptions, I mean—God!

Soon Tyler's bigwig Hollywood producer, Tony (Mazursky), comes to Beijing to try to clean up the mess. After Tyler refuses to create "celluloid junk, uninspired trash that doesn't have any truth in it," Tony unceremoniously tells him he'll be replaced as director by an "MTV kid" whom nobody has heard of.

In a turning point in the film, Tyler again walks with Lucy and Yoyo in a stereotypically Oriental setting—this time a Buddhist monastery—and after pontificating about the Buddhist conception of the afterlife, Tyler, with Lucy as translator, asks Yoyo whether he believes in reincarnation. Noting that Tyler is depressed, Lucy refuses to translate Yoyo's initial answer: "I don't believe it. It's all a big hoax. After you die, there's nothing." So, on second thought, Yoyo serves up a "Chinese saying" that the sooner one dies, the sooner one is reborn (*zao si zao chaosheng*). He explains, through Lucy, that not only is death "not such a bad thing," but that an old person's funeral is on the contrary an occasion for celebration. Soon Tyler and Yoyo are interrupting Lucy to (mis)communicate with each other directly, and they more or less mutually come up with the idea of a "comedy funeral" (*xiju zangli*), a funeral that will provide "the same feeling you get when you see a really witty comedy." The scene as a whole thus milks more humor from the figure of the Westerner seeking mystical truths from his Oriental other,[58] while also introducing the farcical project that will soon spiral out of control—the "comedy funeral." For, soon afterward, Tyler requests just such a funeral from Yoyo before collapsing in a trailer back at the movie set and sinking into a coma.

Most of the remainder of the film is taken up with the increasingly outrageous funeral arrangements made by Yoyo, who enlists the help of a pompous promoter friend, Louis Wang (played by Ying Da, the popular television and film comedy actor who had played the Patton pretender in *Party A, Party B*). While waiting for Tyler to die, the two concoct an elaborate pageant filled with famous singers, actors, and directors that will be set in the Forbidden City itself and broadcast live via satellite throughout the world. To fund the production, Yoyo and Louis decide to sell advertising for the funeral and take on sponsors in the style of the Olympics (no random parallel, considering the imminent 2008 summer games in Beijing). In a series of parodic vignettes, a satirical eye is cast on the contemporary culture of celebrity in China and, most of all, the rampant commercialism that has swept the country since the early 1990s. In a reductio ad absurdum of product placement, the funeral becomes so saturated with advertising that even each of Tyler's corpse's feet is to be clad in different shoe brands, while his unseeing eyes will sport a specific brand of contact lens. Although some of the products mentioned are fictional parodies of real products—such as a cola called *kexiao kele*, a pun on the Chinese name for Coca-Cola that translates as "laughable cola"—others are in fact real products, so that the parody of product placement is simultaneously actual product placement for the sponsors of *Big Shot*, which included BMW, Sony, and several Chinese companies. *Big Shot*'s critique of commodification thus also constitutes, very self-consciously, its own autocritique—or, put less charitably, its critique is undermined by its own complicity with the object of critique.[59]

This reflexive consciousness of the film's own commodity form is just one way in which a disorienting circular logic becomes an essential part of *Big Shot*'s structure. Even more intriguing than the unmistakable self-inclusive admonitions of commercialism are the rich web of intertextual references in the film and the metacinematic elements that foreground the film's own process of production and repeatedly raise the question of precisely who is authoring the film.[60] *The Last Emperor* is an obvious touchstone for the film's parody, with some early scenes of Tyler filming in the Forbidden City skillfully mimicking the quality of light and the golden and red hues with which Bertolucci had captured interiors in the Forbidden City in the first part of his own film. As had been the case with the *Patton* imitation in *Party A, Party B*, such a gesture flaunts Feng Xiaogang's skill as a filmmaker while simultaneously undercutting the supposed cultural authority of its referent, if only by showing how easily it is imitated. Other references to *The Last Emperor* in *Big Shot* include the symmetrical arrays of uniformed people in the vast outdoor plazas of the compound that are reviewed by the boy emperor in both Bertolucci's film and in Tyler's remake of it (in which his majesty yawns and takes a swig from a bottle of cola). In *Big Shot*, these are further parodied during the funeral preparations, when armies of extras on the plaza, for example, form the international MTV corporate logo using a multitude of umbrellas raised in precise formations. Still other intertextual filmic references range from the obvious, as when Louis says "Sorry, baby!" (the English title of one of Feng's earlier *hesuipian*) to someone in English, to the obscure, such as the fact that more than three decades earlier Paul Mazursky had himself directed *Alex in Wonderland* (1970), a film starring none other than Donald Sutherland as a self-important director thrown into a creative crisis when he decides he wants to make a film of lasting social importance rather than the entertainment product he had previously been peddling—a plot that in turn recalls the Preston Sturges classic *Sullivan's Travels* (1941) as well as Fellini's *8½* (1963).[61]

At least as tortuous to trace as the intertextuality of *Big Shot*, however, is its

FIG. 6.3. Young emperor in the Forbidden City in *The Last Emperor*.

house-of-mirrors structure. We have already seen how the film includes within itself at least two other films, Tyler's remake of *The Last Emperor* and Yoyo's "making-of" documentary; but on top of that, in an ending that spirals nearly out of control and presents the kind of epistemological quandary mentioned earlier, the spectator is challenged to reconsider the authorship of the entire film just viewed and faced with the prospect of infinite regression. As it turns out, Tyler does not die, but rather emerges from his coma just as his own funeral preparations are picking up steam and becoming a Chinese media sensation in their own right. From his hospital bed, Tyler becomes fascinated with the whole project, declares Yoyo to be "brilliant," and refuses to stop the process by letting Yoyo know that he is not in fact dying.[62] The farce only comes to an end when Lucy finally becomes fed up and tells Yoyo the secret. Then, after an ellipsis of several months, we see Lucy visiting Yoyo in an insane asylum, where he is apparently still convinced that Tyler is dead and that the funeral preparations must go on. (Other inmates are humorously portrayed as capitalists of various sorts making frenzied, deluded plans to cash in on China's growing prosperity.) Lucy assures him that Tyler has fully recovered, has mollified all the angry advertisers by selling the advance rights to his real funeral, and is in fact now making a film about the whole incident. Then, just when Yoyo is about to be given electroshock therapy, he suddenly reveals to Lucy that he has only been feigning madness to escape the wrath of the funeral advertisers. Shortly thereafter, the

FIG. 6.4. Shot from set of *Big Shot's Funeral* (*The Last Emperor* remake).

madcap comedy scenes in the mental hospital are suddenly interrupted by a shout of "Cut!" by Tyler himself. It turns out that the whole scenario was part of Tyler's new film—which raises the question of the "authorship" of everything we have just seen. In the final analysis, could the whole story turn out to have been the version orchestrated and filmed from the perspective of the American auteur, who is thus creating yet another Hollywood image of China?

At this point, however, the multiplicity of possible perspectives and layers of illusion in the end cannot help but call the viewer's attention to *Big Shot's Funeral* itself, an elaborate and feverish fantasy created by the Chinese director who has shown over the years that he can compete with Hollywood at its own game. The tables are turned once again, then, when we realize the Westerner Tyler's direction of the whole caper is in fact just part of the fiction created by Feng Xiaogang himself. This is dramatized in a way that also allows Feng to partially undermine the "clichéd happy ending" that he has said he was forced to add to fit the *hesuipian* formula.[63] With Lucy and Yoyo's complicity, Tyler decides the film ("his" film, that is) must end with the couple kissing, thus finally consummating their previously sublimated romantic-comedy attraction, hints of which had been sprinkled at various points in *Big Shot*, as if as an afterthought, to fit the generic precedents of Feng's previous *hesuipian*. In the (seemingly) final shot, only Tyler is visible, looking directly into the camera and urging the couple, who are being filmed by Tyler's own camera operator: "Come on guys, I'm not going to say 'cut' until you kiss . . . Cut!" The screen then goes blank as we hear Tyler repeat "Cut!" twice more to let us know that the kiss continues. Here the soundtrack music surges and the movie seems to end on this romantic-comedic note, but then the image suddenly returns to show Tyler passing out and collapsing once again, as he had when shooting the earlier film. It quickly turns out that he is only playing a practical joke, but the added scene nevertheless allows Feng Xiaogang to subtly undercut the senti-mental ending of the kiss, framing it with ironic distance as merely the corny ending to Tyler's film-within-the-film.

To sum up, by the end of *Big Shot*, the multiplicity of texts-within-texts has resulted in an unstable *mise-en-abyme* structure that again calls to mind the reflexive self-undermining of Romantic irony.[64] As already noted, *Big Shot* not only makes direct intertextual references to *The Last Emperor* and *Sorry, Baby*; it also contains no fewer than three films-within-the-film: the "shooting-of" documentary shot by Yoyo, the *Last Emperor* remake that Tyler begins to shoot (and an "MTV kid" presumably finishes), and the new film Tyler decides to make about the events surrounding his own "comedy funeral." And while the very last scene inserted after the "Cut!" obviously belongs to the most "outside" layer of the film we are watching, *Big Shot's Funeral* itself, it is nevertheless un-clear whether other parts of what we have seen should be taken as the "real" events as they happened (the same "outside" layer) or as dramatizations for Tyler's second film-within-the-film; that is, since we realize retroactively that the latter was certainly the case for the scenes in the insane asylum, we cannot be entirely sure about all the preceding scenes. Yet if there is such instability of enunciation inside the film, the outside shell, the unseen authorship of Feng Xiaogang, suggests itself as the only stable authority over the text. The most fundamental critical, even political, message of *Big Shot* may in fact lie not in its social satire of rampant commercialization in contemporary China, but rather in the gesture of authorial control of the means of intercultural representation by the director.

The Geopolitics of Spectatorship and
Class Politics of Culture

As mentioned earlier, in the wake of the success of *Crouching Tiger, Hidden Dragon*, which made over $100 million in America and over $200 million worldwide, Columbia Pictures invested in *Big Shot's Funeral* in the hope of cashing in on the sudden, perceived popularity of Chinese-American coproductions starring an international mix of actors. Feng Xiaogang himself had harbored hopes of competing for mass audiences internationally even before *Big Shot*. He had offered *Be There or Be Square*—at the time China's most commercially successful film ever—for a mere $30,000 to anybody in Hollywood who wished to distribute it in America, but he was not so much as given a counteroffer. With *Big Shot*, however, it appears that both the director and Columbia Pictures were hoping for an international hit.[65] Its performance in mainland China, where it earned $4.8 million to beat *Be There*'s record, certainly portended well, but that was followed by a disappointing release in Hong Kong in early 2002.[66] By the time the film was finally released in the West that fall, the studio seemed to have given up on it, failing to give it significant distribution or advertising, so that few American filmgoers would even have been aware of it. Thus it turned out that the geography of *Big Shot*'s commercial success was the exact reverse of that of *Crouching Tiger, Hidden Dragon*, which had bombed in mainland China and made only mediocre sales in Hong Kong after being a sensation in North America.

The reasons for the failure of *Big Shot* to make inroads into the Western mass audience for Feng Xiaogang are no doubt many and varied. One film festival–goer who viewed it at the Toronto International Film Festival described it thus in his blog: "the film tries to do too much, goes on too long, is badly acted whenever some of the Chinese cast speak in English . . . and is way too slapstick."[67] The film is indeed uneven, and most bilingual viewers would agree that Ge You is not nearly as funny in broken English as he is in Chinese, and that Rosamund Kwan strikes a discordant note acting in English next to Sutherland—not because her English is less than fluent, but because her acting is far less assured than his. Perhaps more important, so much of the film's satire is specific to the Chinese context that Western audiences would be unable to get

many of the specific jokes, even though the broad outlines of the satirical targets would be clear (commodification, fame, greed, and so on). In fact, Feng's
films in general are so regionally flavored with Beijing slang and in-jokes that
they tend to make an inordinately large percentage of their profits in the vicinity of the capital, being much less popular in the Chinese south.[68]

In another sense, however, the problem of *Big Shot* in America may have
been not so much its unfamiliarity in some respects as its excessive familiar-
ity in others. Western audiences—from the mass audience of *Crouching Tiger,
Hidden Dragon* to the more limited art-house audiences of the Fifth Generation—have long shown their willingness to consume cinematic depictions of
a mythical, exotic China. Also, as the previous chapter describes, they will turn
out for films that excel at a cinematic style currently fashionable on the art-film
circuit, such as the aestheticized long-take realism of Jia Zhangke, or for films
that, like his, offer views of Chinese poverty or social oppression. However,
Westerners are apparently far less inclined to consume images of a China that
looks not so different from any other contemporary urban milieu. In fact, there
is a certain irony when we compare the geographical success of the directors
that have been the focus of the last two chapters. Jia Zhangke's first three feature
films, depicting ordinary Chinese people in the interior provinces, got great
attention abroad but no domestic distribution, despite the director's craving
for recognition at home; in contrast, Feng Xiaogang's early *hesuipian*, depicting
savvy, worldly consumers in a cosmopolitan metropolis, found phenomenal
success at home but little distribution abroad, despite the director's craving for
audiences in the West.

At this writing, Feng in fact may be poised to score a hit with Western audiences, but only by catering to their appetite for a mythical, exotic China characterized by martial arts battles and beautiful, doomed women. His period martial arts piece *Ye yan* (The banquet, 2006), very loosely based on *Hamlet*, is a
coproduction of Huayi Brothers—the Beijing-based coproducers of *Big Shot's
Funeral*—and the Hong Kong-based Media Asia. With major stars including
Feng regular Ge You, Hong Kong's Daniel Wu (Wu Yanzu), and internationally
known mainland starlets Zhang Ziyi and Zhou Xun, the film is a big-budget
(nearly US$19 million) production that aims at the type of over-the-top visual
impact achieved by such global hits as *Crouching Tiger, Hidden Dragon* and

Yingxiong (Hero; dir. Zhang Yimou, 2002; to be discussed in the next chapter). However, it received a decidedly unenthusiastic critical response both in China and at its initial Western screenings in film festivals including Cannes and Toronto in 2006. Moreover, in both China and the West, audiences responded to the film with laughter—presumably not the intended effect—at its overwrought melodrama and awkwardly classical dialogue.[69] Nevertheless, less than three weeks after its release, *The Banquet* (which does not count as *hesuipian* due to its early autumn release) was reportedly on track to break the box-office records of all of Feng Xiaogang's previous films.[70]

In fact, in retrospect, the set of films examined in this chapter appear to constitute an initial phase of Feng's directing career that has since ended. The basic formula of his early *hesuipian*—romantic comedy combined with an ironic sense of humor and a great deal of metacinematic play (with emphasis moving from the former to the latter in the progression from *Party A* to *Be There* to *Big Shot*)—was replaced at first by a much more didactic, moralizing formula that even bordered on the thematic territory of the state-sponsored "main melody" films.[71] This began with *Sigh* in 2000 and continued, after *Big Shot's Funeral*, with *Cell Phone* and *Tianxia wu zei* (A world without thieves, 2004), all of which were essentially moral fables in which threats to ethics raised by contemporary postsocialist society are overcome by characters who learn to become better, more altruistic people in the course of the film. This type of feel-good pedagogical drama seemed to have become a mini-genre in itself engaged in by China's elite directors around the turn of the century, a phenomenon deserving a study in its own right.[72] In any case, such films appear to depart greatly from the films examined in this chapter.

Feng's turn to more solemn topics may have been due in part to the critical dismissal of his earlier films by the cultural establishment in China. That is, while the director attained the very type of celebrity he spoofed in *Big Shot*—frequently appearing on television talk shows and in press gossip pages, for example—what he did not achieve was wide acceptance by the Chinese intellectual and critical community. Particularly in the late 1990s, when his first three *hesuipian* had their great commercial success, the Chinese intelligentsia viewed him as just another of the crass "hooligans" who were merely "pandering to the vulgar" and "mocking everything" (see Chapter Two). Leading Beijing film scholar and cultural critic Dai Jinhua dismissed Feng's *hesuipian* as "cultural fast food."[73] An associate of Fifth Generation auteur Zhang Yimou remarked that "Feng is brilliant at taking piles of rubbish and turning it into a delicious Coca-Cola. It's a tragedy for the culture."[74] Similarly, film critic Wang Zhen was quoted as huffing, "We are shocked by Feng's superficial motives, outdated film skills and astonishing lack of creativity. It falls under the banner of commercial filmmaking."[75] This was no doubt due partly to his frequent association with the chief cultural "hooligan" himself, novelist and media entrepreneur Wang Shuo, but it also betrays a more general anxiety over the appearance of entertainment cinema in PRC filmmaking, one of the defining characteristics of which had for several decades been a "deep-rooted seriousness in its self-conception and presentation."[76]

These critics were in part reacting against the fact that the domestic entertainment cinema of Feng Xiaogang brings Chinese film inexorably into the new era of globalized commercial culture. It offers an alternative form of national cinema, but one that concedes in advance many of the axioms of mainstream Hollywood: that cinema is a profit-driven business, that audiences first and foremost seek pleasure rather than edification, and that there are certain tried-and-true formulas which, however clichéd they may be, can reliably produce audience pleasure and thus profits. These premises are at loggerheads with the maxims of Chinese artists and intellectuals that prevailed through much of the twentieth century, when domestic political crises and external threats engendered an unceasing, deadly serious search for truth combined with a functionalist view of art as a means for fashioning public consciousness for higher purposes.

By the turn of the century, the dizzying pace of change in China no longer felt like a crisis to Feng: "I think China now is in a comic era. A lot of things that scholars see as problems or as tragic I see as very comical."[77] While this may fit critics' views of Feng as one who merely "mocks everything," it actually belies the self-critical element inherent in the reflexivity that Feng had built into his early *hesuipian*. Recalling again Robert Stam's distinction, particularly with *Big Shot's Funeral* Feng's reflexivity becomes not merely ludic—that is, simply entertaining—but also partly "didactic" as in the case of Godard, with his incessant interrogation of cinematic convention. This aspect makes it no less enjoyable as a comedy, but it is a comedy in an ironic mode that demands significant distanciation by the viewer. The tremendous popularity of the film in fact suggests an extremely sophisticated Chinese viewing public, which delights in sorting through a variety of cinematic and cultural codes and conventions without entirely investing in any of them. Such viewing habits are no doubt due partly to the skill, highlighted by James Donald and Stephanie Hemelryk Donald, the Chinese public developed at reading the political subtexts or constituting absences of films made from the Mao era onward to fashion particular forms of political subjectivity or allegiance. For such a public, "a system of textual referentiality is organized around ironic involvement in a shared history."[78] At the same time, the ironic aesthetic in contemporary China manifested by Feng Xiaogang's *hesuipian* indicates as well a healthy dose of skepticism toward the new age of globalized capitalism with Chinese characteristics, including the forms of consumption and enjoyment it promotes. In fact, for a population that continues to study Marx as part of the standard curriculum in public education, humorous critiques of commercialization and the commodity form may attract a more discerning enjoyment in China than in North America.

Speculation on the psychology of their consumption aside, there is no doubt that Feng's *hesuipian* have been on the cutting edge of changes in film production in the age of privatization and globalization of the Chinese film industry. Especially telling is the mutually profitable collaboration between private capital and public agencies to produce the early *hesuipian*. Clearly the mainstream of Chinese film production is no longer heteronomously organized by the state to serve straightforward ideological purposes (nor even to produce groundbreaking art, as was the case in certain state studios of the 1980s). Nor, however, is mainstream film production now generated entirely by private capital responding to market forces. Instead, the combination—some might say unholy alliance—of private and state concerns produces a cinema that takes some chances, aims to make money, and yet is sufficiently politically connected to leap through the bureaucratic hoops that continue to be presented by the institutions controlling censorship, distribution, and exhibition in China. This combination of heteronomy and autonomy, public and private, in the film industry represents a microcosm of the Chinese economy as a whole under postsocialist modernity.

Moving on to the new century and the later films of Feng Xiaogang, he has exemplified yet more important new trends, most notably the globalization of Chinese film production. The participation of Sony/Columbia Pictures in *Big Shot's Funeral*, even if it did not lead to overseas commercial success for the film, nevertheless combines with such films as *Crouching Tiger, Hidden Dragon* and *Kill Bill* (dir. Quentin Tarantino, 2003/2004) to represent a new level of cooperation between the Chinese film industry and its counterparts overseas. Contrary to what might be expected, such cooperation does not merely result in a master-disciple relationship in which Chinese film professionals learn from their more sophisticated counterparts in the West. In the case of *Big Shot*, press reports noted that the Westerners involved in the film were very impressed with the different working habits and skills of Feng Xiaogang and his crew.[79] The making of *Kill Bill* also resulted in a deluge of press reports on the financial efficiency (due partly to lack of unionization) and professional talent available to filmmakers in China, to the point that the Chinese industry almost came to represent an "outsourcing" threat to film professionals in Hollywood. Finally, with *A World Without Thieves*, Feng was at the forefront of yet another new development in the rapidly transforming Chinese film industry. A 2003 agreement exempting Hong Kong films from the import quotas that had previously applied equally to Hong Kong and Hollywood meant that as long as they passed censorship (often achieved by having two different final cuts of a film), an unlimited number of Hong Kong films could be shown in China. More important, the new rules encouraged the already rising fluidity of film talent and capital between Hong Kong and the mainland, making coproductions more attractive to both industries. The Hong Kong studio Media Asia Films, fresh from the financial success of its *Infernal Affairs* trilogy, signed Feng in early 2004 to make *A World Without Thieves* as one of the earliest projects developed in response to the new rules. Such growing Hong Kong and international influence is viewed by some as a boon to mainland Chinese national cinema and by others as its death knell—a distinction that may well revolve around the question of precisely what vision of a national cinema is in question, rather than whether an industry in some form will survive and even thrive.

Returning finally to the films examined at length in this chapter, we can interpret the metacinematic element of Feng Xiaogang's early *hesuipian* along a number of different lines of reasoning. First, as mentioned earlier, it would seem to fit the historical argument that metacinema appears in popular films precisely when the industry is thrown into crisis—in this case, by the multiple threats of foreign competition in the newly opened market combined with the spread of television ownership and video piracy in the course of the 1990s. In this reading, Feng's metacinematic films represent an interrogation of the dynamics of the Chinese film industry and its place in world cinema: in *Party A, Party B*, the "One-Day Dream Trip" company approximates the fantasy-fulfillment business that is popular cinema, even borrowing its name from Feng's own earlier film and television production company; *Be There or Be Square* depicts a Chinese film crew operating in Los Angeles, just as Feng's own crew was, showing the effort of Chinese filmmakers to turn the representational tables on Hollywood; *Big Shot*, finally, sends up the other side of the coin by showing a Western auteur failing in an attempt to render an exoticized, mythical China onscreen. Aside from such obvious metacommentary on the conditions of film production, however, there is a second and more fundamental metacinematic element of these films, which is precisely the self-conscious toying with the basic dynamics of viewer pleasure and identification, as mentioned earlier. By reflexively presenting and then undermining the cinematic illusion, I have argued, Feng gets at an essential element of film as entertainment that precedes even film itself and goes back to the "magic theater" and the Phantasmagoria of the nineteenth century, showing that audiences' enjoyment at being immersed in an illusion comes partly from their simultaneous awareness of its status as illusion.

The investigation into the form of entertainment cinema carried out by Feng's early *hesuipian* thus amounts to a reflection on *entertainment* itself as an autonomous cinematic function. That is, the need for metacinematic discourse comes not just from an industrial crisis but also from the ideological crisis facing postsocialist Chinese cinema and culture in general. After decades in which entertainment value, while certainly present, was nonetheless always placed in the service of some higher purpose—whether that of instilling revolutionary consciousness in the 1950s–70s or that of promoting cultural enlightenment in the 1980s—it would now stand as a goal in its own right; a film could be made to entertain holiday audiences and nothing else. Of course, following the pattern we have seen frequently in preceding chapters, the autonomy of entertainment from political or social agendas is in the final analysis only a relative one generated by the market; the reason entertainment arises as an apparent end in itself is in fact that it produces box-office revenues and thus profits for both public and private studios and production companies facing unprecedented competition. Consequently, the crisis of the Chinese cinema, both industrial and ideological, is characteristic of the postsocialist condition of newly marketized societies in general, in which relative autonomy appears as an aspect of a transition from state heteronomy to market heteronomy. In Russia as well, for example, the post-Soviet "crisis" in the film industry resulted both from economic difficulties and from the domestic audience's turn to foreign films. Thus Feng Xiaogang might find his counterpart in Aleksei Balabanov, who, as Susan Larsen notes, went from directing "defiantly uncommercial" art films in the early 1990s to choosing "aggressively commercial material" a few years later. In doing so, he followed the principle that, as Russia's Association of Young Filmmakers put it, "It is the audience's love that must become in future the fundamental and most natural form of support for national cinema."[80] Indeed, although national cinemas, in their traditional conception as an alternative to Hollywood, are generally thought of in their art-film manifestations (German Expressionism, Italian Neorealism, the French New Wave, and so on), in the economic environment of global capitalism and "free" trade, the survival of a significant domestic Chinese film industry may well depend more upon the apparent new autonomy of entertainment value than the excellence of a handful of art-film auteurs.

7

Conclusion:
Postsocialist Modernity's Futures

One of the paradigmatic geographical settings dramatizing the recent rise of China as a world power is the Pudong district of Shanghai, where some of the world's tallest skyscrapers are rising. More precisely, the setting I have in mind is the spectacular Pudong skyline as seen from the Bund (*Waitan*), the stretch of riverfront in Puxi across the Huangpu River from Pudong. It has become a cliché to describe this setting as the point where China's past and future meet: on the west side of the river are the neoclassical and art deco buildings of Shanghai's former colonial occupiers from the late nineteenth to early twentieth centuries, while on the east are twenty-first-century high-rises and the fanciful futuristic design of the Pearl Tower, rising like a giant Tinkertoy construction to fairly scream the news of China's forward march into the new millennium.[1] Implied in the comparison is the idea that China has finally "stood up" (*zhan-qilaile*), first by shaking off its imperialist occupiers through the anti-Japanese war and the communist revolution, and then by advancing to the forefront of the world economy during the post-Mao economic miracle.

What interests me about this image is the question of who is gazing from the Bund, metaphorically in "old" China, to the Pudong skyline, emblematic of the "new" China of the future. It may of course be a Shanghai commuter changing buses, a businessperson out to grab lunch, or a foreign tourist following the advice of a guidebook. However, one thing such a tourist would note is that, while the Bund is one of the most likely places to find plenty of foreigners in China, ironically it is also one of the few places in Shanghai where a foreigner is apt to attract many stares of curiosity. The reason for this is of course that the throngs of sightseers on the Bund are dominated not by foreigners, nor by Shanghainese, but rather by domestic tourists—people who come from all over China, including many from the overlooked cities, small towns, and rural villages where most Chinese live, but which are largely absent from accounts of Chinese culture and society today, which generally highlight metropolises on the vanguard of postsocialist modernization. For these tourists, foreigners are part of the spectacle of the Bund, just as is the dramatic Pudong skyline.

If we imagine for a moment a rural Chinese resident embodying this gaze—perhaps not even a tourist but a migrant worker who has come to live illegally in Shanghai in a desperate attempt to get ahead, pay for a child's schooling or a sick parent's health care, or any number of other reasons—we can discern the very structure of the ideology of postsocialist modernity in China. This traveler or migrant worker does not belong in a Pudong skyscraper, will certainly never work in an office or live in an apartment there, but the spectacle of this "new China" is enticing and even in some sense a source of pride. Is this strikingly modern China not what the Chinese people have worked so hard and suffered so much for? And yet the wide Huangpu River lies in between the gazer and the object of the gaze, and it requires an ideological leap of faith for the identification of the viewer with the object to succeed, for the illusion of a look into the future to be convincing to a particular individual who seems to exist in a different world from Pudong's sleek, shiny modernity.

Teleological Ideology and Abjection

In the importance of the *future* to the ideology of postsocialist China, we find yet another justification for insisting on postsocialist *modernity*. Postmodernity has long been defined in part as the condition after the end of teleology, after the loss of faith in all sorts of master narratives.[2] However, the legitimacy of the political and economic power structure of post-Mao China has relied more than anything else on a master narrative of progress, which is fundamental to the ideology of modernity. As Christopher Prendergast argues, modernity should not "be identified with a 'completed' form (or as far as we have got with it) of industrial and technological modernization, which is, rather, a feature of postmodernity. Instead, modernity is tied to a situation of 'incomplete' modernization. It is a structure of hope, fear and fantasy invested in an emergent formation and a possible future."[3] In the case of postsocialist China, this future is no longer as definable as was the communist utopia promised by Maoism, but the rhetoric of progress remains nonetheless. This rhetoric is evident in the prominence of the suffix *-hua* (equivalent to the English *-ize* or *-ization*) in so many buzzwords of the reform era, from the "Four Modernizations" (*si ge xiandaihua*) of the Deng Xiaoping era to the marketization (*shichanghua*), pluralization (*duoyuanhua*), individualization (*gerenhua*), and differentiation (*fenhua*) of the period covered in this book. In all of these cases, the suffix *-hua* indicates a dynamic process of becoming, marking the reform era as a period of transition rather than simply a "new state of affairs."[4]

Kevin Latham has argued that this is the key to the continued ideological legitimacy of the Chinese Communist Party (CCP) after the end of communism, as "the hegemony of the Party works discursively through a number of 'rhetorics of transition' . . . which require the notion of a rapidly changing and developing society. If China were to be perceived to stop changing, these rhetorics of transition would become meaningless, or—worse—they would be seen to be false."[5] These rhetorics involve not a singular telos but rather "a whole spectrum of alternative teleologies"—a transition to a market economy and consumer paradise, a transition to a civil society and democracy, or indeed, officially, still a transition to socialism of some vague nature.[6] Under these rhetorics of transition, "any discontent with the present is downplayed in order not to endanger the imagined future."[7] Thus, returning to our imaginary visitor to the Bund, the question is whether the vision of the Pudong skyline is sufficient to gain the ordinary Chinese citizens' imaginary investment in the promised future of a modernized China, to make them feel that they are somehow included in that vision despite their demonstrable current distance from it.

In previous chapters, we have encountered a number of real and fictional characters who appear in danger of being left behind in various ways by postsocialist China's march into the future—the Shanghai "humanist spirit" scholars, the listless monads of Zhu Wen's fiction, the impotent former village chief in *Ermo*, the small-town slackers and migrant workers of Jia Zhangke's cinema. In the novel *Shouhuo*, gifted satirical author Yan Lianke sketches an entire hamlet that has somehow been left behind by China's modern history.[8] "Shouhuo" is a difficult-to-translate regional colloquialism that has been rendered as "enjoyment" in English, though "grin and bear it" might be more accurate. In any case, in Yan Lianke's novel it is the name of a fictional southern village that is so cut off from society as a whole that it has had little interaction with the outside world and does not even appear on maps. Moreover, the entire population of the village suffers from one or another physical deformity or disability. After the village has encountered various tribulations during the Mao years, in the reform era County Magistrate Liu tries to make it the base of a new effort to survive in the market age through a harebrained scheme to buy Vladimir Lenin's embalmed corpse and put it on display as a tourist attraction—a perfect, darkly comic illustration of postsocialist marketization. The crippled folk of Shouhuo Village are enlisted to help realize this plan by touring the region as a traveling freak show. Much of the novel consists of bitingly humorous commentary on the typical characters and slogans of postsocialist China, with its get-rich-at-any-cost mentality. In the end, of course, the plan fails, and not only do the villagers decide to drop out of the wider society (*tuishe*) again, but County Magistrate Liu chooses to join them, even intentionally maiming himself so that he will be a "normal" Shouhuo villager.

While the satire of *Shouhuo* is multifaceted and often hilarious, its most basic ideological intervention is arguably to reject the very "rhetorics of transition," with their implied teleologies, that Latham has described. The crippled villagers of Shouhuo represent a fantasized existence outside of history itself, suggesting the possibility of escaping both revolutionary communist modernity and postsocialist capitalist modernity to retreat into a timeless alternate universe invisible to the outside world. While such a space is presented as utopian only in a parodic sense, it nonetheless represents at least the yearning for something else, some escape from the madness of modernity in general. The greatest irony may be that this fantasized Chinese space that can escape modernity is populated entirely by deformed people, who still in some sense appear less sick than the society they seek to escape. Thus, now that China has "stood up" and may finally take its rightful place as an equal to the nations that had once colonized it and exploited its weakness, there paradoxically appears a nostalgia for the "sick man of Asia," the condition associated with the original confrontation with an invasive capitalist modernity during the Qing Dynasty. Just as the villagers of Shouhuo experience their condition as normal and see outsiders as freaks, the "sick man of Asia" was likewise a matter of perspective, of being defined by an external power and placed within an imperialist world-system that was itself fundamentally pathological. In seeking to step off the juggernaut of modernity,[9] the Shouhuo villagers in fact suggest the utopian potential of a state of *abjection*—in the original meaning of the word as being cast off, rejected, or excluded. Their physical abnormalities are a metaphor for their desire to exist outside of modern history, a desire as aberrant as it is perhaps sane.

Globalized Primitive Accumulation

The fantastical nature of the fictional Shouhuo Village, however, indirectly points to the inescapable reality of postsocialist modernity. In fact, the destitution of many of the rural people in the novel *Shouhuo* in part realistically portrays the actual conditions that yet prevail in much of China, complicating all the rhetoric about an economic miracle. Returning to the broad question, introduced in Chapter One, of the place of postsocialist modernity in the history of global capitalism, it should be emphasized that much of the economic growth of post-Mao China has occurred under conditions of primitive accumulation, or what David Harvey prefers to call "accumulation by dispossession" to accentuate the fact that it in many cases involves a direct, involuntary transfer of wealth from the many to the few.[10] As all kinds of collective enterprises in China, from vast state-owned factories to small village workshops, have been closed or sold off to private interests, all too often the workers who ostensibly shared ownership in them have been inadequately compensated, have not been compensated at all, or have lost associated pension benefits, housing, health care, and so on.[11] As urban areas sprawl, development increases, and property values appreciate, countless corrupt village chiefs have sold land that was supposed to be collectively owned and pocketed most or all of the profits themselves.[12] Even rural local governments that are not corrupt have in many cases fallen into bankruptcy, forcing them to sell off collective property.[13] In urban areas as well, the nationwide dismantling of much of the social welfare infrastructure has deprived people of many of their former social assets. As people across China lose their "iron rice bowl" (guaranteed employment and benefits for life) and go to work in privately owned Chinese or foreign enterprises, they not only give up their previous welfare and security but also completely lack the crucial right to form unions and make collective demands of their new employers; the only unions that can legally represent them are those under the CCP-dominated All-China Federation of Trade Unions, which in fact generally represents the priorities of management rather than workers (so much so that even the notoriously antiunion Wal-Mart has welcomed their presence in its stores in China).

One result of this capitalist accumulation by dispossession has been a most-ly invisible but growing revolt of workers and peasants across China. According to official government statistics, there were no fewer than 74,000 violent mass protests in 2004 and 87,000 in 2005, some of them fierce battles of entire rural populations against hundreds or even thousands of police, often spurred by the theft of peasant land by corrupt officials or broken promises to laid-off work-ers.[14] Though triggered by specific incidents, this violence is in part an erup-tion of generalized anger over the vast disparities in China today. The current urban-rural income gap is officially given as 3.3 to 1, but the Chinese Academy of Social Sciences puts it at 7 to 1 when factors like social services, health care, and education are included.[15] Besides instances of violent revolt, across rural China many of the dispossessed have taken up various strategies of "rightful resistance," which "operates near the boundary of authorized channels, em-ploys the rhetoric and commitments of the powerful to curb the exercise of power, hinges on locating and exploiting divisions within the state, and relies on mobilizing support from the wider public." In particular, given the legacy of socialism and its continued nominal validity in official discourse, the weak and disenfranchised can in some cases effectively use existing "laws, policies, and other officially promoted values" to oppose local political and economic elites.[16] Despite the various forms of resistance offered by the rural poor, how-ever, the overall trend of growing income disparity continues.

I have argued that postsocialist modernity is a global condition. Nowhere is this more evident than when one traces the intimate connections between the contemporary economic conditions of the PRC and the United States, which in some ways recall the Cold War's irrational structure of "mutually assured destruction" (MAD). Much attention has been focused, for example, upon the way the two states have together propped up the value of the dollar, creating a bubble that neither side can afford to see burst.[17] The essential dynamic is that China (along with Japan, Taiwan, and South Korea) finances U.S. public and private spending in various ways, allowing the U.S. government and consumers to accumulate unprecedented debt without suffering the usual consequences of high interest rates, tax hikes, and a currency crash. If China were to cease buttressing the dollar, the resulting U.S. recession would send the world economy into decline and stall the engine of China's own economic boom. The question of how this unsustainable situation resolves itself will likely be a major factor determining the fate of U.S. global hegemony as well as whether and how the Chinese and other East Asian economies can emerge from any future global economic crisis and possibly even come to dominate the world economy, in whatever form it will take as the twenty-first century progresses.

Perhaps more relevant to the daily lives of ordinary people today, though, is the growing income inequality in both the United States and China. None other than Morgan Stanley's own chief economist, Stephen Roach, has exposed the tenet that globalization is a "rising tide that lifts all boats" as a delusion, at best.[18] In a global economy in which the Internet and other technologies collapse all distances, the phenomenon of "global labor arbitrage" allows capital throughout the world to take advantage of China's low labor costs and lack of union empowerment while outsourcing the jobs of first-world workers. As a result, while the rich get richer in both the United States and China, most of the population experiences "brutal wage compression." The Gini indexes (the standard measure of income disparity, in which zero represents total equality and 100 total inequality) of China and the United States are among the highest of all the world's major economies, and both have risen to an identical level in recent years. American workers have seen their wages stagnate in the last several decades even as productivity skyrocketed, and the U.S. Gini index rose steadily from 35 in 1970 to 45 in 2004.[19] The change in China is even more dramatic, with the exact same rise—from 35 to 45—occurring just between 1990 and 2003 (roughly the period covered in this book). In an ostensibly socialist society, the average income of the richest 20 percent of Chinese workers is now more than twenty times that of the poorest 20 percent. Moreover, in an age when TV and video make it even into impoverished rural regions, the poor are well aware of the hedonistic new consumer lifestyle they are being left out of (and indeed helping to pay for), which no doubt in part fuels the growing instances of unrest mentioned above.

Contradiction and Critique

As Roach makes clear, the economic trends in China and America cannot be fully understood without reference to each other, since both take place in the context of globalization. Moreover, as I argued in the introductory chapter, globalization must be understood more broadly as a phenomenon of world-wide postsocialist modernity. In the case of China, globalization is inseparable from the transition from socialism to capitalism, a transformation that in turn changes the landscape of the global economy. The primitive accumulation and rising income disparities that have accompanied this process have provoked increasingly direct opposition, from the peasant revolts in China to the protests against the World Trade Organization in Seattle in 1999. Thus capitalism's global triumph in the postsocialist age inevitably generates its own contradiction—and the "post" in *postsocialism* may well turn out to be as premature as that in *postmodernity*. In Latin America, for example, after two decades of rightist economic restructuring failed miserably in its promise to alleviate poverty among ordinary people, a new leftist movement has been ascendant from Cape Horn to the Rio Grande, with socialist-leaning governments taking power in more than a half dozen countries and falling short in Mexico only through massive electoral fraud.

In China itself the New Left (*xin zuopai*) has arisen among intellectuals to challenge what had been largely a liberal consensus. In 1997 Wang Hui published the landmark essay "Contemporary Chinese Thought and the Question of Modernity" in the journal *Tianya* (Frontiers), arguing that many of China's current problems arose from capitalist modernization itself, not from the remnants of traditional feudalism or Maoist communism.[20] Moreover, Wang wrote, after the demise of communism in Eastern Europe and the former Soviet Union, "global capitalism has advanced to a new historical stage and China's postsocialist reforms have already led to the complete incorporation of the country's economic and cultural processes into this global market."[21] Wang concludes that if "East Asia could be turning its accustomed peripheral position in the former world capitalist system into the economic center of the new world capitalist order," then the important task before scholars is to explore "the internal contradictions of the capitalist mode of production in the twenty-first century."[22] Wang argues that the idea that continued globalization, capitalist modernization, and the legitimizing "teleology of progress" would solve China's problems must be opposed by critical thinkers. In fact, since "the future designs of global capitalism . . . do not promise to overcome the crisis of modernity," Chinese intellectuals now have "a historic opportunity for theoretical and institutional innovation."[23]

While Wang Hui's pioneering essay was roundly criticized by liberal Chinese intellectuals at the time, several events of the next few years—including the Asian financial crisis, the increases in corruption and income disparity in China, and the growing suspicions of American power following the NATO bombing of the Chinese embassy in Belgrade, the American spy plane incident in 2001, and the U.S. war in Iraq—led increasing numbers of scholars and students to oppose the uncritical acceptance of globalization and capitalist modernization as natural and positive developments.[24] Even some ostensible liberals, such as He Qinglian, dared to write detailed, damning, and widely read exposés on the corrupt practices of primitive accumulation in the new economy.[25] While they certainly do not yet equal—either in numbers or proximity to power—the legions of followers of Friedrich Hayek and Milton Friedman among China's economists and other social scientists, the rise of the New Left among intellectuals nonetheless has shown beyond any doubt that a comprehensive and clear-sighted critique of China's contemporary situation (far beyond the "humanist spirit" arguments of the early and mid-1990s), is not only possible but well under way, driven by the increasingly strained contradictions of Chinese culture and society.

In fact, there appears to be a resurgence of socialist consciousness even within the CCP leadership (a phenomenon that reveals a dirty secret long overlooked by American politicians and media: that throughout the reform era there has arguably been more ideological diversity *within* China's one party than there is between the mainstreams of America's two). In early 2006 the National People's Congress was expected to rubber-stamp a new law to protect private property ownership, but instead sharp criticism by legislators concerned about rising income inequality and social unrest caused the bill to be shelved for a year before finally being quietly passed under a near media blackout. Despite proceeding with such measures, the new leadership after Jiang Zemin's retirement, President Hu Jintao and Premier Wen Jiabao, significantly shifted the rhetoric of top officials to emphasize social equity and the fight against corruption rather than just rapid development and growing wealth. Political leaders and the official press have trumpeted a campaign for a "new socialist countryside," including the restoration of basic health insurance and free public education for poor rural children.

The Conscience of a Poet

None of this, of course, yet represents any fundamental turn away from global postsocialist modernity in China. Unlike the Shouhuo villagers, most Chinese are inescapably swept along by the tides of marketization and globalization. However, just as a number of scholars in China are reflecting increasingly critically on these phenomena, critiques by artists are also becoming more developed. By way of a conclusion, I will briefly discuss a few examples, tracing in particular the theme of various sorts of global imaginaries—which sometimes contradict one another—in these works.

One example is the independent film *Xiang jimao yiyang fei* (Chicken poets, dir. Meng Jinghui, 2002), a visually flamboyant, absurdist black comedy that is also an ultimately moving fable on the fate of the arts in China's economic boom as well as the difficulty of maintaining the idealism of youth. Frustrated poet Ouyang Yunfei arrives in the Beijing suburbs to visit his old friend Chen Xiaoyang, who had also been a poet but is now a successful young entrepreneur who farms black-feathered chickens and markets their black eggs. Yunfei meets Fang Fang, a local colorblind woman who keeps trying and failing to get a job as a flight attendant. In a series of incidents of escalating absurdity, Yunfei wrestles with his acute claustrophobia, the temptation to sell out his art, and his complicated relationships with his old friend and his new love interest.

Facing a writer's block in his pursuits in pure literature, he helps the chicken entrepreneur Xiaoyang to write catchy advertising slogans. Then he makes a Faustian bargain with a hawker of pirated video disks, buying a CD-ROM that promises to make its user a successful poet. Carefully shielding his actions from others, Yunfei overcomes his creative drought by entering parameters (a title and a poetic school or style) into the computer program, which then mysteriously churns out complete, well-formed poems. Soon Yunfei has achieved incredible fame as a poet, appearing on television talk shows and writing advertising jingles with catchy choruses like "This is our poetic life!" However, by the end of the film Xiaoyang has abandoned his chicken farm, Fang Fang has disappeared as well, and Yunfei's guilt over selling out has caught up with him.

Yunfei's conscience, and by extension that of the arts in contemporary society, is represented throughout the film by the Soviet poet Vladimir Mayakovsky. The first shot of the film is a dramatic close-up of a photograph of Mayakovsky's face, in which the poet stares intently into the camera. Yunfei's voiceover narration states: "The Soviet poet who died at thirty-seven loved to recite in places where people gathered. They say his voice was loud and clear and his mind was nimble. The young men and women of his time were crazy with love for him. They would recite along with him just like young people today sing along with their favorite pop singers."

The next shot is of Yunfei himself facing the camera. A tomato flies from offscreen and smashes against his head, after which the photo of Mayakovsky reappears, this time with tomato juice dripping over the image of the poet's face. The framing tightens until just the poet's intense, almost angry eyes fill the screen. This image of Mayakovsky reappears several times during the film (which features periodic cutaways to nondiegetic shots that provide a sort of cryptic, imagistic commentary on the diegetic events). In the end, Yunfei drops his sham career as a celebrity and concludes, "If I want to be a poet, I should live a completely different life." In the last scene he has shaved his head to look like Mayakovsky himself, and his final voiceover narration quotes Mayakovsky's maxim that "people must choose their way of life and have the courage to uphold it."[26]

Chicken Poets as a whole thus serves as a parable on the selling out of the arts in an age of commerce, and in fact it is in many ways a high-culture, art-cinema version of the social satire of Feng Xiaogang's *Big Shot's Funeral*, as described in the previous chapter. Mayakovsky symbolizes the spirit of pure art that is being drowned under the tidal wave of commodification, but which returns as a specter to cast its damning gaze on the present. The symbol is particularly powerful considering that Mayakovsky, and the Soviet avant-garde of the 1920s as a whole, represents a utopian moment in which the arts achieved both an incredibly vital creativity and freedom of experimentation *and* an unprecedented centrality to social life in their role as instruments of revolutionary transformation. Among other things, this is a reminder that, as an alternative modernity, communism too shared a global imaginary, one which has not completely disappeared. In postsocialist China, presented this way as an ideal, Mayakovsky evokes the revolutionary aspirations of Chinese artists and intellectuals during much of the twentieth century, when art was viewed as integral to the political project of achieving a more fulfilling life; at the same time, his representation in *Chicken Poets* preserves the modernist ideal of artistic autonomy that the vision of art as revolutionary instrument eventually suppressed so thoroughly, in both the Soviet Union and Maoist China. *Chicken Poets* seems to darkly suggest that in the new market age of consumer capitalism, art can be integrated with social practice only insofar as it becomes advertising, while artistic integrity can be maintained only through the rarest of ascetic, individual personal commitments, such as that made by the solitary Yunfei at the film's end.

Aside from its broader historical concerns, *Chicken Poets* is very much a depiction of a certain generation of Chinese intellectuals, those for whom great aspirations and artistic visions formed in the 1980s gave way to all the compromises and disappointments that would end that decade's idealism in the following years. In the course of this study we have touched upon the historical reasons for this, from the violent suppression of the youth movement in Tiananmen Square to the subjugation of the culture industry to the market during the 1990s; yet the struggles of Yunfei, who is thirty-one years old when the film begins, also suggest a more universal melancholy over the lost idealism of youth and the effort needed to sustain or rekindle the passion for art that burns especially brightly when it is young.

In spite of its critique of the state of the arts in contemporary China, *Chicken Poets* paradoxically provides much evidence for the *vitality* of the arts in the same China. It was made not by a studio director, nor by an independent film auteur, but rather by China's leading avant-garde theater director, Meng Jing-hui, who cast longtime members of his own acting troupe in most of the principal roles. Despite its roots in theater, the film is a showcase of startling, stylized cinematography and daring editing. In fact, it is very difficult to imagine such a film coming out of China even a decade earlier, such is its combination of formalist experimentalism, riotous satire, confident cosmopolitanism, and direct social critique. If its story provides ample grounds for pessimism about the direction of the arts in China, its form simultaneously makes the case for a small-scale avant-garde renaissance in China—driven in large part by resistance to cultural commodification, yet often implicated in that same process.

Nostalgia and the Institutionalization of the Avant-Garde

Another recent example from the arts in China offers a similar sense of melancholy and anxiety over the direction of contemporary society, in which a more favorable environment for art must be weighed against the new, increasingly global market conditions that determine cultural output. In the video piece *Wo de weilai bu shi meng* (My future is not a dream), made in 2000 and exhibited in the massive *First Guangzhou Triennial* that opened at the Guangdong Museum of Art in late 2002, Hainan-based artist Weng Fen (*aka* Weng Peijun) edited together scenes from thirteen different Chinese films dating back to the 1950s. Selected, taken out of their original context, and juxtaposed with each other, the scenes create a new, loose narrative for the video piece.[27] The scenes from the first set of films, all either dating from or set in the Mao era, feature characters talking hopefully about their futures, which promise personal fulfillment through participation in a larger collective project: becoming a teacher after liberation, making the country prosperous, raising a flag on a new navy vessel, having better food to eat after the revolution, defeating the United States and the USSR in World War III, becoming a doctor, overthrowing oppression. A typical example is a clip from the revolutionary classic *Hongse niangzi jun* (Red detachment of women; dir. Xie Jin, 1960), in which the young heroine and her friend lie in bed together discussing their dream of someday joining the Communist Party. In the scenes from the second set of films—which includes one each from Taiwan and Hong Kong, indicating the diaspora's new relevance to the mainland imagination—the setting is contemporary and the aspirations expressed by the characters are very different. Many of them discuss making money or other personal material advancement, while two scenes from different films placed together have blind characters whose hopes are raised that their eyesight might be restored.[28]

Taken as a rough narrative in itself, the video thus traces a loss of the idealism and collective identifications of the Mao era in favor of much more personal, practical, and arguably selfish or myopic ("blind") goals, particularly the pursuit of money. Like *Chicken Poets*, it evokes a nostalgia for a lost period of idealism, this time not that of the cultural enlightenment movement in the 1980s but that of the previous age of revolution. Such nostalgia for the idealism of the Mao era reminds us that communist ideology was not simply a distant and alienating official discourse but also informed the daily lives of ordinary people. As Alexei Yurchak points out in the case of Russia:

for great numbers of Soviet citizens, many of the fundamental values, ideals, and realities of socialist life (such as equality, community, selflessness, altruism, friendship, ethical relations, safety, education, work, creativity, and concern for the future) were of genuine importance, despite the fact that many of their everyday practices routinely transgressed, reinterpreted, or refused certain norms and rules represented in the official ideology of the socialist state. . . .

An undeniable constitutive part of today's phenomenon of "post-Soviet nostalgia," which is a complex post-Soviet construct, . . . is the longing for the very real humane values, ethics, friendships, and creative possibilities that the reality of socialism afforded—often in spite of the state's proclaimed goals—and that were as irreducibly part of the everyday life of socialism as were the feelings of dullness and alienation.[29]

In China, too, nostalgia for the Mao era is widespread and takes many forms, from the bittersweet Fifth Generation film romanticizing the 1950s, Zhang Yimou's *Wo de fuqin muqin* (The road home, 1999), to the enthusiastic amateur performances of revolutionary songs and dances by middle-aged and elderly park-goers across China to the present day. The fondness with which revolutionary ideals are commemorated itself acts as an implicit rebuke to the much more individualized and commercialized values of the postsocialist era.

Indeed, it is worth reflecting upon the fact that in the video *My Future Is Not a Dream*, even some of the film clips recalling the Mao era are in fact from films made in the 1990s but *set* in the revolutionary period. Given the contemporaneity of those films, not to mention the video piece that edits them together, it is evident that the idealism of the 1950s and 1960s is not simply a past state of being but something that is actively reconstructed through representation under postsocialist modernity; a feeling of meaningfulness and utopian purpose is constituted retroactively in a move that is as much a productive resituating of the present via the (imagined) past as it is mere nostalgia for the past.

In this sense, all such contemporary expressions of yearning for a bygone era of idealism, meaning, and purpose should perhaps not be taken at face value, since in some fundamental way they contradict their own premise. That is, the *imagination* of the state of idealism or collectivity occurs in an ongoing present, so that insofar as the resources of past imaginaries are deployed actively to critique the present, their ideals (or at least the ideal of *having* ideals) must still remain in effect, if only in an often repressed form in the current consumer culture. Such expressions should not be taken to mean that significant numbers of artists or intellectuals in fact wish for a return to the days of Maoism, nor even to the inspiring but (in retrospect) naive "culture fever" of the 1980s; instead, the memory of past idealisms serves as a reminder that the Chinese public has not in fact entered some eternal postmodern present in which the cultural slate is simply wiped clean and ready for an endless play of consumer stimulations and simulations. History cannot be so easily excised, and if China is now in a new age of postsocialist modernity, it nonetheless bears the imprint of the unique path it took to get there, which could yet influence its trajectory into the future.[30]

Returning to *My Future Is Not a Dream*, a final lesson may be drawn from this rather melancholy and undeniably powerful video when one steps back from the piece itself to consider the context in which it appeared. The *First Guangzhou Triennial* was unprecedented in its scope, quality, and institutional support structure. An obvious point of comparison would be the *China/Avant-Garde* exhibition from over a decade earlier, in which 297 works from across China were displayed at the National Gallery in Beijing in 1989, only weeks before the students would begin gathering in Tiananmen Square. Much of the art in that exhibit was political and confrontational, and in fact the authorities closed the exhibition twice, the first time only hours following the opening after the artist Xiao Lu shot a pistol at a reflection of herself in a mirror during a performance. No further such large exhibits were attempted inside China during the next decade, up until the *First Guangzhou Triennial* itself. Thus the exhibition not only documented a decade of Chinese art following the *China/Avant-Garde* show but also was something of a milestone in its own right. In contrast to the controversy and political confrontation of the earlier show, the *Triennial* was successfully held in the new public exhibition space provided by the Guangdong Museum of Art, which had opened only five years earlier, and the exhibition was curated by the American-based Chinese art historian Wu Hung and kicked off with an international conference of scholars and museum professionals. In short, the show evinced the far greater space of autonomy that had opened for art over the previous decade, even in the case of publicly financed institutions. Moreover, the art itself had not necessarily grown tamer; the guiding label of *experimental* (*shiyan*) was explicitly defined as indicating an alternative, marginal, and even oppositional space for art and artists in relation to mainstream society.[31]

Then again, the institutionalization of the avant-garde as it enters the major museums and the academy is itself a way of taming its radical tendencies, as is already an old story in the West. Chinese artists might well barely finish celebrating their new freedom before they lament their concurrent lack of political relevance, in an echo of the dilemmas of the "humanist spirit" scholars examined in Chapter Two. Such are the ironies of the arts in contemporary China; as a Beijing punk rocker is quoted as saying, "because the government doesn't care about us, we are not forbidden from playing. Maybe we are not dangerous. It's sad."[32]

The international collaboration that occurred for the *First Guangzhou Triennial* indicates a general trend over the course of the reform era, during which the international market for visual art has absorbed a striking number of Chinese artists, to the point that many are now essentially within the mainstream of global artistic discourse. A transnational network of elite galleries and museums—from Beijing, Shanghai, and Hong Kong to Manhattan, London, and Chicago—now regularly features contemporary Chinese artists, and a casual browse through a current issue of *Art Forum* or *Art in America* would verify that Chinese artists are no longer peripheral oddities on the world art scene.

However, much as was the case with independent Chinese filmmakers succeeding on the transnational art-film market (see Chapter Five), this phenomenon has also generated a backlash among artists in China, who criticize some of their peers for cravenly catering to foreign collectors and curators at the expense of their integrity and their integral connection to conditions in China itself. Some exhibitions in China even began to take the form of a sometimes grotesque protest against the international art market. For example, a two-day show in Beijing entitled *Post-Sense, Sensibility, Alien Bodies, and Delusion* included works that featured a real human cadaver and a stillborn fetus encased in ice, a severed human arm hanging from a ceiling, and a live goose with its feet glued to the floor, slowly starving to death. Despite the possible inspiration of such controversial Western artists as Damien Hirst, this show was no desperate attempt to gain more attention from the world art market; instead, according to an assistant curator at one of Beijing's most prestigious galleries, these artists were "purposefully trying to create works that can't be sold, especially not to Westerners."[33] In other words, from the apparent political subversion against the communist state a decade earlier by artists who had thereby gained access to a share of the world art market, now an entirely new form of radical resistance was appearing in the Chinese art world, taking the most negative form possible and opposing none other than the world art market that had become the dominant force in the contemporary Chinese visual art scene, at least at its most elite levels.

Heroes and Migrants in the World

In the realm of popular culture as well, a few artists have managed to make a significant impact on the global cultural market. One example is the blockbuster film *Yingxiong* (Hero; dir. Zhang Yimou, 2002), which broke all the domestic box-office records that had been set by the series of Feng Xiaogang's *hesuipian* discussed in the previous chapter. *Hero* told the story of legendary assassins who plotted to kill the Qin Dynasty emperor Shihuang, who first unified China in the third century B.C., as vengeance for the acts of violence he had perpetrated in extending his rule across the land. In the end, the assassin Wu Ming ("no name"), after finally facing the emperor and thus becoming able to attempt the assassination, is instead persuaded to sacrifice his own life in the recognition that the emperor's previous harsh measures were necessary in order to fulfill the higher cause of China's unity. The film attracted some criticism in the Western media for being an ideological justification for China's authoritarian government, which had used violence to rein in peripheral territories such as Tibet and threatened to do the same in Taiwan, and for which the causes of national unity and social stability are often invoked to justify repressive measures. Interestingly, some criticisms that popped up on Chinese Web sites took an alternate view, parodying the film as a justification for George W. Bush's unfettered application of military power throughout the world at a time when the American administration was building up to its disastrous invasion and occupation of Iraq in the name of an elusive higher good.[34]

As these contrasting views indicate, *Hero* was a complex phenomenon which I will only touch upon briefly, but a few of its aspects are especially worthy of attention in the present context. First, it is another example (after *Big Shot's Funeral*, as discussed in the previous chapter) of a film that attempted to recreate the international success of *Crouching Tiger, Hidden Dragon* with a production that drew big-name talent from a number of different sources to make a Chinese film that would have worldwide appeal. It included some of the top stars from both mainland China (Zhang Ziyi) and Hong Kong (Jet Li, Maggie Cheung, Tony Leung) and employed Christopher Doyle, the Australian cinematographer who had played a key role in the distinctive look of the films of the internationally acclaimed Hong Kong director Wong Kar-wai. The fight sequences also followed the venerable Hong Kong tradition of martial-arts cinema, being choreographed by Hong Kong industry veteran Ching Siu-tung, who had also directed such genre classics as *Qiannü youhun* (A Chinese ghost story, 1987) and *Xiao ao jianghu zhi Dongfang bubai* (Swordsman II, 1991). Finally, *Hero* was perhaps the most spectacular visual statement yet made by Zhang Yimou himself, whose early films, with their careful color schemes and striking compositions, had done much to establish the lush visual style of the Fifth Generation.

Miramax bought the rights to release *Hero* in North America, but its distribution was delayed for over a year and a half as the company pondered whether to cut it severely or possibly not release it at all. When in 2004 it was finally released in a full-length cut at Quentin Tarantino's urging, the film led the United States box office—a first for a Chinese film—for two weeks and earned over $50 million during its American run. In other words, it accomplished what Feng Xiaogang had hoped to achieve in getting North American distribution for *Big Shot's Funeral*: it became a record-breaking blockbuster in both China and the West.

Such global attention is still rare for Chinese popular cultural products; as discussed in the first chapter, even growing economic hegemony by no means ensures a prominent place in world cultural space. Nevertheless, the box-office success of *Crouching Tiger, Hidden Dragon*, *Hero*, and *House of Flying Daggers* has established that at least a certain middle-brow combination of Hong Kong–style martial-arts action and Fifth Generation aestheticism has been inscribed as representing Chinese culture in the global popular cinema marketplace. Moreover, as we have seen, since the early reform era the Chinese presence has expanded remarkably in the arenas of high visual culture, including gallery and museum art as well as art cinema.

For example, since making the films explored in detail in Chapter Five, Jia Zhangke's global reputation has only grown. His first film to pass the censors and gain official distribution in China, *Shijie* (The world, 2004), continued the attempt to realistically represent those generally unrepresented in contemporary China—the poor, migrant workers, youth with no actual prospects to match the aspirations raised by globalization. At the same time, the stylistic aestheticization discussed earlier in the cases of *Platform* and *Unknown Pleasures* was expanded, particularly with the addition of oneiric animation sequences that are interspersed in the narrative.

The World takes its name from the Beijing theme park in which it is set—an attraction consisting of reduced-scale replicas of major global landmarks, ranging from the Notre Dame Cathedral to the lower Manhattan skyline.[35] The park's slogan, "See the world without leaving Beijing," combined with its staff of migrant workers from the interior provinces that had been the setting for Jia Zhangke's previous films, set up an obvious (indeed, at times almost *too* obvious) allegory about the empty promises that globalization holds for the ordinary people of China. The opening sequence of the film establishes a front-/backstage distinction, as the main protagonist, Tao (played by Jia favorite Zhao

Tao, who had acted in *Platform* and *Unknown Pleasures* as well), who works as a dancer for the theme park, interacts with her fellow employees backstage while preparing for an elaborate dance routine to entertain the park customers. The relaxed chitchat of the dancers backstage, as costumes are donned and make-up applied, contrasts with the formal elegance of their onstage dance routine. These dances, which appear several times in the film, are faux cultural experiences reminiscent of Las Vegas–style entertainment; in one routine, for instance, the dancers vaguely mimic a stereotype of Egyptian pharaoh culture.[36] Most of the film, however, concentrates on the real lives and relationships of the park's low-wage workers, who have been drawn to Beijing due to lack of opportunity at home, only to become stuck in dead-end jobs in the tourist industry. This front-/backstage dynamic, alternating between the illusory cosmopolitanism peddled by the theme park and the actual hardscrabble lives of its workers, is a reworking of one of Jia Zhangke's claims to realism that goes back to his first feature-length film, *Xiao Wu*: a contrast is drawn between representation and reality, between spectacle and "real" life, or indeed between the new teleologies of progress, globalization, and consumerism on the one hand, and most people's actual, intractable conditions of existence on the other. The distinction is baldly spelled out during the title sequence of the film. The shot that accompanies the film's title, "The World," is of a hunched-over old peasant figure, bearing an impossibly huge load on his back, walking across the screen in the foreground as the surreal image of the theme park's fake Eiffel Tower looms behind him in the background; here the rhetoric of globalization's illusions versus the postsocialist real is asserted from the outset of the film.

The World, however, brings to the fore a complication in this portrayal that had been more or less implicit in *Xiao Wu*, *Platform*, and *Unknown Pleasures*: the "real" experiences of the films' characters are themselves not distinct from the representations and technologies of mass communications but rather are unavoidably already mediated through them. Thus Xiao Wu's last remaining shred of hope, to which he clings even after his arrest at the end of the film, is that his negligent girlfriend will contact him via the pager he bought for that purpose. The young cultural troupe members in *Platform*, while straining against the straitjacket of the cultural ideology left over from the Mao era, forge their new identities partly through the new imaginaries of youth fashion and pop music, their "real" lives being not distinct from mass-mediated representations so much as caught between those of the official discourse and the emerging consumer culture. In *Unknown Pleasures* as well, to the extent that the young slacker-protagonists have utopian ideals, they are embodied through media representations such as the cartoons of the "Monkey King" Sun Wukong, who personifies the absolute freedom they so clearly lack.

The World, while still depending for its narrative force upon the distinction between the illusions of media and ideology on the one hand and the hard conditions of real life on the other, nonetheless makes this distinction even more problematic than in the previous films. This is nowhere more evident than in the five animation sequences in the film, all of which are motivated by text messages received by the characters on their cell phones. These sequences present a bit of a puzzle of enunciation: are we to take these as being imagined by the characters receiving the text messages, or are they rather an interpretive commentary provided by the narrative as a whole? Since the mood of the animation seems to reflect that of the characters, it would seem to be at least in part a representation of their imagination, showing that their relations to their own "real" conditions of existence are mediated through an imaginary best captured by the popular cultural form of animation. These semisubjective fantasy sequences range from uplifting images of aerial flight during moments of joy or release, to a melancholy sequence following Tao's revelation, made by the accidental viewing of a cell phone message, that her boyfriend has been having an affair (a discovery reminiscent of Feng Xiaogang's *Cell Phone*, discussed in Chapter Four).

The cell phone/animation sequences of *The World*, combined with the similar evidence from Jia Zhangke's earlier films, imply a view of these young migrant workers' lives that is not as simple as the illusion-versus-reality rhetoric suggested elsewhere in the same films. Instead, we are forced to recognize that in some very basic sense the "reality" of postsocialist modernity lies not in a "real" life condition that simply belies the illusions of global capitalism, nor in the utopian consumer imaginary of the contemporary mainstream media discourse in China—but rather precisely in the gulf between the two, a distance that is materialized in the lives of the films' characters. The protagonists of *The World* strive, partly through the mediations of technologies such as cell phones and animation, to build new networks of both relationships and meaning out of the rubble of postsocialism. Their real lived condition is neither that of family-based traditional society, nor that of revolutionary communism, nor the promised consumer paradise of global capitalism. Instead, they struggle to make a new life caught between all of these—attempting to preserve the kinship ties to their hometowns while simultaneously making new connections within the newly globalized labor force that has absorbed them, all the while negotiating the elusive temptations of media spectacle and commodification.

The World depicts these struggles and negotiations of the postsocialist condition as globalized in a concrete sense beyond the global imaginary of the media, the most striking example being the friendship between women workers who can communicate not by language but only by their shared suffering and exploitation. Soon after four new Russian women arrive at the "World" theme park to work as performers, Tao strikes up a friendship with one of them, named Anna. Communicating despite their lack of a common language, Tao learns that Anna has left a husband and two children in Russia and has a long-lost sister in Ulan Bator, whom it is her "dream" to save up enough money to visit. The women bond at least in part due to their shared experience of displacement by the global postsocialist economy and their common plight as commodified—and, as it turns out, trafficked—bodies on display. This is made more explicit as the film progresses and we find that the performers are also expected to accompany wealthy guests in karaoke bars. In a key sequence, a crass, rich Chinese businessman attempts to talk Tao into accompanying him on a business trip to Hong Kong in a thinly veiled solicitation of prostitution. She manages to extract herself from the situation, only to run into Anna, whom she discovers has, in her desperation, succumbed to a similar offer. The two devastated women weep in each other's arms, an image of transnational postsocialist solidarity as well as despair.

Indeed, the vision of postsocialist modernity offered by *The World* darkens by degrees as the film progresses. Circumstances force Anna into prostitution, a hometown relative of Taisheng's is killed in a construction accident while working overtime at night, and finally Tao and Taisheng both die mysteriously in what might have been a joint suicide or a murder-suicide. The solemn final scene of their bodies being removed is mitigated by the enigmatic insertion of a voiceover in which Taisheng asks, "Are we dead?" and Tao replies, "No. We only just began." This hint of optimism, however meager and illogical, adds to the dollops of hope found earlier in the film—the cross-cultural friendship of Tao and Anna, the loyalty of hometown friends to each other, the flights of fancy of the animation sequences.

In spite of these uplifting moments, *The World*, as with Jia Zhangke's films in general, can be taken as the cinematic equivalent of the trenchant critiques of postsocialist modernity in China offered by New Left intellectuals such as Wang Hui. In this context, however, it is interesting to note that Jia Zhangke's sympathy for the losers within the new globalized economy comes despite the fact that he has become quite the "successful personage" (*chenggong renshi*— see Chapter Five) himself. Not only did *The World* win censorship approval and official distribution in China—a first for Jia's films—but it also benefited from his usual international funding (receiving production funds from Japan and France in addition to China) and distribution (it premiered at the Venice International Film Festival and went on to festivals worldwide). As of this writing, his follow-up feature, *Sanxia haoren* (Still life, 2006) has won the Golden Lion in Venice and is set to be officially distributed in China. A companion piece, the documentary *Dong* (2006), filmed simultaneously, appears to reflect critically on the filmmaker's own stance in depicting the plight of postsocialist modernity's vast underclass. Here the apparent proxy for the director is the artist Liu Xiaodong, who paints portraits of such subjects as demolition workers at the Three Gorges Dam project in China and young female prostitutes in Thailand. Though the film is not unsympathetic to Liu Xiaodong, it does implicitly meditate upon the inevitable distance between the painter and the subjects he seeks to represent. As an intellectual and a successful artist based in Beijing, how indeed can Liu—or Jia Zhangke himself, for that matter—be completely comfortable in his capacity to speak for postsocialist modernity's dispossessed?

Viewers of China in the West, no matter their ideological bent, also suffer from a bit of the megalomania occasionally evident in the musings of the painter in *Dong* insofar as they take it upon themselves to diagnose China's current conditions and prescribe the proper way forward—whether that is conceived as democratic political reform, socialist economics, or theoretical projects such as deconstructing the nation and so on. The question of what sort of future global postsocialist modernity has will likely prove to be less a matter for people or powers in the West to decide than is now imagined. Though problems from cultural vulgarization to economic exploitation and ecological catastrophe now recognize no state boundaries, it may increasingly be within China that the decisions determining modernity's future are made. Nevertheless, we can perhaps begin to imagine a transnational solidarity that arises in recognition of a common fate and seeks to make that fate a product of popular will and conscious critical reflection rather than impersonal processes.

Reference Matter

Notes

1. According to Perry Link's comprehensive study, the "socialist Chinese literary system" ended in "about 1990": "By the early 1990s, extreme disillusionment with the socialist bureaucracy and a rapidly increasing role for commercialism in literary publication made the official literary establishment increasingly irrelevant." Perry Link, *The Uses of Literature: Life in the Socialist Chinese Literary System* (Princeton, NJ: Princeton University Press, 2000), 5.

2. Jiang Zemin began speaking about the Three Represents in 2000, it was officially adopted and promulgated by the Sixteenth Party Congress in late 2002, and finally the national constitution was amended to include it in 2004.

3. *China Daily*, October 18, 2002. For the section of Jiang's speech devoted to culture, see http://news.xinhuanet.com/english/2002-11/18/content_632562.htm.

4. See Shuyu Kong, "Between a Rock and a Hard Place: Chinese Literary Journals in the Cultural Market," *Modern Chinese Literature and Culture* 14 (spring 2002): 93–144; also a chapter in the same author's *Consuming Literature: Best Sellers and the Commercialization of Literary Production in Contemporary China* (Stanford, CA: Stanford University Press, 2005).

5. Cooperative publishing began in the 1980s as a way for research and educational organizations to publish their materials through the official publishing houses, but by the late 1980s it had become in many cases simply a front behind which private concerns published profitable entertainment fiction.

6. The term *post–new era* was coined by Beijing-based critic Zhang Yiwu in his article "Houxinshiqi wenxue: Xinde wenhua kongjian" (Post–new era literature: A new cultural space), *Wenyi lilun* (Literary theory) 1 (1993).

7. See, for example, Sheldon H. Lu, *China, Transnational Visuality, Global Postmodernity* (Stanford, CA: Stanford University Press, 2001); and Arif Dirlik and Xudong

Zhang, eds., *Postmodernism and China* (Durham, NC: Duke University Press, 2000). For a discussion of how the term *postmodernism* functioned within Chinese intellectual discourse, see Haun Saussy, "Postmodernism in China: A Sketch and Some Queries," in his *Great Walls of Discourse and Other Adventures in Cultural China* (Cambridge, MA: Harvard University Asia Center, 2001), 118–45.

8. This was sparked by Fredric Jameson's series of lectures on postmodernism at Peking University in 1985, though it is notable that the scholars who afterward took up the banner in China, such as Zhang Yiwu and Chen Xiaoming, did not maintain Jameson's critical distance toward postmodernism but instead embraced the concept as liberating.

9. Gao Minglu, "Post-Utopian Avant-Garde Art in China," in *Postmodernism and the Postsocialist Condition: Politicized Art Under Late Socialism*, ed. Aleš Erjavec (Berkeley: University of California Press, 2003), 247–48.

10. Fredric Jameson, *Postmodernism, Or, the Cultural Logic of Late Capitalism* (Durham, NC: Duke University Press, 1987), 45–46.

11. Niklas Luhmann, *The Differentiation of Society* (New York: Columbia University Press, 1982), 231.

12. Ibid., 198–99. Emphasis in original.

13. Karl Polanyi, *The Great Transformation* (New York: Farrar & Rinehart, 1944), 57.

14. Ibid., 71.

15. Karl Marx and Frederick Engels, "Manifesto of the Communist Party," in Marx and Engels, *Selected Works* (New York: International Publishers, 1968), 38.

16. Gilles Deleuze and Félix Guattari, *Anti-Oedipus: Capitalism and Schizophrenia* (Minneapolis: University of Minnesota Press, 1983), 33.

17. For Adorno on the contradiction between aesthetic autonomy and exchange-driven heteronomy, see, for example, Theodor W. Adorno, *Aesthetic Theory* (Minneapolis: University of Minnesota Press, 1997), 225–61.

18. My thanks to Sumanth Gopinath for suggesting this terminological distinction.

19. See, for example, the essays in the collection Gil Eyal, Iván Szelényi, and Eleanor Townsley, eds., *Making Capitalism Without Capitalists: The New Ruling Elites in Eastern Europe* (London: Verso, 1998).

20. Kevin Latham, "Rethinking Chinese Consumption: Social Palliatives and the Rhetorics of Transition in Postsocialist China," in *Postsocialism: Ideals, Ideologies and Practices in Eurasia*, ed. C. M. Hann (London: Routledge, 2002), 218.

21. Aleš Erjavec, introduction to *Postmodernism and the Postsocialist Condition: Politicized Art Under Late Socialism*, ed. Aleš Erjavec (Berkeley: University of California Press, 2003), 3.

22. Fredric Jameson, *A Singular Modernity: Essay on the Ontology of the Present* (London: Verso, 2002), 12.

23. Eyal, Szelényi, and Townsley, 3.

24. David Harvey, *The New Imperialism* (Oxford: Oxford University Press, 2003), 39.

25. Giovanni Arrighi, *The Long Twentieth Century* (London: Verso, 1994).

26. Giovanni Arrighi, "Hegemony Unravelling—1," *New Left Review* 32 (March–April 2005): 51.

27. Harvey, esp. 109, 115.

28. See Leo Panitch and Sam Gindin, "Superintending Global Capital," *New Left Review* 35 (September–October 2005): 101–23.

29. Here the terms *center* and *periphery* are intentionally borrowed from Immanuel Wallerstein's world-system theory. In a recent article, Wallerstein himself speculates that an "East Asian union" of China, Japan, and Korea could emerge as the strongest center among the "Triad of the North"—the E.U., North America, and East Asia—and that the United States may eventually even be drawn "into its camp as a sort of combined elder statesman/junior partner." Immanuel Wallerstein, "The Curve of American Power," *New Left Review* 40 (July–August 2006): 93–94.

30. Pascale Casanova, *The World Republic of Letters* (Cambridge, MA: Harvard University Press, 2004), 10–11; Casanova, "Literature as a World," *New Left Review* 31 (January–February 2005): 84–85.

31. Antoaneta Bezlova, "China's New Cultural Revolution," *Asia Times*, July 29, 2006.

32. Susan Larsen, "In Search of an Audience: The New Russian Cinema of Reconciliation," in *Consuming Russia: Popular Culture, Sex, and Society since Gorbachev*, ed. Adele Marie Barker (Durham, NC: Duke University Press, 1999), 192–93.

33. Wang Xiaoming et al., "Kuangye shang de feixu: wenxue he renwen jingshen de weiji" (Ruins in the wilderness: The crisis of literature and humanist spirit), in *Renwen jingshen xunsi lu* (Thoughts on the humanist spirit), ed. Wang Xiaoming (Shanghai: Wenhui chubanshe, 1996), 8, 13.

34. Wang Xiaoming, "Jiushi niandai yu 'xin yishixingtai'" (The 1990s and the "new ideology"), in *Jiushi niandai wen cun: 1990–2000* (Collected writings on the 1990s, 1990–2000), ed. Lin Dazhong (Beijing: Zhongguo shehui kexue, 2001), 2:286.

35. Wang Gan, Zhang Yiwu, and Zhang Weimin, "'Xin zhuangtai wenxue' san ren tan" ("New state of affairs literature" three-way discussion), in *90 Niandai piping wenxuan* (Selected works of 1990s criticism), ed. Chen Sihe and Yang Yang (Shanghai: Hanyu dacidian chubanshe, 2001), 444.

36. Wang Xiaoming et al., 11.

37. Wang Hongsheng et al., "Xiandai renwen jingshen de shengcheng" (The generation of modern humanist spirit), in *Renwen jingshen xunsi lu* (see note 33), 231.

38. Erjavec, 26.

39. Ibid., 28.

40. Ibid., 38.

41. See Slavoj Žižek, "The Fetish of the Party," in *Lacan, Politics, Aesthetics,* ed. Willy Apollon and Richard Feldstein (Albany: State University of New York Press, 1996), esp. 27.

42. C. T. Hsia, *A History of Modern Chinese Fiction* (New Haven, CT: Yale University Press, 1971), 553–54.

43. For a study of the "individualization" that accompanies the "disintegration of previously existing social forms," see Ulrich Beck and Elisabeth Beck-Gernsheim, *Individualization: Institutionalized Individualism and Its Social and Political Consequences* (London: Sage, 2002).

44. For a paradigmatic discussion of how this shift to interiority plays out in cultural texts from advertising to fiction in postsocialist China, see Xiaobing Tang, "Decorating Culture: Notes on Interior Design, Interiority, and Interiorization," in *Chinese Modern: The Heroic and the Quotidian* (Durham, NC: Duke University Press, 2000), 295–315.

45. Jason McGrath, "The New Formalism: Mainland Chinese Cinema at the Turn of the Century," in *China's Literary and Cultural Scenes at the Turn of the 21st Century,* ed. Jie Lu (London: Routledge, forthcoming).

46. Cornelius Castoriadis, *World in Fragments: Writings on Politics, Society, Psychoanalysis, and the Imagination,* ed. and trans. David Ames Curtis (Stanford. CA: Stanford University Press, 1997).

47. Ibid., 17, 86, 165. Alexei Yurchak makes a similar point in his description of ideology in Stalin's USSR, in which he cites "Lefort's paradox," that ideological rule must appear to transcend its origins, leading to the false impression of a "master" figure who is "presented as standing *outside* ideological discourse and possessing *external* knowledge of the objective truth," thus concealing the historical contingency of ideology by acting something like an ideological prophet who brings the Truth from beyond. See Alexei Yurchak, *Everything Was Forever, Until It Was No More: The Last Soviet Generation* (Princeton, NJ: Princeton University Press, 2006), 10. (Emphases in original.)

48. Ibid., 62.

49. Chen Sihe, ed. *Zhongguo dangdai wenxue shi jiaocheng* (A course in the history of contemporary Chinese literature) (Shanghai: Fudan University Press, 1999), 338.

CHAPTER TWO

1. Wang Xiaoming, "Women nengfou zouchu shiyu de kunjing" (Can we escape the predicament of aphasia), *90 niandai sixiang wenxuan* (Selected works of 1990s thought), ed. Luo Gang and Ni Wenjian (Nanning: Guangxi renmin chubanshe, 2000), 1:430; originally published in Wang Xiaoming, *Cicongli de qiusuo* (Searching in the briar patch) (Shanghai: Shanghai yuandong chubanshe, 1995).

2. Ben Xu, following Dong Zhilin, traces the origin of the discussion to a defense of

Wang Shuo and his so-called hooligan literature published by leading author and critic Wang Meng earlier in 1993. This essay is indeed significant for the later development of the debate insofar as Wang Meng may have taken the Shanghai scholars' following critique of Wang Shuo as an indirect attack on himself. However, most sources acknowledge the panel discussion in *Shanghai wenxue* as the instigator of the "humanist spirit" phenomenon, and I follow this view on the grounds that it was the first publication to foreground the very concept of "humanist spirit." See Ben Xu, *Disenchanted Democracy: Chinese Cultural Criticism after 1989* (Ann Arbor: University of Michigan Press, 1999), 37; and Wang Meng, "Duobi chonggao" (Avoiding nobility), *Dushu* no. 1 (1993): 10–17.

3. By September 1995, Wang Xiaoming estimated the number of articles he had personally seen in the "humanist spirit" discussion at over one hundred, and Huang Lizhi later put the figure at "nearly 200." See Wang Xiaoming, ed., *Renwen jingshen xunsi lu* (Thoughts on the humanist spirit; hereafter *RJXL*) (Shanghai: Wenhui chubanshe, 1996), 270; and Huang Lizhi, *Zhongguo huayu: dangdai shenmei wenhua shilun* (Chinese discourse: historical essays on contemporary aesthetic culture) (Beijing: Zhongyang bianshi chubanshe, 2001), 211.

4. Zhu Xueqin, in Zhang Rulun et al., "Renwen jingshen: shifou keneng yu ruhe keneng" (Humanist spirit: Is it possible and how is it possible), in *RJXL*, 32; originally published in *Dushu* no. 3 (1994).

5. Wang X. et al., "Kuangye shang de feixu: wenxue he renwen jingshen de weiji" (Ruins in the wilderness: The crisis of literature and humanist spirit), in *RJXL*, 1–2; originally published in *Shanghai wenxue* no. 6 (1993).

6. Ibid., 2.

7. Ibid., 2.

8. Liang Qichao, "On the Relationship Between Fiction and the Government of the People," in *Modern Chinese Literary Thought: Writings on Literature, 1893–1945*, ed. Kirk Denton (Stanford, CA: Stanford University Press, 1996), 74–81.

9. Hu Shi, "Some Modest Proposals for the Reform of Literature," in *Modern Chinese Literary Thought: Writings on Literature, 1893–1945*, ed. Kirk Denton (Stanford, CA: Stanford University Press, 1996), 123–39.

10. *Meisu*, which I am translating here as "pandering to the vulgar," has also been used as a Chinese translation for *kitsch* since the 1980s; however, here the meaning clearly is not simply *kitsch*, so the reverse translation is inappropriate. Geremie R. Barmé, who translates *meisu* as "kowtowing to the vulgar," traces the genealogy of the term in *In the Red: On Contemporary Chinese Culture* (New York: Columbia University Press, 1999), 301–2.

11. Wang X. et al., 3, 5. As a result of such "identification with the ruins," Wang Shuo's novels were said to amount to "a ruin mocking a ruin" (ibid., 9). This analysis recalls Horkheimer and Adorno's description of "the self mockery of man" through the

culture industry: "One needs only to become aware of one's nullity, to subscribe to one's own defeat, and one is already a party to it." Max Horkheimer and Theodor Adorno, *Dialectic of Enlightenment: Philosophical Fragments* (Stanford, CA: Stanford University Press, 2002), 123.

12.   Wang X. et al., 6. In their critique of Zhang Yimou, the panel participants repeatedly condemn as "imitation postmodernism" the style of films such as *Da hong denglong gaogao gua* (Raise the red lantern). However, here *postmodernism* seems to function as a catchphrase for what might more accurately be called a kind of modernist formalism, or a mannerism in cinematography and mise-en-scène that calls attention to itself. The film's visual style (long-shot compositions, minimal camera movement, repetition, obsessively symmetrical framing, heavy-handed symbolism) has little to do with postmodernism but much to do with the established (modernist) aesthetics of international art cinema.

13.   Ibid., 8.

14.   The limited English literature on the humanist spirit debate disagrees over whether *zhongji guanhuai* should be translated as singular (ultimate concern) or plural (ultimate concerns). Moreover, Sheldon H. Lu shifts the grammar of the phrase by translating it as "concern with the ultimate," which indeed occasionally seems most appropriate. Sheldon H. Lu, *China, Transnational Visuality, Global Postmodernity* (Stanford, CA: Stanford University Press, 2001), 81. I choose to translate it generally as plural (since the singular falsely implies that the humanist critics had a specific, identifiable "concern" in mind), but I vary my usage according to what seems to render the Chinese source most intelligibly.

15.   Zhang R. et al., "Renwen jingshen," 19, 22.

16.   This is a notable phenomenon in itself, often visible in the humanist spirit discussion and in academic discourse in general during the reform era: when criticizing an opponent's perceived reliance on some imported theoretical orientation, the theory itself is rarely attacked; instead, the domestic manifestation of it is described as fake, immature, or lacking in genuine understanding of the Western original. Thus, for example, postmodernism's denial of transcendence is excoriated in China but declared as valid in the West because it "came after a build-up process." Even nihilism is condemned only in its Chinese form, with the critic careful to exclude the more authentic Western nihilism, which is said in contrast to leave the "possibility of creating an even higher meaning" (thus paradoxically becoming a form of idealism). See Wang X. et al., 11, 10. The broader irony of this phenomenon is of course that, in effect, the authority of the West is invoked in order to discredit those who make use of "Western" theories.

17.   Zhu Xueqin, in Zhang R. et al., "Renwen jingshen," 20.

18.   Zhang Rulun, in Zhang R. et al., "Renwen jingshen," 20.

19.   Wang X. et al., 12. This idea of disguised retreat and self-deception provoked one

of the more memorable images of the "humanist spirit" debate, given by Cui Yiming in the same panel discussion. Deploring the "self-satisfied" commercial literature of the day, he compared it to "a tubercular patient preening his muscles on the bodybuilding stage. Actually it's only powerful lights and a thin film of olive oil that gives people a kind of sensory stimulation." Wang X. et al., 15.

20. Wang X. et al., 10. The term refers to the famous Lu Xun character, who convinces himself that his humiliations are actually triumphs.

21. Over many articles, the humanist critics made multiple references to several Western sources including Kant, Hegel, Marx, Wittgenstein, Habermas, Gadamer, the Frankfurt School (en masse), and Daniel Bell, to name some of the more prominent examples.

22. See especially Zhang R. et al., "Renwen jingshen," 20–31. For a lengthy discussion of the distinction between the ostensibly broader notion of *renwen jingshen* and the narrower Western *humanism,* see Zhang Rulun and Lin Hui, "Guanyu renwen jingshen" (On the humanist spirit), in *RJXL,* 156–60; originally published in *Wen lun bao* (15 January 1995).

23. See, for example, Chen Sihe's comments on Confucius in Zhang R. et al., "Renwen jingshen," 21; and Chang Guangyuan's citation of the Confucian concept of "benevolence" (*ren*) as a manifestation of "humanist spirit" in Chang Guangyuan, Zhang Li, and Meng Dengying, "Zai shiji bianyuan muge: renwen jingshen duihua lu" (Pastoral song at the brink of the century: record of a conversation on the humanist spirit), in *RJXL,* 255; originally published in *Zuojia bao* (Author report) (29 July 1995).

24. Chen Sihe, "Guanyu 'renwen jingshen' taolun de liang feng xin" (Two letters concerning the 'humanist spirit' discussion), in *RJXL,* 154.

25. Meng Fanhua, "Xin lixiangzhuyi yu zhishifenzi yishixingtai" (The new idealism and intellectual ideology), in *RJXL,* 250; originally published in *Guangming ribao* (Guangming daily), July 5, 1995.

26. Zhang Zhizhong, "Renwen jingshen er bian" (Humanist spirit debate again), in *RJXL,* 176.

27. Ibid., 177.

28. On the sought-after humanist spirit as a "sublation" of that of the 1980s, see Wang Yichuan, "Cong qimeng dao goutong: 90 niandai shenmei wenhua yu renwen jingshen zhuanhua lungang" (From enlightenment to communication: the aesthetic culture of the 1990s and an outline for the transformation of the humanist spirit), in *RJXL,* 208–9; originally published in *Wenyi zhengming* (Literature and arts contention) no. 5 (1994). For an example of the view of the 1980s as a now-faded "renaissance" of the May Fourth spirit, see Gao Ruiquan et al., "Renwen jingshen xun zong" (Tracking the humanist spirit), in *RJXL,* esp. 35–37; originally published in *Dushu* no. 4 (1994).

29. Xudong Zhang also divides the critical response to the humanist critique into

two camps, "the old liberal-humanist establishment" and a "younger generation of literary and cultural critics." My formulation differs only in that I add the (young) Wang Shuo and his cohorts to the former camp. See "Nationalism, Mass Culture, and Intellectual Strategies in Post-Tiananmen China," in *Whither China? Intellectual Politics in Contemporary China*, ed. Xudong Zhang (Durham, NC: Duke University Press, 2001), 328–29.

30. Wang Meng, "Renwen jingshen wenti ougan" (Random thoughts on the question of the humanist spirit), in *RJXL*, 116; originally published in *Dongfang* (Orient) no. 5 (1994).

31. Bai Ye et al., "Xuanze de ziyou yu wenhua taishi" (Freedom of choice and cultural trends), in *RJXL*, 87, 89, 90; originally published in *Shanghai wenxue* no. 4 (1994). The latter two comments must be understood as having a certain tongue-in-cheek quality.

32. Ibid., 97–98.

33. Ibid., esp. 88–91.

34. Ibid., 95.

35. Wang M., "Renwen jingshen," 108, 111.

36. Ibid., 108–9.

37. Ibid., 111.

38. Ibid., 113.

39. Wang Meng, "Hushang si xu lu" (Long-winded record of thoughts in Shanghai), *Shiji zhi jiao de chongzhuang: Wang Meng xianxiang zhengming lu* (Clash at the turn of the century: record of controversy over the Wang Meng phenomenon), ed. Ding Dong and Sun Min (Beijing: Guangming ribao chubanshe, 1995), 78.

40. See Thomas Frank, *One Market Under God: Extreme Capitalism, Market Populism, and the End of Economic Democracy* (New York: Anchor Books, 2000).

41. Ibid., esp. 30–31.

42. Qu Weiguo, "Weiji? Jinbu?" (Crisis? Progress?), in *RJXL*, 104; originally published in *Dushu* no. 8 (1994).

43. Bai et al., 97.

44. Chen Xiaoming, "Renwen guanhuai: yizhong zhishi yu xushi" (Humanist concerns: a kind of knowledge and narrative), in *RJXL*, 120–28; originally published in *Shanghai wenxue* no. 5 (1994).

45. Ibid., 122–23.

46. Zhang Yiwu, "Renwen jingshen: zuihou de shenhua" (Humanist spirit: the last mythology), in *RJXL*, 137–41; originally published in *Zuojia bao*, May 6, 1995.

47. The most notable example was Zhang Rulun, who by 1995 was arguing that "actually the appearance of this crisis or the loss of the humanist spirit did not occur with the development of the market economy," and in fact, "quite the opposite, the develop-

ment of the market and the improvement of the material life conditions of the Chinese people should actually become crucial conditions for the renewal and development of the humanist spirit." Zhang and Lin, 164–65. The previous year, before the counteraccusations of Wang Shuo, Wang Meng, and Chen Xiaoming, the same critic had been blaming "the irreversible spread of instrumental reason" and "the great clamor of consumerism" for the loss of "ultimate values." Zhang R. et al., "Renwen jingshen," 22.

48. Bai et al., 93.

49. Yuan Jin, in Gao et al., 34.

50. Chen Shaoming, "Ba jieshi jutihua—ye tan renwen qifen de danmo" (Concretize the explanation—on the haziness of the humanist atmosphere), in *RJXL*, 201; originally published in *Xianzai yu chuantong* (Modern and traditional) no. 5 (1994). In reflections written after the debate had died down, Wang Xiaoming would acknowledge the critique of the excessive scope and vagueness of the term *humanist spirit* by scholars such as Chen Shaoming as the most "reasonable" of the attacks against him. See Wang Xiaoming, "'Renwen jingshen' lunzheng yu zhishifenzi de rentong kunjing" (The "humanist spirit" debate and intellectuals' identification difficulties), *90 niandai sixiang wenxuan* (Selected works of 1990s thought), ed. Luo Gang and Ni Wenjian (Nanning: Buangxi renmin chubanshe, 2000), 449; originally published in Chen Qingqiao, ed., *Shenfen rentong yu gonggong wenhua* (Status identification and public culture) (Hong Kong: Niujin Daxue chubanshe, 1997).

51. Zhang and Lin, 158, 164; Wang Y., 206–7.

52. Zhang and Lin, 157.

53. Zhang R. et al., "Renwen jingshen," 26.

54. Zhang and Lin, 158.

55. Zhang Y., 137.

56. Zhang R. et al., "Renwen jingshen," 29.

57. Ibid., 26–27.

58. Ibid., 25.

59. Ibid., 30.

60. See Fredric Jameson, *Postmodernism, Or, the Cultural Logic of Late Capitalism* (Durham, NC: Duke University Press, 1987), 154–80.

61. Ibid., 163–65.

62. Xiaobing Tang, "Melancholy Against the Grain: Approaching Postmodernity in Wang Anyi's Tales of Sorrow," in *Chinese Modern: The Heroic and the Quotidian* (Durham, NC: Duke University Press, 2000), 316–40.

63. Ibid., 339.

64. Wu Xuan et al., "Women xuyao zenyang de renwen jingshen" (What type of humanist spirit do we need?), in *RJXL*, 68; originally published in *Dushu* no. 6 (1994).

65. Ibid., 70.

66. Michael Hardt and Antonio Negri, *Empire* (Cambridge, MA: Harvard University Press, 2000), 21.

67. Ibid., 323. In fact, *Empire* suffers from the same shortcomings as the "humanist spirit" critique, insofar as its presentation of the problem is weakened by the vague and sometimes self-contradictory suggestions it offers to resist it. As a result, it ironically reinforces its own argument that there seems to be "no place left to stand," insofar as it ultimately fails to find any firm new basis of resistance.

68. The loss of legitimacy of a classical Marxist critique of capitalism in China by the early 1990s occurred on many levels, some of which should be obvious from the preceding discussion. An explicitly class-based critique of capitalism would have been accused of simply trying to return to an earlier historical moment even more forcefully than was the "humanist spirit" position. The excesses of Maoism and particularly the Cultural Revolution provided ample fodder for critics such as Wang Meng to guard against any rallying cry of class struggle. Moreover, the official CCP ideology remained ostensibly Marxist, so that such a stance could have seemed to the humanist critics to align themselves once again (albeit in a different way) with the government that had betrayed them in 1989. Nevertheless, as the decade progressed, a class-based critique reappeared in critical discourse in the form of the "New Left" and even in the later writings of Wang Xiaoming himself (see Chapters Five and Seven).

69. Wang Hui, "Contemporary Chinese Thought and the Question of Modernity," *Social Text 55* 16.2 (summer 1998): 12, 37. Originally published as "Dangdai Zhongguo de sixiang zhuangkuang yu xiandai xing wenti" (Contemporary Chinese thought and the question of modernity), *Tianya* (Frontiers) (October 1997), 133–50; English translation also available in Wang Hui, *China's New Order: Society, Politics, and Economy in Transition* (Cambridge, MA: Harvard University Press, 2003), 139–87.

70. For a detailed exploration of these phenomena, see Timothy Brook, *The Confusions of Pleasure: Commerce and Culture in Ming China* (Berkeley: University of California Press, 1998).

71. See, for example, Gao et al., 35; and Zhang and Lin, 164–65.

72. On late-Qing popular fiction, see David Der-Wei Wang, *Fin-de-siècle Splendor: Repressed Modernities of Late Qing Fiction, 1849–1911* (Stanford, CA: Stanford University Press, 1997).

73. Robin Lynne Visser, "The Urban Subject in the Literary Imagination of Twentieth Century China" (Ph.D. diss., Columbia University, 2000), 105–6.

74. Xu Jilin et al., "Daotong, xuetong yu zhengtong" (Moral tradition, scholarly tradition, and political tradition), in *RJXL*, 55; originally published in *Dushu* no. 5 (1994).

75. Ibid., 50.

76. Ibid., 53–54.

77. Ibid., 48–49.

78. Wang Y., 206.

79. Ibid., 212.

80. Arrighi notes that Fernand Braudel views the "flexibility" and "eclecticism" of capital as *the* defining feature of historical capitalism: "Let me emphasize the quality that seems to me to be an essential feature of the general history of capitalism: its unlimited flexibility, its capacity for change and *adaptation*. If there is, as I believe, a certain unity in capitalism, from thirteenth-century Italy to the present-day West, it is here above all that such unity must be located and observed." Quoted in Giovanni Arrighi, *The Long Twentieth Century* (London: Verso, 1994), 4. Emphasis in Braudel's original.

81. Karl Marx, *Grundrisse* (London: Penguin, 1973), 157.

82. Ibid., 156–57.

83. Karl Polanyi, *The Great Transformation* (New York: Farrar & Rinehart, 1944), 57.

84. Gao et al., 43.

85. See "Gongming yu wuming" (Common name and namelessness) in Chen Sihe, *Chen Sihe zixuan ji* (Chen Sihe's selected works) (Guilin: Guangxi shifan daxue chubanshe, 1997), 139–52; originally published in *Shanghai wenxue* no. 10 (1996).

86. Chen Sihe, "Guanyu 'renwen jingshen' taolun," 143.

87. Lu Yingping, "Lifazhe, jieshizhe, youmin" (Lawmakers, explainers, vagabonds), in *RJXL*, 183; originally published in *Dushu* no. 8 (1994).

88. Zhang Y., 137.

89. Chen X., 128.

90. Wang M., "Renwen jingshen," 118.

91. Zhang R. et al., "Renwen jingshen," 23–24.

92. Chen Sihe, "Guanyu 'renwen jingshen' taolun," 144.

93. Zhang Y., 138.

94. Xu et al., 58.

95. Wang Hongsheng et al., "Xiandai renwen jingshen de shengcheng" (The generation of modern humanist spirit), in *RJXL*, 232, 238.

96. Meng, 252–53.

97. Wang X. et al., 9.

98. In other instances, Wang Xiaoming has been among the most candid and direct of the humanist scholars. For example, in contrast to the impersonal "you" in the preceding quotation, a February 1995 essay begins with an explicitly autobiographical account of intense intellectual disillusionment. See Wang X., "Women nengfou," esp. 414–16. In a later essay first published in Hong Kong, he directly addresses the two major events that "shocked" intellectuals out of their belief in "modernization": the June Fourth Incident in 1989 and the acceleration of free market reforms in 1992. See "'Renwen jingshen' lunzheng," 443–44.

99.   Gao Yuanbao, for example, argued that Chinese deconstructionism arose from an academic atmosphere of nihilism. See Zhang Rulun et al., "Wenhua shijie: jiegou haishi jiangou" (The cultural world: deconstruction or construction), in *RJXL*, 76–77; originally published in *Dushu* no. 7 (1994).

100.   Wang H. et al., 231.

101.   Wu et al., 62.

102.   Wang M., "Renwen jingshen," 111.

103.   Zhang Y., 141.

104.   Gao Yuanbao, "Renwen jingshen taolun zhi wo jian," (My view of the humanist spirit discussion), in *RJXL*, 170; originally published in *Zuojia bao* (20 May 1995).

105.   Xu et al., 50.

106.   Ibid., 47–54.

107.   Wang X., "'Renwen jingshen' lunzheng," 451.

108.   Gao Y., "Renwen jingshen taolun," 166–67.

109.   This phenomenon is mentioned in Gao Yuanbao, *Ling yizhong quanli* (Another kind of power) (Shijiazhuang: Huashan wenyi chubanshe, 2001), 153.

110.   Barmé, 286.

111.   Zhang R., "Renwen jingshen," 30.

112.   Gao Y., *Ling yizhong quanli*, 153, 154.

113.   Indeed, it is impossible to define precisely where the "humanist spirit" phenomenon ends and its "ripples" begin. For example, a side tangent of the discussion involved a heated debate between Wang Meng and several other critics and writers, most notably critics Wang Binbin and Xiao Xialin and novelists Liang Xiaosheng, Zhang Wei, and Zhang Chengzhi (whom some of the Shanghai humanists had championed as a contrast to Wang Shuo). The militancy of some of these latter figures far exceeded the intentions of the earlier "humanist sprit" critics and in some cases was directly or indirectly denounced by them—for example, in Gao Yuanbao's critique of the desire to "establish an absolute value" cited in the previous paragraph. In the present chapter, in the interest of space and focus, I have limited my discussion to the individuals, panel discussions, and critical essays in which the concept of the "humanist spirit" itself plays a central role. Barmé provides a critical discussion of these associated intellectual wrangles in *In the Red*, 298–315, as does Gao Yuanbao in *Ling yizhong quanli*, 149–64.

114.   See S. Lu, 39–41, for an overview of these critical developments.

115.   The influence of the humanist spirit discussion is evident in both the liberal and the New Leftist schools of the following years. The liberals continued the critique of Chinese postmodernism and the concern with humanism. However, by criticizing the effects of the market economy and subsequently absorbing and countering the charges that they advocated a return to Mao-era "class struggle," the humanist spirit critics also helped enable the genuine critical renewal of the issue of class in China by the New Left

critics in the latter half of the 1990s (see Chapter Seven). To see the wide repercussions of the debate for these developments, it is interesting to note the later affiliations of the participants in one of the most influential of the early *Dushu* panel discussions, "Renwen jingshen: shifou keneng yu ruhe keneng." Of the four critics, one (Zhu Xueqin) later became a leading figure of the "liberal" school, two others (Wang Xiaoming and Zhang Rulun) became loosely identified with the "New Left" school, and the remaining one (Chen Sihe) stood somewhere in the middle.

CHAPTER THREE

1. Alain Badiou, *Manifesto for Philosophy* (Albany: State University of New York Press, 1999), 55.

2. Jean-Paul Sartre, *Critique of Dialectical Reason, Volume One* (London: Verso, 2004), 258.

3. Wang Gan, Zhang Yiwu, and Zhang Weimin, "'Xin zhuangtai wenxue' san ren tan" ("New state of affairs literature" three-way discussion), in *90 Niandai piping wenxuan* (Selected works of 1990s criticism), ed. Chen Sihe and Yang Yang (Shanghai: Hanyu dacidian chubanshe, 2001), 436.

4. My discussion here is indebted to the overview provided in Hong Zicheng, *Zhongguo dangdai wenxue shi* (History of contemporary Chinese literature) (Beijing: Beijing daxue chubanshe, 1999), 384; and to Shuyu Kong's *Consuming Literature: Best Sellers and the Commercialization of Literary Production in Contemporary China* (Stanford, CA: Stanford University Press, 2005).

5. The elite literary journals paid an average of thirty yuan per thousand characters, while the popular magazines commonly paid over one hundred yuan per thousand characters. Hong, 393n2.

6. For a thorough discussion of these and other changes among literary journals in the 1990s, see the chapter "Literary Journals: Between a Rock and a Hard Place," in Shuyu Kong, *Consuming Literature: Best Sellers and the Commercialization of Literary Production in Contemporary China* (Stanford, CA: Stanford University Press, 2005), 144–69; or see her earlier article version "Between a Rock and a Hard Place: Chinese Literary Journals in the Cultural Market," *Modern Chinese Literature and Culture* 14 (spring 2002): 93–144.

7. On the lack of "movements" in visual art of this time, see Wu Hung, *Transience: Chinese Experimental Art at the End of the Twentieth Century* (Chicago: The David and Alfred Smart Museum of Art, University of Chicago, 1999), 23–24.

8. *Zhongshan* (Zhong mountain), no. 3 (1989).

9. Hong, 340.

10. Ibid., 391.

11. Ibid., 391–92.

12.   In her analysis of Zhang Ailing's fiction, Rey Chow, following Naomi Schor, defines feminine details "as the sensuous, trivial, and superfluous textual presences that exist in an ambiguous relation with some larger 'vision' such as reform and revolution, which seeks to subordinate them but which is displaced by their surprising returns." Rey Chow, *Woman and Chinese Modernity: The Politics of Reading Between West and East* (Minneapolis: University of Minnesota Press, 1991), 85. See also Naomi Schor, *Reading in Detail: Aesthetics and the Feminine* (London: Routledge, 1987).

13.   Shuyu Kong, "Is There a Realism in Neo-Realism?" *British Columbia Asian Review* 8 (winter 1994/1995): 121.

14.   Chi Li, "Leng ye hao, re ye hao, huozhe jiu hao" (Hot or cold, it's good to be alive), in *Chi Li wenji 2: Yi dong wu xue* (Chi Li collected works 2: A snowless winter) (Nanjing: Jiangsu wenyi chubanshe, 1995), 334–51.

15.   Chi Li, *Fannao rensheng* (Troublesome life), in *Chi Li wenji 2*, 53. Translations are my own, though I have consulted the English collection Chi Li, *Apart From Love* (Beijing: Chinese Literature Press, 1994).

16.   Chi, *Fannao rensheng*, 2, 4.

17.   Xiaobing Tang, *Chinese Modern: The Heroic and the Quotidian* (Durham, NC: Duke University Press, 2000).

18.   Chow, 120.

19.   Fredric Jameson, "Beyond the Cave: Demystifying the Ideology of Modernism," in *The Ideologies of Theory: Essays, 1971–1986,* vol. 2, *Syntax of History* (Minneapolis: University of Minnesota Press, 1988), 128.

20.   Liu Chuan'e, *Xiao shimin, ming zuojia: Chi Li lun* (Petty urbanites, famous author: a study of Chi Li) (Wuhan: Hubei renmin chubanshe, 2000), 215.

21.   Ibid., 217.

22.   Zhang Yiwu, "Lixiangzhuyi de zhongjie" (The end of idealism), *Beijing wenxue* (Beijing literature), no. 4 (1989).

23.   Liu, 215.

24.   Ibid., 216. For a discussion of the critical accusation of "pandering to the vulgar," see Chapter Two.

25.   Ibid., esp. 35.

26.   Ibid., 208, 203, 209.

27.   Chi Li, *Lailai wangwang* (Coming and going) (Beijing: Zuojia chubanshe, 1998). An abridged and unreliable English translation appears under the title "To and Fro" in *Chinese Literature* (winter 1999): 14–63.

28.   The novella had been published in short-story form the previous year in *Shiyue* (October) 4 (1997): 4–34.

29.   This sales figure is given in Liu, 198. The number is no doubt much higher if one takes into account pirated copies of the book.

30. Chi, *Lailai wangwang*, 166.

31. Ibid., 177.

32. Ibid., 182. The poem is "The Fairy Cave" (Xianren dong), which goes as follows: "Amid the growing shades of dusk are sturdy pines / Scattered clouds fly calmly by / Nature has created a Fairy Cave / Unbounded scenery dwells in her perilous peaks."

33. Ibid., 185.

34. The questions, all answers, and a statistical summary of the results were provided in Zhu Wen, "Duanlie: yi fen wenjuan he wushiliu fen dajuan" (Rupture: a questionnaire and fifty-six replies), which is reprinted along with other relevant critical essays in Wang Jifang, ed., *Duanlie: shijimo de wenxue shigu—ziyou zuojia fangtan lu* (Rupture: the literary accident at the end of the century—interviews with free authors) (Nanjing: Jiangsu wenyi chubanshe, 2000), 251–306.

35. Geremie Barmé, "Flashback: It's Not All About Money," *Time Asia*, October 23, 2000.

36. Li Xianting, "'Duanlie' shi yi ge xuanyan—Li Xianting fangtan lu" ("Rupture" is a manifesto—interview with Li Xianting), in *Duanlie*, 1.

37. See "Residual Modernism: Narratives of the Self in the 1980s," in Tang, *Chinese Modern*, 196–224.

38. Zhu Wen, "Gou yan kan ren: cong duanlie congshu chuban tanqi" (A dog's-eye view of people: on the publication of the Rupture book series), in *Duanlie*, 330.

39. Ibid., 331.

40. Ibid., 333.

41. Ibid., 331.

42. Fredric Jameson, *A Singular Modernity: Essay on the Ontology of the Present* (London: Verso, 2002), 90.

43. Ibid., 91.

44. From a discussion with novelist and literary scholar Zhang Sheng in Shanghai, March 2003.

45. Chen Xiaoming, *Biaoyi de jiaolü: lishi qumei yu dangdai wenxue biange* (Ideographic anxieties: historical exorcism and contemporary literary transformation) (Beijing: Zhongyang bianyi chubanshe, 2001), 322.

46. Ibid., 320–21.

47. Ibid., 322.

48. Ibid., 323.

49. Ibid., 321. For more on the influence of Wang Shuo in the 1990s, see Chapters Two and Six.

50. Ibid., 339–41.

51. Ibid., 323.

52. Ibid., 339–40.

53. Ibid., 340.

54. For a collection of these translated into English, see Zhu Wen, *I Love Dollars and Other Stories*, trans. Julia Lovell (New York: Columbia University Press, 2007).

55. A punk rock movement in Beijing around the turn of the century, for example, called themselves the *wuliao jundui*, or roughly "army of the bored."

56. Wang Xiaoming, "Zai 'wuliao' de bishi xia—cong Zhu Wen bixia de Xiao Ding shuo qi" (Under the stare of 'wuliao'—proceeding from Xiao Ding under the pen of Zhu Wen), in *Zai xin yishi xingtai de longzhao xia: 90 niandai de wenhua he wenxue fenxi* (Under the shroud of the new ideology: culture and literary analysis of the 1990s), ed. Wang Xiaoming (Nanjing: Jiangsu renmin, 2000), 204, 205.

57. See my quotations of Wang Xiaoming in Chapter Two.

58. Wang X., 205.

59. Ibid., 214–15.

60. Walter Benjamin, "The Return of the Flaneur," in *Selected Writings: 1927–1934* (Harvard University Press, 1999 [1929]), 2:313.

61. Zhu Wen, *Xiao Ding gushi* (Stories of Xiao Ding), in *Yinwei gudu* (Because of loneliness) (Chengdu: Sichuan wenyi chubanshe, 1996), 1–95.

62. Zhu Wen, *Shenme shi laji shenme shi ai* (What's trash, what's love) (Nanjing: Jiangsu wenyi chubanshe, 1998), 103.

63. Sartre, 256.

64. Ibid., 262.

65. Wang G., Zhang, and Zhang, 445.

66. In Chi Li's early fiction, the narrator sometimes even flaunts this superior epistemological position by addressing an unhearing character in the second person, as in this example:

> "What a beautiful daughter!" the delivering doctor marveled. "Thank you!" Li Xiaolan's gratitude came from her deepest heart.
>
> Doctor, are you aware that before this she had never expressed heartfelt thanks to anyone?
>
> Chi Li, *Taiyang chushi* (The sun comes out), in *Chi Li wenji* 2, 142. Translation by Scudder Smith in Chi, *Apart From Love*, 301–2.

67. Zhang Jun, "Xinshengdai: gerenhua xiezuo de shuangzhong zijue" (The newly born generation: the dual forms of self-consciousness of individualized writing), in *90 Niandai piping wenxuan* (Selected works of 1990s criticism), ed. Chen Sihe and Yang Yang (Shanghai: Hanyu dacidian chubanshe, 2001), 331–33. In describing the previous condition, Zhang cites Chen Sihe's notion of the "common name" (*gongming*) of previous times in contrast to the "namelessness" (*wuming*) of the 1990s, as I discussed in Chapter Two.

68. Ibid., 336.

69. Zhu, *Shenme shi laji*, 287.

70. Huang Fayou, "Zai youdangzhong qiu kun—Zhu Wen he *Shenme shi laji shenme shi ai*" (Trapped in idleness—Zhu Wen and *What's trash, what's love*), *Wenyi zhengming* (Literature and arts contention), no. 2 (2002): 78.

71. Fredric Jameson, *The Seeds of Time* (New York: Columbia University Press, 1994), 37.

72. Wang Hongsheng et al., "Xiandai renwen jingshen de shengcheng" (The generation of modern humanist spirit), in *Renwen jingshen xunsi lu* (Thoughts on the humanist spirit), ed. Wang Xiaoming (Shanghai: Wenhui chubanshe, 1996), 231.

73. Song Mingwei, "Piaoliu de fangzi he xuwang de lütu—lijie Zhu Wen" (Floating houses and fabricated journeys—understanding Zhu Wen), *Shanghai Wenxue* (September 1997): 67.

74. Ibid., 70.

75. Ibid., 69.

76. Ibid., 70.

77. Wang H. et al., 231.

78. This contrast corresponds to the distinction Alain Badiou makes between *knowledge*—that which can be represented and ordered encyclopedically in a given situation—and *truth*—which is rather a matter of "creating a hole in knowledge." Xiao Ding himself approximates Badiou's idea of a "wandering excess" that fails to fit into the new society and thus appears as a nihility from the ideological perspective of that society. Badiou, 37, 80–81.

79. In contrast to a *symptom*, which demands to be interpreted, Lacan labeled as *sinthome* that which appears as fundamentally unanalyzable, beyond the realm of the symbolic order.

80. Geremie Barmé, "Time's Arrows: Imaginative Pasts and Nostalgic Futures," in *Voicing Concerns: Contemporary Chinese Critical Inquiry,* ed. Gloria Davies (Lanham, MD: Rowman and Littlefield, 2001), 236.

81. A similar rush to publish a novel as essentially a product tie-in, in this case for a film, would be seen in 2004 with the popular culture sensation *Shouji* (Cell phone; dir. Feng Xiaogang), in which Liu Zhenyun, another major writer previously labeled as New Realist, wrote both the screenplay and a novel based upon it that was released almost simultaneously. See Chapter Four for more on *Cell Phone*.

82. See Liu, 198–99.

83. For an analysis of one of the turn-of-the-century Chinese noir films, see Zhang Zhen, "Urban Dreamscape, Phantom Sisters, and the Identity of an Emergent Art Cinema," in *The Urban Generation: Chinese Cinema and Society at the Turn of the Twenty-first Century* (Durham, NC: Duke University Press, 2007), 344–87. For a discussion of

the "new formalism," see my essay "The New Formalism: Mainland Chinese Cinema at the Turn of the Century," in *China's Literary and Cultural Scenes at the Turn of the 21st Century*, ed. Jie Lu (London: Routledge, forthcoming 2008).

84. The script's co-writer, novelist Yu Hua, claimed to be largely responsible for the final version of the script, with Zhu Wen's work coming on an earlier draft. Conversation in Chicago, November 4, 2003.

CHAPTER FOUR

1. For more on the ironies of product placement in Feng Xiaogang's films, see Chapter Six.

2. See Wang Xiaoming, "Banzhanglian de shenhua" (Myth of the half-faced portrait), in *Zai xin yishi xingtai de longzhao xia: 90 niandai de wenhua he wenxue fenxi* (Under the shroud of the new ideology: culture and literary analysis of the 1990s), ed. Wang Xiaoming (Nanjing: Jiangsu renmin, 2000), 29–36. For more on this critique of contemporary media culture, see Chapter Five.

3. For one summary of the *Cell Phone* phenomenon, see Mark Magnier, "Hit Movie Rings True in China," *Los Angeles Times*, April 12, 2004. For much more on director Feng Xiaogang, see Chapter Six.

4. The phenomenon of *hesui pian* is discussed at length in Chapter Six.

5. In his groundbreaking study of Chinese popular fiction in the early twentieth century, Perry Link identified "the issue of free versus arranged marriage" as the defining theme of the first "wave" of Mandarin Duck and Butterfly fiction during the early 1910s. E. Perry Link, Jr., *Mandarin Ducks and Butterflies: Popular Fiction in Early Twentieth-Century Chinese Cities* (Berkeley: University of California Press, 1981), 22.

6. Rey Chow, *Woman and Chinese Modernity: The Politics of Reading Between West and East* (Minneapolis: University of Minnesota Press, 1991), 39.

7. *In the Wild Mountains* made several breakthroughs in cinematic technique relative to its predecessors in mainland China during the Mao and immediate post-Mao era. These included the use of realist methods such as natural lighting and sound, overlapping dialogue, exclusively on-location shooting in the countryside, and some unusually long takes. In addition, like many Fifth Generation films that would follow shortly, it turned a seemingly detached ethnographic gaze on the lives and customs of rural peasants.

8. Xiaobing Tang, "Rural Women and Social Change in New China Cinema: From *Li Shuangshuang* to *Ermo*," *Positions: East Asia Cultures Critique* 11 (winter 2003): 655.

9. On the implications of these truck-driver characters, see Tang, 669–71.

10. Jacob Eyferth, Peter Ho, and Eduard B. Vermeer, "Introduction: The Opening-Up of China's Countryside," *Journal of Peasant Studies* 30 (April/July 2003): 3.

11. For an account of Zhou Xiaowen's career up to *Ermo*, much of it told in his own

words, see Tony Rayns, "The Ups and Downs of Zhou Xiaowen: In Beijing the Director Discusses His Troubled Career and His New Film *Ermo,*" *Sight and Sound* 5 (July 1995): 22–24.

12. Ibid., 23.

13. Several readings of Ermo have noted the eroticization of Ermo's dough-kneading. Tani E. Barlow calls such scenes "hilarious, painful (and yet unspeakably carnal)," Beth Notar describes them as "extraordinarily sensual," and Judith Farquhar notes that they "are filmed in a distinctly erotic fashion." David Leiwei Li asserts that "the camera work drives home Ermo's direct channeling of her repressed sexuality into noodle making," an activity that thus becomes "the transmutation of love into labor." Sheldon H. Lu and Anne T. Ciecko similarly describe Ermo's noodle-making as "elliptically masturbatory" and "a displaced expression of female sexuality," and they attribute the "showcasing [of] Ermo's distinctive and erotically charged mode of making noodles with her feet" in these scenes to the self-orientalizing strategies of Fifth Generation filmmakers seeking recognition abroad. See Tani E. Barlow, "'green blade in the act of being grazed': Late Capital, Flexible Bodies, Critical Intelligibility," *Differences: A Journal of Feminist Cultural Studies* 10, no. 3 (1998): 145; Beth Notar, "Blood Money: Woman's Desire and Consumption in *Ermo,*" *Asian Cinema* 12, no. 2 (2001): 135; Judith Farquhar, "Technology of Everyday Life: The Economy of Impotence in Reform China," *Cultural Anthropology* 14, no. 2 (1999): 160; David Leiwei Li, "'What Will Become of Us If We Don't Stop?' *Ermo*'s China and the End of Globalization," *Comparative Literature* 53, no. 4 (2001): 447; and Anne T. Ciecko and Sheldon H. Lu, "*Ermo*: Televisuality, Capital, and the Global Village," in Sheldon H. Lu, *China, Transnational Visuality, Global Postmodernity* (Stanford, CA: Stanford University Press, 2001), 92.

14. This scene of sexualized labor can easily be read according to a sublimation model, in which Ermo's sexual frustration due to her impotent husband finds release in physical work; thus Beth Notar's conclusion that, "As Freud might deduce, Ermo's sexual frustrations are redirected into productive labor" (135). However, one could also take the scene as an apparent illustration of Deleuze and Guattari's thesis that social production is not a sublimated form of libidinal urges (as in the Freudian model), but rather is immanently and directly invested with desire. Gilles Deleuze and Félix Guattari, *Anti-Oedipus: Capitalism and Schizophrenia* (Minneapolis: University of Minnesota Press, 1983), 29. Judith Farquhar also rejects the sublimation thesis (see note 46 below).

15. Karl Marx, "Results of the Immediate Process of Production," included as an appendix in Karl Marx, *Capital: Volume 1* (London: Penguin, 1976), 950, 951.

16. Wang Dehou, "*Ermo*: zhuozhuang yu mangmu de jiejing" (*Ermo*: a crystallization of sturdiness and blindness), *Dianying yishu* (Film art) no. 5 (1994): 38.

17. The anthropomorphism evoked by these shots is captured by Xiaobing Tang's description: "A mutual gaze between the enrapt viewer and the TV screen is established

through a sequence of shot and reverse-shot that resembles a dialogue between two subjects." Tang, 667.

18.   Marx's vivid description of the fetishism that ensues after a table "emerges as a commodity" goes as follows: "It not only stands with its feet on the ground, but, in relation to all other commodities, it stands on its head, and evolves out of its wooden brain grotesque ideas, far more wonderful than if it were to begin dancing of its own free will." Karl Marx, *Capital: Volume 1*, 163–64. In this context, it is interesting to recall that Marx annotates this passage with a complex reference to the revolutionary potential of the Chinese peasantry: "One may recall that China and the tables began to dance when the rest of the world appeared to be standing still—*pour encourager les autres*." Ibid., 164n27. Here the dancing tables refer to the fad of spiritualism in Germany in the years following the failed 1848 revolts, while China is said to have begun "dancing" in the same period with the Taiping Rebellion and its proto-communist collectivism. Thus, nearly 130 years after Marx implicitly contrasted the revolutionary potential of the nineteenth-century Chinese peasantry with the commodity fetishism of the European bourgeoisie, *Ermo* ironically depicts the same peasantry in the postsocialist era fetishizing an object that conveys a Western bourgeois imaginary.

19.   See Alfred Gell, "Newcomers to the World of Goods: Consumption among the Muria Gonds," in *The Social Life of Things: Commodities in Cultural Perspective*, ed. Arjun Appadurai (Cambridge: Cambridge University Press, 1988), 113–15.

20.   Farquhar, 160.

21.   Anthony Giddens, *The Consequences of Modernity* (Stanford, CA: Stanford University Press, 1990), 24.

22.   Tang, 668. Emphasis added.

23.   Ciecko and Lu, 98.

24.   Ibid., 102.

25.   On Ermo's TV set as a Benjaminian commodity spectacle, see Ping Fu, "*Ermo*: (Tele)Visualizing Urban/Rural Transformation," in *Chinese Films in Focus: 25 New Takes*, ed. Chris Berry (London: British Film Institute, 2003), 76.

26.   Thus Xiaobing Tang points out that the TV set's role as Ermo's *objet petit a* means that in essence it functions "only as an empty space or void, necessarily unobtainable and always metonymic of something else and/or more" (Tang, 667). While this has been the TV set's essential role since Ermo's first encounter with it in the department store, it is only with this final look at it that the film invites her (and the audience) to literally see it *as* void.

27.   Zhang Yiwu, "*Ermo*: xiandai zhi kunhuo" (*Ermo*: confusions of the modern), *Dangdai dianying* (Contemporary cinema), no. 5 (1994): 48.

28.   Beth Notar, for example, sums up the film thus: "Set in China's reform era transition from a socialist planned economy to a capitalist market economy, the film critiques commodity fetishism through a sympathetic portrayal of a stubborn and naïve

village woman, Ermo" (132). The film's depressing conclusion, according to Ping Fu, is that "what most represses rural women like Ermo is no longer traditional ethics but modern civilisation itself in the form of the commodity" (75).

29. Luo Yijun, "Guanyu Ermo" (On Ermo), Dangdai dianying (Contemporary cinema), no. 5 (1994): 45–46.

30. Tao Dongfeng, "Huangtang de fuchou: Ermo yu ta de da caidian" (Absurd revenge: Ermo and her large color TV), Dangdai dianying (Contemporary cinema), no. 5 (1994): 52.

31. Zhang, 48.

32. In her essay on the film, Dai Jinhua has noted that the villagers' continued use of "Village Chief" in addressing Ermo's husband was less a matter of residual respect for his position than pity, or perhaps even mockery. Dai Jinhua, "Ermo: xiandai yuyan kongjian" (Ermo: modern allegorical space), Dianying yishu (Film art), no. 5 (1994): 41.

33. Notar highlights the differences, in clothing and otherwise, between the Chief and Xiazi in the context of her overall reading of the film as a national allegory: "Ermo tries to abandon the impotent Chief for what she sees as the potent Blindman. Allegorically, we can read this as China trying to abandon Socialism for Capitalism" (139).

34. Ciecko and Lu, 94.

35. Shao Mujun, "Tan Ermo" (On Ermo), Dangdai dianying (Contemporary cinema), no. 5 (1994): 46.

36. Dai, 41. Given this interpretation, Dai goes on to note that the irony would then be that Ermo's actions are in fact speeding up the historical processes that led to her family's loss of status rather than slowing down or reversing them. Nevertheless, Dai concludes that the film does not depict actual historical change so much as a more or less static situation in which real change is longed for but never quite achieved. Ibid., 43.

37. I base this evaluation not only on my own response but on the raucous audience reaction I witnessed during a screening at a Shanghai movie theater holding a retrospective series of Chinese films of the reform era in early 2003.

38. Tang, 647–74.

39. Fredric Jameson, The Seeds of Time (New York: Columbia University Press, 1994), 29–30.

40. Stephen J. Gould and Nancy Y. C. Wong, "The Intertextual Construction of Emerging Consumer Culture in China as Observed in the Movie Ermo: A Postmodern, Sinicization Reading," Journal of Global Marketing 14 (2000): 160. Among the authors' recommendations are the following: "It is not enough to consider Chinese consumers as members of some broad social class, but rather, they should be seen as a part of product and/or work-related lifestyle tribes which drive their behavior." And, "We learn in the movie that a television is a social center (more so than in the West), that its size is a symbol of status, that a piece of furniture could be marketed to hold the television,

and that consumers project the dramas of their lives on it, among other things. Such findings thus can inform the development of product and promotional strategies." Ibid., 164, 165.

41. Ibid., 156.

42. This is a primary concern of much of the "root-seeking" (*xungen*) movement in literature of the 1980s in addition to several contemporary films of the Fifth Generation and the much-heralded TV series *He shang* (River elegy, 1988).

43. I have not included in my analysis some other films of the 1980s and 1990s depicting adultery due to the fact that they are set in the past and thus do not explicitly represent the reform era. This includes, for example, the "Fifth Generation" classic *Ju Dou* (dir. Zhang Yimou, 1990).

44. For a much more thorough discussion of *The Day the Sun Turned Cold*, see the chapter "Oedipus Comes to Hong Kong: *The Day the Sun Turned Cold*," in Jerome Silbergeld, *Hitchcock with a Chinese Face* (Seattle: University of Washington Press, 2004), 47–72.

45. Tang, 650.

46. As Judith Farquhar argues: "It is not just that people had few opportunities to indulge individual passions; rather, they lived within a whole built world that was structured as if privacy had no uses, as if the personal could only detract from the eventual triumph of the people in true communism." Instead of seeing this as a Maoist sublimation or repression of libidinal drives, Farquhar supports a model of "subjectivity in which desire can just as naturally be directed toward abstract objects like the state, the people, and the Great Helmsman as toward other mundane individuals" (168).

47. Drawing on the work of Miriam Hansen, James Donald and Stephanie Hemelryk Donald apply such an argument to Chinese cinema of the 1980s in "The Publicness of Cinema," in *Reinventing Film Studies*, ed. Christine Gledhill and Linda Williams (London: Arnold, 2000), 114–29.

48. See Zhang Nuanxin and Li Tuo, "Tan dianying yuyan de xiandaihua" (On the modernization of cinematic language), in *Bainian Zhongguo dianying lilun wenxuan* (Selected works of one-hundred years of Chinese film theory), ed. Ding Yaping (Beijing: Wenhua yishu chubanshe, 2002), 2:10–36; originally published in *Dianying yishu* (Film art) no. 3 (1979). This landmark article, to be discussed in the next chapter, advocated Bazin's notion of cinematic realism as a model for study in the PRC.

49. Liu Zhenyun had been considered one of the leading writers of "New Realist" fiction (*xin xieshi xiaoshuo*) in the late 1980s. Consequently, his collaborations with Feng Xiaogang in TV and entertainment cinema fifteen years later represents a career trajectory similar to that of Chi Li, another leading New Realist writer discussed at length in Chapter Three. Both novelists managed not just to survive but to thrive in the new, highly commercialized culture market wrought by the 1990s.

CHAPTER FIVE

1. Jia Zhangke, "Jia Zhangke: zai 'zhantai' shang dengdai" (Jia Zhangke: waiting on the "Platform"), interview by Cheng Qingsong and Huang Ou, in *Wo de sheyingji bu sahuang: liushi niandai Zhongguo dianying daoyan dang'an* (My camera doesn't lie: files on the '60s generation of Chinese film directors), ed. Cheng Qingsong and Huang Ou (Beijing: Zhongguo youyi chuban gongsi, 2002), 356–57.

2. André Bazin, "An Aesthetic of Reality: Neorealism," in *What Is Cinema? Vol. II* (Berkeley: University of California Press, 1971), 26.

3. I highlight the period from 1984 to 1993 because many of the later Fifth Generation films show a notable change in tone, setting, and apparent intended audience.

4. Jia is usually labeled as a "Sixth Generation" filmmaker; however, the concept of a Sixth Generation is not, I believe, the most useful way to approach his films. "Sixth Generation" generally refers to directors who began working from the late 1980s to the mid-1990s, and in fact it covers a wide range of filmmakers, cinematic styles, and modes of production. The label is perhaps useful only by way of contrast with the Fifth Generation. Thus, compared to their immediate predecessors, the Sixth Generation are said to favor urban and contemporary settings rather than rural and historical or mythical ones, and immediate, observable life circumstances rather than abstract allegorical tales. However, one can cite many exceptions even to such basic distinctions, and in any case the contrast I wish to highlight is that between independent and state studio productions, not that between "generations" of filmmakers.

5. For example, Ulrich Gregor, the German critic and major force in the Berlin and Cannes Film Festivals, has called Jia "the dazzling light of hope flashing like lightning in Asian cinema." In the wake of the release of *Platform*, in particular, J. Hoberman of the *Village Voice* called the film "a major work by a striking new talent" and "one of the richest films of the past decade," while Jonathan Rosenbaum of the *Chicago Reader* proclaimed it "one of the most impressive Chinese films I've ever seen" and even said it "might be the greatest film ever to come out of mainland China." See Chen Pingshu, "Jia Zhangke, Wang Xiaoshuai huigui zhuliu: dianying 'diliudai' jiedong?" (Jia Zhangke and Wang Xiaoshuai return to the mainstream: the thaw of cinema's "sixth generation"?), *Zhongguo qingnian bao* (China youth daily), January 17, 2004; J. Hoberman, "Conflict Management," *Village Voice*, March 2, 2001; J. Hoberman, "Cults of Personality," *Village Voice*, March 12–18, 2003; Jonathan Rosenbaum, "Critic's Choice: *Platform*," *Chicago Reader*, May 17, 2002; and Jonathan Rosenbaum, *Essential Cinema: On the Necessity of Film Canons* (Baltimore: Johns Hopkins University Press, 2004), 191.

6. These include *Beijing zazhong* (Beijing bastards, 1992) and *Donggong xigong* (East palace, west palace, 1996).

7. Yet other directors also generally grouped within the Sixth Generation, such as Guan Hu (*Toufa luanle* [Dirt, 1994]) and Lou Ye (*Zhoumo qingren* [Weekend lovers,

1995]), were making their first films within the studio system, which is one reason the generational label does not lend itself to my analysis.

8. For example, after a string of independent works, Zhang Yuan began making films through the official studios with *Guonian huijia* (Seventeen years, 1999) and *Wo ai ni* (I love you, 2002). He Jianjun and Wang Xiaoshuai also have vacillated between independent or internationally financed productions such as *Youchai* (Postman, 1995) and *Jidu hanleng* (Frozen, 1995), respectively, and state studio works such as He's *Hudie de weixiao* (Butterfly smile, 2002) and Wang's *Biandang guniang* (So close to paradise, 1998).

9. For a more thorough discussion of the various forms of postsocialist realism in Chinese cinema, see Chris Berry, "Getting Real: Chinese Documentary, Chinese Postsocialism," in *The Urban Generation: Chinese Cinema and Society at the Turn of the Twenty-first Century*, edited by Zhang Zhen (Durham, NC: Duke University Press, 2007), 115–34. I am also grateful for his sharing his essay "*Xiao Wu*: Watching Time Go By," forthcoming in *Chinese Films in Focus*, 2nd ed. (London: British Film Institute); and the text of his presentation "Postsocialist Realism: Towards a Genealogy of Jishizhuyi in the Chinese Cinema," given at the Annual Meeting of the Association for Asian Studies, New York City, March 28, 2003. As these references indicate, my ideas regarding postsocialist realism evolved in dialogue with Chris Berry.

10. Thus it is clear that a gesture of some kind of *unmasking* is essential to both socialist and postsocialist realism, the distinction between them being dependent on their historical chronology and changed ideological circumstances. Here is perhaps a universal trait underlying any rhetorical claim to an aesthetic of realism—the presence, whether implicit or explicit, of some previously existing artistic form that is held to be less "real."

11. "'Xin xieshi xiaoshuo da lianzhan' juanshou yu" ("Grand exposition of new realist fiction" volume preface), *Zhongshan* (Zhong mountain), no. 3 (1989): 4.

12. Yin Hong, "Shiji zhi jiao: jiushi niandai zhongguo dianying beiwang" (The turn of the century: memo on Chinese cinema in the nineties), in *Bainian Zhongguo dianying lilun wenxuan* (Selected works of one-hundred years of Chinese film theory), ed. Ding Yaping (Beijing: Wenhua yishu chubanshe, 2002), 2:678. Lü Xiaoming, "90 niandai Zhongguo dianying jingguan zhi yi: 'diliu dai' ji qi zhiyi" (One of the landscapes of 1990s Chinese film: the "Sixth Generation" and doubts thereof), *Dianying yishu* (Film art) (May 10, 1999): 24.

13. André Bazin, "The Ontology of the Photographic Image," in *What Is Cinema? Vol. I* (Berkeley: University of California Press, 1967), 11.

14. André Bazin, "The Evolution of the Language of Cinema," in *What Is Cinema? Vol. I* , 40; and "An Aesthetic of Reality," 25.

15. In an interview, Jia discusses his use of long-shot compositions and the

consequent freedom of the audience to choose what details to take notice of, concluding as follows: "Through all these, I am imparting a director's attitude, how he sees the world and the cinema. What I mean to say is that it's only an attitude because you can never be absolutely objective. When you need somebody to look at something, it's no longer objective. There is no absolute objectivity, there is attitude, and through this attitude, there is an ideal." See Stephen Teo, "Cinema with an Accent: Interview with Jia Zhangke, Director of *Platform*," *Senses of Cinema*, no. 15, July/August 2001, http://www. sensesofcinema.com/contents/01/15/zhangke_interview.html. In another interview, Jia summed up his realism in the following way: "For me, all the realist [*jishi*] methods are there to express the real world of my inner experience. It is almost impossible for us to approach reality in itself, and the meaning of cinema is not simply to reach the level of reality. I pursue the feeling of the real in cinema more than I pursue reality, because I think the feeling of the real is on the level of aesthetics whereas reality just stays in the realm of sociology." See Sun Jianmin, "Jingyan shijiezhong de yingxiang xuanze: Jia Zhangke fangtan lu" (Selecting images in the experiential world: an interview with Jia Zhangke), *Jinri xianfeng* (Avant-garde today) 12 (March 2002): 31.

16. Zhang Nuanxin and Li Tuo, "Tan dianying yuyan de xiandaihua" (On the modernization of cinematic language), in *Bainian Zhongguo dianying lilun wenxuan* (Selected works of one-hundred years of Chinese film theory), ed. Ding Yaping, 2:10–36; originally published in *Dianying yishu* (Film art) no. 3 (1979).

17. See Roland Barthes, *Camera Lucida: Reflections on Photography* (New York: Hill and Wang, 1981); and Siegfried Kracauer, *Theory of Film: The Redemption of Physical Reality* (New York: Oxford University Press, 1960). For an overview of the introduction of Western film theories to China in the reform era, see Hu Ke, "Contemporary Film Theory in China," *Dangdai dianying* (Contemporary cinema) no. 2 (1995), 65–73. The article is translated into English by Ted Wang, Chris Berry, and Chen Mei at http://www. latrobe.edu.au/www/screeningthepast/reruns/hkrr2b.html.

18. For a description of the rise of this movement, see Dai Jinhua, "A Scene in the Fog: Reading the Sixth Generation Films," in *Cinema and Desire: Feminist Marxism and Cultural Politics in the Work of Dai Jinhua*, ed. Jing Wang and Tani E. Barlow (London: Verso, 2002), esp. 85–88. For several other relevant essays on the new documentary scene in China, published after this chapter was drafted, see Paul G. Pickowicz and Yingjin Zhang, eds., *From Underground to Independent: Alternative Film Culture in Contemporary China* (Oxford: Rowman & Littlefield, 2006).

19. Marston Anderson, *The Limits of Realism: Chinese Fiction in the Revolutionary Period* (Berkeley: University of California Press, 1990), 202.

20. This short was the latest in a series of documentaries on Tiananmen Square by young directors in the early 1990s. Wu Wenguang's *Tiananmen* (1991) had featured interviews with people in the vicinity of the square, while the feature-length *The Square*

(*Guangchang*, 1994), directed by Zhang Yuan and Duan Jinchuan, focused like Jia's shorter project on the everyday activities of the site.

21. For a detailed firsthand account of the Beijing Film Academy Youth Experimental Film Group, see Gu Zheng, "Women yiqi lai pai dianying ba: hui wang 'qingnian shiyan dianying xiaozu'" (Let's make a movie together: a look back at the "Youth Experimental Film Group"), in *Xianchang* (Document), vol. 1, ed. Wu Wenguang (Tianjin: Tianjin shehui kexueyuan chubanshe, 2000), 213–22. The group also made a VHS short video, *Dudu* (1996), after *Xiaoshan Going Home*.

22. *Cinéma vérité* originally referred to the French version of a broader film movement of the 1960s (known elsewhere as *direct cinema, free cinema,* or *candid eye*). It indicates a style of documentary filmmaking that places the highest priority on directly recording unscripted events as they unfold in the uniqueness of a moment. While its roots go back to the age of silent cinema, the style flourished as a series of technological innovations in mobile cameras and synchronized sound from the late 1950s to the digital age allowed filmmakers much greater freedom in following and responding to spontaneous events.

23. I borrow the term *on-the-spot* from Chris Berry's translation of *jishizhuyi*; for a discussion of on-the-spot realism and its importance to the style of both the new documentary movement and the postsocialist realist fiction filmmakers, see Chris Berry, "Getting Real," esp. 122–23.

24. Yu Lik Wai had directed the documentary *Meili de hunpo* (Neon goddesses, 1996) and would later direct *Tianshang renjian* (Love will tear us apart, 1999) and *Mingri tianya* (All tomorrow's parties, 2003). As Jia has often made clear in interviews, Yu Lik Wai would play a key role in realizing the stylistic vision of Jia's feature films, and Jia has paid tribute by inserting in-jokes about him in the scripts. (A character in Jia's *Unknown Pleasures* tries to buy Yu's *Love Will Tear Us Apart* from a vender of pirated DVDs, and there is a background loudspeaker announcement at a bus station in *Platform* telling people to be on the lookout for criminals, including one Yu Liwei, who is said to "speak with a heavy Cantonese accent" and be "proficient in French"; the name as written in the Chinese subtitles is an exact homophone for the cinematographer's name, while the English-subtitled version uses the Cantonese spelling "Yu Lik Wai.")

25. This fact is prominently noted, as a kind of neorealist badge of honor, in the first title following the final shot of the film. An extended interview with Jia by independent documentary filmmaker Wu Wenguang offers many details about how the cast members of *Xiao Wu* were recruited and directed during the twenty-one days it took to shoot the film. Aside from three of the main characters, all actors were found in the Fenyang area, and actors even for speaking roles were often found on the day of the shooting and directed to improvise situations. See Wu Wenguang, "Fangwen 'Xiao Wu' daoyan Jia Zhangke" (Interview with *Xiao Wu* director Jia Zhangke), *Xianchang*, vol. 1, 184–212.

26. Jia Zhangke, "Zhongguo de duli dianying ren" (China's independent filmmaker), interview, in *Dianying chufang: dianying zai Zhongguo* (Film kitchen: film in China), ed. Wang Shuo (Shanghai: Shanghai wenyi chubanshe, 2001), 152.

27. Chris Berry, "*Xiao Wu.*"

28. Wang Xiaoming, *Banzhanglian de shenhua* (Myth of the half-faced portrait) (Guangdong: Nanfang ribao chubanshe, 2000), 11–19. A nearly identical version of the essay appears in Wang Xiaoming, "Banzhanglian de shenhua" (Myth of the half-faced portrait), in *Zai xin yishi xingtai de longzhao xia: 90 niandai de wenhua he wenxue fenxi* (Under the shroud of the new ideology: culture and literary analysis of the 1990s), ed. Wang Xiaoming (Nanjing: Jiangsu renmin, 2000), 29–36. A more extended analysis of the *xin furen* class appears in the same author's "Jiushi niandai yu 'xin yishixingtai'" (The 1990s and the "new ideology"), in *Jiushi niandai wen cun: 1990–2000* (1990s collected writings: 1990–2000), ed. Lin Dazhong (Beijing: Zhongguo shehui kexue, 2001), 2:284–305.

29. Kevin Latham, "Rethinking Chinese Consumption: Social Palliatives and the Rhetorics of Transition in Postsocialist China," in *Postsocialism: Ideals, Ideologies and Practices in Eurasia*, ed. C. M. Hann (London: Routledge, 2002), 231.

30. Here the film is in a sense retelling Marx's story of "The Secret of Primitive Accumulation," with which most Chinese students would be familiar. A "successful personage" such as Xiaoyong is claimed, in capitalist ideology, to be benefiting from legitimate hard work and sacrifice, while a member of the "floating population"—in fact deprived of his previous means of livelihood in the collectivized rural economy—is dismissed as being simply shiftless and lazy. See Karl Marx, *Capital: Volume 1* (London: Penguin, 1976), 873–76.

31. The Faye Wong (Wang Jingwen) song "Sky" (Tiankong) became popular in the mid-1990s and expressed a powerful feeling of mournfulness and yearning. The two verses sung by Meimei, as translated ably into English on a fan Web site (http://c.1asphost.com/aiyulong/), go as follows: "Why is my sky filled with tears? / Why does my sky always have a grey face? / Wandering on the other side of the world / Letting loneliness invade again and again / The sky is streaked with longing // Is your sky filled with clouds of thought? / Does your sky have a cold moon? / Banished to the other side of the sky / Letting loneliness take over night after night / The sky is filled with hidden longing."

32. Aside from the fulfillment of his pledge to his best friend upon the latter's marriage, other details bear witness to the code of honor paradoxically upheld by the pickpocket—most notably his habit of returning the identification cards of his victims by anonymously dropping them into public mailboxes, so that, while stealing their money, he spares them the inconvenience of losing their all-important identification.

33. The effect is similar to that of the 360-degree panning shot in *Il Bandito* (Al-

berto Lattuada, 1946), in which the combination of mobile framing and shot length seem to transform an objective shot into a subjective shot without editing. See Bazin, "An Aesthetic of Reality," 32.

34. Several seminal modern stories by Lu Xun in the late 1910s to early 1920s, including "The True Story of Ah Q" and "Medicine," depict crowds of Chinese people enjoying a public execution, and in his preface to his first volume of short stories Lu Xun himself credits his inspiration to take up writing literature to witnessing a similar scene of cruel voyeurism during a slideshow of news photography. Since the present chapter was first drafted, Jia has confirmed that, at the time he got the inspiration for this closing shot, "naturally, I also thought of Lu Xun's conception of the crowd." See "Jia Zhangke: Capturing a Transforming Reality," in Michael Berry, *Speaking in Images: Interviews with Contemporary Chinese Filmmakers* (New York: Columbia University Press, 2005), 203.

35. The director has verified that the crowd was composed entirely of random passersby attracted not simply by a handcuffed man but by a handcuffed man being filmed. Jia Zhangke, interview by author, Beijing, April 26, 2003.

36. This T-Mark producer, Shozo Ichiyama, had been the producer of Hou's *Hao nan hao nü* (Good men, good women, 1995), *Nanguo, zaijian nanguo* (Goodbye south goodbye, 1996), and *Haishang hua* (Flowers of Shanghai, 1998). As Jia later said of the producer, "I deeply love Hou Hsiao-hsien's movies, and thought if he could work with Hou Hsiao-hsien over a long period, he must be a trustworthy person, or at the very least be someone who likes this kind of film." Jia, "Jia Zhangke," 344. Aside from Hou Hsiao-hsien's films, other influences Jia acknowledges are *Nanook of the North* (1922; dir. Robert J. Flaherty), *Malu tianshi* (Street angels, 1937; dir. Yuan Muzhi), *Xiaocheng zhi chun* (Spring in a small town, 1948; dir. Fei Mu), and the films of Yasujiro Ozu. See Jia, "Zhongguo de duli dianying ren," 154, 162; and Teo, "Cinema with an Accent." In most interviews he also cites a 1991 initial viewing of Chen Kaige's *Huang tudi* (Yellow earth, 1984) as first inspiring him to pursue an education in filmmaking, though he usually adds that he has liked few other Fifth Generation films.

37. Michael Berry, 190.

38. Jia, "Jia Zhangke," 343.

39. Sheldon H. Lu, *China, Transnational Visuality, Global Postmodernity* (Stanford, CA: Stanford University Press, 2001), 198.

40. Michael Berry, 190.

41. See Jia, "Jia Zhangke," 346; and *Nanfang dushi bao* (Nanfang metropolitan news), "Jia Zhangke fangtan—you yigu qi zhengzai ningju" (Jia Zhangke interview—there's a puff of vapor that's now condensing), March 4, 2002.

42. André Bazin, "De Sica: Metteur en Scène," in *What Is Cinema? Vol. II*, 66.

43. Ibid., 76. Speaking here of Vittorio De Sica's *Umberto D* (1952), Bazin defines "life time" as "the simple continuing to be of a person to whom nothing in particular happens."

44. The Four Modernizations—of industry, agriculture, national defense, and science and technology—were the ideological mantra of the Deng Xiaoping era and are dutifully recited at one point by the main protagonist of *Platform* at the request of his troupe leader. Jia has related the preference for the combination of ellipses and quotidian duration in shot selection to the geographical location: "When I started shooting this film, it was as if I had two alternatives. One was to film the very strong changes of the era, and the other was to show more deeply the experience of this in the hinterlands, so that it seems as if nothing has happened, and yet everything is happening." See Jia, "Zhongguo," 159.

45. Svetlana Boym, *The Future of Nostalgia* (New York: Basic Books, 2001), esp. 49–55.

46. Ibid., 49.

47. When one of the main characters tearfully revolts against getting an abortion, for example, the entire scene is shot from the other end of a hospital corridor, so that the viewer lacks even clear access to the facial expressions of the characters as they speak.

48. In an aside about Hollywood editing, Boym asserts that the avoidance of real time is the "one inviolable code in Hollywood cinema," in which "it is no longer the content of the images but the pace of editing itself that has a visceral impact on the viewer and puts an invisible taboo on any form of reflective longing." Boym, 38.

49. See David Bordwell, *Ozu and the Poetics of Cinema* (Princeton, NJ: Princeton University Press, 1988), 84.

50. The exchange between the two potential lovers atop the old city wall recalls, in its setting and its undercurrent of repressed emotion, the two scenes from the 1948 classic *Spring in a Small Town,* during which the former sweethearts Yuwen and Zhichen simultaneously face and evade their feelings for each other during pauses in strolls on an old city wall.

51. Despite their stylistic similarities, I do not mean to imply that these filmmakers share identical concerns. For example, many films of Kiarostami and some of his contemporaries in Iran contain a self-critique of their own realist impulses and are at least partially about the invasiveness of the very attempt to capture the real on film and the impossibility of its success. Examples include Jafar Panahi's *The Mirror* (1997) and Kiarostami's *Close-Up* (1990), *The Taste of Cherry* (1997), and *The Wind Will Carry Us* (1999).

52. Dogma 95 aimed to counter the conception of cinema as illusion with a manifesto-like "vow of chastity," drafted by Lars von Trier and Thomas Vinterberg, in which the filmmakers swear to uphold such restrictions as natural light and sound, on-location shooting, realistic subjects, and contemporary settings. Representative films include Vinterberg's *The Celebration* (1998) and von Trier's *The Idiots* (1998).

53. Andrew Grossman blasts this aesthetic as an "alleged minimalist solution to Hollywood bombast" and mocks "the fallaciously 'transcendental' promise of uneventfulness," and in particular the critical reception of *The Wind Will Carry Us*: "We must en-

dure tired formalist arguments from Kiarostami cultists who insist that the film's medi-
tative uneventfulness is in fact an intellectually demanding existential challenge—as if
this were the cinematic equivalent of Kierkegaard—and that the film's organic structure
transcends the mundanity of its content by paradoxically presenting something more
real than reality through a monastically ascetic style. (So, then, is style reality?) The
mere recognition of conspicuously realistic time in a medium known for its temporal
trickery becomes a *de facto* false ideology of naturalist realism." See Andrew Grossman,
"The Wind Will Carry Us," *Scope: An On-line Journal of Film Studies*, Institute of Film
Studies, University of Nottingham, May 2001, http://www.nottingham.ac.uk/film/jour-
nal/filmrev/the-wind-will-carry-us.htm. While I do not share Grossman's evaluation of
The Wind Will Carry Us, his broadside effectively points to the fine line between naturalist realism and minimalist formalism in recent art cinema.

54.   Gilles Deleuze, *Cinema* (Minneapolis: University of Minnesota Press, 1986). As
different as their concerns are—Deleuze the poststructuralist philosopher and Bazin
the humanist critic—both share a direct debt to Bergson in their theories of cinematic
time.

55.   See Chris Berry, "*Xiao Wu:* Watching Time Go By," for an application of Deleuze's notion of the time-image to *Xiao Wu*.

56.   In the course of the 1990s, Hollywood went from having no presence in the
mainland Chinese film market to being the dominant force at the box office. For details,
see Stanley Rosen, "The Wolf at the Door: Hollywood and the Film Market in China,"
in *Southern California and the World*, ed. Eric J. Heikkila and Rafael Pizarro (Westport,
CT: Praeger, 2002), 49–77. Despite their lack of official distribution, Jia's early films still
constitute an alternative viewing experience in mainland China if one considers video-
watching in private homes, cafés, and bars, which is dominated by pirated video compact disks (VCDs) and DVDs. *Xiao Shan Going Home* is available in a small number of
video shops on poor-quality, home-burned VCDs, and most of Jia's films can also be
downloaded to computers. Moreover, pirated high-quality DVDs of all of Jia's feature
films became widely available in Chinese video stores soon after their release in Japan
and the West.

57.   *Qingnian bao* (Youth daily), "Jia Zhangke: keyi shuo shi yi zhong tuoxie" (Jia
Zhangke: you can say it's a kind of compromise), April 15, 2003.

58.   In an interview published after this chapter was drafted, Jia confirmed that he
intended to show that the generation of youth depicted in *Unknown Pleasures* "are faced
with a new kind of cultural oppression. This is in part due to the lifestyles they hear and
learn about through the media—especially the Internet and cable television—which exist on a completely different plane from their everyday reality. It is this radical contrast
between the reality of their environment and the picture of the world they get through
the media that creates an enormous pressure in their lives." Michael Berry, 193.

59. Chen Pingshu.

60. In the documentary *My Camera Doesn't Lie* (2003; dir. Solveig Klassen and Katharina Schneider-Roos), for example, some independent Chinese directors express their disappointment with Zhang Yuan for working in the mainstream studio system. Jia is a notable exception, saying that Zhang Yuan had built up enough credibility to be trusted to maintain his integrity in any system within which he chose to work.

61. Yu Aiyuan, "Tuwei, taoli, luowang" (Breakthrough, escape, ensnarement), *Jinri xianfeng* (Avant-garde today) 12 (March 2002): 39. Despite my slight disagreement here, this is a very insightful discussion of Jia's films. I would also like to note that, since the drafting of this chapter, a much more thorough discussion of the issue of Jia's "banned" status has appeared in Valerie Jaffee, "Bringing the World to the Nation: Jia Zhangke and the Legitimation of Chinese Underground Film," *Senses of Cinema*, no. 32 (July–September 2004), http://www.sensesofcinema.com/contents/04/32/chinese_underground_film.html.

62. In a Chinese interview, for example, Jia was told that "there are many people who feel that you and some other young directors are achieving 'premeditated success' by shooting films for the West." (The director replied simply that he does not allow criticism to guide his work.) See Jia, "Jia Zhangke," 261–62. I heard criticism expressed in the same way—that the film was "made for Westerners"—after a private DVD viewing of *Platform* with several graduate students in Shanghai during the fall of 2002. Evidently sensitive to such criticism, Jia himself raised and adamantly rejected the accusation that his films are aimed specifically at a foreign audience both in the documentary *My Camera Doesn't Lie* and in my April 2003 interview with him.

63. For example, Jim Jarmusch—one of America's few genuinely independent feature filmmakers—has a much larger following in Europe than in the United States.

64. Such an implication crops up even in the discussions of some of China's most well-known critics. For instance, Dai Jinhua ridiculed the enthusiasm of an American film festival organizer for He Jianjun's *Youchai* (Postman, 1995), which Dai felt was inferior to other Chinese films in the festival but was received more favorably only because of its novelty at the time as a Sixth rather than Fifth Generation film. Given that *Postman* is both innovative in its narrative and accomplished in its technique, one wonders why the festival organizer is assumed to have such superficial reasons for liking the film. The seemingly immaterial but nonetheless highlighted fact that the festival organizer was "a blonde, blue-eyed American lady" indicates how precariously reflexive accusations of orientalism can verge on becoming their own kind of essentialism. See Dai, 77.

65. Pascale Casanova, "Literature as a World," *New Left Review* 31 (January–February 2005): 79n.

66. Ibid., 83.

67. These comments by Russian film critic Irina Shilova are quoted in Susan Larsen,

"In Search of an Audience: The New Russian Cinema of Reconciliation," in *Consuming Russia: Popular Culture, Sex, and Society since Gorbachev*, ed. Adele Marie Barker (Durham, NC: Duke University Press, 1999), 198.

68. Tarr's early films include *Family Nest* (1979), *The Outsider* (1982), and *Prefab People* (1982). Like Jia, Tarr was not an isolated phenomenon but was part of a broader aesthetic movement toward a raw documentary-style realism—in Tarr's case the "Budapest school," which favored "black-and-white photography, hand-held cameras, a deliberated lack of smoothness in the editing, large degrees of improvisation and use of amateur actors." John Cunningham, *Hungarian Cinema: From Coffee House to Multiplex* (London: Wallflower Press, 2004), 136.

69. Cunningham, *Hungarian Cinema*, 116.

70. Tarr's films of this time include the epic *Satantango* (1994) and the more modest but still staggering *Werkmeister Harmonies* (2000).

CHAPTER SIX

1. Feng Xiaogang himself credits his fellow director and sometime collaborator Zheng Xiaolong with the idea of applying the *hesuipian* strategy to the mainland market with the television series *Wanshiruyi* (As you wish), which ran during the 1997 Spring Festival. Feng Xiaogang, *Wo ba qingchun xian gei ni* (I devoted my youth to you). (Wuhan: Changjiang wenyi, 2003), 100.

2. Crystyl Mo, "Feng Xiaogang Sets His Sights on Hollywood," http://www.chinanow.com/english/shanghai/city/movies/fengxiaogang.html.

3. Three years later, *Cell Phone* earned more than *Big Shot's Funeral*, but in the meantime *Yingxiong* (Hero; dir. Zhang Yimou, 2002) had taken the title of highest-grossing mainland production ever. (See Chapter Seven for more on *Hero*.)

4. Quoted in Hannah Beech, "Keeping It Reel," *Time Asia*, July 23, 2001. http://www.time.com/time/arts/article/0,8599,167619,00.html.

5. Feng's full statement (made in 2000) is as follows: "If you consider the market effect of films, from 1997 to 2000, it was my movies that saved the Chinese film industry, not Chinese film that saved me." Quoted in Shuyu Kong, "Big Shot from Beijing: Feng Xiaogang's *He Sui Pian* and Contemporary Chinese Commercial Film," *Asian Cinema* 14, no. 1 (spring/summer 2003): 178.

6. Probably the most celebrated Western instance of metacinema in a time of industrial crisis is Billy Wilder's *Sunset Boulevard* (1950), produced just when Hollywood appeared to be in serious economic decline. See, for example, Robert Stam, *Reflexivity in Film and Literature: From Don Quixote to Jean-Luc Godard* (New York: Columbia University Press, 1992), 85–90.

7. The idea of a national cinema can easily lead to the kind of hypostatization of the "nation" that much recent scholarship has sought to problematize. The term *national*

cinema has likewise been called into question by sinological and other scholars. See, for example, Stephen Crofts, "Reconceptualizing National Cinema/s," *Quarterly Review of Film and Video* 14, no. 3 (1993): 49–67; Chris Berry, "If China Can Say No, Can China Make Movies? Or, Do Movies Make China? Rethinking National Cinema and National Agency," in *Modern Chinese Literary and Cultural Studies in the Age of Theory: Reimagining a Field*, ed. Rey Chow (Durham, NC: Duke University Press, 2000), 159–80; and Chris Berry and Mary Farquhar, "From National Cinemas to Cinema and the National: Rethinking the National in Transnational Chinese Cinemas," *Journal of Modern Literature in Chinese* 4, no. 2 (2001): 109–22. I thus use the term *national cinema* not as an obvious or natural category but rather as a discursive formation (though it may well deploy various forms of "strategic essentialism") that arises partly in resistance to Hollywood's hegemony.

8. According to Hansen, "Hyperbolically speaking, one might say that Russian cinema became Soviet cinema by going through a process of Americanization." Miriam Bratu Hansen, "The Mass Production of the Senses: Classical Cinema as Vernacular Modernism," in *Reinventing Film Studies*, ed. Christine Gledhill (London: Oxford University Press, 2000), 334.

9. The classical Hollywood style established conventions of temporal and spatial organization that have remained remarkably resilient to fundamental change even after the end of the golden age of the studio production system. For one influential analysis and description of this mode's formal characteristics, see David Bordwell, Janet Staiger, and Kristin Thompson, *The Classical Hollywood Cinema: Film Style and Mode of Production to 1960* (New York: Columbia University Press, 1985). See also the chapter "Classical Narration: The Hollywood Example" in David Bordwell, *Narration in the Fiction Film* (Madison: University of Wisconsin Press, 1985), 156–204; and for an alternative model, see Tom Gunning, *D. W. Griffith and the Origins of American Narrative Film* (Urbana: University of Illinois Press, 1991).

10. See Miriam Bratu Hansen, "Fallen Women, Rising Stars, New Horizons: Shanghai Silent Film as Vernacular Modernism," *Film Quarterly* 54, no. 1 (2000): 10–22; and Zhang Zhen, *An Amorous History of the Silver Screen: Shanghai Cinema, 1896–1937* (Chicago: University of Chicago Press, 2005).

11. For overviews of Chinese cinema history, including both the Shanghai golden age and the Mao era that followed, see Zhiwei Xiao, "Chinese Cinema," in *Encyclopedia of Chinese Film*, ed. Yingjin Zhang and Zhiwei Xiao (New York: Routledge, 1998), 3–30; Yingjin Zhang, *Chinese National Cinema* (London: Routledge, 2004); and Paul Clark, *Chinese Cinema: Culture and Politics Since 1949* (New York: Cambridge University Press, 1988). Clark in particular discusses changes in film culture in terms of a dichotomy between the progressive, cosmopolitan Shanghai style and the revolutionary, nationalist Yan'an style.

12.   This practice continued into the reform era in the case of some patriotic "main melody" films, for which complimentary tickets were often distributed through work units, artificially inflating box-office figures for such films.

13.   Indeed, as Rey Chow has demonstrated at length, the foreign gaze not only constitutes the Chinese national cinema in the eyes of the world but also mediates the understanding within China of its own national cinema, including its possibilities for intervention in the ways China is constructed in the global imaginary. See Rey Chow, *Primitive Passions: Visuality, Sexuality, Ethnography, and Contemporary Chinese Cinema* (New York: Columbia University Press, 1995).

14.   The seven types are (1) European-model art cinemas, which target a specialized audience rather than competing directly with Hollywood; (2) "third" cinema, which directly critiques Hollywood; (3) commercial entertainment cinemas, which both imitate and compete directly with Hollywood for the same domestic audience; (4) cinemas which ignore Hollywood and successfully develop a very different sort of industry and aesthetic (namely, India and Hong Kong cinemas); (5) Anglophone cinemas that try to beat Hollywood at its own game by capturing a popular American audience; (6) totalitarian cinemas, which are state-controlled and predominantly socialist realist in aesthetic; and (7) regional/ethnic cinemas that mobilize minority cultures and languages within a nation. Crofts, 50–57.

15.   Crofts, 50.

16.   For more details, see Stanley Rosen, "The Wolf at the Door: Hollywood and the Film Market in China," in *Southern California and the World*, ed. Eric J. Heikkila and Rafael Pizarro (Westport, CT: Praeger, 2002), 49–77.

17.   Jin Bo, "Imported Movies: Entertainment or Hegemony?" *China Daily*, April 8, 2002, http://www1.chinadaily.com.cn/cndy/2002-4-8/64606.html.

18.   For a more detailed account of changes in film distribution in China, including the impact of the VCD format and the new Hollywood imports, see Shujen Wang, *Framing Piracy: Globalization and Film Distribution in Greater China* (Lanham, MD: Rowman & Littlefield, 2003). She points out, for example, that by limiting foreign films to only about a third of those distributed, domestic film distribution was indirectly subsidized by the same imports it was competing against, since distribution profits from the imports helped to compensate for distribution losses from many domestic productions. Ibid., 63.

19.   Jin Bo.

20.   For more on Wang Shuo and the cultural politics surrounding him, see Chapter Two. For a more detailed discussion of Wang Shuo and the *liumang* phenomenon, see Geremie Barmé, *In the Red: On Contemporary Chinese Culture* (New York: Columbia University Press, 1999), 62–98; and Jing Wang, *High Culture Fever: Politics, Aesthetics, and Ideology in Deng's China* (Berkeley: University of California Press, 1997), 261–86.

21. Aleš Erjavec, introduction to *Postmodernism and the Postsocialist Condition: Politicized Art Under Late Socialism*, ed. Aleš Erjavec (Berkeley: University of California Press, 2003), 4.

22. Xiaobing Tang, "The Function of New Theory: What Does It Mean to Talk About Postmodernism in China?" in *Politics, Ideology, and Literary Discourse in Modern China: Theoretical Interventions and Cultural Critique*, ed. Liu Kang and Xiaobing Tang (Durham, NC: Duke University Press, 1993), 294. For another discussion of the prevalence of irony in early 1990s Chinese culture, see Barmé, 281–83.

23. J. Wang, 262.

24. *Wanzhu* has been variously translated as *Troubleshooters, Troublemakers, Three-T Company*, and *The Operators*.

25. For a discussion of *Stories of an Editorial Board*, see Claire Huot, *China's New Cultural Scene: A Handbook of Changes* (Durham, NC: Duke University Press, 2000), 50–55.

26. For an in-depth ideological analysis of this TV series, see Lydia H. Liu, "Beijing Sojourners in New York: Postsocialism and the Question of Ideology in Global Media Culture," *Positions: East Asia Cultures Critique* 7 (winter 1999): 763–97. See also Huot, 60–64.

27. An adaptation of Wang Shuo's novel *Wo shi ni baba* (I am your father) was blocked, apparently because of the potential for the story to be read allegorically as a critique of political authority. Another collaboration with Wang Shuo, this time a non-moralizing treatment of a man having an extramarital affair, was shut down ten days into shooting—although, as we have seen in Chapter Four, Feng would go on to make two of his later films with a similar theme after he had established himself a few years later. Another banned project of his during this time featured a bank robber who ends up being caught and executed.

28. Feng, 44.

29. Ibid., 102–4.

30. Compromises such as these in Feng's *hesuipian* helped lead to an estrangement from his old friend Wang Shuo, who would later comment that Feng had suffered from the "pathetic" necessity that a film director achieve box-office success and "give us some scant celebration of stability and unity" (the latter being a mocking reference to the Maoist slogan *anding tuanjie*). Wang Shuo, *Meiren zeng wo menghanyao* (A beauty presents me with knock-out drops) (Wuhan: Changjiang wenyi, 2000), 127. The author's related critique that the subversive popular culture (*dianfu tongsu wenhua*) of the late 1980s and early 1990s had degenerated into an obsequious mass culture (*meitai dazhong wenhua*) by the late 1990s due to the rule of the free market perhaps downplays the extent to which his own "subversion" had embraced commodification from the beginning. Ibid., 67–68.

31. The picture announces its "New Years film" status immediately, opening with a brief image of an animated tiger and then the greeting "Wishing citizens across the country a highly auspicious Year of the Tiger."

32. Chinese box-office figures are of course misleading by Western standards, since even in the late 1990s many movie theater tickets still cost little more than a dollar.

33. Yingjin Zhang, *Screening China: Critical Interventions, Cinematic Reconfigurations, and the Transnational Imaginary in Contemporary Chinese Cinema* (Ann Arbor: Center for Chinese Studies, University of Michigan, 2002), 319.

34. Ge You had in the meantime won a best actor award at Cannes for his role in *Huozhe* (To live; dir. Zhang Yimou, 1994), but he is best loved in China for his deadpan humor in comedy roles.

35. Similarly, the landlords whom the bullying husband serves in another "dream" sequence parody those from the classic revolutionary film *Bai mao nü* (White-haired girl; dir. Shui Hua and Wang Bin, 1950).

36. Tan Ye, "Hollywood and the Chinese Other," *Cineaction* , no. 60 (2003): 16.

37. The distinction here being one between the (fictional) customer's experience of only the profilmic battlefield tableau and the (actual) spectator's experience of the filmmaker's framing and editing *of* the customer's experiences.

38. Zhang, *Screening China*, 318.

39. Hortense Powdermaker, *Hollywood: The Dream Factory* (Boston: Little, Brown, 1950).

40. For a discussion of the film-as-daydream, following Ernst Bloch, see Jane M. Gaines, "Dream/Factory," in *Reinventing Film Studies*, ed. Christine Gledhill (London: Oxford University Press, 2000), 100–113.

41. Stam, xviii.

42. Ibid., xvi–xvii.

43. Kenneth Klinkner has identified this *tiaokan* play as a central element to Feng Xiaogang's *hesuipian* formula in "Lightening Up China: The Holiday Films of Feng Xiaogang" (paper presented at the China Pop Culture Conference, University of Illinois, Urbana, April 20, 2002).

44. Zhou Shaoming, "Making Money Can Be Funny," *Cinemaya*, no. 52 (2001): 14.

45. Various citations of Chinese box-office figures seldom agree exactly, but the consensus is that *Be There* took in something over 40 million yuan, or about 5 million dollars. Of course, given that there would have been many more viewings of the film on video than in the theater, and that the vast majority of those would have been of pirated VCDs, it is impossible to measure the film's actual audience in China. For *Big Shot's Funeral*, Feng himself estimated that there were a million pirated copies, and if each were watched by an average of five viewers, the total box-office revenues lost would have been three times the film's actual box-office gross. Jaime FlorCruz, "Piracy Cripples China's Film Industry," Cnn.com. (No longer posted.)

46. Scarlet Cheng, "There's Nothing Like Being There," *Los Angeles Times*, November 1, 1998.

47. FUBU, an acronym for "For Us, By Us," was initially conceived as a line of urban sportswear created "for African Americans by African Americans" in an expression of black empowerment.

48. Tom Gunning defines the "cinema of attractions" as "a conception that sees cinema less as a way of telling stories than as a way of presenting a series of views to an audience, fascinating because of their illusory power . . . and exoticism." Such an "exhibitionist cinema" dominated film before about 1906–7, after which it "does not disappear with the dominance of narrative, but rather goes underground, both into certain avant-garde practices and as a component of narrative films." See Tom Gunning, "The Cinema of Attraction: Early Film, Its Spectator and the Avant-Garde," *Wide Angle* 8 (1986): 64.

49. Cheng.

50. Stam, xiii.

51. Tom Gunning, "An Aesthetic of Astonishment: Early Film and the (In)Credulous Spectator," in *Film Theory and Criticism: Introductory Readings,* 5th ed., ed. Gerald Mast, Marshall Cohen, and Leo Braudy (New York: Oxford University Press, 1999), 821.

52. The Phantasmagoria was an optical illusion dating to the late eighteenth century that used a "magic lantern" to project vivid apparitions in darkened rooms for the astonishment and amusement of audiences.

53. Tom Gunning, "Illusions Past and Future: The Phantasmagoria and Its Specters," Media Art Histories Archive, http://www.mediaarthistory.org/Programmatic%20key%20texts/pdfs/Gunning.pdf. I am also grateful to Tom Gunning for sharing the text of his paper "Phantasmagoria and the Manufacturing of Illusions and Wonder: Towards a Cultural Optics of the Cinematic Apparatus" (presented at the Domitor Conference, Montreal, Canada, June 2002).

54. The word *funeral* was removed from the Chinese title after the director took ill during shooting and deemed the word unlucky. Feng, 183–84.

55. Feng Xiaogang has reported that Marlon Brando had initially agreed to play the role that eventually went to Sutherland. According to Feng, Brando backed out for no apparent reason after all the arrangements had been made with his agent. Other actors Feng considered trying to get for the part included Al Pacino and Warren Beatty. See Mo; and Stephen Short, "'As Sex Scenes Are Banned, We Need to Be Creative': Web-Only Interview with Director Feng Xiaogang," *Time Asia* (October 26, 2000), http://www.time.com/time/asia/features/ interviews/2000/10/26/int.feng_xiaogang.html.

56. Shujen Wang makes a similar point in her insightful reading of the film: "This scene is significant because it touches on one of the most important themes of the film: looking and the power of representation." Shujen Wang, "*Big Shot's Funeral*: China, Sony, and the WTO," *Asian Cinema* 14, no. 2 (fall/winter 2003): 150.

57. For an extended analysis of the cultural politics of Bertolucci's representational strategies in *The Last Emperor* and the position of a Chinese "ethnic spectator" for the film, see Rey Chow, "Seeing Modern China: Toward a Theory of Ethnic Spectatorship," in *Woman and Chinese Modernity: The Politics of Reading Between West and East* (Minneapolis: University of Minnesota Press, 1991), 3–33.

58. For more on the cross-cultural politics of representation in the film, see Wang, "*Big Shot's Funeral*," 149–50.

59. As Shuyu Kong notes, "despite the fact that the theme of *Big Shot's Funeral* is to mock the commercialism which has permeated every part of social and cultural life, exemplified by advertising in this case, and also to expose in an exaggerated manner 'people's insane lust for money,' the film itself is made possible by various international and local sponsorships, from Columbia Pictures to local luxury hotels, and various actual goods, from women's products to cigarettes to furniture, are all advertised items in the funeral scene, thus making *Big Shot's Funeral* itself an example of exactly what it is mocking." Kong, 186. Carlos Rojas also notes how Feng's *hesuipian* in general are often found to be "alluding ironically to their own status as cultural commodities." Carlos Rojas, "A Tale of Two Emperors: Mimicry and Mimesis in Two 'New Year's' Films from China and Hong Kong," *Cineaction*, no. 60 (spring 2003): 3.

60. For an essay on reflexivity in an array of films about filmmaking, see the chapter "The Process of Production" in Stam, 71–126.

61. Underscoring the reference, Fellini makes a cameo appearance as himself in Mazursky's film.

62. The fictional Tyler's appreciation of the cynical travesty of advertising and product placement that his Chinese friends were making of his "funeral" contrasts greatly with his real predecessor's condescending fondness for his Chinese hosts. Bertolucci has said of China, "For me it was love at first sight. I loved it. I thought the Chinese were fascinating. They have an innocence. They have a mixture of a people before consumerism, before something happened in the West. Yet in the meantime they are incredibly sophisticated, elegant and subtle, because they are 4,000 years old." Quoted in Chow, 4.

63. Quoted in Kong, 181.

64. This kind of layering of narratives also has important precedents in premodern Chinese literature. For example, a Qing Dynasty ghost story in the classical style by Ji Yun contains a total of six enunciators, beginning with the author himself, each of which is enclosed by the preceding one, and three of which turn out to be ghosts. Ji Yun, *Yuewei caotang biji* (Notes from the thatched cottage of careful reading) (Beijing: Zhongguo wenlian chubanshe, 1996), 119–20. (My thanks to Judith Zeitlin for sharing a draft of her English translation of this story.) A more obvious example of the reflexive structure of multiple enclosed narrators in Chinese fiction is the classic vernacular novel *Honglou-*

meng (Dream of the red chamber), which has a complexity of enunciative voices to rival any work of high modernism in the West.

65. On the international hype preceding *Big Shot's Funeral* as well as Feng's own hopes for an international audience, see Mo as well as Erik Eckholm, "Leading Chinese Filmmaker Tries for a Great Leap to the West," *New York Times*, June 21, 2001.

66. Wendy Kan, " 'Big Shot' Doesn't Win Over Locals," *Variety* 387, no. 2 (May 27, 2002): 8.

67. Craig White, "Craig's Toronto FilmFest News and Reviews," September 10, 2002, http://filmfest.tnir.org/archives/2002_09.html.

68. Rosen, 70. An exception to this rule was the popularity of *Big Shot's Funeral* in Shanghai, where Feng's previous *hesuipian* had not done nearly as well as in Beijing. (See Wang, "*Big Shot's Funeral*," 148.) Perhaps that film's send-up of commercialization and get-rich-quick madness could find no more knowing public than in the metropolis that had boomed like no other in China during the preceding decade.

69. On the reactions of foreign and domestic audiences and critics at the film's various "premiers," see, for example, Zhang Rui, "*The Banquet* World Premiere," China.org. cn, Sep. 11, 2006, http://www.china.org.cn/english/2006/Sep/180709.htm. In contrast to this article's description of audience reaction at Cannes, the audience at the screening I attended during the 2006 Toronto Film Festival was clearly amused by the film and laughed frequently at ostensibly melodramatic situations.

70. "More Detail on Feng Xiaogang's *The Assembly Call*," *MonkeyPeaches*, Sep. 26, 2006, http://www.monkeypeaches.com/thebanquet.html.

71. For a much more detailed discussion of the progression of Feng Xiaogang's career, see Rui Zhang, "Feng Xiaogang and Chinese Cinema after 1989," Ph.D. diss., Ohio State University, 2006. I am also indebted to Robin Visser's paper "Pop Art Conscience? Middle-Brow Aesthetics in the Film/Novel *Cell Phone*," presented at the annual meeting of the Association for Asian Studies, Chicago, April 1, 2005.

72. Other examples would include Zhang Yimou's *Xingfu shiguang* (Happy times, 2000) and Chen Kaige's *He ni zai yiqi* (Together, 2002).

73. Quoted in Zhang, *Screening China*, 318.

74. Paul F. Duke, "China's Feng Will 'Be There': Helmer Hot O'seas," *Variety* 377, no. 8 (January 10, 2000): 6–7.

75. Beech. The same source records Feng's view of the intelligentsia, offered while he is eating a meal: "Feng responds to such sniping by dislodging [an] offending bit of dinner from his teeth. It is a piece of dried chili pepper. He takes it from his tongue and places it on the table. 'This is me,' he says, pointing with a toothpick. Then he picks up a shrimp from a plate next to him. 'This is the intellectuals.' Feng places the shrimp on top of the chili; the red flake disappears from view. Then Feng leans in, his raspy voice rising

as he approaches the punch line. 'But tomorrow morning, when you're sitting on the toilet'—he pops both the shrimp and chili in his mouth—'which one do you remember more: the shrimp or the chili?'"

76. Xiaobing Tang, "Rural Women and Social Change in New China Cinema: From *Li Shuangshuang* to *Ermo*," *Positions: East Asia Cultures Critique* 11 (winter 2003): 648.

77. Eckholm.

78. James Donald and Stephanie Hemelryk Donald, "The Publicness of Cinema," in *Reinventing Film Studies*, ed. Christine Gledhill and Linda Williams (London: Arnold, 2000), 125.

79. See, for example, Eckholm.

80. Susan Larsen, "In Search of an Audience: The New Russian Cinema of Reconciliation," in *Consuming Russia: Popular Culture, Sex, and Society since Gorbachev*, ed. Adele Marie Barker (Durham, NC: Duke University Press, 1999), 196.

CHAPTER SEVEN

1. The cartoonish futurist aesthetic of the Pearl Tower recently lent itself to B-level Hollywood when it was used as a setting for the throwaway science fiction film *Ultraviolet* (2006). Though the film is not explicitly set in China, the choice of the architecture of Pudong to represent the stereotypical technological dystopia of the future is a backhanded compliment that lends credence to the idea that the Pudong skyline signifies the twenty-first century to come.

2. See, for example, Jean-Francois Lyotard, *The Postmodern Condition: A Report on Knowledge* (Minneapolis: University of Minnesota Press, 1979).

3. Christopher Prendergast, "Codeword Modernity," *New Left Review* 24 (Nov.-Dec. 2003): 103.

4. As noted in Chapter Three, even those who christened the "new-state-of-affairs" literature described it as a "transition mechanism" that marked the transformation of society and culture. See Wang Gan, Zhang Yiwu, and Zhang Weimin, "'Xin zhuangtai wenxue' san ren tan" ("New state of affairs literature" three-way discussion), in *90 Niandai piping wenxuan* (Selected works of 1990s criticism), ed. Chen Sihe and Yang Yang (Shanghai: Hanyu dacidian chubanshe, 2001), 436.

5. Kevin Latham, "Rethinking Chinese Consumption: Social Palliatives and the Rhetorics of Transition in Postsocialist China," in *Postsocialism: Ideals, Ideologies and Practices in Eurasia*, ed. C. M. Hann (London: Routledge, 2002), 223.

6. Ibid., 230.

7. Ibid., 231. For a discussion of the "deeply problematic" concept of *transition* in studies of postsocialist societies in general, see "Introduction: Transitions to Post-Socialism and Cultures of Survival," in Frances Pine and Sue Bridger, eds., *Surviving Post-*

Socialism: Local Strategies and Regional Responses in Eastern Europe and the Former So-viet Union, (London: Routledge, 1998), 2–3.

8. Yan Lianke, *Shouhuo* (Enjoyment) (Shenyang: Chunfeng wenyi chubanshe, 2004).

9. On the image of modernity as a juggernaut, see Anthony Giddens, *The Consequences of Modernity* (Stanford, CA: Stanford University Press, 1990), 139.

10. David Harvey, *The New Imperialism* (Oxford: Oxford University Press, 2003), 137–82. On the specific case of postsocialist China, see 153–54.

11. This process is depicted nowhere as thoroughly as in Wang Bing's epic nine-hour documentary *Tiexi qu* (West of the tracks, 2003), a beautiful, sprawling, and ultimately devastating account of the closing of factories that had supported generations of workers and the razing of the neighborhood in which many of them lived in the rust-belt city of Shenyang.

12. Stephen Roach, "Globalization's New Underclass: China, the US, Japan, and the Changing Face of Inequality," *Japan Focus*, March 3, 2006, http://www.japanfocus.org/products/details/1923.

13. Swati Lodh Kundu, "Rural China: Too Little, Too Late," *Asia Times*, July 19, 2006.

14. These figures have been widely cited in the Western media. For one example, see Isabel Hilton, "Karl, China Needs You," *New Statesman*, February 20, 2006.

15. Joseph Kahn, "A Sharp Debate Erupts in China Over Ideologies," *New York Times*, March 12, 2006; Kundu.

16. Kevin J. O'Brien and Lianjiang Li, *Rightful Resistance in Rural China* (Cambridge: Cambridge University Press, 2006), 2.

17. See, for example, Craig Karmin and Henny Sender, "If U.S. Presses China on Yuan, a Delicate Scale Could Tip," *Wall Street Journal*, June 29, 2005; R. Taggart Murphy, "East Asia's Dollars," *New Left Review* 40 (July–August 2006): 39–64.

18. Roach.

19. The latter figure, updating the statistic Roach gives from the turn of the century, is taken from "The World Factbook" of the U.S. Central Intelligence Agency, https://www.cia.gov/library/publications/the-world-factbook/fields/2172.html. Compare, for example, the Gini indexes of Denmark (23.2) or Sweden (25).

20. Wang Hui, "Dangdai Zhongguo de sixiang zhuangkuang yu xiandai xing wen-ti" (Contemporary Chinese thought and the question of modernity), *Tianya* (October 1997): 133–50; translated by Rebecca Karl in Wang Hui, *China's New Order: Society, Politics, and Economy in Transition* (Cambridge, MA: Harvard University Press, 2003), 139–87.

21. Wang Hui, *China's New Order*, 145. This, needless to say, summarizes my justi-

fication for using the term *postsocialist modernity* to refer not just to the condition in China or other formerly communist societies, but to the contemporary capitalist world-system as a whole.

22. Ibid., 181–82.

23. Ibid., 186–87.

24. For an excellent overview of intellectual debates of the 1990s, including the rise of the New Left, see Wang Chaohua's "Introduction: Minds of the Nineties," in *One China, Many Paths*, ed. Chaohua Wang (London: Verso, 2003), 9–45.

25. See He Qinglian's book *Xiandaihua de xianjing: dangdai Zhongguo de jingji she-hui wenti* (Modernization's pitfall: contemporary China's economic and social questions) (Beijing: Jinri Zhongguo chubanshe, 1998)—originally published as *China's Pitfall* the previous year in Hong Kong.

26. I have discussed *Chicken Poets* in a different context in my essay "The New Formalism: Mainland Chinese Cinema at the Turn of the Century," in *China's Literary and Cultural Scenes at the Turn of the 21st Century*, ed. Jie Lu (London: Routledge, forthcoming).

27. The form of this work of video art recalls experimental filmmakers such as Matthias Müller, whose experimental short films use found footage from feature films to construct pseudonarratives that reveal the sexual and political unconscious of Hollywood clichés. Weng Fen's piece, as originally exhibited, showed the edited film clips side by side with another video of interviews with ten contemporary people in Hankou talking about their hopes for the future, but this was not included in the Guangzhou Triennial exhibit.

28. These clips are from *Xiao jie* (The alley; dir. Yang Yanjin, 1981) and *Xingfu shi-guang* (Happy times; dir. Zhang Yimou, 2000).

29. Alexei Yurchak, *Everything Was Forever, Until It Was No More: The Last Soviet Generation* (Princeton, NJ: Princeton University Press, 2006), 8.

30. For a study of contemporary Chinese culture that elaborates the persistence of revolutionary culture and ideals even amid the globalization of the post-Deng era, see Liu Kang, *Globalization and Cultural Trends in China* (Honolulu: University of Hawai'i Press, 2004).

31. See Wu Hung, Wang Huangsheng, and Feng Boyi, *The First Guangzhou Triennial—Reinterpretation: A Decade of Experimental Chinese Art (1990–2000)* (Guangzhou: Guangdong Museum of Art, 2002), 11–12. The only political problem experienced by the show occurred when authorities refused to allow Huang Yongping's installation of a replica of the American spy plane that recently had collided with a Chinese fighter jet.

32. Maureen Fan, "Punks and Posers in China," *Washington Post*, August 9, 2006.

33. Ian Johnson, "New Chinese Art: Revolting …," *Wall Street Journal*, May 5, 1999.

34. One parody, "Bushe Zongtong kanwan *Yingxiong* zhihou" (President Bush after

watching *Hero*), which has been posted on over a thousand Chinese Web sites, has President Bush himself watching *Hero* and taking it as a legitimization of his foreign policies. See, for example, http://www.pdsw.net/asp/comm_show.asp?id=209641.

35. The actual attraction in Beijing is called "Window of the World" (*Shijie zhi chuang*). A twin theme park in Shenzhen served as a shooting location as well.

36. The dance has an interesting precedent in early Chinese cinema. In the metacinematic 1931 film *Yinhan shuang xing* (Two stars in the Milky Way; dir. Shi Dongsan), film industry figures scout a potential young movie starlet by watching her perform a stylized "Egyptian dance" as part of a program on a modern, Art-Deco theater stage. The comparison of these two instances of commodified exoticism indicates the sometimes striking parallels between China under semicolonial modernity in the Republican era and China under postsocialist modernity today.

Works Cited

Adorno, Theodor W. *Aesthetic Theory*. Minneapolis: University of Minnesota Press, 1997.

Anderson, Marston. *The Limits of Realism: Chinese Fiction in the Revolutionary Period*. Berkeley: University of California Press, 1990.

Arrighi, Giovanni. "Hegemony Unravelling—1." *New Left Review* 32 (March–April 2005): 23–80.

———. *The Long Twentieth Century*. London: Verso, 1994.

Badiou, Alain. *Manifesto for Philosophy*. Albany: State University of New York Press, 1999.

Bai Ye, Wang Shuo, Wu Bin, and Yang Zhengguang. "Xuanze de ziyou yu wenhua taishi" (Freedom of choice and cultural trends). In *Renwen jingshen xunsi lu* (Thoughts on the humanist spirit), edited by Wang Xiaoming, 84–99. Shanghai: Wenhui chubanshe, 1996.

Barlow, Tani E. "'green blade in the act of being grazed': Late Capital, Flexible Bodies, Critical Intelligibility." *Differences: A Journal of Feminist Cultural Studies* 10, no. 3 (1998): 119–58.

Barmé, Geremie. "Flashback: It's Not All About Money." *Time Asia*, October 23, 2000.

———. *In the Red: On Contemporary Chinese Culture*. New York: Columbia University Press, 1999.

———. "Time's Arrows: Imaginative Pasts and Nostalgic Futures." In *Voicing Concerns: Contemporary Chinese Critical Inquiry*, edited by Gloria Davies, 227–57. Lanham, MD: Rowman and Littlefield, 2001.

Barthes, Roland. *Camera Lucida: Reflections on Photography*. New York: Hill and Wang, 1981.

Bazin, André. *What Is Cinema? Vol. I*. Berkeley: University of California Press, 1967.

————. *What Is Cinema? Vol. II.* Berkeley: University of California Press, 1971.

Beck, Ulrich, and Elisabeth Beck-Gernsheim. *Individualization: Institutionalized Individualism and Its Social and Political Consequences.* London: Sage, 2002.

Beech, Hannah. "Keeping It Reel." *Time Asia,* July 23, 2001. http://www.time.com/time/asia/arts/magazine/0,9754,167619,00.html.

Benjamin, Walter. "The Return of the Flaneur." In *Selected Writings: 1927–1934,* 2:262–67. Cambridge, MA: Harvard University Press, 1999 [1929].

Berry, Chris. "Getting Real: Chinese Documentary, Chinese Postsocialism." In *The Urban Generation: Chinese Cinema and Society at the Turn of the 21 Century,* edited by Zhang Zhen. Durham, NC: Duke University Press, 2007.

————. "If China Can Say No, Can China Make Movies? Or, Do Movies Make China? Rethinking National Cinema and National Agency." In *Modern Chinese Literary and Cultural Studies in the Age of Theory: Reimagining a Field,* edited by Rey Chow, 159–80. Durham, NC: Duke University Press, 2000.

————. "*Xiao Wu*: Watching Time Go By." In *Chinese Films in Focus,* 2nd edition. London: British Film Institute, forthcoming.

Berry, Chris, and Mary Farquhar. "From National Cinemas to Cinema and the National: Rethinking the National in Transnational Chinese Cinemas." *Journal of Modern Literature in Chinese* 4, no. 2 (2001): 109–22.

Berry, Michael. *Speaking in Images: Interviews with Contemporary Chinese Filmmakers.* New York: Columbia University Press, 2005.

Bezlova, Antoaneta. "China's New Cultural Revolution." *Asia Times,* July 29, 2006.

Bo, Jin. "Imported Movies: Entertainment or Hegemony?" *China Daily,* April 8, 2002. http://www1.chinadaily.com.cn/cndy/2002-04-08/64606.html.

Bordwell, David. *Narration in the Fiction Film.* Madison: University of Wisconsin Press, 1985.

————. *Ozu and the Poetics of Cinema.* Princeton, NJ: Princeton University Press, 1988.

Bordwell, David, Janet Staiger, and Kristin Thompson. *The Classical Hollywood Cinema: Film Style and Mode of Production to 1960.* New York: Columbia University Press, 1985.

Boym, Svetlana. *The Future of Nostalgia.* New York: Basic Books, 2001.

Brook, Timothy. *The Confusions of Pleasure: Commerce and Culture in Ming China.* Berkeley: University of California Press, 1998.

Casanova, Pascale. "Literature as a World." *New Left Review* 31 (January–February 2005): 71–90.

————. *The World Republic of Letters.* Cambridge, MA: Harvard University Press, 2004.

Castoriadis, Cornelius. *World in Fragments: Writings on Politics, Society, Psychoanalysis, and the Imagination.* Edited and translated by David Ames Curtis. Stanford, CA: Stanford University Press, 1997.

Cavell, Stanley. *Pursuits of Happiness: The Hollywood Comedy of Remarriage*. Cambridge, MA: Harvard University Press, 1981.

Chang Guangyuan, Zhang Li, and Meng Dengying. "Zai shiji bianyuan muge: renwen jingshen duihua lu" (Pastoral song at the brink of the century: record of a conversation on the humanist spirit). In *Renwen jingshen xunsi lu* (Thoughts on the humanist spirit), edited by Wang Xiaoming, 254–58. Shanghai: Wenhui chubanshe, 1996.

Chen Pingshu. "Jia Zhangke, Wang Xiaoshuai huigui zhuliu: dianying 'diliudai' jiedong?" (Jia Zhangke and Wang Xiaoshuai return to the mainstream: the thaw of cinema's "sixth generation"?). *Zhongguo qingnian bao* (China youth daily), January 17, 2004.

Chen Shaoming. "Ba jieshi jutihua—ye tan renwen qifen de danmo" (Concretize the explanation—on the haziness of the humanist atmosphere). In *Renwen jingshen xunsi lu* (Thoughts on the humanist spirit), edited by Wang Xiaoming, 201–5. Shanghai: Wenhui chubanshe, 1996.

Chen Sihe. *Chen Sihe zixuan ji* (Chen Sihe's selected works). Guilin: Guangxi shifan daxue chubanshe, 1997.

———. "Guanyu 'renwen jingshen' taolun de liang feng xin" (Two letters concerning the 'humanist spirit' discussion). In *Renwen jingshen xunsi lu* (Thoughts on the humanist spirit), edited by Wang Xiaoming, 142–55. Shanghai: Wenhui chubanshe, 1996.

———, ed. *Zhongguo dangdai wenxue shi jiaocheng* (A course in the history of contemporary Chinese literature). Shanghai: Fudan University Press, 1999.

Chen Sihe and Yang Yang, eds. *90 niandai piping wenxuan* (Selected criticism of the 1990s). Shanghai: Hanyu dacidian, 2001.

Chen Xiaoming. *Biaoyi de jiaolü: lishi qumei yu dangdai wenxue biange* (Ideographic anxieties: historical exorcism and contemporary literary transformation). Beijing: Zhongyang bianyi chubanshe, 2001.

———. "Renwen guanhuai: yizhong zhishi yu xushi" (Humanist concerns: a kind of knowledge and narrative). In *Renwen jingshen xunsi lu* (Thoughts on the humanist spirit), edited by Wang Xiaoming, 120–28. Shanghai: Wenhui chubanshe, 1996.

Cheng, Scarlet. "There's Nothing Like Being There." *Los Angeles Times*, November 1, 1998.

Chi Li. *Apart From Love*. Beijing: Chinese Literature Press, 1994.

———. *Chi Li wenji 2: Yi dong wu xue* (Chi Li collected works 2: A snowless winter). Nanjing: Jiangsu wenyi chubanshe, 1995.

———. "Lailai wangwang." *Shiyue* (October) 4 (1997): 4–34.

———. *Lailai wangwang* (Coming and going). Beijing: Zuojia chubanshe, 1998.

———. "To and Fro." *Chinese Literature* (Winter 1999): 14–63.

Chi, Robert. "*The Red Detachment of Women*: Resenting, Regendering, Remembering." In *Chinese Films in Focus: 25 New Takes*, edited by Chris Berry, 152–59. London: British Film Institute, 2003.

China Daily, "Shanghai Has Higher Divorce Rate," November 23, 2002.

Chow, Rey. *Primitive Passions: Visuality, Sexuality, Ethnography, and Contemporary Chinese Cinema.* New York: Columbia University Press, 1995.

———. *Woman and Chinese Modernity: The Politics of Reading Between West and East.* Minneapolis: University of Minnesota Press, 1991.

Ciecko, Anne T., and Sheldon H. Lu. "*Ermo*: Televisuality, Capital, and the Global Village." In *China, Transnational Visuality, Global Postmodernity,* by Sheldon H. Lu, 89–103. Stanford, CA: Stanford University Press, 2001.

Clark, Paul. *Chinese Cinema: Culture and Politics Since 1949.* New York: Cambridge University Press, 1988.

Crofts, Stephen. "Reconceptualizing National Cinema/s." *Quarterly Review of Film and Video* 14, no. 3 (1993): 49–67.

Cunningham, John. *Hungarian Cinema: From Coffee House to Multiplex.* London: Wallflower Press, 2004.

Dai Jinhua, *Cinema and Desire: Feminist Marxism and Cultural Politics in the Work of Dai Jinhua.* London: Verso, 2002.

———. "*Ermo*: xiandai yuyan kongjian" (*Ermo:* modern allegorical space). *Dianying yishu* (Film art), no. 5 (1994): 39–43.

Deleuze, Gilles. *Cinema.* Minneapolis: University of Minnesota Press, 1986.

Deleuze, Gilles, and Félix Guattari. *Anti-Oedipus: Capitalism and Schizophrenia.* Minneapolis: University of Minnesota Press, 1983.

Dirlik, Arif, and Xudong Zhang, eds. *Postmodernism and China.* Durham, NC: Duke University Press, 2000.

Donald, James, and Stephanie Hemelryk Donald. "The Publicness of Cinema." In *Reinventing Film Studies,* edited by Christine Gledhill and Linda Williams, 114–29. London: Arnold, 2000.

Donald, Stephanie Hemelryk. *Public Secrets, Public Spaces: Cinema and Civility in China.* Lanham, MD: Rowan and Littlefield, 2000.

Duke, Paul F. "China's Feng Will 'Be There': Helmer Hot O'seas." *Variety* 377, no. 8 (January 10, 2000): 6–7.

Eckholm, Erik. "Leading Chinese Filmmaker Tries for a Great Leap to the West." *New York Times,* June 21, 2001.

Erjavec, Aleš. Introduction to *Postmodernism and the Postsocialist Condition: Politicized Art Under Late Socialism,* edited by Aleš Erjavec, 1–54. Berkeley: University of California Press, 2003.

Eyal, Gil, Iván Szelényi, and Eleanor Townsley, eds. *Making Capitalism Without Capitalists: The New Ruling Elites in Eastern Europe.* London: Verso, 1998.

Eyferth, Jacob, Peter Ho, and Eduard B. Vermeer. "Introduction: The Opening-Up of China's Countryside." *Journal of Peasant Studies* 30 (April/July 2003): 1–17.

Fan, Maureen. "Punks and Posers in China." *Washington Post*, August 9, 2006.

Farquhar, Judith. "Technology of Everyday Life: The Economy of Impotence in Reform China." *Cultural Anthropology* 14, no. 2 (1999): 155–79.

Feng Xiaogang, *Wo ba qingchun xian gei ni* (I devoted my youth to you). Wuhan: Changjiang wenyi, 2003.

FlorCruz, Jaime. "Piracy Cripples China's Film Industry." CNN.com. No longer posted.

Foucault, Michel. "Of Other Spaces: Utopias and Heterotopias." *Diacritics* 16, no. 1 (1986): 22–27.

Frank, Thomas. *One Market Under God: Extreme Capitalism, Market Populism, and the End of Economic Democracy.* New York: Anchor Books, 2000.

Fu, Ping. "*Ermo*: (Tele)Visualizing Urban/Rural Transformation." In *Chinese Films in Focus: 25 New Takes*, edited by Chris Berry, 73–80. London: British Film Institute, 2003.

Gaines, Jane M. "Dream/Factory." In *Reinventing Film Studies*, edited by Christine Gledhill, 100–113. London: Oxford University Press, 2000.

Gao Minglu. "Post-Utopian Avant-Garde Art in China." In *Postmodernism and the Postsocialist Condition: Politicized Art Under Late Socialism*, edited by Aleš Erjavec, 247–83. Berkeley: University of California Press, 2003.

Gao Ruiquan, Yuan Jin, Zhang Rulun, and Li Tiangang, "Renwen jingshen xun zong" (Tracking the humanist spirit). In *Renwen jingshen xunsi lu* (Thoughts on the humanist spirit), edited by Wang Xiaoming, 33–45. Shanghai: Wenhui chubanshe, 1996.

Gao Yuanbao. *Ling yizhong quanli* (Another kind of power). Shijiazhuang: Huashan wenyi chubanshe, 2001.

———. "Renwen jingshen taolun zhi wo jian," (My view of the humanist spirit discussion). In *Renwen jingshen xunsi lu* (Thoughts on the humanist spirit), edited by Wang Xiaoming, 166–71. Shanghai: Wenhui chubanshe, 1996.

Gell, Alfred. "Newcomers to the World of Goods: Consumption among the Muria Gonds," In *The Social Life of Things: Commodities in Cultural Perspective*, edited by Arjun Appadurai, 110–38. Cambridge: Cambridge University Press, 1988.

Giddens, Anthony. *The Consequences of Modernity.* Stanford, CA: Stanford University Press, 1990.

Gould, Stephen J., and Nancy Y. C. Wong. "The Intertextual Construction of Emerging Consumer Culture in China as Observed in the Movie *Ermo*: A Postmodern, Sinicization Reading." *Journal of Global Marketing* 14 (2000): 151–67.

Grossman, Andrew. "The Wind Will Carry Us." *Scope: An On-line Journal of Film Studies.* Institute of Film Studies, University of Nottingham, May 2001. http://www.nottingham.ac.uk/film/journal/filmrev/the-wind-will-carry-us.htm.

Gu Zheng. "Women yiqi lai pai dianying ba: hui wang 'qingnian shiyan dianying xiaozu'"

(Let's make a movie together: a look back at the "Youth Experimental Film Group"). In *Xianchang* (Document), vol. 1, edited by Wu Wenguang, 213–22. Tianjin: Tianjin shehui kexueyuan chubanshe, 2000.

Gunning, Tom. "An Aesthetic of Astonishment: Early Film and the (In)Credulous Spectator." In *Film Theory and Criticism: Introductory Readings*, 5th ed., edited by Gerald Mast, Marshall Cohen, and Leo Braudy, 818–32. New York: Oxford University Press, 1999.

———. "The Cinema of Attraction: Early Film, Its Spectator and the Avant-Garde." *Wide Angle* 8 (1986): 63–70.

———. *D. W. Griffith and the Origins of American Narrative Film*. Urbana: University of Illinois Press, 1991.

———. "Illusions Past and Future: The Phantasmagoria and Its Specters." Media Art Histories Archive. http://www.mediaarthistory.org/Programmatic%20key%20texts/pdfs/Gunning.pdf.

———. "Phantasmagoria and the Manufacturing of Illusions and Wonder: Towards a Cultural Optics of the Cinematic Apparatus." Paper presented at the Domitor Conference, Montreal, Canada, June 2002.

Hansen, Miriam Bratu. "Fallen Women, Rising Stars, New Horizons: Shanghai Silent Film as Vernacular Modernism." *Film Quarterly* 54, no. 1 (2000): 10–22.

———. "The Mass Production of the Senses: Classical Cinema as Vernacular Modernism." In *Reinventing Film Studies*, edited by Christine Gledhill, 332–50. London: Oxford University Press, 2000.

Hardt, Michael, and Antonio Negri. *Empire*. Cambridge, MA: Harvard University Press, 2000.

Harvey, David. *The New Imperialism*. Oxford: Oxford University Press, 2003.

He Qinglian. *Xiandaihua de xianjing: dangdai Zhongguo de jingji shehui wenti* [Modernization's pitfall: contemporary China's economic and social questions]. Beijing: Jinri Zhongguo chubanshe, 1998.

He Zhenbang. *Jiushi niandai wentan saomiao* (A scan of the 1990s literary scene). Kunming: Yunnan renmin chubanshe, 2000.

Hilton, Isabel. "Karl, China Needs You." *New Statesman*, February 20, 2006.

Hoberman, J. "Conflict Management." *Village Voice*, March 2, 2001.

———. "Cults of Personality." *Village Voice*, March 12–18, 2003.

Hong Zicheng. *Zhongguo dangdai wenxue shi* (History of contemporary Chinese literature). Beijing: Beijing daxue chubanshe, 1999.

Horkheimer, Max, and Theodor Adorno. *Dialectic of Enlightenment: Philosophical Fragments*. Stanford, CA: Stanford University Press, 2002.

Hsia, C. T. *A History of Modern Chinese Fiction*. New Haven, CT: Yale University Press, 1971.

Hu Ke. "Contemporary Film Theory in China." Translated by Ted Wang, Chris Berry and Chen Mei. http://www.latrobe.edu.au/www/screeningthepast/reruns/hkrr2b.html.

Hu Shi. "Some Modest Proposals for the Reform of Literature." In *Modern Chinese Literary Thought: Writings on Literature, 1893–1945*, edited by Kirk Denton, 123–39. Stanford, CA: Stanford University Press, 1996.

Huang Fayou. "Zai youdangzhong qiu kun—Zhu Wen he *Shenme shi laji shenme shi ai*" (Trapped in idleness—Zhu Wen and *What's trash, what's love*). *Wenyi zhengming* (Literature and arts contention), no. 2 (2002): 75–80.

Huang Lizhi. *Zhongguo huayu: dangdai shenmei wenhua shilun* (Chinese discourse: historical essays on contemporary aesthetic culture). Beijing: Zhongyang bianshi chubanshe, 2001.

Huot, Claire. *China's New Cultural Scene: A Handbook of Changes*. Durham, NC: Duke University Press, 2000.

Jaffee, Valerie. "Bringing the World to the Nation: Jia Zhangke and the Legitimation of Chinese Underground Film." *Senses of Cinema*, no. 32 (July–September 2004). http://www.sensesofcinema.com/contents/04/32/chinese_underground_film.html.

Jameson, Fredric. *The Ideologies of Theory: Essays, 1971–1986*. Vol. 2, *Syntax of History*. Minneapolis: University of Minnesota Press, 1988.

———. *Postmodernism, Or, the Cultural Logic of Late Capitalism*. Durham, NC: Duke University Press, 1987.

———. *The Seeds of Time*. New York: Columbia University Press, 1994.

———. *A Singular Modernity: Essay on the Ontology of the Present*. London: Verso, 2002.

Ji Yun. *Yuewei caotang biji* (Notes from the thatched cottage of careful reading). Beijing: Zhongguo wenlian chubanshe, 1996), 119–20.

Jia Zhangke. "Jia Zhangke: zai 'zhantai' shang dengdai." (Jia Zhangke: waiting on the "Platform"). Interview by Cheng Qingsong and Huang Ou. In *Wo de sheyingji bu sahuang: liushi niandai Zhongguo dianying daoyan dang'an* (My camera doesn't lie: files on the '60s generation of Chinese film directors), edited by Cheng Qingsong and Huang Ou, 341–64. Beijing: Zhongguo youyi chuban gongsi, 2002.

———. "Zhongguo de duli dianying ren" (China's independent filmmaker). Interview in *Dianying chufang: dianying zai Zhongguo* (Film kitchen: film in China), edited by Wang Shuo, 146–63. Shanghai: Shanghai wenyi chubanshe, 2001.

Johnson, Ian. "New Chinese Art: Revolting . . . ," *Wall Street Journal*, May 5, 1999.

Kahn, Joseph. "A Sharp Debate Erupts in China Over Ideologies." *New York Times*, March 12, 2006.

Kan, Wendy. "'Big Shot' Doesn't Win Over Locals." *Variety* 387, no. 2 (May 27, 2002): 8.

Karmin, Craig, and Henny Sender. "If U.S. Presses China on Yuan, a Delicate Scale Could Tip." *Wall Street Journal*, June 29, 2005.

Klinkner, Kenneth. "Lightening Up China: The Holiday Films of Feng Xiaogang." Paper presented at the China Pop Culture Conference, University of Illinois, Urbana, April 20, 2002.

Kong, Shuyu. "Between a Rock and a Hard Place: Chinese Literary Journals in the Cultural Market." *Modern Chinese Literature and Culture* 14 (spring 2002): 93–144.

———. "Big Shot from Beijing: Feng Xiaogang's *He Sui Pian* and Contemporary Chinese Commercial Film." *Asian Cinema* 14, no. 1 (spring/summer 2003): 175–87.

———. *Consuming Literature: Best Sellers and the Commercialization of Literary Production in Contemporary China.* Stanford, CA: Stanford University Press, 2005.

———. "Is There a Realism in Neo-Realism?" *British Columbia Asian Review* 8 (winter 1994/1995): 117–27.

Kracauer, Siegfried. *Theory of Film: The Redemption of Physical Reality.* New York: Oxford University Press, 1960.

Kundu, Swati Lodh. "Rural China: Too Little, Too Late." *Asia Times,* July 19, 2006.

Larsen, Susan. "In Search of an Audience: The New Russian Cinema of Reconciliation." In *Consuming Russia: Popular Culture, Sex, and Society since Gorbachev,* edited by Adele Marie Barker, 192–216. Durham, NC: Duke University Press, 1999.

Latham, Kevin. "Rethinking Chinese Consumption: Social Palliatives and the Rhetorics of Transition in Postsocialist China." In *Postsocialism: Ideals, Ideologies and Practices in Eurasia,* edited by C. M. Hann, 217–37. London: Routledge, 2002.

Li, David Leiwei. "'What Will Become of Us If We Don't Stop?' *Ermo*'s China and the End of Globalization." *Comparative Literature* 53, no. 4 (2001): 442–61.

Li Xianting. "'Duanlie' shi yi ge xuanyan—Li Xianting fangtan lu" ("Rupture" is a manifesto—interview with Li Xianting). In *Duanlie: shijimo de wenxue shigu—ziyou zuojia fangtan lu* (Rupture: the literary accident at the end of the century—interviews with free authors), edited by Wang Jifang, 1–6. Nanjing: Jiangsu wenyi chubanshe, 2000.

Liang Qichao. "On the Relationship Between Fiction and the Government of the People." In *Modern Chinese Literary Thought: Writings on Literature, 1893–1945,* edited by Kirk Denton, 74–81. Stanford, CA: Stanford University Press, 1996.

Link, E. Perry, Jr. *Mandarin Ducks and Butterflies: Popular Fiction in Early Twentieth-Century Chinese Cities.* Berkeley: University of California Press, 1981.

Link, Perry. *The Uses of Literature: Life in the Socialist Chinese Literary System.* Princeton, NJ: Princeton University Press, 2000.

Liu Chuan'e. *Xiao shimin, ming zuojia: Chi Li lun* (Petty urbanites, famous author: a study of Chi Li). Wuhan: Hubei renmin chubanshe, 2000.

Liu, Dalin, Man Lun Ng, Li Ping Zhou, and Erwin J. Haeberle. *Sexual Behavior in Modern China: Report on the Nationwide Survey of 20,000 Men and Women.* New York: Continuum Publishing, 1997.

Liu Kang. *Globalization and Cultural Trends in China*. Honolulu: University of Hawai'i Press, 2004.

Liu, Lydia H. "Beijing Sojourners in New York: Postsocialism and the Question of Ideology in Global Media Culture." *Positions: East Asia Cultures Critique* 7 (winter 1999): 763–97.

Lu, Sheldon H. *China, Transnational Visuality, Global Postmodernity*. Stanford, CA: Stanford University Press, 2001.

Lu Yingping. "Lifazhe, jieshizhe, youmin" (Lawmakers, explainers, vagabonds). In *Renwen jingshen xunsi lu* (Thoughts on the humanist spirit), edited by Wang Xiaoming, 181–84. Shanghai: Wenhui chubanshe, 1996.

Lü Xiaoming. "90 niandai Zhongguo dianying jingguan zhi yi: 'diliu dai' ji qi zhiyi" (One of the landscapes of 1990s Chinese film: the "Sixth Generation" and doubts thereof). *Dianying yishu* (Film art) (May 10, 1999): 24.

Luhmann, Niklas. *The Differentiation of Society*. New York: Columbia University Press, 1982.

Luo Yijun. "Guanyu Ermo" (On *Ermo*). *Dangdai dianying* (Contemporary cinema), no. 5 (1994): 45–46.

Lyotard, Jean-Francois. *The Postmodern Condition: A Report on Knowledge*. Minneapolis: University of Minnesota Press, 1979.

Magnier, Mark. "Hit Movie Rings True in China." *Los Angeles Times*, April 12, 2004.

Marx, Karl. *Capital: Volume 1*. London: Penguin, 1976.

———. *Grundrisse*. London: Penguin, 1973.

Marx, Karl, and Frederick Engels. "Manifesto of the Communist Party." In *Selected Works*, by Karl Marx and Frederick Engels, 35–63. New York: International Publishers, 1968.

McGrath, Jason. "The New Formalism: Mainland Chinese Cinema at the Turn of the Century." In *China's Literary and Cultural Scenes at the Turn of the 21st Century*, edited by Jie Lu. London: Routledge, forthcoming 20008.

Meng Fanhua. "Xin lixiangzhuyi yu zhishifenzi yishixingtai" (The new idealism and intellectual ideology). In *Renwen jingshen xunsi lu* (Thoughts on the humanist spirit), edited by Wang Xiaoming, 250–53. Shanghai: Wenhui chubanshe, 1996.

Meng Fanhua and Lin Dazhong, eds. *Jiushi niandai wen cun: 1990–2000* (Collected writings on the 1990s, 1990–2000). 2 vols. Beijing: Zhongguo shehui kexue chubanshe, 2001.

Mo, Crystyl. "Feng Xiaogang Sets His Sights on Hollywood." http://www.chinanow.com/english/shanghai/city/movies/fengxiaogang.html.

"More Detail on Feng Xiaogang's *The Assembly Call*." *MonkeyPeaches*. September 26, 2006. http://www.monkeypeaches.com/thebanquet.html.

Murphy, R. Taggart. "East Asia's Dollars." *New Left Review* 40 (July–August 2006): 39–64.

Nanfang dushi bao (Nanfang metropolitan news), "Jia Zhangke fangtan—you yigu qi zhengzai ningju" (Jia Zhangke interview—there's a puff of vapor that's now condensing), March 4, 2002.

Notar, Beth. "Blood Money: Woman's Desire and Consumption in *Ermo*." *Asian Cinema* 12, no. 2 (2001): 132–53.

O'Brien, Kevin J., and Lianjiang Li. *Rightful Resistance in Rural China*. Cambridge: Cambridge University Press, 2006.

Panitch, Leo, and Sam Gindin, "Superintending Global Capital." *New Left Review* 35 (September–October 2005): 101–23.

People's Daily, "Divorce Rate in China Will Increase," April 21, 2002.

Pickowicz, Paul G., and Yingjin Zhang, eds. *From Underground to Independent: Alternative Film Culture in Contemporary China*. Oxford: Rowman & Littlefield, 2006.

Pine, Frances, and Sue Bridger, eds. *Surviving Post-Socialism: Local Strategies and Regional Responses in Eastern Europe and the Former Soviet Union*. London: Routledge, 1998.

Polanyi, Karl. *The Great Transformation*. New York: Farrar & Rinehart, 1944.

Powdermaker, Hortense. *Hollywood: The Dream Factory*. Boston: Little, Brown, 1950.

Prendergast, Christopher. "Codeword Modernity." *New Left Review* 24 (November-December 2003): 95–111.

Qingnian bao (Youth daily), "Jia Zhangke: keyi shuo shi yi zhong tuoxie" (Jia Zhangke: you can say it's a kind of compromise), April 15, 2003.

Qu Weiguo. "Weiji? Jinbu?" (Crisis? Progress?). In *Renwen jingshen xunsi lu* (Thoughts on the humanist spirit), edited by Wang Xiaoming, 100–105. Shanghai: Wenhui chubanshe, 1996.

Rayns, Tony. "The Ups and Downs of Zhou Xiaowen: In Beijing the Director Discusses His Troubled Career and His New Film *Ermo*." *Sight and Sound* 5 (July 1995): 22–24.

Roach, Stephen. "Globalization's New Underclass: China, the US, Japan, and the Changing Face of Inequality." *Japan Focus*, March 3, 2006. http://www.japanfocus. org/products/details/1923.

Rojas, Carlos. "A Tale of Two Emperors: Mimicry and Mimesis in Two 'New Year's' Films from China and Hong Kong." *Cineaction*, no. 60 (spring 2003): 2–9.

Rosen, Stanley. "The Wolf at the Door: Hollywood and the Film Market in China." In *Southern California and the World*, edited by Eric J. Heikkila and Rafael Pizarro, 49–77. Westport, CT: Praeger, 2002.

Rosenbaum, Jonathan. "Critic's Choice: *Platform*." *Chicago Reader*, May 17, 2002.

———. *Essential Cinema: On the Necessity of Film Canons*. Baltimore: Johns Hopkins University Press, 2004.

Sartre, Jean-Paul. *Critique of Dialectical Reason, Volume One*. London: Verso, 2004.

Saussy, Haun. *Great Walls of Discourse and Other Adventures in Cultural China*. Cambridge, MA: Harvard University Asia Center, 2001.

Schor, Naomi. *Reading in Detail: Aesthetics and the Feminine*. London: Routledge, 1987.

Shao Mujun. "Tan *Ermo*" (On *Ermo*). *Dangdai dianying* (Contemporary cinema), no. 5 (1994): 46.

Short, Stephen. "'As Sex Scenes Are Banned, We Need to Be Creative': Web-Only Interview with Director Feng Xiaogang." *Time Asia*, October 26, 2000. http://www.time.com/time/asia/features/interviews/2000/10/26/int.feng_xiaogang.html.

Silbergeld, Jerome. *Hitchcock with a Chinese Face*. Seattle: University of Washington Press, 2004.

Song Mingwei. "Piaoliu de fangzi he xuwang de lütu—lijie Zhu Wen" (Floating houses and fabricated journeys—understanding Zhu Wen). *Shanghai Wenxue* (September 1997): 66–71.

Stam, Robert. *Reflexivity in Film and Literature: From Don Quixote to Jean-Luc Godard*. New York: Columbia University Press, 1992.

Sun Jianmin. "Jingyan shijiezhong de yingxiang xuanze: Jia Zhangke fangtan lu" (Selecting images in the experiential world: an interview with Jia Zhangke). *Jinri xianfeng* (Avant-garde today) 12 (March 2002): 18–33.

Tan Ye. "Hollywood and the Chinese Other." *Cineaction* , no. 60 (2003): 10–20.

Tang, Xiaobing. *Chinese Modern: The Heroic and the Quotidian*. Durham, NC: Duke University Press, 2000.

———. "The Function of New Theory: What Does It Mean to Talk About Postmodernism in China?" In *Politics, Ideology, and Literary Discourse in Modern China: Theoretical Interventions and Cultural Critique*, edited by Liu Kang and Xiaobing Tang, 278–99. Durham, NC: Duke University Press, 1993.

———. "Rural Women and Social Change in New China Cinema: From *Li Shuangshuang* to *Ermo*." *Positions: East Asia Cultures Critique* 11 (winter 2003): 647–74.

Tao Dongfeng. "Huangtang de fuchou: Ermo yu ta de da caidian" (Absurd revenge: Ermo and her large color TV). *Dangdai dianying* (Contemporary cinema), no. 5 (1994): 52–53.

Teo, Stephen. "Cinema with an Accent: Interview with Jia Zhangke, Director of *Platform*." *Senses of Cinema*, no. 15, July/August 2001. http://www.sensesofcinema.com/contents/01/15/zhangke_interview.html.

Tianfu Wang, William Parish, Edward Laumann, and Kwai Hang Ng, "Trends in Chinese Sexual Behaviors," unpublished manuscript, Department of Sociology, University of Chicago.

Visser, Robin Lynne. "Pop Art Conscience? Middle-Brow Aesthetics in the Film/Novel *Cell Phone*." Panel paper, annual meeting of the Association for Asian Studies, Chicago, April 1, 2005.

———. "The Urban Subject in the Literary Imagination of Twentieth Century China." Ph.D. diss., Columbia University, 2000.

Wallerstein, Immanuel. "The Curve of American Power." *New Left Review* 40 (July–August 2006): 77–94.

Wang, Ban. *The Sublime Figure of History: Aesthetics and Politics in Twentieth-Century China*. Stanford, CA: Stanford University Press, 1997.

Wang, Chaohua, ed. *One China, Many Paths*. London: Verso, 2003.

Wang, David Der-Wei. *Fin-de-siècle Splendor: Repressed Modernities of Late Qing Fiction, 1849–1911*. Stanford, CA: Stanford University Press, 1997.

Wang Dehou. "*Ermo*: zhuozhuang yu mangmu de jiejing" (*Ermo*: a crystallization of sturdiness and blindness). *Dianying yishu* (Film art) no. 5 (1994): 36–38.

Wang Gan, Zhang Yiwu, and Zhang Weimin. "'Xin zhuangtai wenxue' san ren tan" ("New state of affairs literature" three-way discussion). In *90 Niandai piping wenxuan* (Selected works of 1990s criticism), edited by Chen Sihe and Yang Yang, 434–51. Shanghai: Hanyu dacidian chubanshe, 2001.

Wang Hongsheng, Geng Zhanchun, He Xiangyang, Zeng Fan, and Qu Chunjing. "Xiandai renwen jingshen de shengcheng" (The generation of modern humanist spirit). In *Renwen jingshen xunsi lu* (Thoughts on the humanist spirit), edited by Wang Xiaoming, 222–38. Shanghai: Wenhui chubanshe, 1996.

Wang Hui. *China's New Order: Society, Politics, and Economy in Transition*. Cambridge, MA: Harvard University Press, 2003.

———. "Contemporary Chinese Thought and the Question of Modernity." *Social Text* 55 16.2 (summer 1998): 9–44.

———. "Dangdai Zhongguo de sixiang zhuangkuang yu xiandai xing wenti" (Contemporary Chinese thought and the question of modernity). *Tianya*. (October 1997): 133–50.

Wang Jifang, ed. *Duanlie: shijimo de wenxue shigu—ziyou zuojia fangtan lu* (Rupture: the literary accident at the end of the century—interviews with free authors). Nanjing: Jiangsu wenyi chubanshe, 2000.

Wang, Jing. *High Culture Fever: Politics, Aesthetics, and Ideology in Deng's China*. Berkeley: University of California Press, 1997.

Wang Meng. "Duobi chonggao" (Avoiding nobility). *Dushu* no. 1 (1993): 10–17.

———. "Hushang si xu lu" (Long-winded record of thoughts in Shanghai). In *Shiji zhi jiao de chongzhuang: Wang Meng xianxiang zhengming lu* (Clash at the turn of the century: record of controversy over the Wang Meng phenomenon), edited by Ding Dong and Sun Min. Beijing: Guangming ribao chubanshe, 1995.

———. "Renwen jingshen wenti ougan" (Random thoughts on the question of the humanist spirit). In *Renwen jingshen xunsi lu* (Thoughts on the humanist spirit), edited by Wang Xiaoming, 106–19. Shanghai: Wenhui chubanshe, 1996.

Wang, Shujen. "*Big Shot's Funeral*: China, Sony, and the WTO." *Asian Cinema* 14, no. 2 (fall/winter 2003): 145–54.

————. *Framing Piracy: Globalization and Film Distribution in Greater China.* Lanham, MD: Rowman & Littlefield, 2003.

Wang Shuo. *Meiren zeng wo menghanyao* (A beauty presents me with knock-out drops). Wuhan: Changjiang wenyi, 2000.

————. *Ni bu shi yi ge suren* (You're not a commoner). *Shouhuo* (Harvest), no. 2 (1992).

————. *Please Don't Call Me Human.* New York: Hyperion East, 2000.

Wang Xiaoming. *Banzhanglian de shenhua* (Myth of the half-faced portrait). Guangdong: Nanfang ribao chubanshe, 2000.

————. "Jiushi niandai yu 'xin yishixingtai'" (The 1990s and the "new ideology"). In *Jiushi niandai wen cun: 1990–2000* (Collected writings on the 1990s, 1990–2000), edited by Lin Dazhong, 2:284–305. Beijing: Zhongguo shehui kexue, 2001.

————. "'Renwen jingshen' lunzheng yu zhishifenzi de rentong kunjing" (The "humanist spirit" debate and intellectuals' identification difficulties). *90 niandai sixiang wenxuan* (Selected works of 1990s thought), edited by Luo Gang and Ni Wenjian, 1:443–55. Nanning: Guangxi renmin chubanshe, 2000.

————, ed. *Renwen jingshen xunsi lu* (Thoughts on the humanist spirit). Shanghai: Wenhui chubanshe, 1996.

————. "Women nengfou zouchu shiyu de kunjing" (Can we escape the predicament of aphasia). *90 niandai sixiang wenxuan* (Selected works of 1990s thought), edited by Luo Gang and Ni Wenjian, 1:414–31. Nanning: Guangxi renmin chubanshe, 2000.

————. "Zai 'wuliao' de bishi xia—cong Zhu Wen bixia de Xiao Ding shuo qi" (Under the stare of 'wuliao'—proceeding from Xiao Ding under the pen of Zhu Wen). In *Zai xin yishi xingtai de longzhao xia: 90 niandai de wenhua he wenxue fenxi* (Under the shroud of the new ideology: culture and literary analysis of the 1990s), edited by Wang Xiaoming, 203–15. Nanjing: Jiangsu renmin, 2000.

————, ed. *Zai xin yishi xingtai de longzhao xia: 90 niandai de wenhua he wenxue fenxi* (Under the shroud of the new ideology: culture and literary analysis of the 1990s). Nanjing: Jiangsu renmin chubanshe, 2000.

Wang Xiaoming, Zhang Hong, Xu Lin, Zhang Ning, and Cui Yiming. "Kuangye shang de feixu: wenxue he renwen jingshen de weiji" (Ruins in the wilderness: The crisis of literature and humanist spirit). In *Renwen jingshen xunsi lu* (Thoughts on the humanist spirit), edited by Wang Xiaoming, 1–17. Shanghai: Wenhui chubanshe, 1996.

Wang Yichuan, "Cong qimeng dao goutong: 90 niandai shenmei wenhua yu renwen jingshen zhuanhua lungang" (From enlightenment to communication: the aesthetic culture of the 1990s and an outline for the transformation of the humanist spirit). In *Renwen jingshen xunsi lu* (Thoughts on the humanist spirit), edited by Wang Xiaoming, 206–21. Shanghai: Wenhui chubanshe, 1996.

White, Craig. "Craig's Toronto FilmFest News and Reviews." September 10, 2002. http:// filmfest.tnir.org/archives/2002_09.html.

Wu Hung. *Transience: Chinese Experimental Art at the End of the Twentieth Century.* Chicago: The David and Alfred Smart Museum of Art, University of Chicago, 1999.

Wu Hung, Wang Huangsheng, and Feng Boyi. *The First Guangzhou Triennial— Reinterpretation: A Decade of Experimental Chinese Art (1990–2000).* Guangzhou: Guangdong Museum of Art, 2002.

Wu Wenguang. "Fangwen 'Xiao Wu' daoyan Jia Zhangke" (Interview with *Xiao Wu* director Jia Zhangke), *Xianchang* (Document), vol. 1, edited by Wu Wenguang, 184– 212. Tianjin: Tianjin shehui kexueyuan chubanshe, 2000.

Wu Xuan, Wang Gan, Fei Zhenzhong, and Wang Binbin. "Women xuyao zenyang de renwen jingshen" (What type of humanist spirit do we need?). In *Renwen jingshen xunsi lu* (Thoughts on the humanist spirit), edited by Wang Xiaoming, 59–71. Shanghai: Wenhui chubanshe, 1996.

Xiao, Zhiwei. "Chinese Cinema." In *Encyclopedia of Chinese Film*, edited by Yingjin Zhang and Zhiwei Xiao, 3–30. New York: Routledge, 1998.

"'Xin xieshi xiaoshuo da lianzhan' juanshou yu" ("Grand exposition of new realist fiction" volume preface) *Zhongshan* (Zhong mountain) no. 3 (1989): 4.

Xu, Ben. *Disenchanted Democracy: Chinese Cultural Criticism after 1989.* Ann Arbor: University of Michigan Press, 1999.

Xu Jilin, Chen Sihe, Cai Xiang, and Gao Yuanbao. "Daotong, xuetong yu zhengtong" (Moral tradition, scholarly tradition, and political tradition). In *Renwen jingshen xunsi lu* (Thoughts on the humanist spirit), edited by Wang Xiaoming, 46–58. Shanghai: Wenhui chubanshe, 1996.

Yan Lianke. *Shouhuo* (Enjoyment). Shenyang: Chunfeng wenyi chubanshe, 2004.

Yin Hong. "Shiji zhi jiao: jiushi niandai zhongguo dianying beiwang" (The turn of the century: memo on Chinese cinema in the nineties). In *Bainian Zhongguo dianying lilun wenxuan* (Selected works of one-hundred years of Chinese film theory), edited by Ding Yaping, 2:658–89. Beijing: Wenhua yishu chubanshe, 2002.

Yu Aiyuan. "Tuwei, taoli, luowang" (Breakthrough, escape, ensnarement). *Jinri xianfeng* (Avant-garde today) 12 (March 2002): 34–39.

Yurchak, Alexei. *Everything Was Forever, Until It Was No More: The Last Soviet Generation.* Princeton, NJ: Princeton University Press, 2006.

Zhang Jianqun. "Jia Zhangke kewang zhuliu: haishi xian pai heibang pian" (Jia Zhangke seeks the mainstream: will shoot a gangster film first). *Qingnian bao* (Youth daily), April 15, 2003.

Zhang Jun. "Xinshengdai: gerenhua xiezuo de shuangzhong zijue" (The newly born generation: the dual forms of self-consciousness of individualized writing). In *90 Niandai piping wenxuan* (Selected works of 1990s criticism), edited by Chen Sihe and Yang Yang, 331–43. Shanghai: Hanyu dacidian chubanshe, 2001.

Zhang Nuanxin and Li Tuo. "Tan dianying yuyan de xiandaihua" (On the modernization of cinematic language). In *Bainian Zhongguo dianying lilun wenxuan* (Selected works of one-hundred years of Chinese film theory), edited by Ding Yaping, 2:10–36. Beijing: Wenhua yishu chubanshe, 2002.

Zhang, Rui. "*The Banquet* World Premier." China.org.cn. Sep. 11, 2006. http://www.china.org.cn/english/2006/Sep/180709.htm.

———. "Feng Xiaogang and Chinese Cinema after 1989." Ph.D. diss., Ohio State University, 2006.

Zhang Rulun, Li Guibao, Gao Yuanbao, and Chen Yinchi. "Wenhua shijie: jiegou haishi jiangou" (The cultural world: deconstruction or construction). In *Renwen jingshen xunsi lu* (Thoughts on the humanist spirit), edited by Wang Xiaoming, 72–83. Shanghai: Wenhui chubanshe, 1996.

Zhang Rulun and Lin Hui. "Guanyu renwen jingshen" (On the humanist spirit). In *Renwen jingshen xunsi lu* (Thoughts on the humanist spirit), edited by Wang Xiaoming, 156–65. Shanghai: Wenhui chubanshe, 1996.

Zhang Rulun, Wang Xiaoming, Zhu Xueqin, and Chen Sihe. "Renwen jingshen: shifou keneng yu ruhe keneng" (Humanist spirit: Is it possible and how is it possible). In *Renwen jingshen xunsi lu* (Thoughts on the humanist spirit), edited by Wang Xiaoming, 18–32. Shanghai: Wenhui chubanshe, 1996.

Zhang, Xudong. *Chinese Modernism in the Era of Reforms: Culture Fever, Avant-garde Fiction, and the New Chinese Cinema.* Durham, NC: Duke University Press, 1997.

———. "Nationalism, Mass Culture, and Intellectual Strategies in Post-Tiananmen China." In *Whither China? Intellectual Politics in Contemporary China*, edited by Xudong Zhang, 315–48. Durham, NC: Duke University Press, 2001.

Zhang, Yingjin. *Chinese National Cinema.* London: Routledge, 2004.

———. *Screening China: Critical Interventions, Cinematic Reconfigurations, and the Transnational Imaginary in Contemporary Chinese Cinema.* Ann Arbor: Center for Chinese Studies, University of Michigan, 2002.

Zhang Yiwu. "*Ermo*: xiandai zhi kunhuo" (*Ermo*: confusions of the modern). *Dangdai dianying* (Contemporary cinema), no. 5 (1994): 47–48.

———. "Houxinshiqi wenxue: Xinde wenhua kongjian" (Post–new era literature: A new cultural space). *Wenyi lilun* (Literary theory) 1 (1993).

———. "Lixiangzhuyi de zhongjie" (The end of idealism). *Beijing wenxue* (Beijing literature), no. 4 (1989).

———. "Postmodernism and Chinese Novels of the Nineties." In *Postmodernism and China*, edited by Arif Dirlik and Xudong Zhang, 325–36. Durham,NC: Duke University Press, 2000.

———. "Renwen jingshen: zuihou de shenhua" (Humanist spirit: the last mythology). In *Renwen jingshen xunsi lu* (Thoughts on the humanist spirit), edited by Wang Xiaoming, 137–41. Shanghai: Wenhui chubanshe, 1996.

Zhang, Zhen. *An Amorous History of the Silver Screen: Shanghai Cinema, 1896–1937.* Chicago: University of Chicago Press, 2005.

———. "Urban Dreamscape, Phantom Sisters, and the Identity of an Emergent Art Cinema." In *The Urban Generation: Chinese Cinema and Society at the Turn of the Twenty-first Century*, edited by Zhang Zhen, 344–87. Durham, NC: Duke University Press, 2007.

Zhang Zhizhong. "Renwen jingshen er bian" (Humanist spirit debate again). In *Renwen jingshen xunsi lu* (Thoughts on the humanist spirit), edited by Wang Xiaoming, 172–80. Shanghai: Wenhui chubanshe, 1996.

Zhou Shaoming. "Making Money Can Be Funny." *Cinemaya*, no. 52 (2001): 13–18.

Zhu Wen, "Duanlie: yi fen wenjuan he wushiliu fen dajuan" (Rupture: a questionnaire and fifty-six replies). In *Duanlie: shijimo de wenxue shigu—ziyou zuojia fangtan lu* (Rupture: the literary accident at the end of the century—interviews with free authors), edited by Wang Jifang, 251–306. Nanjing: Jiangsu wenyi chubanshe, 2000.

———. "Gou yan kan ren: cong duanlie congshu chuban tanqi" (A dog's-eye view of people: on the publication of the Rupture book series). In *Duanlie: shijimo de wenxue shigu—ziyou zuojia fangtan lu* (Rupture: the literary accident at the end of the century—interviews with free authors), edited by Wang Jifang, 323–34. Nanjing: Jiangsu wenyi chubanshe, 2000.

———. *I Love Dollars and Other Stories.* Translated by Julia Lovell. New York: Columbia University Press, 2007.

———. *Shenme shi laji shenme shi ai* (What's trash, what's love). Nanjing: Jiangsu wenyi chubanshe, 1998.

———. *Yinwei gudu* (Because of loneliness). Chengdu: Sichuan wenyi chubanshe, 1996.

Žižek, Slavoj. "The Fetish of the Party." In *Lacan, Politics, Aesthetics*, edited by Willy Apollon and Richard Feldstein, 3–29. Albany: State University of New York Press, 1996.

List of Chinese Characters

Anyang de gu'er 安阳的孤儿

ban zhanglian de xiaoxiang 半张脸的肖像

banzuo chuban 伴做出版

bei choukong 被抽空

Beijing ren zai Niuyue 北京人在纽约

beng 崩

bengkui 崩溃

bengta 崩塌

Bianjibu de gushi 编辑部的故事

Bu tan aiqing 不谈爱情

Bujian busan 不见不散

Cai Mingliang (Tsai Ming-liang) 蔡明亮

canquezhong ziyou 残缺中自由

chai 拆

Chen Kaige 陈凯歌

Chen Sihe 陈思和

Chen Xiaoming 陈晓明

chenggong renshi 成功人士

Chi Li 池莉

chun wenxue 纯文学

cubihua 粗鄙化

dapian 大片

Dawan 大腕

Deng Lijun 邓丽君

duanlie 断裂

duoyuanhua 多元化

Ermo 二嫫

Fang Fang 方方

Fannao rensheng 烦恼人生

Feng Xiaogang 冯小刚

fengci 讽刺

fenhua 分化

foudingxing 否定性

fuxing 复兴

gaige-kaifang 改革开放

gang 纲

gangling 纲领

Gao Yuanbao 郜元宝

Ge You 葛优

gerenhua 个人化

gerenhua xiezuo 个人化写作

gongju lixing 工具理性

gongming 共名

Guonian huijia 过年回家

guoxue 国学

Haishang hua 海上花

Haixian 海鲜

Han Dong 韩东

Haomeng yiriyou 好梦一日游

He Jianjun 何建军

He Qinglian 何清涟

hesuipian 贺岁片

Hong gaoliang 红高粱

Hongse niangzi jun 红色娘子军

Hou Xiaoxian (Hou Hsiao-hsien) 侯孝贤

hou xin shiqi 后新时期

houxinshiqi wenxue 后新时期文学

houxue 后学

-*hua* 化

Huang tudi 黄土地

huanyuan 还原

Jia Zhangke 贾樟柯

Jiafang yifang 甲方乙方

jiahuo 家伙

jishizhuyi 纪实主义

Ju Dou 菊豆

kexiao kele 可笑可乐

Lailai wangwang 来来往往

"Leng ye hao, re ye hao, huozhe jiu hao"
    冷也好，热也好，活着就好

Lianlian fengchen 恋恋风尘

Lihun le jiu bie zai lai zhao wo 离婚了就
    别再来找我

Liu Chuan'e 刘川鄂

liudong renkou 流动人口

Liulang Beijing 流浪北京

liumang 流氓

maimai shuhao 买卖书号

Mama 妈妈

Mang jing 盲井

maoyi 贸易

meisu 媚俗

Meiwan meiliao 没完没了

Meng Jinghui 孟京辉

mingong 民工

Nanguo zaijian, nanguo 南国，再见南国

Ni bu shi yi ge suren 你不是一个俗人

pizi 痞子

posui 破碎

Qianxi manbo 千禧曼波

qimeng 启蒙

qing yinyue 轻音乐

Qingnian dianying shiyan xiaozu 青年电
    影实验小组

Qiu Ju da guansi 秋菊打官司

qushi 去势

Ren xiaoyao 任逍遥

rendaozhuyi 人道主义

rensheng sanbuqu 人生三部曲

renwen jingshen 人文精神

renwenzhuyi 人文主义

Sanxia haoren 三峡好人

shengming zhuangtai de huanyuan 生命
    状态的还原

Shenme shi laji shenme shi ai 什么是垃圾
    什么是爱

shichanghua 市场化

Shijie 世纪

Shijie zhi chuang 世界之窗

shiluo 失落

shisuhua 世俗化

shiyan 实验

Shouhuo 受活

Shouji 手机

Shuohao bu fenshou 说好不分手

shushang 书商

si ge xiandaihua 四个现代化

sui 碎

Sun Wukong 孙悟空

Taiyang chushi 太阳出世

tansuo pian 探索片

Tianguo nizi 天国逆子

Tianxia wu zei 天下无贼

tiaokan yiqie 调侃一切

tiaokan 调侃

Tongnian wangshi 童年往事

tongsu wenxue 通俗文学

tuishe 退社

waidi ren 外地人

Waitan 外滩

Wang Hongsheng 王鸿生

Wang Hui 汪晖

Wang Meng 王蒙

Wang Shuo 王朔

Wang Xiaoming 王晓明

Wang Xiaoshuai 王小帅

Wang Yichuan 王一川

wanshengdai 晚生代

Wanzhu 玩主

Weng Fen 翁奋

wengongtuan 文工团

wenhua re 文化热

Wo de fuqin muqin 我的父亲母亲

Wo de weilai bu shi meng 我的未来不是梦

Wohu canglong 卧虎藏龙

wuliao 无聊

wuming 无名

Wushan yunyu 巫山云雨

xiahai 下海

xianchang 现场

xiandaihua 现代化

xianfeng xiaoshuo 先锋小说

xianfeng 先锋

Xiang jimao yiyang fei 像鸡毛一样飞

Xianghun nü 香魂

Xiao Ding gushi 小丁故事

Xiao Shan huijia 小山回家

Xiao Wu 小武

xiaofeizhuyi 消费主义

xiaoyao 逍遥

xiju zangli 戏剧葬礼

xin furen 新富人

xin shimin xiaoshuo 新市民小说

xin shiqi 新时期

xin tiyan xiaoshuo 新体验小说

xin xieshi xiaoshuo 新写实小说

xin xieshi 新写实

xin zhuangtai wenxue 新状态文学

xin zuopai 新左派

xingwei yishu 行为艺术

xingwei 行为

xinshengdai 新生代

xinzuopai 新左派

Xiyou ji 西游记

xungen 寻根

xuwu 虚无

xuwuzhuyi 虚无主义

Yan Lianke 阎连科

yange 阉割

yangqi 扬弃

Ye shan 野山

Ye yan 夜宴

yi jieji douzheng wei gang 以阶级斗争为纲

Yi sheng tanxi 一声叹息

yige suipianzhong de shijie 一个碎片中的世界

yihua 异化

yilei 异类

Yingxiong 英雄

yitihua 一体化

yiyuanhua de daotong 一元化的道统

yiyuanhua 一元化

You yitian, zai Beijing 有一天，在北京

youshou-haoxianzhe 游手好闲者

Yu Liwei (Yu Lik Wai) 余力为

yuansheng xingtai 原生形态

yuanshengtai 原生态

yuanyang-hudie pai 鸳鸯蝴蝶派

yulepian 娱乐片

yuleye 娱乐业

Yun de nanfang 云的南方

yundong 运动

zao si zao chaosheng 早死早超生

Zhang Rulun 张汝伦

Zhang Yimou 张艺谋

Zhang Yiwu 张颐武

Zhang Yuan 张元

Zhantai 站台

Zhao Xiansheng 赵先生

zhe tama 这他妈

zhebi 遮蔽

zhongji guanhuai 终极关怀

zhongji jiazhi 终极价值

Zhou Xiaowen 周晓文

Zhu Wen 朱文

zhuxuanlü 主旋律

Zijincheng yingye gongsi 紫禁城影业公司

ziyou zuojia 自由作家

ziyoupai 自由派

ziyou zhuangaoren 自由撰稿人

ziyu 自娱

zizhuquan 自主权

zousi 走私

Index

Made in the USA
Monee, IL
28 August 2021